Democratic Spaces

A Volume in the Series
ENVIRONMENTAL HISTORY OF THE NORTHEAST
Edited by
Richard W. Judd

Democratic Spaces

Land Preservation in New England, 1850–2010

RICHARD W. JUDD

University of Massachusetts Press
AMHERST AND BOSTON

Copyright © 2023 by University of Massachusetts Press
All rights reserved
Printed in the United States of America

ISBN 978-1-62534-757-2 (paper); 758-9 (hardcover)

Designed by Sally Nichols
Set in Adobe Jenson Pro
Printed and bound by Books International, Inc.

Cover design by adam b. bohannon
Cover photo by Dr. Frog, *World's End, Hingham, Massachusetts.* 2008 CC.O.

Library of Congress Cataloging-in-Publication Data
Names: Judd, Richard William, author.
Title: Democratic spaces : land preservation in New England, 1850–2010 / Richard W. Judd.
Description: Amherst : University of Massachusetts Press, [2023] | Series: Environmental history of the Northeast | Includes bibliographical references and index.
Identifiers: LCCN 2023013535 (print) | LCCN 2023013536 (ebook) | ISBN 9781625347572 (paperback) | ISBN 9781625347589 (hardcover) | ISBN 9781685750381 (ebook)
Subjects: LCSH: Nature conservation—New England—History—19th century. | Nature conservation—New England—History—20th century. | Nature conservation—New England—History—21st century. | Natural areas—New England—History—19th century. | Natural areas—New England—History—20th century. | Natural areas—New England—History—21st century.
Classification: LCC QH76.5.N45 J83 2023 (print) | LCC QH76.5.N45 (ebook) | DDC 508.74—dc23/eng/20230907
LC record available at https://lccn.loc.gov/2023013535
LC ebook record available at https://lccn.loc.gov/2023013536

British Library Cataloguing-in-Publication Data
A catalog record for this book is available from the British Library.

FOR PAT AND KIERAN

Contents

Acknowledgments ix

INTRODUCTION

1

CHAPTER 1
The Art of Public Improvement
Iconography in Rural New England

7

CHAPTER 2
Awakening the Preservation Spirit
The Trustees of Public Reservations

43

CHAPTER 3
Stewardship Strategies
The Trustees in the Twentieth Century

77

CHAPTER 4
The Land Trust Explosion
Grassroots Preservation in the 1960s and 1970s

114

CHAPTER 5
Reimagining Urban Spaces
Preservation in the City, 1980–2000

154

CHAPTER 6
Middle-Way Preservation in the Era of Ecosystem Management, 1990–2010

187

CONCLUSION

226

Notes 231

Index 287

Acknowledgments

All scholarly research is a collaborative effort, but in the age of Covid this collaboration takes different forms. Fortunately, I was able to spend several wonderful days before the onset of the pandemic at the Trustees of Reservations Archives & Research Center in Sharon, Massachusetts, working with an invaluable collection of materials relating not only to the trustees but to land preservation projects generally throughout the region. I am deeply indebted to Sarah Hayes and Alison Bassett for their suggestions and help with these materials. The pandemic prevented me from traveling to other archives, but it also forced me to dig deeper into the available digital resources. I have used these in the past, but never as diligently. I was happy to discover the broad and ever-growing coverage of preservation issues in online books, newspapers, pamphlets, theses, and dissertations. I am particularly obliged to Archive.org, which offers an incredible range of older books and journals, and to the Trustees' own site, which contains a trove of primary documents and newspaper clippings. While this project has been lonelier than I had anticipated, I am indebted to several others for their help and encouragement, including Brian Halley and Rachael DeShano at University of Massachusetts Press; Annette Wenda for her diligent copyediting; David Hart, director of the Senator George J. Mitchell Center for Sustainability Solutions at the University of Maine who read portions of an earlier version of chapter 6; the anonymous readers who offered helpful suggestions on the manuscript; and Beth Clevenger at MIT Press for first suggesting the project to me. As always with my research, Pat and Kieran listened patiently to my arcane theories about land preservation throughout the life of this project.

Democratic Spaces

INTRODUCTION

A contemporary map of New England, scaled at the township level brings to light a dense pattern of protected areas ringing almost every town and city in the region. Big and small, rural and urban, these green spaces represent more than a century of preservation effort on the part of philanthropic foundations, planning professionals, state agencies, and, most important, community-based organizations. Because these spaces are so diverse in size, shape, and origin, they do not appear in any clear way in the chronicles of American preservation accomplishments, but taken together, they represent one of the most significant advances in land stewardship in US history. *Democratic Spaces* explains how these green spaces came to be and what they represent for New Englanders and the nation at large.

This book grew out of an exploration I began many years ago into the origins and accomplishments of the conservation movement in New England. Turning from the government experts and scientists most historians credit with having formulated conservation ideology in the Progressive Era, I became interested in ordinary New England folk who used experience-based conservation arguments to protect local fish, timber, and game resources from outside exploiters. This grassroots perspective informed my first book on the subject, *Common Lands, Common People: The Origins of Conservation in Northern New England*, and also my later studies of water-pollution control, wild and scenic river legislation, and coastal resource protection in the environmental era. *Democratic Spaces* looks at another facet of this grassroots tradition:

the land trusts and other community-based preservation organizations that inscribed their accomplishments on the township-scale map of New England.

Land preservation has a venerable history in this country beginning, to be somewhat arbitrary, with federal attempts to protect southern live-oak stands in the early national period and continuing through Henry David Thoreau's plea for protecting the woods fringing Walden Pond. Preservation reached epic proportions when Congress began setting aside portions of the federal domain that were notable for natural beauty or geological wonders. Congress dedicated Yellowstone National Park in 1872 and added more parks to the system in the 1890s. The National Park Service (NPS) was founded in 1916. Another dimension of the preservation story emerged in the 1950s with popularization of the wilderness movement. Historians often combine the story of preservation with a history of natural resource conservation, which began effectively with the 1891 Forest Reserve Act and the founding of the US Forest Service in 1905.

Historians gravitate to these epic events due to their national visibility, and today the preservation story is told almost exclusively in terms of national parks and wilderness areas. Among the earliest of these histories was Peter Schmitt's *Back to Nature: The Arcadian Myth in Urban America*, which detailed America's growing appreciation for natural scenery and wild places. Elmo Richardson's *Dams, Parks, and Politics: Resource Development and Preservation in the Truman-Eisenhower Era* combined a history of preservation and conservation in a formative period of modern federal policymaking. These and other early works aside, preservation history is grounded in two seminal volumes: Roderick Nash's *Wilderness and the American Mind*, first published in 1967, and Alfred Runte's *The National Parks: The American Experiences*, which appeared in 1979. These books were followed by numerous revisions and refinements, but it is clear that Nash and Runte established a lasting paradigm: preservation is a tale of epic landscapes and their salvation by nationally known thinkers or politicians—towering personalities like Henry David Thoreau, John Muir, and Theodore Roosevelt. Philip Terrie's *Forever Wild: A Cultural History of Wilderness in the Adirondacks* and Hal Rothman's *Preserving Different Pasts: The American National Monuments* describe different preservation achievements, but both follow the formula established by Nash and Runte.

Democratic Spaces steps outside this paradigm to look at landscapes preserved not because they were monumental and pristine but because they were examples of a familiar local environment. Their champions were not nationally known writers and politicians but ordinary citizens concerned about the visual, recreational, and ecological health of their neighborhoods and communities. Locally based preservation underscores the activist-volunteers in hundreds of towns and cities across America who created a vast network of reservations, parks, greenways, greenbelts, nature sanctuaries, and other preserved places that today totals more than fifty-six million acres, an aggregation nearly three-quarters the size of the National Park System.

Of all the regions in the country, New England best exemplifies the hidden side of the American preservation movement and demonstrates the importance of land stewardship at the community level. The New England story begins in the mid-nineteenth century with a small class of professional horticulturists and gardeners who worked as patrons on country estates along the Eastern Seaboard. Struggling to adapt European principles of landscape design to American conditions, they disseminated their vision of country cottages, tidy villages, sculpted groves, and lush gardens in books, manuals, journals, and country life magazines. Writers, artists, and essayists working in the same era gave these images moral meaning, and together these cultural brokers created a landscape archetype—an ideal representation of rural New England—that played on the imagination of those who came to see the region as the embodiment of rural America. Viewing the countryside as an objet d'art, upcountry town elites, working with wealthy urbanites who owned homes in the country, sponsored village improvement societies and set out to translate the principles of landscape design into everyday preservationist practice. How these elite visions diffused into a generalized love of New England landscapes is the focus of the first chapter.

These events culminated in the founding of the Trustees of Public Reservations, the first private land-stewardship organization in America. Formed in Boston in 1891, the TPR became the voice of New England preservation in the first half of the twentieth century by acquiring land with scenic, cultural, recreational, or ecological value and managing it for the common good. The second and third chapters show how the TPR translated this simple strategy into a sophisticated preservation agenda. The fourth chapter explores the rise of community-based land trusts in the shadow of the TPR, and the fifth traces the new uses urban activists found for open spaces in their cities. The final chapter looks at yet another turning point in New England preservation history: the effort to protect entire landscapes in accordance with the new science of ecosystem management.

Across a century of dramatic change, New England preservationists held to a common goal of protecting valued open spaces and ensuring access for an ever-widening circle of citizens. Their accomplishments have received little attention in the annals of the preservation movement, despite the fact that New England's mountains, coastlines, harbors, villages, and farms are keystone features in our national identity. When we view the movement from the ground up, New England's role becomes even more pivotal. Here, at the birthplace of community-based preservation, Americans first learned to value the seemingly inconspicuous green spaces that gave texture and meaning to the world around them. It was here that the preservation movement, having fixed the nation's attention on parks in the Great West, turned to the familiar places that defined a community for those who lived there.

To understand New England's attachment to these common landscapes, I turned to another of my earlier research projects. In *Second Nature: An Environmental History of New England*, published in 2014, I argued that the region's long postfrontier Euro-American occupancy allowed for centuries of interaction with nature across a varied and ever-changing landscape. This extended period of adjustment between land and people blurred the boundaries between nature and culture, yielding a series of hybrid landscapes known to students of environmental history as second nature. Philosopher René Debos captured the essence of the term in describing the centuries-old agricultural landscapes of Europe and Asia. These long-domesticated scenes, he remarked, had become "so familiar to us that we tend to forget their origin; we contemplate them in a mood of casual acceptance and reverie without giving thought to those parts of primeval nature that had to be profoundly transformed, or destroyed, to make them fit not only our biological needs but also our esthetic longings." In New England, preservationists valued these second-nature landscapes no less than they valued the wild mountains and deep forests on the far northern fringes of the region. They understood the powerful symbolic meanings communities attached to these familiar places, and they fought to protect them. Harvard professor Charles W. Eliot II, a leading figure in the TPR in its middle years, pointed out that the open spaces in and around the towns and cities of New England are not simply vacant lands waiting development. "On the contrary they are the essential voids which give meaning to the solids. They are the essential contacts with the natural in an artificial environment." Land stewardship begins, as Eliot suggested, when communities discover "the positive uses and values of [their own] open spaces."[1]

New England is also important because it underscores the complexity of the movement at the grassroots level. Community-based organizations, as Cody Ferguson writes, hold "important insights for how we understand the history of the preservation movement and the role of citizen activists." What emerges from this understanding, he continues, "is a complicated picture of environmental activism based not on a single coherent environmentalism . . . but on common calls for fairness, justice, and access to the decisions that affect the land, air, water, and public health."[2] The preservation movement, on this level, was incredibly diverse, ranging from neighborhood organizations fighting to save a nearby property to multiorganizational alliances orchestrated to protect entire ecosystems. From this complicated bottom-up perspective, we learn first that preservation history encompasses more than just the national parks and wilderness areas that stand as the movement's most visible accomplishment. Second, we learn that these more modest forms of preservation had deeply personal meanings. Americans cherished their national parks, but they experienced them mostly as abstractions. Trust lands preserved features vital to the scenic and ecological integrity of their towns; it was here that residents could truly immerse themselves in nature by wandering out at any convenience to rediscover their natural heritage and find solace from a world of concrete and steel.[3] New England complicates our understanding of preservation history, but it brings us closer to appreciating what the movement meant to everyday citizens.

I pieced together this story of land stewardship by observing land trusts and other stewardship organizations from the ground up, as I did in tracing the history of conservation in *Common Lands*. This meant examining the goals and accomplishments of hundreds of local land trusts in newspaper accounts across the region and in documents housed in the Trustees of Reservations Archives & Research Center in Sharon, Massachusetts. These varied experiences revealed two common themes in more than a century of preservation activity: the halting movement toward a more inclusive and democratic definition of public access and the expanding geographical scope of preservation projects. The former culminated in the conversion of thousands of unused inner-city spaces into pocket parks, urban wilds, greenways, community gardens, affordable-home lots, and other stewardship lands that served diverse neighborhoods across the metropolitan area. The latter came to a head in the preservation of hundreds of thousands of acres of timberland in northern New York and New England as a first step in implementing the new science of region-wide ecosystem management.

These two trends demonstrate a third common thread in these stories: the key role ordinary people played in the modern land-preservation movement. Like the New England farmers and fishers who fought for equitable conservation rules a century earlier, volunteers in local and regional preservation organizations shouldered the burden of protecting wildlife habitats, increasing recreational opportunities, defending historically significant structures, and preserving the charm and character of their neighborhoods and towns. "Conservation was a social movement," I wrote in *Common Lands*; "it could hardly be otherwise."[4] Land preservation was likewise a social movement. It was grounded in the social experiences of ordinary people, and it derived its legitimacy not from the scientific merit or political opportunity it represented but from the social values it embodied: a love of place, a faith in collective action, and a commitment to democratic process. It is my hope that this study will convince readers that they, too, can contribute to the preservation cause by finding their own meaning in nature and place and working with others who share these values. The region is unique in some ways but representative in others. For more than a century, people in communities all across the nation have gathered together to protect a cherished natural landscape here or a venerable cultural landmark there. A careful study of this activity in New England expands our understanding of preservationist possibilities not only in this region but across America.

CHAPTER 1

The Art of Public Improvement
Iconography in Rural New England

Writing in the *Atlantic Monthly* in 1896, New England artist and gardener Mary Caroline Robbins described a recent tour of England that left her deeply impressed by the way nature and culture could be woven together to beautify the countryside. The varying moods of North Atlantic weather—wild and stern, placid and calm—conditioned the "rugged British race, with its underlying tenderness," and the people in turn adorned their countryside in a tradition derived through the ages from these climatic influences. Nature served as "brush and canvas, chisel and stone," and virtually everyone, from manor lord to humble peasant, used these tools in the "unconscious obedience to the highest principles of landscape-art."[1]

Inspired by this example, Robbins imagined rural America as medium for a new form of art embraced by "the humblest and the wisest alike." The embellishment of great estates, the improvement of villages, and the creation of vast national parks and preserves would come together as the nation's greatest aesthetic achievement. Because of its democratic heritage, America would excel in this endeavor. "Each of us can contribute after his fashion,—the workman with his spade, the farmer with the neat tilling and fencing of his broad acres, the small householder with a well-kept yard, the rich man with his stately pleasure-grounds, the village with its common and well-shaded streets, the town with its squares and greens and broad avenues, the city with its generous park systems, the nation with its vast reservations." This broad-based and democratic reform would uplift the entire nation. "We claim that the art for America, the art in which we may hope to set an example to the world, is the Art of Public Improvement."[2]

The inspiration for Robbins's ardent preservationist appeal was neither the symbol-laden nature conjured by midcentury transcendentalists nor the pristine wilderness romanticized by landscape artists, mountaineers, and other seekers of the sublime. Rather, it was the familiar world of farm, woods, and village that textured the New England landscape. Although the region's reformers were involved in a variety of preservation activities at the turn of the century, their concerns were grounded in Robbins's Art of Public Improvement: the arrangement of rural landscapes into an appealing blend of nature and culture. This "aestheticization of the rural," as historian Kirin Makker puts it, launched a preservation movement that, in the twentieth century, embraced hundreds of organizations, thousands of volunteer activists, and millions of acres of natural, scenic, and recreational reserves.[3]

The Art of Public Improvement fits into a broader legacy of American preservationist achievements that began with the dedication of Yellowstone National Park in 1872. The preservation movement gained momentum at the turn of the century when additional parks and monuments were established, and it culminated in the Wilderness Act in 1964, which today protects more than 111 million acres of "untrammeled" land. Preservation also refers to saving historic structures and sites, a trend that began as early as 1853 with the restoration of George Washington's Mount Vernon estate. Federal agencies took up historic preservation with passage of the Lacey Antiquities Act of 1906, which authorized the president to set aside historic aboriginal sites, along with geological curiosities, as national monuments, and passage of the 1966 National Historic Preservation Act. Preservation is closely related to conservation, and the complicated interaction between the two begs some clarification. Speaking generally, preservation aims at protecting lands or historic sites by preventing their use in ways that compromise their ecological or cultural value. Preservation implies permanence and stability. Conservation—again generally speaking—implies somewhat the opposite: the ongoing use of timber, grasslands, water, fisheries, soils, wildlife, and minerals in sustainable ways. Both terms came into general use during the Progressive Era, although both have historical antecedents. Watershed events in the conservation movement include creation of the US Forest Service in the Progressive Era and the Soil Conservation Service and Tennessee Valley Authority during the New Deal.

In some instances preservation and conservation were almost indistinguishable. President Theodore Roosevelt, for instance, was both: he created several conservation agencies during his administration and set aside more federal land for national parks, monuments, and wildlife preserves than all previous presidents combined. In other instances the two movements were at odds. The battle over Hetch Hetchy Valley in Yosemite National Park at the turn of the century pitted preservationists, who saw the valley as a sacred trust, against conservationists, who argued that the valley would serve the greater good as a reservoir for the city of San Francisco. New Deal officials combined conservation and preservationist goals in programs like the Civilian Conservation Corps and the Agricultural Adjustment Act, but the wilderness movement once again set preservationists and conservationists at odds. Preservation usually implies leaving nature to its own devices, as stipulated in the Wilderness Act, but this is not always the case. Every park, whether the carefully landscaped urban retreats that grace our larger cities or the vast natural reserves in our national park system, has been manipulated in some fashion to address popular impressions of a "natural" environment. "Preservation," in short, is a term that must be understood in context.

The preservation story has been told and retold, and each telling emphasizes the vast swaths of western federal land sequestered into parks, monuments, wildlife refuges, and wilderness areas. These achievements were indeed epic, but they represent only a portion of the story. The national preservation achievements most familiar to us are the result of presidential or congressional action, typically prompted by powerful preservationist organizations. New England offers a different perspective that highlights ordinary landscapes and the ordinary men and women who saved them. That this side of the story is seldom told is not surprising. Traditionally, historians wrote from the vantage of nationally known literary, scientific, or political figures, and environmental historians generally followed this tradition. Samuel Hays, in his pathbreaking 1959 *Conservation and the Gospel of Efficiency*, emphasized the scientific experts who used their political connections to usher in the conservation movement, and Roderick Nash, in his 1967 *Wilderness and the American Mind*, focused on the writings of well-known naturalists like Henry David Thoreau, John Muir, and Aldo Leopold. Alfred Runte's seminal work on national parks likewise highlighted the work of well-positioned writers and politicians. It is only recently that environmental historians have given voice to ordinary people who pursued their own ideas of nature's proper use.[4] The New England preservation story builds on this "history from the ground up" perspective, underscoring the accomplishments of activist-volunteers in creating a vast network of reservations, parks, greenways, greenbelts, nature sanctuaries, and other preserved places throughout the region. These scattered stewardship lands drew far more people into the bosom of nature and protected a greater diversity of ecosystems than those carved out of the western federal domain. New England exemplifies the hidden side of the American preservation movement and demonstrates the vital importance of saving nature on a community-by-community basis. As a beginning, this chapter traces the Art of Public Improvement—the ideological foundation for New England's preservation legacy—through four manifestations: the landscaping of country estates, the accomplishments of Victorian-era village improvement societies, the conservation of northern New England forests, and the campaign for urban parks.

The Art of Public Improvement

The New England preservation story begins with the aesthetics of place: the visual images, encoded meanings, and moral messages that made up rural New England iconography. Although it seems a somewhat capricious beginning, landscape appreciation, as historian Norman Newton points out, set the scene for the preservation and conservation impulses that followed. Scenery, like other natural resources, was a finite resource; its protection and elaboration required scientific expertise; and its preservation was critical to a healthy, democratic society.[5] Landscape appreciation in New England began in the middle of the nineteenth century when the regional landscape was "invented" or "imagined," as historians Dona Brown and Joseph Conforti put it, in landscape art, literature, journalism, Fourth of July speeches, and other cultural expressions. These symbol-laden images crystallized in the mind of the reformer and set the tone for preservation initiatives into the twenty-first century.[6]

The most important benchmark in the aesthetic crusade Mary Caroline Robbins envisioned was the founding of the Trustees of Public Reservations in Boston in 1891. As the nation's first private preservationist association, the TPR captured the spirit of nineteenth-century landscape appreciation and transformed it into a preservationist crusade, and after a half century of this pioneering work, the TPR was joined by smaller land trusts throughout New England and across the country. By the end of the century these smaller versions of the TPR had protected millions of acres of recreationally, aesthetically, and ecologically critical landscapes—an underappreciated accomplishment that ranks among the greatest legacies of the environmental movement. "Within a few hours' drive of anywhere in the United States," Chris Elfring wrote in 1989, "there is a patch of open space that exists solely because a group of local citizens joined ranks to save it. . . . Most likely, the group members would not consider themselves activists, just neighbors who value open space and all it brings."[7] This movement began as an effort to preserve rural character in towns across New England, an idea that first took shape in the nineteenth-century Art of Public Improvement.

Land trusts filled an important niche in the environmental movement. National environmental organizations, caught up in the crusade to save vast tracts of western wilderness, seldom involved themselves in protecting landscapes important only in a local context, yet these smaller reserves were vitally important in preserving wildlife habitat and introducing millions of ordinary citizens to nature. Moreover, the accomplishments of these community-based organizations offer insight into the dynamics of the broader environmental movement. In 1977 Gerald Barney counted some three thousand environmental organizations of various sorts across the nation. Most were small groups dependent on individual contributions and volunteer staff, but in the aggregate they were vital to the preservation of nature in America.[8] Understanding how they were formed, how they defined the nature they hoped to preserve, and what they accomplished is crucial to understanding the environmental movement as a whole.

The goals and strategies pursued by local land trusts changed between the 1960s and the early 2000s. Trusts first appeared in the wealthier towns in eastern Massachusetts and southeastern Connecticut where rapid development threatened the village character of the states' suburban communities. Too frequently, these early trusts saw open-space preservation as a means of exclusion, but with the rise of the environmental movement, officers and volunteers turned to a more inclusive goal of protecting habitat and introducing townspeople to nature in their own backyards. In the next decade the focus of land preservation became even more inclusive as activists transformed thousands of vacant inner-city lots into urban wilds, community gardens, greenways, and space for affordable housing, and at the turn of the century trusts tackled larger, ecologically centered projects like protecting watersheds, farmlands, and entire ecosystems. Accomplishing these ambitious goals required complex coalitions of local, regional, and national trusts; philanthropic foundations; state and federal land-management agencies; nearby residents; landowners; and other stakeholders. Between 1960 and 2010, in short, land trusts matured, diversified, and embraced an ever-larger constituency, both human and natural, even while they retained their grassroots character.

From the founding of village improvement societies to the campaigns for ecosystem protection, preservationists pursued a common goal in preserving open spaces for the enjoyment of ordinary citizens. While the goals were inclusive, the movement itself carried an undercurrent of elitism, particularly in its early phases. Nineteenth-century constructs of rural beauty originated with the European gentry, and, as Richard Bushman notes, it was difficult to see how Americans reconciled these aristocratic landscapes with American notions of republicanism. Preservation in any context is a dialogue between experts and privileged reformers, on the one hand, and ordinary people, on the other, and indeed those who first professed the Art of Public Improvement were men and women of wealth and standing. Well traveled, well read, and well positioned, they sought to reproduce in America the beauty they saw in European country estates, with their thick layers of tradition and aristocratic overtones. These elites, Mary Caroline Robbins among them, imposed their own idea of aesthetic appreciation on the land they protected, even while they remained dedicated to values they thought would appeal, as Robbins said, to the "humble and the magnificent alike." This tension remained embedded in the Art of Public Improvement throughout the nineteenth century, but eventually the preservationist banner passed to grassroots activists whose goals were more closely attuned to the concerns of the surrounding community.[9] Private land stewardship is, like so much in American politics and society, a story of gradual and nonlinear progression toward more inclusive and democratic ideals. Exclusionary notions lingered, but over time preservation accomplishments became egalitarian and participatory in concept and execution.

Defining Rural Atmosphere

Since the days of Thomas Morton and Anne Bradstreet, poets and writers have associated rural atmosphere with health, moral order, and beauty. As Thomas Jefferson made clear in his 1785 *Notes on the State of Virginia*, rural landscapes were at the core of American identity, and in a nation of diverse peoples still unsure of their civic institutions, this identity was important.

Early on, New England farmers contributed to this iconography by forging the landscapes that later romantics idealized. Pioneer farming in the region was as rapacious as anywhere—a "sorrowful sight . . . to see extensive hill-sides," a midcentury editor observed, "which only twenty years ago refreshed the eye with their summer green, . . . now bald and bare." The "uprooting of nature," as geographer David Lowenthal puts it, was "harsh and ugly," but as farmers cleared away the trees, removed the stumps and charred logs, and paid off their mortgages, they cast a more appreciative eye on their surroundings. Gradually, the raw edges of the cleared lands grew smooth, and fields, meadows, pastures, and woodlots mingled pleasantly with the forests on the borders of the scene. Postpioneering families developed a powerful attachment to this landscape.[10]

Farm beautification had broad appeal in the second half of the century, particularly as railroads, horse-drawn machinery, and Peruvian guano enhanced the prosperity of the New England farm. The seemingly boundless expanse of farmland west of the Appalachians weighed on the minds of these New Englanders, and they understood that landscape beauty was an important consideration in keeping their sons and daughters at home. Farm-journal editors warned that yards and fields blemished by rusting equipment, toppled stone walls, and other visual scars discredited the rural neighborhood and compromised the moral character of its inhabitants. They urged farmers to square up their fields and fences, grub up the weeds, remove stumps and stones, apply more manure, and make their farms not only more productive but more beautiful.[11] This appeal was not a preservationist theme in the usual sense, but it illustrates the symbolic attachment to the landscape ideals emerging in the rural mind at midcentury. Geographer Kent Ryden summarized an understanding that informed so much of the commentary on nineteenth-century rural New England: "The region's old agricultural landscape could be seen as nothing less than a work of folk art on an epic scale, a place where natural materials were reshaped according to the patterns held in human minds in order to not only do a job but to exhibit a sense of visual rightness, to inspire a sense of creative satisfaction in its makers, and a degree of aesthetic pleasure in its viewers."[12]

Among New Englanders generally, the Art of Public Improvement crystallized at a time when cities were being transformed by the twin forces of immigration and industrialization. The contrast between city and country provided a benchmark for rural aesthetics: the former was worldly, mechanical, greedy, and hurried, and the latter, innocent, open-handed, organic, and timeless.[13]

Responding to these cultural preferences, writers and artists added a poetic overlay to the farm improvers' quest for a tidy and productive farm-and-village scene. "Everything from houses to barns to village streets," historian Richard Bushman writes, "was to be made beautiful; every scene was to be turned into a picture."[14] Guided by their belief in the fundamental rightness of rural life, nineteenth-century reformers and romantics formulated the issues that would define New England preservation.

Transforming the countryside into an art form was no easy task. New England villages lacked the ancient monuments that textured and enriched their counterparts in Europe. Sara Josepha Hale, whose widely read books and articles on domestic life depended heavily on rural imagery, admitted that the New England hills appeared to most travelers as only "piles of earth and rock." New England was not a "finished scene," as Joseph Conforti put it. "While Goethe and Coleridge walked through European landscapes fraught with cultural memories, Americans moved through scenes almost completely devoid of Western institutions."[15]

The layers of memory were thin, perhaps, but New England's culture brokers went to work transforming these piles of earth and rock into a vast store of picturesque imagery. As a number of historians have pointed out, America compensated for its lack of Old World monuments by grounding its cultural identity in nature. By the middle of the nineteenth century, the "forest primeval," as Longfellow and others called it, had become an intriguing metaphor for the uniqueness of American character. Wilderness, still the vast bulk of the continental land base, took on biblical and romantic associations as a source of redemption, renewal, and national distinction: a place for playing out the frontier myth of escape and self-reliant individualism. Romantics saw in these wild and lonely places a chance for sublime experience; viewers would be overwhelmed by the vast power and cosmic indifference of unending forests, deep chasms, and soaring mountain peaks. Religion, as Mark Stoll points out, "irradiated" the wilderness, defining it as a place where America could "begin again and build a perfect society according to God's plan."[16]

In the second half of the nineteenth century, the focus of wilderness imagining shifted to the West, where, as Alfred Runte points out, the quest for American distinctiveness could be more easily fulfilled. As wilderness romance moved westward, New Englanders discovered their own connection to nature, not in the grandeur of mountain peaks but in the artful juxtaposition of village and forest that reformers saw as the epitome of country life.

By midcentury, according to art historian Angela Miller, "the taste for wilderness had largely given way to a preference for the pastoral landscape. Sublime wilderness appealed less to metropolitan audiences than did the shared pleasures of a nature increasingly enjoyed for its parklike qualities, mirroring the middle-class discomfort with the intense, spiritually demanding nature of the Romantics."[17]

The pivotal figure in this shift from mountain sublime to pastoral iconography was Henry David Thoreau. Having spent time in the Maine woods and on the desolate shores of Cape Cod, Thoreau understood the psychic impact of wilderness travel, but he experienced these regions as a tourist or sightseer rather than a fellow traveler with nature. Wilderness, to his thinking, was a place to refresh the poetic soul but not to experience the organic world on an intimate level. Roderick Nash, who pioneered the study of wilderness in America, was correct in pointing out Thoreau's contribution to wilderness imagery, but he missed Thoreau's subtle distinction between wilderness and wildness. Thoreau's most compelling odes to nature were framed in the latter, which he saw everywhere in his daily saunters through the fields and woods of Concord. Here the wildness of the domesticated landscape was palpable. "He tasted it in the huckleberries growing along the farmer's fences and felt it in the minnow's impulsive struggle upstream against the current. His favorite season was springtime, when nature exploded in a chaos of new life—swampside frog choruses, meadows bursting into color, and clouds of insects 'ushered into being' on warm evenings." This passion for wildness, evident in all Thoreau's Concord-based essays, invested ordinary landscapes with metaphorical meaning. If any single writer was responsible for romanticizing the rural New England landscape, it was Henry David Thoreau.[18]

As Thoreau's writings suggest, much of New England literature involved nature in a domestic context. James Russell Lowell sought inspiration not in the mountains "where nature rules man" but in the humanized landscapes around his Cambridge home, where he could "luxuriate in . . . the soft lapping of the summer breeze coming over the meadows with the fragrance of buttercups and clover and the tinkling rapture of the bobolink." Although he traveled to the Maine woods, the Adirondacks, and the West, he, like Thoreau, wrote less fervently about these places than he did about the woods and fields of the Boston suburbs. Emerson too derived his multifaceted transcendental philosophy by wandering the hills of Concord. As a Neoplatonic idealist, he saw nature as a reflection of universal ideas, but time and again he was drawn back to the "independent existence of the world about him." Writers like Lowell and Emerson saw these landscapes as tokens of national identity.[19]

The most powerful expression of rural iconography came from a group of painters known collectively as the Hudson River School. Seated in patron-rich New York City, they spent summers painting in the heavily forested upper Hudson River basin, and by the 1840s they were exploring mountain and coastal landscapes in New England. In detailed renderings, they freighted the hills and valleys with symbols of deeply felt ideas relating to God, nature, simple rural virtues, and national destiny. That this artistic celebration emerged in the industrializing Northeast suggests a subtle tension in the expression of rural life. Thomas Cole, the genre's most influential spokesperson, conveyed these anxieties in scenes suggesting primordial struggle between living nature and base elements like wind, rain, and rocks. While he spoke confidently of American democracy, Cole suggested in his art a rural world threatened by the transition from agrarian republic to industrial titan.[20]

In popular literature these concerns were submerged beneath a thick layer of sentimentalism. Susan Fenimore Cooper, author of *Rural Hours* and *The Rhyme and Reason of Country Life*, praised the solace of rustic life in an age of frenzied commercial growth and personal ambition. If the countryside lacked tradition, it was, as Cooper put it, "surrounded by great natural teachers, by noble monitors, in the works of the Deity." Writers like Donald Grant Mitchell (Ik Marvel), Frederick William Shelton, S. H. Hammond, and L. W. Mansfield crafted romantic images of wooded valleys, quiet villages, and rustic farmsteads. Mrs. A. J. Graves's *Girlhood and Womanhood* taught middle-class Americans to associate beauty, health, virtue, and religious sensitivity with rural life, while folio pictorials like Nathaniel Parker Willis's *American Scenery* and George Putnam's *Home Book of the Picturesque* idealized rural America in scenes rendered by some of the nation's most gifted artists, illustrators, and essayists. Books, essays, prints, lithographs, engravings, paintings, and other landscape interpretations, along with scores of articles in journals like *Harper's*, *Scribners's Monthly*, *Graham's*, and *Godey's Lady's Book*, signaled an emerging rural aesthetic. As historian Judith Major wrote, the term "rural" became "the purest adjective ... in the language."[21]

Despite its rapidly industrializing cities, New England was widely perceived as the archetype of the American countryside. The West was still too raw to embody fundamental American values and the South too tainted by slavery. For this reason, landscape architect Egbert Hans wrote, "old New England and its charming characteristics, ... should be preserved." Henry Ward Beecher's popular *Norwood; or, Village Life in New England* confirmed the impression that this was a land of simple habits, plain speech, and sturdy independence. In the most widely read midcentury affirmation of New England village iconography, Congregational minister Horace Bushnell commemorated the centennial of Litchfield, Connecticut, in an essay titled "The Age of Homespun." Penned in 1851, Bushnell's reminiscence was reproduced in magazines across America, and it struck a chord with Americans searching for a sense of national identity. John Greenleaf Whittier's epic *Snow-Bound* added new layers of meaning to the New England countryside, and histories by Herbert Baxter Adams, Edward Perkins Channing, and James Truslow Adams portrayed the New England village as the font of America's democratic values. Regionalist writers like Harriet Beecher Stowe, Rose Terry Cooke, Mary E. Wilkins Freeman, Sarah Orne Jewett, Rowland Robinson, Alice Brown, and Celia Thaxter immortalized rural New England using a heady mix of nostalgia and nature appreciation. In a nation deeply divided over slavery, New England villagers' independence and love of liberty confirmed the moral superiority of the free-labor system.[22]

Country Estates and the Art of Public Improvement

The Art of Public Improvement gained concrete form as wealthy merchants and industrialists, chasing images projected in landscape art and literature, purchased homes and laid out estates in the country. In colonial times wealthy landowners like Thomas Jefferson, John Rutledge, and Thomas Lee Shippen explored ways of modifying the English style of landscaping to suit American conditions, and after the Revolution others followed, seeking to create "real-world counterparts to the landscape painting they loved." Rather than ape the European landed aristocracy, they created estates that were more productive than elegant. They saw themselves not as aristocrats but as reformers. Having read the great historians of the age, they saw the course of civilization as cyclical, beginning with a simple pastoral way of life and proceeding through stages of prosperity and luxury to decay and decline. They hoped to sustain America's republican values by shoring up its agricultural base. To this end, they experimented with improved methods of farming, livestock breeding, and horticulture, hoping through example to enlighten nearby farmers.[23]

Viewed skeptically by most ordinary farmers, these wealthy improvers accomplished little through direct example, but they advanced the cause of landscape appreciation in four ways. First, they supported the local agricultural clubs and horticultural societies that came together in the 1850s as state boards of agriculture—the region's earliest conservation agencies. These societies awarded premiums for superior produce and livestock, sponsored fairs and exhibitions, and promoted more efficient farming, but as historian Richard Cloues points out, they went beyond field and livestock experiments to serve as "broad-based improvement organization[s] for reforming, literally as well as figuratively, farming, country life, and the rural landscape." The boards promoted the idea that productivity depended on keeping homes and farms orderly, uncluttered, and efficient—a message that gave rural beautification a practical justification. Second, estate owners advanced the idea that landscape and moral character were one and the same. They groomed their own properties to reflect their standing in society, and they interpreted ordinary farms similarly as a reflection of family standing. Insisting that tidy neighborhoods promoted sound moral bearing, they made beautification a matter of high principle. Third, the estate owners reinforced the idea that the countryside appealed, as geographer Blake Harrison put it, "because of rather than in spite of its humanized feel." Nature had to be cultivated to be made beautiful—a principle that landscape professionals would later claim as an article of faith. Fourth, antebellum gentleman-farmers laid a foundation for country estates of a different kind. In the middle decades of the century, they narrowed their agricultural endeavors to cultivating fruit trees, since vegetables were too earthy for gentlemen growers and flowers too showy for republican sensibilities. In horticulture aesthetic principles came to the fore. "Lingering doubts about the legitimacy of ornament . . . vanished," historian Tamara Thornton writes, as the owners rededicated their lands to the display of wealth.[24]

These display-oriented estates appealed to a new class of industrial tycoons. Traditionally, upper-class families demonstrated their wealth through a European practice called the grand tour; they "vacated" the city during the pestilential season for a months-long excursion to points of interest across the East. The alternative to the grand tour, increasingly popular among wealthy but culturally insecure postbellum plutocrats, was a country seat, which met the need for sumptuous display but provided additional opportunities for privacy and prestige. Estates validated the owner's class standing. "One must *live in the country* with all the appliances and comforts of *home* about them," a contemporary writer opined, "not as a visitor or an occasional sojourner, but as one 'to the manor born.'"[25] The country estate, unlike the circuit of hotels and spas on the grand tour, was a permanent physical embodiment of the owner's wealth and status. It was, as a contemporary described it, sumptuous: "built at large expense, often palatial in its dimensions, furnished in the richest manner and placed on an estate perhaps large enough to admit of independent farming operations, and in most cases with a garden which is an integral part of the architectural scheme." With their vast grounds and virtually unlimited budgets, estate owners experimented with Old World gardening principles adapted to New World conditions. Still holding to the idea of a didactic landscape, they created bastions of beauty and grace in the still somewhat raw and coarse northeastern countryside.[26]

The middle decades of the century saw three centers of estate building along the Eastern Seaboard, each adopting slightly different principles, but each with European antecedents. The prerevolutionary estates, mostly along the Southern Seaboard, were designed in the Formal style: a Renaissance tradition characterized by a geometric arrangement of paths, shrubs, and flower beds and a sprawling greensward with trees arranged in clumps and bowers. In the huge colonial-era patroon estates along the Hudson River, owners experimented with long, straight crushed-limestone walks and extensive, geometrically arranged lawns. Lines of formal lawn, hedges, and gardens reached down toward the Hudson River, with a gazebo or summerhouse overlooking the expanse of water. In the towns around Boston, in the Berkshire Hills, and on the coast of Maine, estates were generally smaller and the grounds left in more natural conditions, with curved walkways and driveways and creative approaches to grouping foliage. An early observer reasoned that the Bostonian, brought up in a city of "crooked and curved streets," was conditioned to reject the "stiff and straight lines" that characterized southern and mid-Atlantic estates. Theirs were largely Gardenesque arrangements featuring luxuriant growth and flowing lines that followed an undulating surface, or Picturesque, with edges set off in rugged outlines bordered by sturdy, wild-looking trees like oak and pitch pine. Typically, these estates were opened to the public on certain days to introduce people of the lesser sort to various principles of landscape design. Together, their lavish gardens, lush lawns, and exquisite landscapes embellished the idea of the countryside as a place of beauty and grace.[27]

To create estate grounds that met the standards of their class and region, owners turned to a new group of professionals dedicated to the Art of Public Improvement. Estate gardeners drew their inspiration from European landscape design, and particularly from Humphrey Repton, who dominated

English landscaping in the early nineteenth century, and somewhat later from Scottish horticulturist John Loudon who also wrote extensively about gardening and landscaping. America's first nationally recognized landscape designer was André Parmentier, a Belgian immigrant who in 1824 established a nursery on twenty-four acres of rough, stony soil in Brooklyn. Parmentier's Horticultural and Botanic Garden displayed various species of fruit-bearing vines and trees, but it also featured ornamentals set out in a garden of sinuous walks, stone walls, and irregular flower beds. As his reputation grew, Parmentier began planning estate grounds around New York, working in the Gardenesque style advocated by Repton, who rejected the geometric forms in contemporary Italian and French gardens and designed landscapes that mimicked the English countryside. Parmentier's widely circulated pamphlet, *Landscapes and Picturesque Gardens*, extolled what he termed the "modern style" patterned after Repton.[28]

Parmentier's successor, Andrew Jackson Downing, was the first American to write extensively about the principles of landscaping. Downing was born in Newburgh on the Hudson River near some of the finest country estates in America. As a boy he learned the landscaping trade from his father, a wheelwright and nurseryman, and after his father died he joined his brother in managing the nursery business. Like Parmentier, he traded on the status consciousness of upper-class families, but he also appealed to a love of rural life among all citizens. He understood, as Judith Major relates, that "the benefits of rural retirement ... had attained the level of moral truth in America" and offered advice to modest home owners seeking to express their own "ardent love of rural life."[29]

Like Parmentier, Downing promoted naturalistic design. Americans, so wary of wilderness in the Puritan days, had grown accustomed to the wild look of their countryside, and they were ready, he reasoned, to incorporate these forms into their domestic arrangements. His 1841 *Treatise on the Theory and Practice of Landscape Gardening Adapted to North America* borrowed heavily from Loudon, but he modified the Scotsman's principles using lines, spaces, mass, force, and texture in slightly different ways to suggest America's wilder and more rugged settings. Although his principles were not original, his writing carried a strong sense of conviction, and his timing was fortunate: his *Treatise* appeared just as Thoreau and the other transcendentalists were giving new meaning to nature, and just as gardening was becoming an acceptable pastime for middle-class women and men. Downing's goal was to create a "little-humanized Nature in which a man might lose his consciousness of self," as Samuel Parson wrote in his 1915 *Art of Landscape Architecture*. Like the transcendentalist writers of the same era, Downing saw nature as an allegory for moral truths, and he assigned these attributes to the landscapes he created. The *Treatise* laid out the "great principles of taste" upon which the Art of Public Improvement would be founded.[30]

Eight years after he published his *Treatise*, Downing launched the *Horticulturist*, a magazine devoted to beautifying rural landscapes from the great estate to the humble suburban home. Downing's magazine blended moral insights with practical advice, appealing, as Richard Cloues writes, "directly to the American predisposition . . . [to] do-it-yourself." In its pages Downing denounced the geometric school as a relic of European imperialism aimed at dominating nature and urged gardeners to take their inspiration from the beauty of natural form. Paths and lines of shrubbery would follow the "natural shape of the surface, and avoid all abrupt angles." Gardenesque and Picturesque principles complemented the lightly domesticated or wild nature on the estate's borders. "If the adjacent grounds are wild and picturesque, the architectural style will admit of more irregularity, and of a ruder kind of ornamentation." In the French or Italian style, "one seeks the effects of art slightly assisted by nature"; in the American style, the designer creates a "primeval paradise whose pervading beauty was found in the unstudied simplicity of nature."[31] In the pages of the *Horticulturist* Downing crafted the Art of Public Improvement using stylized representations of rural New England as his archetype.

Downing was noted for his patronizing attitude toward status-conscious estate owners, but like Mary Robbins he saw landscaping as the "great humanizer of the age"—an art form that would unite the estate owner, the suburbanite, and the humble villager. His patronage was narrow, but his vision was broad. Like gentlemen farmers before him, he saw a correlation between landscapes and morals. As a later disciple put it, "The homes of the people . . . openly reveal their civilized or their barbarous condition—their thrift and advancement, or their sloth and consequent degradation." Slovenly neighborhoods bred "coarse, groveling manners," while beautiful yards and grounds uplifted the entire community. The "apostle of taste" need only erect a graceful home, and others would follow. The Art of Public Improvement would thus radiate outward from the great estates.[32]

Downing, like Robbins, believed that individuals regardless of circumstances could contribute to the Art of Public Improvement. His landscaping principles were crafted to the needs of an American aristocracy, but his fondness for the simplicity of nature hinted at his democratic instincts. In the *Horticulturist* he offered advice to farmers, artisans, and suburbanites as well as owners of great estates. In accord with the nation's republican values, he urged home builders to observe the strictures of their own class: "Let the cottage be a cottage—the farm-house a farm-house—the villa a villa, and the mansion a mansion." For those of limited means, he simplified and miniaturized his estate plans and extolled the satisfactions of a modest but cheerful home. The pleasures of rural life required no "baronial possessions"—only a refined sense of harmony in home, grounds, and modes of life. Combining the high principles of British landscaping and the vernacular styles of the villages around him, he democratized landscape ideals by bridging the gap between prestige-seeking estate owners and a new class of suburbanites equally anxious to express their status through landscape art.[33]

Reforming the New England Village

The Art of Public Improvement shifted to a more democratic plane in the second half of the century with the appearance of village improvement societies. The first in a long succession of community-based land-preservation initiatives, improvement societies grew out of social changes in rural New England in the mid-nineteenth century. Early villages were typically little more than scattered collections of farms and shops strung out along a road or river with the land between them cluttered with vegetable gardens, wood piles, poultry sheds, pig pens, and small pastures. In the nineteenth century, lawyers, doctors, merchants, clergy, and tavern keepers moved to central locations to take advantage of a faster pace of commercial exchange, while mills and artisan shops gravitated to waterpower sites that became nodes of an emerging industrial economy.[34] At midcentury artists, poets, and essayists reimagined this unassuming cluster of homes, businesses, and shops as a core feature of republican ideology, and when railroads reached these villages in the second half of the century, urban families purchased summer homes and quickened the sense of village self-consciousness. The improvement societies grew out of the attempt to bring rural reality into line with New England village iconography.[35]

Village leaders, hoping to attract investment from these urban admirers, welcomed the influx of summer residents and vacationers. In his 1887 *Book of Berkshire*, Clark Bryan applauded the Boston socialites who built homes in the western Massachusetts highlands. In due time, Bryan predicted, "the sides and tops of every hill and mountain here and the best valley locations will all be taken up with the houses of [these] ... people." The hill country would be converted "into a vast inhabited park, charming the senses, invigorating the health, [and] prompting thought and imagination." Cornell horticulturist Liberty Hyde Bailey expressed the ebullient optimism of these village reformers: "We shall construct great pictures out-of-doors. We shall assemble the houses, control the architecture, arrange the trees and the forests, direct the roads and fences, display the slopes of the hills, lay out the farms, remove every feature that offends a sensitive eye; and persons will leave the [art] galleries, with their limitations and imitations, to go to the country to see some of the greatest works of art that man can assemble and produce."[36]

The imagery that animated village improvement derived not only from regional literature and art but from the Colonial Revival, a cultural expression that drew support from old-stock upper-class urbanites seeking self-affirmation amid the cities' growing ethnic and religious heterogeneity. The Colonial Revival was a national movement, but it was particularly strong in New England, partly because Americans associated New England Puritanism with national beginnings and partly because so many colonial structures had been preserved by New England's lingering rural stagnation. Highlighting the architecture, domestic furnishings, literature, and arts of a supposedly simpler time, the Colonial Revival was an ironic blend of elite esteem for vernacular culture and snobbish criticism of the rural folk who fashioned it. With summer homes in the uplands, upper-class Yankees recast the village to reflect the images portrayed so vividly in New England art and literature. According to historian William Butler, summer residents in Litchfield, arguably the birthplace of the Colonial Revival, "delighted in showing off their ideal town," although they made it "virtually inaccessible to the common folk." Evidence of ordinary farm-town activity such as stables, shops, animal pens, and vegetable gardens disappeared as the town center took on the "look of the flourishing federal village minus the signs of the period's commercialism and industrialism."[37]

While urbanites were romanticizing rural life, farm families were leaving the upland regions in record numbers, causing concern among northeastern cultural elites. Rural emigration was common across the eastern states, but it was particularly noticeable in New England due to the symbolic significance attached to the Yankee farmer. "There was a time when New England was looked upon as a sort of reservoir of the true American spirit," Geoffrey

Champlin wrote in the *North American Review* in 1888. "No one, knowing what the New England characteristics were, two score years ago, can to-day travel through New England and fail to note the changes which time has made in the habits and characters of the people." The anticipation that Yankee traditions would dissipate as old-stock families sold out to French Canadian, Scandinavian, and Irish farmers gave the Colonial Revival a preservationist edge.[38]

Mindful of the high cultural stakes in Yankee persistence, reformers launched a campaign to enhance the appeal of the farm-and-village landscape. They realized that the openness of the rural landscape, although a staple of landscape art, was at odds with the social needs of its inhabitants. Living in isolation, rural folk expressed little pride in place. Roads were all but impassible, streets and yards barren, fences broken, outbuildings in ruin, and even the more prosperous homesteads cluttered with cast-off equipment and piles of refuse lumber and firewood. A touring Englishman concluded that land in America was too plentiful and too newly cultivated to be cherished in the English fashion; Americans had "lost the love of gardening." A disappointed landscape artist surveyed the "slatternly confusion of unhoused and ill used implements, of uncovered wood-pile and scattered odds and ends of rubbish" and dismissed the New England village as affording "little material for the [artistic] imagination." Landscape designer Robert Morris Copeland expressed hope that villagers would one day take up the Art of Public Improvement, but he was uncertain how this would happen. In Europe owners of great estates were bound by noblesse oblige to care for the surrounding villages and farms, but those in America felt no such responsibility. As Liberty Hyde Bailey said, estate owners contributed "little or nothing to real country welfare."[39]

The solution came, in fact, not at the hands of estate owners but rather from upper-middle-class urbanites who purchased modest homes in the upland towns and refurbished them according to Colonial Revival standards. Assuming the noblesse oblige lacking among the gentry, they formed alliances with local elites to beautify the village just as landscapers had beautified the country estate. "We have cause for rejoicing," Mary Caroline Robbins wrote in an essay on the subject, "that in many of our rural New England communities the awakening has come through the presence of summer visitors . . . who bring with them from the city habits of comfort and convenience . . . which result in improvements everywhere."[40]

Stockbridge, a Berkshire County community well known to Bostonians familiar with Andrew Jackson Downing's work, hosted the first of these village improvement societies. In 1853 local resident Mary G. Hopkins formed the Laurel Hill Association and with a group of dedicated volunteers set to work landscaping streets, expelling cows and hogs from the town center, removing rubbish from the nearby Housatonic River, laying out small parks at intersections, and transforming the once shabby town into an urbanite's vision of the proper New England village. The society planted some two thousand shade trees and recruited children to care for them. They refurbished civic buildings, churches, and stores and encouraged home owners to beautify their premises. Members purchased Laurel Hill, west of the town center, and after clearing underbrush and removing dead trees placed it under the care of a committee of trustees. The society also worked with the owner of nearby Ice Glen to improve the recreational potential of the mountain gorge with a footbridge, paths, and an observation tower. Stockbridge, in the words of sanitary engineer George Waring, came to wear "a look of neatness and intelligence, tasteful care."[41]

Dozens of villages followed the Stockbridge example as the movement radiated outward across the Northeast. By 1913 Massachusetts alone counted more than two hundred village improvement societies tidying up public places, planting trees, grading streets, landscaping public squares or greens, painting bridges and public buildings, improving sanitary conditions, protecting sources of drinking water, seeding street borders, fencing burying grounds, rebuilding stone walls, planting flowers, and installing benches—all to give the village "the effect of a park."[42] Having participated in Progressive Era reforms in the cities, summer residents insisted that improving the physical aspects of the village would strengthen moral character, foster pride in place, and instill a sense of industry.[43] Ambitious leaders insisted that all yards on the main streets be aligned and bordered with "simple fences" and all "meretricious ornamentation" removed to ensure "perfect neatness." All cattle, pigs, and poultry would be confined to backyard enclosures. "Every street shall be graded, every sidewalk shaded, every noxious weed eradicated, every water-course laid and perfected, and every nook and corner beautified." Most societies, to be sure, expressed these goals in more modest terms, content with the power of example to bring villagers into conformity. One tidy, well-kept yard would lead to another, and the gospel of improvement would spread through an entire village. "The whole history of rural affairs," according to one commentator, "shows the action of this principle of imitation."[44]

Like Progressives, village improvers used the rhetoric of democracy. "Even the very poor and ignorant should be invited to become members, out of good fellowship, and as a step in the general civilization," Susan Fenimore Cooper wrote. Improvers appealed to women of all classes, pointing out that yards, sidewalks, streets, and parks were simply extensions of the home. According to sanitation expert George Waring, village improvement required "the sort of systematized attention to detail, especially in the constantly-recurring duty of 'cleaning up,' that grows more naturally out of the habit of good housekeeping than out of any occupation to which men are accustomed."[45] Despite this egalitarian rhetoric, leadership in the societies suggests a tight-knit coalition of local elites and wealthy summer visitors—"judicious persons," as Cooper put it bluntly, "of respectable character . . . [acting] . . . as a general stimulant to torpid [village] corporations and . . . unmanageable individuals." In Stockbridge summer residents owned nearly 75 percent of the farmland and forest within a mile of the town center. Kirin Makker, who studied the Laurel Hill meeting minutes, found that "aesthetics mattered more than commerce to upper-class part-time residents." The affairs of the farm community would yield to "the superior claims of natural beauty," as a Stockbridge society annual report put it. Although improvers hoped to address the needs of all citizens, neither artisan shops nor year-round business establishments entered their field of vision. Inspired by magazines like the *Horticulturist*, they imagined rural New England variously as a park, playground, or objet d'art, with every aspect of village life "pitched in a nobler key."[46]

Despite their elitist overtones, village improvers recognized that the rural landscapes they hoped to preserve were essentially democratic creations. Improvers, George Waring remarked, should keep these humble origins in mind, removing only the "objectionable features" to highlight the simple charm of the village center. He cautioned against extravagant buildings or lavish gardens; rather, the charm of the village lay in its "coziness, neatness, simplicity, and . . . homely air." Hartford clergyman Nathaniel Egleston urged wealthy summer folk to honor the republican simplicity of the village. Summer residences should be "homes rather than showplaces." Whatever embellishment hid this simple beauty, Frederick Law Olmsted cautioned, "however beautiful in itself, is in effect a blemish."[47]

In 1908 President Theodore Roosevelt inaugurated the Commission on Country Life, which studied rural reform from a point of view that included such unromantic considerations as economic viability, educational and cultural opportunity, cooperative marketing, road maintenance, improved domestic conditions for farm wives, parcel-post delivery, sanitation, and soil and forest conservation. Although village improvement societies continued their work into the twentieth century, their leaders were no doubt sobered by the priorities listed in the report the commission issued in 1909. Perhaps, as one historian surmises, the movement was also weakened by the "pervasive feeling that everything useful or neat already had been done, that there was nothing much left to do except care for established improvements." More likely, wealthy urbanites shifted their focus from the village to the suburb, which offered another middle ground between city and country and another field for civic improvement. What remained of the village improvement spirit was expended in more mundane pursuits such as maintaining streets, sidewalks, streetlights, and sewers. Although reformers may have been oblivious to the deeper problems of rural life in America, their imprint is "still widely evident in New England's many 'picture postcard' villages." Their well-publicized campaigns, as Mark Stoll relates, became "intensely moral, with New England leading all other regions in its devotion to the cause." Later, when the city began encroaching on these villages in the 1960s, local citizens revived the spirit of village improvement, touching off the modern preservationist movement in New England.[48]

Tourism, Village, and Forest

The ideals formulated by midcentury estate designers and village improvers were popularized by a third essentially urban influence as middle-class families, taking advantage of cheaper rail transportation, adopted the idea of leisure travel. Working-class recreationists followed when bicycling became fashionable in the 1880s. Responding to this growing recreational interest, railroad and steamship companies, hotel owners' associations, boards of trade, agriculture commissions, and hiking, bicycling, mountaineering, hunting, and fishing clubs promoted rural New England in travel magazines, pamphlets, brochures, and guidebooks. Villages became, in the words of historians Ian McKay and Robin Bates, a "zone of contact between the visitor and the visited." Paintings, prints, and lithographs of lichen-shrouded farmhouses, weather-worn sheds, abandoned mills, narrow country roads, and rambling stone walls imprinted the New England village on the American mind.[49]

Midcentury landscape painting, with its meticulous accuracy, symbolic representations, and panoramic scenes, schooled viewers in the proper emotional reactions to the mountain sublime, and this sensitivity was essential to the early tourist experience. Nathaniel Southgate Shaler, Harvard geologist and sometime poet, warned that the contemplative attitude in landscape appreciation had to be carefully cultivated. "He who would become a lover of the landscape must accustom himself to seek it alone, and must learn to know that his mere presence at its doors will not make him free to its treasures."[50] The artists' language of place conditioned tourists to think of landscapes as an art form, and the ability to articulate this symbolism became the mark of a successful vacation.

Rural New England's first tourist economy was centered around rustic mountain hotels in New Hampshire, mineral springs in Vermont, seaside resorts in Maine, and religious encampments on Martha's Vineyard and Cape Cod. From these recreational outposts tourists fanned out into the lowlands at a time when declining agricultural prospects left rural New Englanders ready to embrace the "summer trade." Tourist promoters capitalized on the region's reputation for healthy living and sound morals, and middle-class visitors, raised in an atmosphere of severe self-denial, found this emphasis on hygienic and spiritual rejuvenation a convenient entrée into the world of leisure and display. Over time, farmhouses and taverns become inns and spas, and summer-home ownership grew in northern New England. Guidebooks adapted the symbol-rich discourse of mountain sublime to the farm-and-village scenery in the lowlands. The modulated topography of this middle landscape—neither wilderness nor urban—implied stability and simplicity in a period of rapid change. Small-town provincialism became a celebration of Yankee wit and native intelligence, hardscrabble farms personified the tenacity of pioneering America, and abandoned mills and fishing vessels became quaint artifacts of days gone by.[51]

In the second half of the century, it became clear that the forests that served as backdrop for these tourist retreats were under threat from logging companies. Among the first to bring this realization to public attention was George Perkins Marsh, lawyer, farmer, congressman, diplomat, and naturalist from Woodstock, Vermont. While ambassador to Italy, Marsh traveled the Mediterranean Rim, read widely, and wrote a brilliant study of deforestation and its consequences in Europe and America. Published in 1864, only two years after Henry David Thoreau's death, *Man and Nature* reminded Americans that improper use of the forest could upset the balance of nature. Although the farm press had raised the alarm about forest clearing decades earlier, Marsh's apocalyptic tone, as biographer David Lowenthal points out, underscored the dangers. "Formerly an emblem of pioneering progress, the hewn tree stump came via Marsh to symbolize wanton destructiveness."[52]

Marsh argued the need to preserve forest cover on the hills and mountains of New England. Trees broke the force of the summer's heavy rains, and their roots anchored soils to the bedrock. Forest litter and thick moss retained rain and snowmelt and gave back the moisture in time of drought. Forests hindered the south winds in summer and north winds in winter, moderating the climate and ensuring rain through the growing season. Written in the tradition of farm-press conservation jeremiads, his ideas were quickly picked up by rural editors. Quoting *Man and Nature*, the *Maine Farmer* reported that people everyone were noticing a diminution in streams and springs. "Brooks where we went trouting fifteen years ago, and which never failed in the driest seasons, are now mere rivulets."[53]

Concerns over logging practices mounted in the 1880s when the industry shifted from the production of lumber, which required mature pine and spruce, to pulpwood, which could be marketed at virtually any size. More intensive logging threatened a "frightful slaughter of the forest" and jeopardized the sublime scenery so important to the tourist industry. By the 1890s around 80 percent of Vermont's forest had been cut over, and loggers in New Hampshire were moving up the slopes of the Presidential Range. In Rhode Island, forester Bernhard Fernow found that "forests in the strict sense of the word can hardly be said to exist," and Harvard botanist Charles Sprague Sargent, who compiled statistics on forests for the 1880 US Census, pronounced these valuable resources "nearly exhausted" in state after state. In recognition of the coming timber famine, Congress passed the Forest Reserve Act in 1891, withdrawing selected federal lands from public sale and providing for their maintenance as forest reserves. Well before this federal initiative, however, New England states had established temporary forestry commissions, first in Maine in 1869, then in Connecticut in 1877, New Hampshire in 1881, Vermont in 1882, and Massachusetts in 1890. These commissions became permanent agencies in the 1890s and 1910s, and legislatures authorized them to accept gifts of land for demonstration forests and to promote fire safety, supervise town-based firefighting organizations, and provide tree seedlings free or at cost to landowners.[54]

The tourist industry was in good part responsible for these and other initiatives. For decades conservationists, quoting Marsh, had argued that forests preserved the balance of nature, but the advent of mountain tourism shifted the focus of these arguments to aesthetic considerations. Conservationist Joseph Chamberlain pointed out that forests grew back with "astonishing vigor" after they were cut or burned, and in the interim dams and reservoirs kept stream flow steady. Still, he saw good reason for conservation. "Sentimental considerations, I suppose, are to be held secondary to the practical in the matter; but they are powerful, and should be aroused in behalf of . . . the woods." Charles Sargent likewise believed that the strongest argument for forest conservation, if not the most practical, was their "irresistible inducement to people in the city who are looking for summer resorts." Tourists paid liberally for their sojourns to mountain hotels, but this liberality depended on protecting the beauty of the surrounding woods and mountains. Women's clubs, as Kimberly Jarvis points out, joined in this conservation campaign for both practical and sentimental reasons. Conservationists rallied to preserve the wilderness backdrop for New England's iconic villages. Trees, they pointed out, were "worth more to look at as they stand than they will be after they are sawed up into lumber."[55] Landscape appreciation, a mainstay of New England rural iconography, took a preservationist turn with the forest conservation campaigns of the 1890s.

The Suburban Village

In an 1858 essay, Andrew Jackson Downing suggested that Americans defined themselves by their "taste for rural beauty," and Nathaniel Egleston added that this love of open country was a "peculiarly Anglo-Saxon trait, . . . come down to us even from our Teutonic ancestors." Susan Fenimore Cooper, whose *Rural Hours* explored the moral landscapes and botanical treasures of the upper Susquehanna Valley, forecast the day when rural living would be near universal. Cities would be "chiefly abandoned to the drudgeries of . . . commerce and manufactures during the hours of day, and deserted at night." Others, however, cautioned against emptying the city of residents. Cities were the engines of economic and artistic progress, they argued, places where the constant exchange of ideas expanded the boundaries of knowledge, stimulated innovation, and dissipated prejudice. The synthesis that emerged out of this ongoing debate was the suburb, a new middle ground where residents could enjoy the tranquility of open spaces and at the same time participate in the lively intercourse that renewed the zest for life. By the end of the century, this solution seemed self-evident. Speaking before the Park and Outdoor Association of America in 1898, L. E. Holden announced a new generation of Americans, neither "country-bred nor city-bred, but suburban-bred, product of neither extreme." The suburb contrived, in David Schuyler's words, a "simultaneous redefinition of agrarianism and urban culture." By combining a rural past and urban present, according to Michael Rawson, New Englanders "invented a suburban future."[56]

At the beginning of the nineteenth century, most of Boston's sixty-one thousand citizens were confined to a square mile of land on the Shawmut Peninsula. As the port grew busier and the waterfront more congested, merchants, bankers, and professionals moved out to Hyde Park, Brookline, Newton, Belmont, Winchester, Melrose, and Malden, where landscaped grounds, winding, tree-lined streets, nearby open fields, and small parks or greens reminded them of a classic New England village. Irish immigrants crowding into Boston's North End tenements in the 1840s augmented this outward flow, as did new transportation technologies introduced at the same time.

Early suburbs were created to house industrial activities too noisy, too dirty, or too large to fit into the city's inner neighborhoods. These outlying towns also hosted a scattering of sumptuous estates belonging to colonial-era merchants. Theodore Lyman's estate in Waltham was laid out "in a manner to rival some of the princely possessions in England," and other towns, particularly Newton and Brighton, were nationally known for their orchards, nurseries, and greenhouses. This began to change in the 1840s when railroads connecting the city to the Midwest added intermediate stops in nearby towns and introduced commuted fares for daily travel. By 1859 some fifty-nine commuter trains arrived in Boston every weekday, giving the city a larger commuter population than any other in America. When horse-drawn street trolleys entered the scene, middle-class families followed their social betters into the suburbs. In the 1890s electric streetcars extended the zone of suburban development. With travel ensured, land syndicates bought up farmland and added middle-class neighborhoods to an urban periphery made up of farms, estates, and clusters of workshops and factories.[57]

In the mid-1850s architect Alexander Jackson Davis created the nation's first fully landscaped suburb, Llewellyn Park, in West Orange, New Jersey, and in the next decade Frederick Law Olmsted and Calvert Vaux designed a much larger sixteen-hundred-acre community about nine miles from Chicago with each home opening on a "pretty little park." Landscaped suburbs grew apace, with developers advertising tree-lined streets, varied architecture, contact with nature, and of course convenient transportation to the city. Olmsted went on to design forty-seven suburban neighborhoods, and his sons, John Charles and Frederick Jr., added some four hundred more across the country. With each home owner a potential gardener or landscaper, suburban growth democratized the Art of Public Improvement, but it also threatened to cheapen it. Designers urged suburbanites to seek professional advice and cautioned against exotic shrubs and ostentatious "chromo-like flower-beds."

Despite the rawness of suburban life, reformers remained optimistic. Properly sculpted, the American suburb would "excite the ... admiration of even our English visitors," landscape architect Charles N. Lowrie predicted. Buoyed by these thoughts, designers plied their trade in towns and villages on the urban fringe.[58]

Suburbs were by no means uniform in their residential makeup. In some cases, farms were subdivided into small lots to be sold to lower-middle-class and upper-working-class residents, while in others the clientele was more exclusive. Concerned about the growing immigrant presence in the city, residents in the wealthier suburbs blocked streetcar extensions in an attempt to slow in-migration and maintain "the appearance of a classic New England village center." Other communities welcomed streetcar extensions as a spur to economic growth, and while some opposed incorporation into metropolitan Boston, others sought the improved infrastructure incorporation would bring. The result was a mosaic of communities arranged according to class and ethnicity, and the appearance of zoning ordinances after midcentury locked these distinctions into place.[59]

As farms disappeared from the suburbs, residents lost touch with the natural world once so apparent in these outlying landscapes. Suburbanites, as Brian Donahue points out, found themselves "living in the midst of a forest with which [they had] ... almost no working relationship." To reconnect with the natural world, they took up nature studies, planted gardens, landscaped their lawns, and hiked or picnicked in the hills that outlined the Boston Basin. Situated at the interface of city and country, they contrived a new pastoral identity that incorporated nature and open spaces as aesthetic and recreational encounters. At the end of the century they took up the challenge of preserving open spaces in order to insulate this pastoral construct from the disorders that came with rapid demographic and commercial growth.[60]

Charles Sprague Sargent and *Garden and Forest*

In the decades after Downing's death in 1852, Charles Sprague Sargent rose to the fore as a leading authority on landscape design, largely due to his work in the burgeoning Boston suburbs. Like Downing, Sargent became a key figure in transforming landscape aesthetics into a preservationist movement. Unlike Downing, Sargent was a member of the class most courted by landscape designers. A Boston blueblood, he grew up on the family's 130-acre Brookline estate, Holm Lea. In 1872 he was charged with creating the Harvard Botanic Garden, as it was then called, on the site of the Benjamin Bussey farm, where four years earlier New Bedford horticulturist James Arnold had willed funds to establish an arboretum. In addition to his Harvard professorship and arboretum work, Sargent published *Garden and Forest: A Journal of Horticulture, Landscape Art, and Forestry*. During its short publication run between 1888 and 1897, the magazine became the most influential guide to landscape design in America, covering such important topics as horticulture, botany, landscaping, parks, roads, and forest conservation. Sargent urged these topics on his readers with articles by leading specialists in each field, calculated, as the *Boston Transcript* put it, "to arouse public attention as few other existing instrumentalities are capable of doing." *Garden and Forest* touched on issues ranging from rapacious logging in the western forests to poverty, inequality, and blight in the eastern industrial cities.[61]

Downing had made his mark in the design of country estates; Sargent, by contrast, was drawn to the suburbs, where a landscape designer could express on a few acres a great deal of creativity in blending art and nature. Sargent understood that designing the suburban residence, far more than landscaping the large estate, would be an artistic illusion. Large estates could be harmonized with the surrounding natural setting with relative ease, but on the outskirts of the city a long history of lumbering, burning, building, pasturing, and cultivation left "at best only a general resemblance of natural scenery." Landscapers could use what remained—a swale, a sprout-wood forest, a tangled bank, or a muddy pond—to create what suburbanites imagined as the iconic New England landscape, but the effect would require a practiced eye.[62]

Garden and Forest presented four themes that helped accommodate rural iconography to the suburban setting. First, its authors followed the example of village improvement societies by focusing primarily on landscapes that were ordinary rather than majestic—places attractive because they were familiar, near at hand, and reminiscent of home. This was clear in their near-universal preference for local plants and trees in their landscaping designs. Second, they privileged lightly modified landscapes over wholly natural scenes—again in the tradition of village improvement. The western wilderness was inspiring, Sargent conceded, but this was due to the novelty of its scale and its primitive appearance. Wilderness scenes evoked an initial sublime reaction, but the observer soon lost interest. The lonely, the savage, or the wild became "oppressive and repellent if long dwelt upon," while the humble humanized landscape endured in the mind. Generations of collective wisdom in clearing land, smoothing contours, and laying out fields and pastures gave the scene a heady republican cast that was far more American than the open spaces of the West.[63]

Third, *Garden and Forest* carried numerous articles advocating preservation of the remaining open spaces in the suburbs, unassuming though these spaces might be. Wooded slopes, wetlands, roadside strips, riverbanks, and other left-behind places were worthless to developers but priceless as relics of the open country that once stretched outward beyond the villages. Sargent, along with Pennsylvania conservationist Myra Dock, articulated perhaps for the first time a rationale for preserving land that contained nothing more significant than the imprint of the original environment. Acknowledging these ordinary places brought landscape designers to the borders of ecological thinking. "It is readily observed that very few species of plants exist . . . alone," Franklin Waugh pointed out. "Practically every one associates habitually with certain other species . . . , and these friendly associations, based upon similarity of tastes and complementary habits of growth, should not be broken up. If we as landscape gardeners desire to preserve the whole aspect of nature, with all its forms intact, we will keep all plants in their proper social groupings."[64]

A fourth recurring theme in *Garden and Forest* involved the status of the landscape designer. Although Sargent paid tribute to the republican values inherent in the vernacular landscape, he insisted on the prerogatives of his rather elite profession when it came to re-creating this landscape in a suburban context. Designing landscapes was like painting with vegetation, he explained; each piece bore a different message, depending on its shape, size, and color. Some leaves were mottled and multicolored, others bright or muted, and still others smooth, shiny, dull, or woolly. Each tree reflected a different mood. Silver maples were "unquiet," sugar maples "restful," and oaks "massive." Professional landscape designers were expected to keep abreast of these principles by reading journals, traveling, assessing the creations of others, and attending conferences.[65]

Intent on professionalizing landscape design, Sargent sent a mixed message about the Art of Public Improvement. Like Downing, he presented technical information in nonspecialist terms, and through the letters-to-the-editor columns he allowed readers to interact with a wide range of experts. Yet he also made it clear that only professionals understood the finer points of landscape art. The juxtaposition of trees and shrubs, with their various shapes, tints, and hues, would have to appeal in all seasons, in all conditions of sun and shade, and in all stages of growth. A truly artistic design required the foresight of the engineer, the taste of the world traveler, and the sensitivity of the poet. Others could plant trees or shrubs, but only the landscape professional could seize an idea from nature and assert it "more perfectly than . . . she herself is often able to express it."[66]

Sargent's crusade to naturalize the suburbs was an important step toward the fierce defense of rural atmosphere that set the land-trust movement in motion in the 1960s, but it is not surprising that this nascent preservationist campaign was both democratic and exclusionist. Sargent understood, as did readers of his *Garden and Forest*, that suburbs were juxtaposed precariously between the isolated and intellectually stagnant countryside and the rapidly expanding and aesthetically distasteful city. Those who lived there were determined to have the best of both worlds and to avoid the pitfalls of both. The Art of Public Improvement required some forms of exclusion to protect the legacy of the New England village. Suburbanites privatized this iconography by joining country clubs, tending spacious lawns, and, in the twentieth century, experimenting with exclusive zoning. They used land trusts to block development on strategic open spaces, but at the same time they made these spaces accessible to everyone. In time, this latter impulse would democratize the Art of Public Improvement.[67]

Mary Caroline Robbins dreamed of an art for all America. *Garden and Forest* clouded this prospect in some ways but legitimized it in others. Contributors to Sargent's journal adopted the principle of genius loci—the inspiration of place—and their attempts to transform common landscapes into a form of publicly accessible art became the standard for preservation campaigns in New England. Operating on this principle, twentieth-century land trusts protected thousands of acres of farms, fields, forests, and other open spaces that had no claim on public attention other than their exquisite ordinariness. Landscapes like these, while neither pristine nor monumental, were important because they were deeply democratic in their expression of regional culture, and for this reason they attracted a great deal of popular loyalty.[68]

Urban Parks and Rural Visions

While suburbanites were moving outward into the nearby countryside, urban reformers were bringing the countryside back into the city. The phrase *rus in urbe*, referring to natural landscaping within the walls of a classic urban villa, appeared prominently in the literature of the 1890s adapted to mean natural landscaping in public places. "Rus in urbe is no more an island. It becomes a river, flowing through all the streets and by-ways, and forming in squares and parks little ponds and lakes of the country." Designers retained the idea of enclosed natural space by bordering parks with thick vegetation to exclude the sights and sounds of the street. Park designers used the landscaping ideals formulated in the countryside to naturalize the city.[69]

Parks are the stepchild of the Industrial Revolution. In the mid-nineteenth century reformers grew concerned about the grime, drudgery, and artificiality that accompanied the rise of industry in the urban environment. Cities had grown so large that strolling out into the countryside for relief was no longer possible, and according to prevailing thought, this loss of contact with nature enervated city people. Americans who traveled abroad were quick to note that landscaped parks, common in Europe, helped remedy this problem. Andrew Jackson Downing saw them as places where "all classes assemble under the shade of the same trees—the nobility, . . . the wealthy citizens, the shopkeepers, and the artisans, etc." Social mixing eased class tensions, while trees and plants removed noxious gasses and odors from the atmosphere. Parks, like great estates, would inspire improvements in the neighborhoods around them. "A beautiful park may awaken a desire for a lovelier home-garden, and the wish for a beautiful home grows into the wish for a beautiful street."[70]

When Downing's detractors suggested that Americans had no interest in parks, he pointed to the crowds of people picnicking in rural cemeteries. The idea of moving cemeteries to the outskirts of a city reflected new attitudes toward death and mourning at a time when sextons were stacking bodies several deep in church cemeteries or exhuming them to make room for the newly departed. The fear of miasmas—fumes from decaying material—and a rise in downtown land values encouraged a search for other means of dealing with the dead. America's first rural cemetery, Mount Auburn, was chartered in 1831 when Harvard botanist Jacob Bigelow, working with the Massachusetts Horticultural Society, landscaped a 170-acre tract of undulating land in Cambridge. Mount Auburn and the rural cemeteries that followed attracted visitors of all classes, and the notion that a natural setting could soothe the overwrought psyche set the scene for bringing English landscaping principles and park ideas to America.[71]

In 1849 Downing and William Cullen Bryant of the *New York Evening Post* began campaigning for a park on the northern outskirts of Manhattan where citizens could enjoy "the substantial delights of country roads and country scenery, and forget, for a time, the rattle of the pavements and the glare of brick walls." Downing and his partner, Calvert Vaux, offered to design the park, but Downing died in a steamboat accident in 1852. A year later, city leaders put out bids for a park plan, and the first premium was conferred on Vaux and Downing's young friend Frederick Law Olmsted. The park movement in America, Olmsted wrote later, dated from "Mr. Downing's writings on the subject in 1849."[72]

Olmsted, who would become America's preeminent landscape designer with the completion of Central Park, was born in Hartford in 1822 and spent much of his boyhood wandering the hills along the Connecticut River. He trained briefly as a civil engineer, served as a dry-goods clerk, apprenticed as a seaman, and took up farming in Connecticut and later on Staten Island. He spent the summer of 1850 in Europe with his brother John and his friend Charles Loring Brace, who would become a leading proponent of country life in America. When Olmsted published *Walks and Talks of an American Farmer in England* in 1852, he included a tribute to England's vernacular farmhouses, lush gardens, thatch-roofed stables, brownstone churches, and bordering hedgerows. Back in America he observed among the urban lower classes "a frantic desire to escape from the dull lives" and concluded that rich and poor alike should be afforded the opportunity to contemplate country scenes like those in England, even in the heart of the city. Combining his interest in landscapes and his compassion for urban working people, he accepted the job as superintendent of the Central Park project.[73]

In one of the great epics of American urban history, Olmsted and Vaux put their laborers to work blasting, grading, excavating, and landscaping a barren 843-acre dumping ground and squatter camp, transforming it into a "model of pastoral freedom." In designing Central Park, Olmsted and Vaux set out the principles that would guide the Art of Public Improvement as it migrated to the cities. Urbanization, they believed, was a positive force in the history of civilization, but its potential was clouded by overcrowding, poor housing and sanitation, class tension, political corruption, and other social afflictions. Like most Progressive reformers, they believed these influences could be mitigated by improving the environmental conditions that fostered them. Although many feared that Central Park would become a "raucous place . . . avoided by the better class," Olmsted and Vaux held firm to the belief that natural environments smoothed the rough edges of working-class life. In their park designs they included greenswards large enough to accommodate thousands of "little family and neighborly parties" and provide opportunities for strolling "for an hour, seeing, hearing, and feeling nothing of the bustle and jar of the streets." On city streets people walked "watchfully, jealously"; in a park they regarded each other with humanity. Convinced that parks would regenerate the human spirit, Olmsted became America's leading advocate for using the moral power of the countryside as an instrument of urban social reform.[74]

Parks, like other forms of landscape improvement, were both democratic and elitist. They were dedicated to the people but designed by those who jealously guarded their "correct knowledge of beautiful forms." Left to popular influences, landscape designers worried, parks would be "spangled with gay exotics, [and] striped with ribbon-borders and beds of brick-colored geraniums uttering their chromatic shrieks on every hand." Park designers protected their creations from "the crude and materialistic impulses of popular culture" by imposing rules that precluded all but "peaceful enjoyment of an idealized rural landscape." They warned against "noisy sports [and the] festivities of the brass band, fireworks, and barbecue order." Despite this bias in design and use, parks were immensely important in popularizing the Art of Public Improvement. Each year, Olmsted pointed out, Central Park exposed four to five million visitors to the "essential esthetic qualities of ... scenery." These visitors returned to the suburb or village with a heightened standard of landscape appreciation, and eventually the whole country, he anticipated, would "feel the impulse which the high culture of the Central Park has given to rural improvements." The park would reform the very countryside it was designed to emulate.[75]

Boston's Common is generally considered America's first municipal park, although it was only one among many examples of public open spaces in colonial-era communities, others being village greens in New England, bowling greens in New Amsterdam, squares in southern cities, and plazas in New Spain. Boston purchased the Common from William Blackstone in 1634, and for several decades it was used as a place for household chores, militia musters, and livestock grazing. Over time, nearby residents realized the benefits of a rural sanctuary, and in response the city planted elms, filled in sloughs, and removed livestock. In 1859 the Massachusetts legislature declared the Common a public park.

Boston was well positioned for park development. Its leading families had made their fortunes outside Boston in the shipping trade, land speculation, or textile manufacturing, and they regarded their city, as Mona Domosh points out, "not as a site of revenue producing ... but as a domestic space, a place to live and play."[76] In 1869, as Central Park was nearing completion, landscape designer Horace W. S. Cleveland published a brief reflection titled "What Boston May Do." The entire Shawmut Peninsula, he recognized, was smaller than Central Park, meaning that to build on a similar scale Boston would have to "go beyond her own limits." Fortunately, the city was surrounded by beautiful natural features, tidy homes and farms, and exquisitely landscaped estates. Pointing to the "thrifty appearance of even the humblest abodes," Cleveland reasoned that the suburbs themselves could provide an alternative to a large central park. "It remains only for Boston to avail herself of the opportunity thus offered by finishing and adorning the roads which wind among these charming scenes in a corresponding style." He was not certain, however, that suburban residents could be trusted "with the preservation of so widely extended a territory, adorned in the style suggested." Since good taste was an untested proposition among suburbanites, Cleveland suggested an additional system of small landscaped parks beginning on the banks of the Charles and extending out to the suburbs. Like Olmsted, he believed that suburbanites would be inspired by the parks' features to maintain their residences in proper fashion, so that those living in the city could "ride for days in succession through continually varying scenes in which the display of individual taste, and the character of refinement and home-comfort . . . is everywhere apparent." In Central Park nature had been "elaborately dressed for the sole and avowed object of display"; in Boston the combination of nature, art, and suburban living would "excite an interest of a more durable nature." The city would adorn itself, not with a "single costly bouquet" but "with a garment of flowers," most of which had been woven already by suburbanites of good taste.[77]

Cleveland's plan borrowed from earlier proposals by Robert Morris Copeland and Uriel Crocker, each of whom envisioned a series of parks linked by parkways designed for carriage travel. Cleveland was unique, however, in drawing "the whole surrounding country" into his system. If suburbs were an embodiment of country life, it was appropriate that they serve as extensions of the urban park system. Although somewhat fanciful, his faith in the Art of Public Improvement carried considerable weight among park enthusiasts, and his call for preserving rural ambience was among the first of many to come.[78]

In 1869, the year of Cleveland's proposal, citizens in the Back Bay neighborhood asked the city council to form a committee to consider park development, and the state's General Court obliged by passing an act authorizing a park system for the city. Bostonians initially voted down the bill, but fierce lobbying kept the idea before the city council. Swayed by the prospect of surpassing New York and Chicago in urban beautification, increasing adjacent property valuations, and providing open space for Boston's working poor, the council finally authorized a park commission. In 1870 Frederick Law Olmsted lectured at the Lowell Institute on "Public Parks and the Enlargement of Towns," and five years later the commissioners asked him to serve as consultant. In designing parks for New York City, Brooklyn, Montreal, Buffalo, and Milwaukee, Olmsted had struggled against city politicians hoping to fill these open spaces with parade grounds, churches, zoos, racetracks, and concessions. In Boston, he realized, the project was firmly in the hands of a Brahmin class well acquainted with the genteel principles that underlaid his own landscaping designs. With elite backing, Olmsted democratized the ideas introduced by Copeland, Crocker, and Cleveland by suggesting a park system accessible to all Bostonians, not just those riding in carriages. He envisioned a series of large and small public spaces running from the Common and Public Garden along the Charles River and Back Bay through the Fens to Jamaica Pond and West Roxbury. Between 1878 and 1895 the commissioners brought this vision to life, holding to Olmsted's landscaping ideas but also including smaller open spaces devoted to less contemplative forms of leisure.[79]

Olmsted began in the Back Bay, then Boston's most fashionable neighborhood, with the troublesome Muddy River, a narrow, winding tidal creek his workers transformed into a "distinctly English waterway flowing peacefully through a natural, yet well ordered landscape." In-filling in Boston Harbor had transformed the creek into a mosquito-breeding, stagnant cattail swamp rank with sewage. Olmsted solved the pollution problem by installing floodgates at the confluence with the Charles and creating a series of holding ponds to ensure steady flowage. "What emerged, after some ten years of construction, was an elegant curving greenway, with willows, oaks, and maples bordering the walkways, carriageways, and bridle paths; all in all, ... a picturesque riverine landscape such as he had found in the marshlands, or fens, of eastern England." The carefully cultivated wild look was innovative, requiring, as a later commentator wrote, "considerable ... professional courage." It was also unique in serving a dual purpose as a parkway and storm drainage system designed to flush contaminated water out into the Charles.[80]

Boston's Emerald Necklace proceeded from the Common, located on the edge of the new Back Bay residential area, and ran to the Charlesbank, built on reclaimed land in one of the poorest districts in the city. To the east, the Fens offered pleasant paths for strolling and riding along two meandering watercourses, and from there the system extended to the Arnold Arboretum, managed jointly by Boston and Harvard University. Between the Fens and the arboretum, a park on Jamaica Pond offered views across an expanse of water. Franklin Park, to the south of the city, featured 527 acres of rolling grassland and woodland. Here Olmsted added a recreational "Ante-Park" neatly segregated from the greensward and featuring sports fields, tennis courts, refreshment stands, an amphitheater, a small zoo and deer park, statues, and swings, tilts, and other "devices for affording pleasure not sufficiently in keeping with the pastoral landscape." The system, preserving more than 2,000 acres of open land, was largely completed by 1895. It offered a variety of recreational features and was accessible to far more citizens than the consolidated 843-acre park in New York City. To resolve the problem of fragmentation, Olmsted connected his parks with parkways, an idea he had improvised in Buffalo. Those in carriages or on foot could travel between parks along undulating roadways landscaped to separate the traveler from the traffic and business of the city.[81] Brilliantly adapted to Boston's varied terrain and diverse neighborhoods, the Emerald Necklace was a masterpiece of park design. It epitomized the high principles landscape art had attained and captured the spirit of those places New England artists, writers, and reformers had molded into a national icon during the previous half century. A graceful blend of culture and nature, the Emerald Necklace was a consummate achievement in the Art of Public Improvement.

Rural Iconography and the Preservationist Spirit

America, as Mary Caroline Robbins suggested in 1896, was a vast and varied canvas for a new form of democratic art predicated on the moral authority of the countryside. Her vision of a coast-to-coast "national parkway" leading from one landscaped pleasure ground to another never came to fruition, but her hope that Americans would grow to appreciate the beauty of their surroundings was anything but far-fetched. Half a century earlier Andrew Jackson Downing had laid the foundation for landscape appreciation in America, admonishing village reformers to create "something more healthful than the ordinary life of cities, and more refining and elevating than the common gossip of country villages." Searching for this illusive middle ground, suburbanites left the city for the countryside, and reformers introduced the countryside into the city in the form of landscaped parks. This exchange confirmed the iconic stature of rural New England and set the stage for a burgeoning preservation movement. In 1902 Boston's Sylvester Baxter sensed this rising interest in landscape beauty and predicted a "Great Civic Awakening in America." The awakening would be more labored than he anticipated, but its arrival had momentous consequences.[82]

Baxter's optimism grew from a landmark event in the Art of Public Improvement. In 1891 he, Charles Eliot, and a small group of Boston luminaries had created the Trustees of Public Reservations, whose mission it was to rally "public-spirited men and women" in a campaign to preserve the best of the New England countryside as reserves set aside for visitors from all walks of life. As the nation's first privately managed land trust, the TPR bridged the chasm between the nineteenth-century country estate and the modern open-space preservation movement. If rural landscapes were the "art of America," as Robbins thought, the TPR's project would be an open-air art museum. From its Olmsted-inspired assumption of patrician stewardship and passive nature contemplation, the TPR went on to inspire a broad-based commitment to the preservation idea. In the 1920s it delegated responsibility for maintaining a growing number of reservations to local residents who shared the TPR's passion for the Art of Public Improvement, and four decades later these far-flung and locally stewarded reservations inspired townspeople across New England to form their own land trusts.[83] In the nineteenth century the Art of Public Improvement meant beautifying the countryside and bringing this beauty back into the cities. In the twentieth century the TPR and other land-preservation organizations extended this commitment by preserving those places that best represented this compelling New England landscape ideal.

CHAPTER 2

Awakening the Preservation Spirit
The Trustees of Public Reservations

The most dramatic advance in land preservation in nineteenth-century New England was the founding of the Trustees of Public Reservations in Boston in 1891. Dedicated to preserving representative landscapes across the Commonwealth, the TPR, the nation's first private land-preservation organization, transformed the Art of Public Improvement into a preservationist agenda that continues to resonate today. Like earlier forms of landscape improvement, it was elite sponsored, but its dedication to providing open spaces for all Massachusetts residents was crucial to democratizing the preservation movement. Beginning with a few small reservations scattered around Boston, the TPR went on to acquire some twenty-seven thousand acres in 116 properties across Massachusetts by the end of the twentieth century.

The TPR pioneered the principles that would guide New England preservation into the twenty-first century, taking on complicated issues such as monitoring public use of delicate natural landscapes, imposing cultural preferences on dynamic natural systems, and promoting the idea that scenery, even on private land, was a public trust. Just as important, the TPR pioneered the democratization of open spaces. Over the years the organization found that managing its widely dispersed reserves was beyond the reach of its Boston area leadership.[1] By necessity and perhaps in response to the changing tone of twentieth-century land conservation, the TPR delegated authority over individual reservations to local volunteers. It remained an essentially top-down organization, but much of its day-to-day decision making was done at a grassroots level. This local management model became the basis for the land-trust movement that grew in its shadow in the 1960s and 1970s.

The TPR originated among a few wealthy and influential men and women in the Boston area who expressed their civic spiritedness by supporting causes like temperance, suffrage, and prison reform and by endowing colleges, museums, hospitals, monuments, and charitable organizations. The TPR, as Gordon Abbott pointed out in his 1993 history of the organization, was a child of this noblesse oblige.

> The early trustees were leaders of their community, and in those days the characteristics of community leadership were easy to identify: a patrician background with a genealogy which often included ancestors who were instrumental in the establishment of the country; marriage to a woman of equal genealogical qualifications; a degree from Harvard College; a religious faith which was Unitarian or Episcopalian; recognized success in what ever field was chosen as a profession; wealth, not ostentatiously displayed, but enough to quietly reflect intellectual tastes in literature, music, and art, and to allow for some measure of personal indulgence such as a summer house or yacht; an involvement in public life in an appointed or elected position.[2]

The TPR was one more way of demonstrating a willingness to take on the burden of uplifting New England civilization.

Boston's elite faced a series of crises at the end of the century. For generations they lived in the shadow of the European gentry, but by the 1890s they were eclipsed by a new class of American industrialists who manipulated wealth and power on a scale unimaginable in Boston's heyday. The city itself slipped behind New York and Chicago as a financial center, and this again affected its leaders' standing as America's cultural arbiters. In addition to the loss of national status, Boston's elites were losing their hold on the city as new political leaders rose out of the immigrant wards. Older residential neighborhoods were becoming less fashionable, and familiar landmarks were giving way to new and more imposing edifices that lacked the patina of age. At the same time, the pastoral landscapes on the metropolitan rim were being despoiled by land speculators and suburban developers. "Besieged on several fronts, many Brahmins entered the last decades of the nineteenth century convinced that their city's best days were behind it."[3]

This combination of civic obligation and cultural anxiety shaped the preservationist movement that grew outward from Boston in the late nineteenth century. Anxious to reassert the city's cultural status and relieve the rising tension in the inner wards, in 1891 influential Bostonians launched the TPR hoping to showcase places of natural charm and historic interest on the Boston fringe. Discomfited by the commercial forces stirring around them, they campaigned to protect selected samples of the familiar New England landscape from "heedless enterprise" and open them to the public.[4] Anticipating a comparable sense of social responsibility among property owners of their class, they appealed for gifts of land to hold in trust as public reserves, and when this proved only modestly successful they broadened their campaign to awaken preservation instincts among all classes of Massachusetts citizens. The appeal to philanthropic landowners and financial donors slowly yielded results, and in the 1930s the TPR invited those living around the reservations to join in preserving the lands they acquired. Having pioneered the twin themes of the coming land-trust movement—private philanthropy and broad public participation—the TPR set the scene for one of the most significant environmental advances in modern American history.

Charles Eliot and the Trustees of Public Reservations

The founder of this high-minded enterprise, Charles Eliot Jr., exemplified both the Brahmin philanthropic outlook and the landscape ideals on which their project was established. Eliot was born in Cambridge in 1859 into a family that traced its wealth back to the early merchant trade out of Boston. His father, Charles William Eliot, was a Harvard professor and later president of the institution. The younger Eliot passed his childhood in a genteel suburban world of well-tended gardens, wide lawns, and stately groves. The Eliot family toured Europe, visiting ancestral gardens and lavish estates. Steeped in the beauty of these hallowed places, Eliot developed a keen appreciation for artfully cultivated natural beauty. When his mother died in 1869, he began spending time with his grandmother and other relatives in Brookline, Chestnut Hill, and Jamaica Plain, forming family connections that became important to his growing interest in landscape design.[5]

Eliot's father remarried in 1877, and with renewed self-confidence young Charles pursued a variety of outdoor activities that included hiking, boating, sketching, and mapmaking. With his family, he summered on Mount Desert Island in Maine, a bucolic retreat framed by rounded granitic peaks, isolated inlets, and rocky headlands. Exploring the hills and shores of the island, he developed a love of nature and, as Melanie Simo writes, a revulsion toward "all attempts to make of these raw materials an English garden or a Newport lawn." At home in Cambridge he wandered through the rural tracts in the Boston Basin, familiarizing himself with the lay of the land, the history of its architecture, and the wild reaches along the rivers. He acquired a deep appreciation for the rural atmosphere of suburban Boston.[6]

At Harvard, Eliot attended lectures on gardening at the Bussey Institute, located on a magnificent estate southwest of Boston. He fell under the influence of poet and geologist Nathaniel Southgate Shaler and through family connections met Frederick Law Olmsted. The former instilled a concern for the "many beautiful places obliterated by human action," and the latter helped focus his understanding of scenic elements. After graduating in 1881, Eliot decided on a career in landscape architecture. The profession included barely a handful of adherents at the time, but demand for their services was growing in the towns on the Boston rim. In 1883 Eliot accepted a position as unpaid apprentice in Olmsted's office, working closely with Olmsted's son John Charles.[7]

In 1885 Eliot interrupted his work with the Olmsteds for a thirteen-month tour of Europe, where he sketched landscapes and read pastoral passages in Petrarch, Boccaccio, Tasso, Dante, Milton, Chaucer, Wordsworth, and others. He traveled without a plan, trusting that almost anywhere in Europe he would stumble across "professionally instructive" scenes. At Portofino a sinuous road skirting a high cliff above the sea led him to a landscape that blended natural and structural form into a "sort of fairyland of fresh green grass and ferns, moss, ivy, and countless flowers, with new-budding trees and singing birds, and cottages hidden away in corners, and steep hill-sides of Olives." In England he walked amid "slopes and swells," admiring huge oaks, beeches, ashes, cedars, and modest cottages bordered with rose and pansy. At Rowsley he found the Chatsworth House tour tedious but drank in the "fine views from the windows."[8] He came to appreciate the manner in which vegetation blended with the cottages, great halls, and sandstone churches to create scenes of overwhelming beauty.

The climax of this experience was Eliot's stay at the estate of Prince Hermann Pückler at Muskau in Silesia. One of the great figures in European landscape art, Pückler designed his grounds as an example of proper spatial relations between natural and human elements. As he explained in his *Hints on Landscape Gardening*, he chose not to clear away the local village, as was common in earlier landscape design; rather, he made the cottages and fields part of his viewshed. He used a flowing network of roads, paths, and small streams to tie the landscape together and planted only native trees and shrubs, explaining that even an artificial landscape "must . . . be true to the character of the country and the climate to which it belongs." The Pückler estate, Eliot wrote, was "one of the loveliest vales on earth—and full to the brim, so to speak, . . . of quieting and often touching beauty." Muskau convinced him that landscaping must reflect the surrounding countryside, be it natural, artificial, or both.[9]

The experience was humbling. In America, Eliot wrote, "buildings, fences, highways and railroads, not to speak of our towns, are often scars, which mar the face of nature." In Europe, "fields, lanes, roads, houses, churches, and even whole villages and towns seem to combine with nature to produce a scenery of a more lovable type than nature working alone can offer us." Still, he remained optimistic about the prospects for landscape art in America. Like his predecessor Andrew Jackson Downing, he returned from Europe convinced that New Englanders could design landscapes worthy of their own more natural environment.[10]

Eliot was similarly influenced by his family's respites on Mount Desert Island. Around 1860 a few well-to-do Bostonians colonized the Maine retreat, and over the next few decades it drew the attention of East Coast urbanites when landscape painters began displaying their island scenes in New York and Boston. In 1881 the Eliot family built a sumptuous home overlooking fjord-like Somes Sound. Sensitized in Europe to the connection between natural form and vernacular architecture, Eliot was impressed by the way the island's humble homes, pathways, and roads blended into the surrounding forest and hills. The island's human story seemed "almost as picturesque and varied as its scenery."[11] Mount Desert provided another important lesson in landscape appreciation. By the time the Eliot family arrived downeast, the finest parts of the Maine Coast had fallen under the control of speculators and land syndicates. Developers divided their holdings into simple rectangular lots that bore no relation to the surrounding landscape and built vulgarly ornamented cottages designed to appeal to middle-class resorters. Wealthy colonists were no less intrusive. Their "absurdly pretentious" estates aped European landscape designs that in local context were garish rather than elegant. Moreover, the intended effect was "unattainable . . . by reason of the shallow soils and frequent droughts." Eliot's commentary on his own class contained a certain irony: "In the treatment of the ground about their houses, the millionaires of Bar Harbor are quite as apt to err as are the humbler cottagers of Squirrel Island."[12]

The beauty and tragedy of Mount Desert Island left a deep impression. Nature combined with art could be scenic, but there were limits to this collaboration, especially where profit was the primary consideration. "A surf-beaten headland may be crowned by a lighthouse tower without losing its dignity and impressiveness, but it cannot be dotted with frail cottages without suffering a woeful fall. A lonely fiord shut in by dark woods, where the fog lingers in wreaths, as it comes and goes, loses its charm whenever even one bank is stripped naked, and streets and buildings are substituted for the spruces and pines." Still, there were no practical constraints on how landowners, rich or poor, native or newcomer, could use their property. He noted that a single hotel company had bought "almost the whole of the wild island of Campobello." The company held the destiny of the island in its hands, and nothing could be done to preserve it for the "common people."[13]

In 1886 Eliot moved to Boston and advertised his services as a professional landscape architect. Like Horace Cleveland before him, he considered ways Boston might highlight the rural charm of its surroundings by bringing together the cultural beauty he saw in Europe and the wildness he relished on Mount Desert. Old World cities had grown up around their ancient royal gardens and estates. Boston would have to plan wisely in order to reserve similar amounts of open land. Moreover, its open spaces would have to reflect American landscape values. "The really beautiful parks of Europe are those which have a character of their own," he concluded, "derived from their own conditions of climate and scene." Only through careful planning could Boston's hinterland achieve the same "smoothness."[14]

Eliot's class standing and upbringing were similar to that of his mentor, Frederick Law Olmsted, but his landscaping philosophy differed. Olmsted's finest creations were centrally located parks built on a grand scale, such as Central Park and Brooklyn's Prospect Park. Eliot cautioned against the extravagance of funding large downtown parks when land was cheaper on the urban periphery, and there the parks could be designed to better reflect the surrounding countryside. Both designers preferred natural ambience to "town-like things" in their parks, but where Olmsted rebuilt nature from the ground up, Eliot preferred to work with existing vegetation. He began with a defining feature of the landscape and imposed only enough art to enhance its inherent beauty. Where Olmsted used vegetation to insulate his parks from their surroundings, Eliot blended his creations into the larger environment, bringing all features, natural and artificial, into a single composition. Centuries of layered use-patterns gave depth and perspective to the countryside, and Eliot's parks accented this regional construct. In Concord, New Hampshire, he transformed twenty-five acres of rough, swampy land into a "quiet resort" for the city's working people—those unable to travel out into the open countryside. He graded the wetland to accentuate a small pond and used the existing terrain around the pond to create an undulating meadow-and-woodland mix, calling to mind "the happy peace of the country." Other parks might feature lawns festooned with flowers and ornamental bushes, but Concord possessed something more valuable: "a typical, strikingly beautiful, and very easily accessible bit of New England landscape."[15]

The Trustees of Public Reservations

In 1890 Eliot brought the preservationist concerns he experienced on Mount Desert Island to bear on a particularly graceful stand of trees called the Waverly (or Waverley) Oaks in the Boston suburbs of Belmont and Waverly. The oaks were not the largest in eastern Massachusetts, but they were the best known, having been immortalized in a poem titled "Beaver Brook" by James Russell Lowell. With a railroad depot nearby, the tract containing the oaks was ripe for development, but because it was divided among several owners and spanned the border of two towns, municipal acquisition seemed out of the question.[16]

Writing in *Garden and Forest*, Eliot proposed an association of citizens "empowered by the state to hold small and well distributed parcels of land free of taxes, just as the public library holds books and the art museum pictures—for the use and enjoyment of the public." Citizens of Cazenovia, New York, had recently come together to purchase land around a falls on Chittenango Creek, and Eliot's idea seemed a logical next step in "securing . . . bits of scenery . . . in what is still the country." Shortly after Eliot's correspondence was published, journalist and reformer Sylvester Baxter wrote a series of articles in the *Boston Herald* highlighting the opportunity for regional parks in the Greater Boston area. Other articles followed, warning against the "steady encroachment of the city upon the unurban towns."[17]

Eliot's concerns were heightened by a disturbing trend he saw in eastern Massachusetts. Property owners were increasingly adamant about excluding the public from land that had been used by walkers and picnickers for generations. New Englanders, according to a contemporary columnist, had been "accustomed . . . to wander at will in the woods, and over fields and seashore, without for a moment considering that the ground under [their] . . . feet was private property." Charles Francis Adams remembered that in the Quincy of his youth, "there was not a grove I could not enter; not a brook on whose banks I could not wander." This changed when city people began buying land on the urban periphery. "At every point signs meet the eye warning the pedestrian that he must not trespass on private property."[18]

In addition, property owners seemed less willing to protect the scenic and historical landmarks that earlier generations considered a part of the public trust. Just months after the Waverly Oaks article appeared, a venerable roadside landmark called the Medford Elm was reduced to cordwood by its owner, causing a stir among Boston-area preservationists. Asserting a public claim to trees on private property seemed somewhat "socialistic," a *Boston Post* correspondent conceded, but "the natural beauties of the land we live in, and the sites which the struggles and valor of the past have made historic, belong to the whole people." Another Massachusetts landmark disappeared in Springfield when a landowner cut down a colonial-era chestnut. "Foolish axes," a protester explained, had "destroyed the most ancient landmark in Springfield." The *Springfield Republican* and the *Worcester Spy* advanced the idea of protecting this arboreal heritage. Trees such as the Waverly Oaks, the Medford Elm, and the Springfield Chestnut had taken "centuries to make," and no proprietor had a right to destroy them. Protests like these suggest a new perception of public rights to scenic and historical places. As a contemporary brochure admonished, "Private ownership of such places deprives the people of a source of education and refreshment which they need to enjoy." Landscape painter John J. Ennekin insisted that all riverbanks "should be owned by towns, and be placed under the control of a general park commission." In 1890, the year of Eliot's Waverly Oaks proposal, Massachusetts passed an act allowing cities and towns to protect ornamental or shade trees growing along highways.[19]

Encouraged by the response to his Waverly Oaks article, Eliot met with officers of the Appalachian Mountain Club (AMC), a Boston-based mountaineering organization whose members were well disposed to scenic preservation, and together they planned a meeting of representatives from historical, antiquarian, horticultural, natural history, and village improvement societies at the Massachusetts Institute of Technology on May 24, 1890. Eliot invited some of the most powerful political and financial figures in the state, including Uriah H. Crocker, who had first proposed the Boston park system three decades earlier; Sylvester Baxter, who had written extensively about Boston's open-space needs; and Charles Sargent, who championed the Waverly Oaks idea in *Garden and Forest*. Henry Sprague, president of the state senate, presided over the meeting, and the many journalists in attendance carried the message to towns and cities across the state.[20]

Attendees formed a committee of twenty-nine members to lobby the legislature, and with support from prominent figures around the state, the committee made a convincing case. A bill of incorporation passed through the General Court a year later, and on May 21, 1891, Governor William Russell signed an act establishing the Trustees of Public Reservations. In addition to giving the organization power to acquire land, the legislature charged it with investigating open spaces across the state, compiling a list of laws regarding these lands, and meeting with park commissioners to encourage statewide cooperation.[21]

Trustees in the Early Years

Eliot's expectation that public land could be acquired through private donation was not unfounded. As early as the 1870s, village improvement societies were accepting small tracts of land to create parks and preserves. Worcester gained Institute Park through private donation in 1887; Quincy townspeople received the seventy-five-acre Merrymount Park as a gift from Charles Francis Adams; and Margaret Merrill of Portland and Nancy Jackson of Boston donated Webb Park to the town of Weymouth. Circus impresario P. T. Barnum, a native of Bridgeport, Connecticut, donated an expansive seaside park to the town and opened his own elegantly landscaped estate to the public. The volunteer forest and park associations formed at the end of the century in each New England state solicited donations of land. While some parks, like Central Park, Prospect Park, and Franklin Park, required immense public outlays, about half the city park investment in the United States came from private individuals, civic associations, women's clubs, art clubs, architectural societies, schools, or universities. A park in New York City, for instance, gained a band pavilion donated by a musical society, a flagstaff and flag given by a mechanics guild, trees planted by children from each school in the city, and benches, seats, and a fountain given by other citizens, while the water company supplied water for the fountain. Antiquarian organizations purchased and preserved historic buildings and battlegrounds. The TPR hoped to institutionalize this random philanthropic practice.[22]

Many New England communities already owned town forests, if not parks. During the colonial era towns held land in common for a variety of reasons, and in the nineteenth century remaining portions of this common, augmented by gifts, tax forfeitures, and occasional purchases, often became town forests. By far the largest of these was the sixteen-hundred-acre Lynn Woods northeast of Boston, and its evolution suggests the casual way so many New England towns acquired public property. The Lynn Woods was originally used for pasture and firewood gathering, but when livestock raising fell off and coal replaced wood for heating, the town retained the woods to protect its water supplies and provide recreational opportunities. In the 1850s Lynn's two outdoor clubs, the Exploring Circle and Boulder Club, joined with the Lynn Natural History Society to advocate for continued public ownership, and in 1871 the town's water board assumed jurisdiction over four reservoirs in the woods. In 1881 the city government incorporated the Trustees of the Free Public Forest of Lynn and charged it with managing the woods and soliciting donations to enlarge it. In 1888 the land became a public park. Frederick Law Olmsted, commissioned to enhance the park's "local character," recommended leaving the forest as a wilderness, and accordingly the trustees limited management to removing fallen trees, cutting back underbrush, enhancing views, and maintaining the trails, bridges, and shelters. As a wilderness park, Lynn Woods was an important source of inspiration for the TPR.[23]

Legislatures encouraged towns to acquire land for public purposes. In 1882 Massachusetts passed a Forest Act that allowed towns to purchase land through eminent domain to be used as working forests or to protect water supplies. Because the act also mentioned recreation, it became known as the Park Act. New York passed a similar act in 1888, allowing citizens to form associations to acquire land for parks or playgrounds, and the following year New Hampshire charged its Forestry Commission with ascertaining the feasibility of purchasing timberland near summer resorts or principal water-supply sources "with the view of preserving the same as public lands and parks."[24]

Despite these precedents, the TPR found itself in uncharted waters. Eliot initially expected the trustees' properties to be called country parks to distinguish them from Olmsted's elaborately landscaped city parks. The federal government designated the Yosemite Valley a state park in 1864 and added Yellowstone National Park in 1872 and Sequoia and Yosemite parks in 1890. But in an eastern context, as Sylvester Baxter pointed out, the term "park" could mean anything from a horse-racing track to a place for storing vehicles, and in his mind parks recalled visions of statuary, bordered walks, clipped greenswards, and other urban trappings. Baxter preferred the term "reservation," as in New York's Niagara Falls Reservation, dedicated in 1885. The term suggested land held in reserve to be converted later into a park if public resources allowed. Eliot and his colleague John Charles Olmsted altered the meaning of the term to suggest a large, intact natural area where visitors could stroll for hours amid natural surroundings. Reservations were akin to the wild lands of the Adirondacks, but with an "air of cheerfulness not always to be found among the gloomy evergreens."[25]

As a first step, the TPR aimed to acquire hilltops, ravines, ocean access points, and narrow strips bordering ponds, streams, and country roads—land useless for development but crucial to preserving the beauty of the countryside. In addition, the TPR would seek out places of antiquarian, historic, or literary interest. And finally, it would accept unique botanical or geological features. Each reservation would highlight a different aspect of the New England landscape. Mountain slopes and hollows would suggest New England's wildness, meadows or pastured woodlands its agricultural past, and swamps, bogs, ponds, pools, and lakes its varied natural history. Landscapers could enhance distant views by cutting or pruning trees or other vegetation. Conversely, views that detracted from the rural atmosphere could be "planted out." Eliot hoped to use the landscaping techniques Olmsted pioneered but only to enhance the unique natural character of each reservation.[26]

Keenly aware of New England's philanthropic tradition, Eliot anticipated that wealthy patrons would shower the organization with gifts of land. To this end, the trustees sent announcements to newspapers across the state, pointing out that even a "few acres of rocks . . . would be of the greatest value to the people." The *Springfield Republican* added a cautionary note: "We would only remark that the lovers of Nature are not so apt to have money as the lovers of art." Indeed, the TPR received numerous suggestions about places needing protection, including the whimsically named Shootflying Hill, Purgatory Hill, Heartbreak Hill, Bash Bish Falls, and Norman's Woe, but despite its well-publicized campaign it received only a few parcels in these early years, partly due to a financial panic coincident with its founding.[27]

In lieu of acquiring lands, the TPR investigated existing open spaces in Massachusetts by searching town histories and other local records, contacting park commissioners and village improvement society officers, and compiling lists of state laws relating to park development. In addition, the TPR made two landmark contributions to conserving open spaces in Massachusetts: it helped create the Boston-area Metropolitan Park Commission and it funded a survey of potential public open spaces along the Massachusetts coast. These two projects generated widespread preservationist enthusiasm in Massachusetts and around New England.[28]

The Metropolitan Park Commission

Realizing that the greatest demand for recreational space was in the Boston area, the trustees decided on an aggressive plan of acquisition in and near the metropolis. There were still thousands of acres of open space in these outlying towns, much of it used informally by recreationists. However, transforming these lands into parks and reserves would be difficult. Fragmented ownership discouraged donations, and ecological boundaries like watersheds, woodlands, and hills seldom coincided with city boundaries. Where Boston had absorbed the surrounding suburbs, park appropriations were feasible, but many towns remained independent, and here large-scale land acquisition was out of the question. Cambridge, for instance, declined an invitation to acquire a portion of the Norton Woods because the recreational benefits would accrue to Somerville as well. Creating parks and reservations would require public funding, eminent domain, and a comprehensive acquisition strategy.[29]

Eliot offered a new vision of Boston's park system based on five trends that had become more pronounced since Olmsted laid out the Emerald Necklace. First, park planning in Boston had been relatively free of political influence in Olmsted's day, but the power of machine-based politics was growing. Thus, Eliot lobbied for an independent park commission well insulated from the shifting political scene. Second, his parks, unlike the Emerald Necklace, would have to serve communities outside Boston proper. Eastern Massachusetts, once an aggregation of small, isolated communities, had become "a land of crowded towns" harboring two-thirds of the state's population. Since these new industrial centers had little room for parks designed in the Olmsted tradition, they would be better served by a comprehensive system that combined in-town parks with reserves carved out of adjacent rural lands. Third, active outdoor pursuits like bicycling, bird-watching, hiking, and botanizing were becoming popular among all classes of New Englanders. Where Olmsted's contemplative park visitors were interested in the illusion of depth, Eliot's more active park-goers would require actual physical space. Fourth, expanded trolley and train service offered Bostonians access to parks and preserves in outlying areas where near-wilderness characteristics could be sustained.[30]

A fifth pressing development was what Eliot termed the "uglification of the Commonwealth." Like many who grew up in the Boston suburbs, Eliot considered his rural environs extraordinarily beautiful. On the urban periphery, a parklike landscape of centuries-old farms and small estates shaded gradually into heavily forested hills farther out from the city. Ancient roadside trees arched over the winding country roads to create a "grateful silence at noonday." In a *Boston Transcript* article aptly titled "To the Rescue," he voiced the fears of many upper-class Bostonians concerned about the defacement of these once secluded places. "The shadowy grove of lofty trees, where we have been refreshed in times past, has been felled. A quarry has been opened in the gateway of our once fine ravine. A once beautiful road leading through a wood of beech and hemlock has been completely despoiled of its shade and its charm." Not only were open spaces disappearing, but the suburbs that replaced them lacked the grace and charm that characterized the old farm-and-estate countryside. The campaign for landscape appreciation that began with Downing's *Horticulturist* seemed to falter in the suburbs, where speculators purchased random parcels of farmland, carved them into uniform blocks convenient for resale, removed any trace of natural vegetation, and built nondescript homes that appealed only in their low cost. The new residents cluttered their lawns with shaped trees, flowerpots, and gaudy garden beds, seemingly content to live in defiance of the countless articles on landscaping published in *Garden and Forest* and other country-life magazines. In time, perhaps, home owners would learn to design in harmony with nature, but even in this optimistic scenario the suburban landscape would remain a private domain. It seemed un-American, Charles Sargent mused, that Boston's popular retreats should be "monopolized for personal profit." Sargent suggested that "we may as well go a step further and hold that all natural beauty is the inheritance of all the people." Boston would have to find ways of curbing the uglification that so troubled Eliot and his colleagues.[31]

In dealing with these developments, Eliot found a valuable ally in Sylvester Baxter, editor of *Outing Magazine* and proponent of Edward Bellamy's futuristic *Looking Backward*, a utopian novel set in Boston in the age of the Cooperative Commonwealth. Baxter had taken an interest in landscaping while he was studying at Leipzig and Berlin, and when he returned to Boston he joined a campaign to preserve the Middlesex Fells northwest of Boston. The experience took him into the realm of park development, and he contributed numerous articles to Boston-area newspapers on parks, landscape architecture, and city planning. In addition to the Fells, he proposed a country park in the Blue Hills south of Boston, a feature that gave Massachusetts its Native American name as the Place of Great Hills. A carriage road connecting the city to the park, Baxter pointed out, would pass through some of the most beautiful country in eastern Massachusetts.[32]

Baxter envisioned another reservation on the banks of the Charles River. Because the ebb and flow of the tide gave the upper basin a "feeling of impermanence" and exposed unsightly and heavily polluted mud flats, he suggested a dam to create a pool of clean, fresh water behind Boston for boating, sailing, and bathing. Still more parks might be built in the marshland fringe along the Mystic and Neponset Rivers. To realize this dream, Baxter proposed a single park board for the entire Boston region: an impartial central body that could rise above purely local or commercial considerations. Eliot endorsed the plan, and together he and Baxter identified several potential reservations in the Blue Hills, the Middlesex Fells, and the city itself, as well as along the Boston Harbor and shore. "Thus easily can Greater Boston save ... her reputation as the most beautiful and most enlightened city in America."[33]

In 1891 Eliot, Baxter, and Charles Sargent began promoting the idea of a Greater Boston park commission. In a widely reproduced statement, Eliot admonished Boston leaders:

> Here is a rapidly growing metropolis planted by the sea, and yet possessed of no portion of the sea-front except what Boston has provided at City Point. Here is a city interwoven with tidal marshes and controlling none of them; so that the way is open for the construction upon them of cheap buildings for the housing of the lowest poor and the nastiest trades. Here is a district possessed of a charming river already much resorted to for pleasure, the banks of which are continually in danger of spoliation at the hands of their private owners.

Eliot attended civic club meetings armed with maps indicating the interesting and beautiful open spaces in and around Boston. He assured wealthy residents living near these sites that their property values would be enhanced, and he courted working-class residents with visions of a fuller, healthier life. Newspapers throughout the region ran articles supporting the park commission.

"The common people want more public spaces and are bound to have it," one cautioned; if the clamor was "wisely led,... good would come of it."[34]

Eliot once again rallied prominent individuals from around the state, and on December 16, 1891, they met to consider a metropolitan park commission. Baxter, inspired by Bellamy's *Looking Backward*, supplied the vision, and Eliot offered a systematic appraisal of potential park and reservation sites. His maps showed that Boston's recreational opportunities rivaled those of London and Paris, and most of the necessary property could be acquired "at slight cost." The governor of Massachusetts and mayor of Boston endorsed the project, and to ensure its success Eliot collected several thousand signatures on a legislative petition. Sargent continued his advocacy in *Garden and Forest*, warning that "every year sees lamentable encroachments upon some of the most charming landscape passages" in the Boston area.[35]

In August 1893, two years after the TPR was formed, the General Court created a three-person Metropolitan Park Commission made up of Charles Francis Adams of Quincy, Philip A. Chase of Lynn, and William de las Casas of Malden. The idea of a regional commission was patterned after a similar authority created in 1889 to administer a Boston-area sewage system and the Rapid Transit Commission established in 1891. The Park Commission was followed by a Metropolitan Water Commission in 1895, and in 1919 these agencies were combined into the Metropolitan District Commission. It is difficult to say how much grassroots support the Park Commission enjoyed, but the enthusiastic reception in the legislature suggests popular endorsement. Boston had been alive to the need for open spaces since the Olmsted park projects of the 1880s, and the new commission, given eminent domain powers and a substantial budget, took advantage of this popularity to extend the park system into the suburban fringe.[36]

Envisioning a Recreational Boston

As the commission's landscape architect, Eliot inventoried open spaces within twelve miles of the statehouse, finding beauty in places others considered waste. Boston, as he pointed out, lay between two wildernesses: "on the one hand the untamed heights of the rock-hills, on the other the untamable sea." Within these bounds lay scenic riches any city would envy—forested peaks, deep woods, freshwater streams and ponds, tidal estuaries and marshes, ocean beaches, and rocky shores. In January 1893 the Park Commission issued its first report, written by Baxter and Eliot, with recommendations for expanding the Emerald Necklace into America's first metropolitan-scale park system.[37]

It was important, Eliot thought, to keep the entire basin in mind while contemplating each park component. The Neponset, Mystic, and Charles River valleys were natural conduits for the breezes sweeping down from the hills and up from the sea. He would keep these open, "leaving the great aerial currents that flow along the lines of their water courses unpolluted." Like Bellamy in *Looking Backward*, he envisioned Boston from the vantage of a future visitor.

> He would see this great city occupying a region of remarkable and diversified landscape interest; a bay with beautiful shores and numerous islands large and small, a country varied with hills and fields, woodland, meadows, lakes and streams. He would find the population . . . provided with extensive facilities for public open-air recreation; an admirable . . . system of parks, parkways and boulevards, public gardens and playgrounds, forming continuous chains of pleasure ground, or sprinkled liberally over the territory.

Eliot, like Bellamy, possessed a remarkable ability to see things not as they were but as they could be. The rivers themselves were unsightly and unsanitary, but he imagined a day when they would be valued playgrounds for the people. He discovered a canal running between the Charles and the Neponset dug in 1639 called Mother Brook, "artificially supplied . . . with an overflow of water from the . . . Charles, so that we find a good canoe stream, which, in the course of two charming miles, brings us among the factories of the town of Hyde Park." An occasional brick building "half concealed by trees" enhanced the scenic effect, and between the buildings he discovered "beautiful views."[38] The Neponset, "fringed with trees and bushy thickets," continued down to Dorchester Bay. Near its mouth the waters rushed between two "great brick chocolate mills" and swept across a pine-clad point before dispersing into the salt marshes. Baxter had proposed transforming its marshes into parks, as Olmsted had done in the Back Bay Fens, and Eliot wrote this proposal into his park plan. The Neponset marsh, "one of the most picturesque spots in the whole neighborhood of Boston," demonstrated that industrial artifacts—wharves, sheds, buildings, derelict schooners—could contribute to the beauty of a scene. In Eliot's enlightened vision, the city's unused spaces took on inestimable value.[39]

To the south and east of the city, Eliot proposed parks of a different sort. Beyond Boston the topography changed gradually from rolling hills to rugged peaks along a fault escarpment thrusting upward to 350 feet. Here park design would shade from the heavily manipulated Back Bay Fens and Franklin Park to a lightly landscaped approximation of primeval nature. Precise, almost surgical adjustments would bring out the beauty in each scene by removing, for example, "a stag-headed tree that over-shadows too much of the progeny, or an old decayed trunk that is not only ugly in its unsoundness, but breeds the enemies of the healthy." Hiking and carriage paths—"slender threads of graded surface winding over and among the huge natural forms"—would link the various observation sites. Landscaping, he recommended, should be limited to mowing or pasturing the grasslands, removing dead and dying trees in the forests, keeping sprout wood from crowding out the venerable oaks and chestnuts, and clearing vegetative screens to open views. Intervention would be "as inconspicuous as possible."[40]

Taking advantage of a surge in park enthusiasm, the commissioners moved ahead with acquisitions. Fortunately, land suited for parks was usually too hilly, rocky, or wet for development and thus could be purchased cheaply. For this and other reasons, the commissioners proceeded with little opposition, although the process involved a complicated series of site surveys and legal negotiations. Almost immediately, the commissioners secured the Waverly Oaks, the eleven prominent summits that made up the Blue Hills, and a tract of woodland in West Roxbury and Hyde Park. In 1895 they acquired land along the Charles and Mystic Rivers and shore land in Revere Beach, the latter being by far the most expensive property in the system.[41]

By 1902 the commissioners had preserved thirty miles of river frontage, ten miles of ocean shoreline, and twenty-two miles of parkways, including three reservations along the Charles River, another embracing the lakes on the upper Mystic, and parkways linking the city to the Blue Hills, the Fells, and Revere Beach. The acquisitions, costing $12 million over an eight-year period, gave Boston an astounding array of recreational choices ranging from swimming and boating to picnicking, sunbathing, hiking, bird-watching, botanizing, carriage and horseback riding, sightseeing, and simply walking. In 1880 Boston had possessed only 106 acres of park space for a population of 363,000; in 1904 the metropolitan area, with a population of 1 million, enjoyed 17,000 acres of parkland, an area twice as large as New York's parks with only one-third its population. The 5,000-acre Blue Hills Reservation was the largest municipal park in the country.[42]

The most complicated purchase was the Middlesex Fells, an area some thought too distant from downtown Boston to attract public support. The Fells was undeveloped due to its steep slopes and marshy ground, and despite repeated incursions by farmers, loggers, and quarry operators, it retained, as Eliot's contemporary Arthur Shurtleff pointed out, "something of the beauty and life-giving qualities of the original forest mantle." Still, conserving it was no accident of topography. Preservationist sentiment began building in the 1880s when social reformer Elizur Wright and naturalist Wilson Flagg launched a campaign to create a park in the still wild region. Wright moved to nearby Medford, purchased land in the Fells around Spot Pond, and lobbied the legislature for protective measures, and when these efforts failed he and Flagg organized the Middlesex Fells Association in 1881. They wrote letters, delivered lectures, published pamphlets, gave tours, and lobbied for the 1882 Forest Act, and when it passed they convinced the water boards in Malden, Medford, and Melrose to purchase land around Spot Pond. After the death of both men, Wright's daughter Ellen devoted herself to the project, eventually donating her father's estate as a "first-of-its-kind wild urban forest park system." What she and her father wanted in the Fells, she wrote, "was a bit of nature so conveniently in our midst that we might watch its workings.... We wanted dark crowded places, even jungles...., marshes into which one might wade after reeds and bright berries, brooks where the border growth and waters frolic together."[43]

Encouraged by this preservationist history, the commission joined with the towns to purchase some 1,600 acres, and this, combined with the Wright donation and water-board lands, brought the Middlesex Fells Reservation to 3,200 acres spread across five cities and towns and accessible from Boston by locomotive and streetcar. Ignoring the history of logging, farming, and quarrying, visitors described the Fells as a primeval wilderness penetrated only by "narrow, winding, natural-seeming roads."[44]

Recreating a Rural Landscape

The commission's second annual report, issued in 1895, included Eliot's "Vegetation and Scenery in the Metropolitan Reservations," a master landscaping plan for the acquisitions. In this seminal document Eliot adapted the landscaping philosophy introduced by Andrew Jackson Downing to conditions that varied from downtown factory districts to wind-torn mountain peaks. According to park commissioner Charles H. Dalton, the report was "one of the most important contributions to the literature of public parks ever made," and its innovative policies were instructive far beyond the Boston Basin. The new parklands, Eliot began, presented an unparalleled opportunity for making Boston the envy of the world, but bringing this to fruition would require careful landscaping and a thorough understanding of each property. This was a project of unprecedented complexity, and Eliot felt the weight of future generations in laying out this legacy.[45]

The idea of "pastoral parks" on the urban periphery was unprecedented. Other cities were building large, carefully landscaped downtown parks like Central Park in New York City, Prospect Park in Brooklyn, Fairmont Park in Philadelphia, Genesee Valley Park in Rochester (New York), and Rock Creek Park in Washington, DC. Protecting the "pleasure forests" on the city outskirts, as forester Bernhard E. Fernow termed them, required a new way of thinking about open spaces. Rather than create an artistic rendering of nature, these parks would rely on the *"natural* naturalness" of the landscape, "with merely a helping hand towards artistic appearance." Here as elsewhere, landscaping would proceed with the understanding that "nature was not always aesthetically pleasing," but the urge to improve would be tempered by the need to keep the reservations as wild as aesthetically possible.[46] Olmsted showed landscape artists how to create the illusion of nature; Eliot showed them how to make an art form out of nature itself.

Eliot began by acknowledging the long history of human interference in the landscapes out of which the reservations were carved. Farming, logging, quarrying, livestock pasturing, fires, and exotic introductions had irrevocably altered the face of the land, and the resulting imbalances left the vegetation extremely dynamic. Places once occupied by stately old-growth pines had been colonized by scrub oak, and clumps of sweet fern grew where hemlock forests once stood. "Bulrushes insist upon crowding every undrained hollow, Bearberry carpets barren rocks, and a great variety of vigorous trees and shrubs have had to be continually and forcibly prevented from reoccupying such parts of the slopes between the rocks and the swamps." Maintaining the "natural" conditions that made the reservations so attractive was now the responsibility of the commissioners and their crews. In addition, they would have to clear vista points, replant burned-over lands, remove sprout wood from pastures and meadows, and liberate old and stately trees from the surrounding brush. "We are well aware that the axe is regarded with a sort of horror by many excellent people," Eliot explained, "but we are equally convinced that . . . the axe, if it be guided wisely, may gradually affect the desired rescue and enhancement of . . . the scenery."[47]

Eliot divided the reservation landscapes into mountain summits, lowland swamps, fields and pastures, and mixed seedling and old-growth forests. The mountaintops represented New England nature in its wildest state. The stunted high-elevation trees had been spared the woodcutter's ax, and the bare ledges that rimmed the hilltops defended the vegetation from fire. The summit growth was "generally low enough to enable the broad prospects . . . , [and] its dwarfness also tends to . . . set off the grand or picturesque . . . ledges and crags." Below the peaks, Eliot suggested managers encourage dogwood on the southern slopes, bearberry on the rocky summits, and white pine and dwarf spruce on the ridges. Pitch pine, cedar, and juniper would grow best on the sunny crags and ledges, and hemlocks in the shady dells at the base of the cliffs. In the valleys, long-lived trees could be planted to replace sprout growth. Managers would have to use a variety of measures to ensure the large or well-grouped trees were not overwhelmed by pioneer growth. Swamps, like mountaintops, were best left in their existing state, since the impenetrable vegetation was most appropriately viewed from afar.[48]

The reservations contained hundreds of acres of pastured woodlands characteristic of the New England countryside, and Eliot offered detailed directions for maintaining them. The vegetation in these lovely glades, he cautioned, would require careful maintenance.

> As soon as cattle cease to browse a piece of land, the common and fast-growing gray birch mingles with the cedar, or takes possession of large areas by itself. . . . With time the bushes of sweet fern, bayberry, blueberry, viburnum, and the like grow more and more numerous and entangled; and their combination with the dark cedars and the white birches often helps to form . . . landscape[s] of rare beauty. . . . Slowly, however, this type of landscape vanishes. From the midst, perhaps, of junipers which browsing cattle have avoided, or from clumps of crowded bushes, slow-growing oaks and other forest trees start up from the seeds brought by the winds, birds, or squirrels . . . Slowly but surely . . . junipers and bushes are overshadowed and as it were suffocated . . . , and in the end the forest of seedling trees takes full possession."

Nature in its early stages tended to monotonous uniformity, and to maintain scenic variety managers would have to keep new growth under control, perhaps by reintroducing livestock.[49]

Because so much of the park lay outside the city, civic planner Charles Robinson concluded that it was "designed to add beauty to the . . . city rather than to benefit its poor." Eliot's recommendations suggest a different conclusion. As

Progressives, Eliot and Baxter were dedicated to the principle of the greatest good for the greatest number, and the activities they deemed appropriate for the reservations, ranging from carriage riding and promenading to more common pursuits like boating, picnicking, bicycling, baseball playing, botanizing, and birdwatching, suggest their concern with serving a broad section of the community. Although they appealed to wealthy landowners for support, they hoped to give ordinary Bostonians an opportunity to get out into the woods. "If our parks ... are to do the most real good to our people," the *Boston Transcript* admonished, "it is not to be by furnishing a place where the prosperous citizen may drive out his family on a Sunday afternoon behind his sleek horses. . . . , but by giving a place where everybody can go and even get lost, enough to give him some training in finding his own way out." Trolley lines reached each of the reservations, ensuring that "ragged boys can go and ... other boys can come home ragged, without disturbing private property and without being told to 'keep off the grass.'"[50]

In a criticism similar to Robinson's, historian Michael Rawson suggested that the commissioners restored Native place-names, removed buildings, and manipulated vegetation in order to transform the reservations into monuments to Boston's Puritan beginnings. There was, he maintains, "something inherently deceptive about the practice, since removing actual historical artifacts to imaginatively recreate a romanticized wilderness past masked the true history of these places." Rawson is correct in assuming Boston elites thought of the reservations as a tribute to their forebears' confrontation with wilderness, but this was not foremost in Eliot's plan for the reservations. Like Alexander Jackson Downing and those who followed him, Eliot saw landscaping as something more than re-creating a wilderness. Pure nature, he felt, was often "insipid and unlovely," while those places where Europeans had "lived longest, or worked hardest, are often beautiful in a high degree." The human legacy was important in landscape art. Why, he asked, was the Middlesex Fells more interesting than the Lynn Woods?

> Largely because the vegetation is more varied. And why is it more varied? Because of Man and not Nature. In the Fells are more pastures, more grassy glades and fields, and there's also more variety in the height and density of forest trees. Nature, indeed, is constantly striving to abolish even the meagre existing variety. . . . Thus, if the reservations are left to Nature, monotony will follow; and not only will the existing scenery be soon obliterated (as one visit to the Woods makes plain), but the existing economical opportunity for securing additional interest and beauty will be lost never to return, unless after a sweeping forest fire.

Eliot's vision was nostalgic but not an assertion of wilderness values. In the vegetation of the Fells he saw the epic creation of the vernacular New England landscape from colonial times forward.[51]

Crews began work on the reservations shortly after Eliot submitted his report. They removed fallen trees, logging debris, and other fire hazards; cleared paths; tore down buildings and fences; and accented watercourses, all to promote the vision of a lightly humanized nature. In the Fells, they lowered the mill dam on a brook flowing out of Spot Pond, returning the water to its natural channels, and built a rustic bridge near the dam. They cleared paths for hiking and horseback riding and rebuilt an old woods road to make it passable by carriage.[52] In Boston the commission adopted Baxter's plan for landscaping the banks of the Charles. Baxter's dam proposal raised controversy, but city administrators on both sides of the river favored the improvement, and the esplanade work was completed in 1910. At Revere Beach the commissioners cleared away squatters' shanties and cottages, moved the railroad tracks, added a promenade along the crest of the beach, and constructed bathhouses and dressing rooms to accommodate more than one hundred thousand bathers each day.[53]

The metropolitan park system was Eliot's finest achievement, but he saw this as only a beginning. Beyond the Boston environs, the trustees would carry the banner of preservation out into the countryside, giving Massachusetts a chain of reservations no less ambitious than the system created by the Metropolitan Commission. The vision of rural New England conjured by earlier landscape designers, artists, writers, and rural improvers beckoned. Rivers flanked by parkways would encourage swimming, boating, fishing, and canoeing, and the state's "exquisitely beautiful" villages would be protected from the blighting hand of commerce. Unfortunately, Eliot did not live to see these ideas realized. While in Hartford overseeing work on the city's Keney Park, he contracted meningitis and died on March 25, 1897, at age thirty-seven. Given his important work on both private and public lands, his death was, as one announcement put it, a "public calamity." He had become, even at this early age, "one of the highest authorities in his profession." But Eliot had already cast his legacy. Even without his guiding hand, the Boston parks he surveyed and designed were, in the words of Mira Dock—herself a notable park promoter—"enduring monuments" to the man who was "happily able to make others see the future value of saving the heights and river shores to any community fortunate enough to live near them."[54] Eliot lived on in the achievements of the TPR and the Metropolitan Commission.

J. B. Harrison and the Coastal Inventory

Having helped launch the Metropolitan Park Commission, the TPR shifted its focus outward, urging local improvement societies to host benefit dinners, dances, or lawn parties to purchase reserves. To help with the campaign the trustees contracted with the energetic reformer Jonathan Baxter Harrison, a native of New Hampshire who had been a member of the state's Forestry Commission, secretary of the American Forestry Congress, and corresponding secretary for the New York State Forestry Association during the campaign for the Adirondack State Park. Most notably, Harrison had been involved in creating the Niagara Falls Reservation when industrial establishments, hotels, resorts, and "tawdry, sensational attractions" threatened to block passage to the world-famous waterfall. Harrison argued strenuously that landmarks of this caliber were by their nature a public trust. Urged by Harrison and others, Governor Grover Cleveland appointed commissioners to select land near the falls, and in 1885 the Niagara Reserve became the nation's second state park after the federal government deeded Yosemite Valley to California in 1864.[55]

The trustees asked Harrison to make a "missionary tour of the state," passing out circulars, engaging the press and local officials, and speaking at local gatherings to generate interest in open-space preservation. At the same time, he was to gather information about existing public lands in each town. Armed with all the legal advice the trustees could muster, Harrison began his tour at the New Hampshire line and worked south through the state's coastal towns. Already sensitized by the commercial preemption of Niagara Falls, he was appalled by the degree to which the coast had been "shut off" from the public. The scenic resources monopolized by "moneyed people from the cities and towns of the whole country" would become even more precious as inland cities became more crowded. Like Eliot, he realized the desperate need to change popular attitudes toward open spaces.[56]

Traveling southward along the coast, Harrison stopped in each town to inquire about public open spaces. Nearly the entire shoreline on Cape Ann, he discovered, was in private hands. Salem's working people were forced to picnic on the town's tiny common, hemmed in by cafés and restaurants that made these excursions "about the same as trying to have a picnic in a crowded street or public hall." Elsewhere, picnickers were driven from the shore "at the behest, as it often happens, of persons who have themselves no real title to the lands from which they want all visitors expelled as trespassers." Harrison corresponded daily with newspapers across the state and contributed a weekly "melancholy chapter" to *Garden and Forest*. This, he hoped, would awaken the same sentiment that resulted in opening Niagara Falls to the public and protecting the Adirondack Mountains.[57]

Harrison employed arguments similar to those used in the Boston suburbs, but in some ways his case was more compelling. The "rugged, reef-ribbed, wreck-strewn shore," he pointed out, framed the history of the state; if access disappeared, with it would go the "pungent aura of freedom that defined the Yankee character." The ocean shore was the Commonwealth's wilderness frontier, a place where "the imagination takes wing, and weaves legends . . . of uncanny deeds done." It was also crucial to the state's tourist industry. Just as logging threatened the mountain forest so essential to New Hampshire and commercialism entangled the approach to Niagara Falls, land speculation threatened the Massachusetts coast.[58]

Harrison's tour was timely. The shoreline in colonial times had been a place for gathering salt hay and seaweed, pasturing livestock, digging clams, netting fish, and launching and hauling vessels. Townspeople understood the value of this community commons and showed foresight in protecting it. When farming and inshore fishing declined in the second half of the nineteenth century, townspeople were slow to realize that these same common lands would be important to the tourist trade that replaced traditional sources of income along the coast. Local landowners were "snappish" in their dealings with strangers, and the accommodations they offered, Harrison remarked, were no better than those in a Rocky Mountain mining camp. They had yet to realize the value inlanders placed on coastal access and were far too casual about protecting it. "One cannot read of highways closed, of grounds [once] dedicated to public use to which the public is now denied admission, . . . of unresisted encroachment upon public lands everywhere, without some indignation."[59]

With these considerations in mind, Harrison described the closing of the seafront commons. Only a few public reserves remained in Newbury, and these were back from the coast and grazed by cattle. Essex and Ipswich offered only two or three shore landings each. At Rockport he found only one or two in the public domain, despite the town's beautiful headlands and the "throngs of visitors" who were sure to come if the town provided access to the sea. Gloucester once had twenty-four public landings but retained fewer than half when

Harrison toured the town. Inhabitants were forced to hold their concerts on a sidewalk. In Bourne local boys played ball on the highway or in a nearby pasture but were frequently warned away. New Bedford's forty-five thousand people had access to just over seven acres of park space. In colonial times, Westport laid out a highway along the beach, but in 1886 several persons built houses in the right-of-way, and "in order to save them the expense of removal," the town relocated the highway behind the houses and out of sight of the ocean. "What might have become one of the most magnificent ocean drives in New England is now a little back road running along the edge of a marsh."[60]

Salisbury had set aside two hundred acres in the 1600s as a training field and public beach, but in 1792 this was appropriated by a body called the Commoners, which later leased it for summer cottages. In 1891 the town investigated the title, but since the Commoners paid taxes on the property, officials concluded that there was "neither law nor justice in an attempt to dispossess them at this late day." Townspeople could use the beach, but only at the corporation's sufferance. The town's training field was lost when an abutter planted a row of apple trees through it. When the fence surrounding the field rotted away, the property owner rebuilt it on the far side of his trees. Rowley had an opposite experience. In 1839 townspeople planted a row of elms along the edge of their four-acre common, and this conspicuous demarcation prevented encroachments. "It would probably have been entirely . . . appropriated by the owners of contiguous private holdings, had it not been for the barrier."[61]

These infringements occurred because townspeople failed to appreciate the scenic resources at their fingertips. In New Bedford, mill owners told Harrison that working families saw no value in parks. "They stay indoors too much, and go to poor, miserable shows in hot, close halls and theatres, when they should be in the open air." The federal government loaned Marblehead its Fort Sewell property to be used as a park, but aside from planting a few shade trees the town neglected the site. Plymouth had an adequate system of parks, Harrison noted, but only because philanthropists donated the land, and even then the town refused to appropriate funds to manage it. In 1852 Beverly ceded its public holdings to a beach association and gave it exclusive access in return for keeping the land in good repair. The association did little to meet its responsibilities. Elsewhere, mutilated trees, torn signs, and other forms of vandalism underscored the low regard for open spaces and landscape beauty. Locals carelessly sold their property to outsiders at minimal prices, "being rather surprised to find they could obtain anything for their land." They seemed as ready to deplete their scenery as they had been to deplete their soils and fisheries.[62]

This lax attitude emboldened trespassers. In Ipswich a man erected a fence across the public highway leading to the beach. Even though he made "no attempt to show any title to the property," it was only after a great deal of hesitation that town authorities removed it. Scituate preserved only two small shore landings and had to survey them frequently to maintain ownership. The other landings had been seized by adjacent property owners who defended their claims with pitchforks while the town "vainly expended thousands of dollars in an effort to defend its rights on the shore." Scituate's training ground was lost in similar fashion. A man squatted on the land "and stayed there, and stayed there, and the town could not get him off, or it did not; and some of his family are living there still."[63] Eventually, townspeople grew weary of struggles like these and lost interest in the land.

The loss of shore access raised economic questions. The decline in fishing, shipbuilding, lumbering, farming, and granite quarrying left tourism the best economic option for many coastal towns, but tourism was viable only where visitors were "free to go where they pleased." A *Cape Ann Breeze* editor noted that in times when "business enterprise seems to languish, it may not be out of place to turn our eyes to the park project." Remarks like these left Harrison optimistic. New Bedford, once "nearly at the bottom of the list of cities," made several large purchases after his tour, and in Marblehead local philanthropists donated land to the city for parks. Harrison's many discussions with local residents and officials were of inestimable value to the nascent preservation movement; they implanted the idea that open spaces were valuable public resources and that access to the great ocean common should be protected at all cost. Stirred to indignation in classic Progressive fashion, shore towns renewed their interest in public lands. Sensing this changing mood, Harrison ended his report envisioning the day when a parkway would run along the entire shore, ensuring public enjoyment of some of the most beautiful scenery in the state.[64]

Saving the Province Lands

Harrison's tour brought to light relatively few remaining public properties, but at Provincetown on the outer Cape he came across an unexpectedly large state domain: some four thousand acres reserved in colonial times as a commons for wharves, landings, and stages for drying fish and still in the hands of the commonwealth. This was the so-called Province Lands, a world of sand dunes, beaches, freshwater ponds, and clumps of tupelo, azalea, clethra, and other "surprisingly beautiful vegetation." The topsoil was thin, but the sand beneath held moisture enough to support groves of trees. As elsewhere, individuals squatted on these lands, creating a great deal of confusion about property rights. Since there were no deeds, residents carved out rights-of-way wherever it was convenient and built close to each other since it was not worthwhile to "grab any great amount of land." Still, about half the land was unoccupied.[65]

The Province Lands were not only a potential recreational resource but also a key to stabilizing the shifting sands that threatened nearby Provincetown Harbor. When the original forest cover was destroyed in the eighteenth century, dunes began migrating. Along the cart paths winds "blew out" areas of bare sand, and when the sand drifted over the paths, new routes were carved into the dunes, each leading to a new line of blowouts. Trees were buried, ponds filled, and salt creeks clogged with sand. By the 1890s about half the Province Lands were deforested, and the sands were on the move. Residents passed several ordinances to control deforestation, and the state and federal governments planted beach grass to stabilize the sand. In 1869 the state appointed a land agent to regulate the removal of trees, brush, and "sods," or root masses used for bulkheads, terraces, banks, and walls. Local residents had little trouble circumventing regulations, and since the agent was usually absent from the town, they seldom troubled themselves with seeking permission.[66]

Harrison was introduced to the Province Lands by Charles W. Felt of Northboro. Like Baxter, Felt was a disciple of Edward Bellamy, who, like Felt, was interested in creating a marine park on the Province Lands and making it accessible from Boston by steamers at low fares. The marine park, as Bellamy saw it, would set off a movement for nationalizing lands all across America. It was "right and proper to begin the New Nation on the spot where the old was formed." In 1891 the Provincetown selectmen invited Bellamy to the Cape to help save the land "from falling into the exclusive possession of wealthy people." Bellamy and his fellow nationalists proposed a massive reforestation, soil enrichment, and highway construction effort to lay public claim to the lands.[67]

For many, the marine park idea seemed too radical. The public domain had been occupied for generations, and the Commonwealth would "never be so cruelly unjust as to take a foot of this land without compensating the present owners." Undaunted, Felt brought a group of state legislators and officials to Provincetown to explore his ideas, and the legislature in turn authorized the

TPR to research the history of the Province Lands, make maps, and propose a plan for disposition of those lands not occupied by squatters. A year later, the trustees submitted a report indicating that unlawful appropriation of firewood and sod left about half the estate treeless, but a thrifty new growth of maple, willow, cottonwood, scrub oaks, beech, pitch pine, tupelo, azalea, clethra, and other vegetation provided evidence that the land was still fertile. Reforestation would not only stabilize the sand ridges but also encourage additional vegetation, and "what is now an eyesore and a standing menace would be converted into a pretty forest." The trustees suggested separating out the unoccupied lands from the settled portion and ceding the latter to the town, which would then lease it or give it to squatters and begin collecting taxes. The unoccupied lands would become the property of the state, and with this would come the responsibility for protecting "one of most important harbors on the Atlantic seaboard for refuge from storms."[68]

On recommendation from the TPR, in 1892 the legislature gave the occupied southern portion of the land to Provincetown and set aside the remaining two thousand acres as a permanent reservation managed by the state commissioners of harbors and lands, who undertook the reforestation project. In 1950 the land was given to the Department of Conservation. Charles Felt had imagined the Province Lands "as a resort for pleasure and health, swept from all sides by the pure air of the surrounding seas," and in 1961 it became exactly that: a part of the new Cape Cod National Seashore. The remaining beach shacks in the federal preserve were placed on the National Register of Historic Places.[69]

Acquiring Reservations

When the Metropolitan Park Commission began acquiring land, the trustees assured the press that there would be "opportunities for such work in all parts of the state," and early donations bore out their expectations. The first property the TPR acquired was a 20-acre woodland in the Middlesex Fells donated by Fanny H. Tudor in 1891 to be named Virginia Wood in memory of her deceased daughter. Members of the TPR and Appalachian Mountain Club inspected the site and found it "eminently suitable for the object intended by the donor" but were wary of accepting the gift without funds to protect it. The AMC circularized the adjacent towns of Melrose, Malden, and Medford requesting donations, and with $2,000 in subscriptions for maintenance, the TPR completed the transfer. In 1895 when the Metropolitan Park Commission acquired the Middlesex Fells, it assumed maintenance of the Virginia Wood, and in 1923 the TPR deeded the parcel to the commission.[70]

In 1897 the trustees received 70 acres of oak woodland in Falmouth to be named Goodwill Park and another 50 acres of pasture and woodland on Mount Anne in Gloucester, given on the condition that it would be "forever maintained as a 'wild park.'" The trustees shared maintenance for Goodwill Park with the town of Falmouth and a custodian "familiar with its attractions." That same year it received a small property known as Rocky Narrows on the Charles River. The heavily forested bend in the river was only eight miles from Boston, but it was again a reminder of New England in its primeval state: "not unlike many of the streams in the woods of Northern Maine." Accessible by canoe, it was difficult to patrol, so the trustees left it under the care of the state fish and game wardens. In 1898 the TPR received portions of the estate of Thomas Hutchinson, the last royal governor of Massachusetts, and raised funds to purchase the adjoining property, thus preserving a "beautiful view ... within a few miles of the centre of the metropolitan district of Boston." The following year Helen Butler of New York gave the trustees 260 acres on Monument Mountain in the Housatonic River valley near Stockbridge. Also in 1899 the trustees acquired the Rufus Putnam homestead in Rutland. Putnam, a land surveyor and cofounder of the Ohio Colony, helped define terms for the Northwest Ordinance—the template for settling lands west of the Appalachian Mountains. Capitalizing on Putnam's importance, the TPR conducted a statewide campaign to raise funds for maintenance costs and, with a sufficient endowment, edged into the business of historic preservation. The lengthy negotiations over its upkeep gave the TPR opportunity to consider carefully the implications of maintaining a structure as opposed to uninhabited land.[71]

These donations completed the TPR's list of acquisitions at the end of the century: seven tracts containing, in all, 431 acres. In 1908 Martha Nash donated Petticoat Hill in Williamsburg as a memorial to her husband, and at this point, the TPR made no new acquisitions until 1929. Its agenda was slowed by a deep recession, preoccupation with the Metropolitan Park Commission and the Harrison tour, a reluctance to take on properties without funds to maintain them, and the untimely death of Charles Eliot.[72]

In lieu of acquiring property, the TPR focused on maintenance, having resolved to be more than "passive holders of the properties entrusted to their care." In his work for the Metropolitan Park Commission, Eliot had provided detailed instructions on maintaining lands under an amazing variety of conditions, and after his death in 1897 the TPR continued landscaping in this spirit, although less aggressively than Eliot would have advised. Volunteers removed dead, "weedy," or blighted trees and planted longer-lived species. They cleared paths to vistas, repaired roads and stone walls, cut back brush to highlight stands of venerable trees, and mowed meadows to keep views open. The town of Falmouth assumed responsibility for Goodwill Park, and since Mount Anne was to be left as a wilderness, the TPR limited upkeep to minor stand improvements supervised by a locally based committee.[73]

Legacies

Although the TPR's acquisitions were limited in these early years, its activities left a powerful preservationist legacy. In addition to sponsoring the Metropolitan Park Commission and the Harrison tour, the TPR conducted lantern-slide lectures, disseminated photographs and maps, distributed copies of its annual reports, issued statements to the press, and worked with village improvement societies, women's clubs, and national organizations like the American Park and Outdoor Art Association. This canvassing awakened the preservation impulse in the countryside, where publicly accessible lands would accommodate new recreational opportunities like camping, hiking, mountaineering, horse riding, boating, and fishing. Following the TPR's lead, the volunteer forestry associations founded in the 1880s and 1890s stepped up their campaigns to create state forests. The Massachusetts Forestry Association, created in 1897, combined public funds and private donations to acquire the state's first public reservation on the summit of Mount Greylock in the Berkshire Hills in 1898. In 1902 the state, with TPR support, purchased a reservation on Mount Tom in the Connecticut Valley and followed this with another on Mount Wachusett in the center of the state. Interest in the Park Act was on the rise, and Massachusetts seemed once again leading the nation in preserving open spaces.[74]

In England Parliament took a lively interest in the TPR and in 1893–94 created the National Trust for Places of Historic Interest or Natural Beauty, with rights and duties similar to those of the Massachusetts organization. In 1895 New York City residents launched a campaign to protect the Hudson Palisades against "unsentimental Jerseymen" who blasted the cliffs for quarry stone. "If the Palisades were on the Charles," a critic remarked, "Massachusetts would whisk them under State protection so quickly that the quarrymen would be obliged to fly in all directions." State legislators first asked Congress to declare the Palisades a national park, and when this effort failed they turned to the Massachusetts plan. In 1899 New York and New Jersey formed the Palisades Interstate Park Commission and with public and private donations established the park the following year.[75]

The TPR's influence spread northward as well. In New Hampshire logging in the White Mountains threatened scenic vistas and important watersheds, and in 1891, the year the TPR was founded, representatives from the hotel industry, women's clubs, state granges, and the AMC met in Concord, New Hampshire, to consider the fate of the forests. The attendees, including several TPR members, founded the Society for the Protection of New Hampshire Forests (SPNHF), which, like the TPR, called for donations of land to be held by a "board of trustees of public reservations." The AMC, like the TPR, gained legislative approval to acquire land and hold it in trust. Acting on the examples of the TPR and the Adirondack Preserve, established in 1892, SPNHF members campaigned for state, and eventually federal purchase of a "national park or forest reserve" in the White Mountains. The campaign came to a successful conclusion in 1911 when Massachusetts representative John W. Weeks shepherded a bill through Congress instructing the US Forest Service to purchase private forestlands in the southern and northern Appalachians. Congress established the White Mountain National Forest in 1918.[76]

The trustees' influence was also apparent in the campaign for a national park on Mount Desert Island in Maine. In 1901 Charles Eliot's father, along with George B. Dorr and other wealthy summer residents, organized the Hancock County Trustees of Public Reservations. Like the Massachusetts Trustees, the Hancock County organization was dedicated to the "perpetual holding of places of interest and beauty," and like its predecessor it accepted gifts of land from wealthy estate owners. With a steady accretion of land on the island, Dorr convinced President Woodrow Wilson to create Sieur de Monts National Monument in 1916. This became Lafayette National Park in 1919 and finally Acadia National Park in 1929.[77]

Emboldened by the campaign for a White Mountain National Forest, in 1905 the Maine Federation of Women's Clubs proposed a similar federal reserve around Katahdin, Maine's highest mountain. At that time Percival P. Baxter, an outdoor enthusiast from a family of wealthy Portland philanthropists, was elected to the state legislature and introduced the first of many unsuccessful bills calling for a state reserve around the mountain. As governor of Maine, Baxter continued to promote the park concept, and in 1930 as a private citizen he purchased 6,000 acres of timberland around Katahdin and deeded it to the state. In the spirit of philanthropic largesse Eliot envisioned for Massachusetts, Baxter continued purchasing land and deeding it to the state and completed the last purchase in 1962, realizing his dream of a wilderness park of more than 200,000 acres at age eighty-seven.[78]

The TPR's brainchild, Boston's Metropolitan Park Commission, became a national model as well, inspiring similar park commissions across the country. Commissioners in New Jersey's Essex County created the nation's first county park system in 1895, and in 1906 Providence established a Metropolitan Park Commission similar to Boston's to lay out a ring of parks and reservations around the city. Philadelphia, Albany, Buffalo, Cleveland, Akron, Toledo, Cincinnati, and Chicago created similar metropolitan park commissions, although Boston's continued to hold by far the largest acreage. Denver's 1912 Mountain Park system led to similar developments in other western cities.[79]

The Harrison tour influenced subsequent preservationist activities as well. In 1889 local benefactors had given the town of Plymouth a 150-acre park, but the town refused to appropriate maintenance funds. Harrison's visit induced the town to set aside funds for upkeep and remove squatters from another 1,400 feet of public beach. Likewise, Charles Francis Adams had donated Merrymount Park to his native Quincy, but only after Harrison's tour did the town appoint park commissioners. Barnstable, Chatham, Wareham, Mattapoisett, and Westport discovered long-forgotten shorefront claims, and New Bedford, Fairhaven Everett, Medford, Hyde Park, Dedham, Salem, Gloucester, Waltham, Beverly, and Malden established park commissions and invested in parks. Lynn complemented its expansive woodland park with public property on the ocean.[80]

The TPR's most important contribution to the preservationist cause was formulating a rationale for extending the park movement out into the countryside. The idea of rural parks took root when the federal government deeded Yosemite Valley to California as a state park in 1864 and set aside Yellowstone National Park in 1872, but these examples were difficult to translate into eastern preservation campaigns. Both were predicated, as Mark Stoll writes, on the "saving power of wilderness," and according to Alfred Runte, they were set aside only because they preserved grand and unique earth monuments that affirmed America's cultural identity. The national parks created in the 1890s continued this focus on exemplary natural wonders, and in most cases the less spectacular lands around these monuments were not, at least initially, considered worthy of protection.[81]

The founding of the TPR coincided with growing interest in state-mandated rural reservations. In 1875 the federal government established Fort Mackinac on Michigan's Mackinac Island as the nation's second national park and deeded it over to the state in 1895 as a state park. New York set aside land around Niagara Falls in 1885, and four years later Minnesota established a state park at Minnehaha Falls. In 1891, the year the TPR was founded, Minnesota established a state park at Itasca Lake, the font of the Mississippi River, and two years later created another at Birch Coulee, the site of a battle in the Sioux War. The state joined with Wisconsin to set aside the Dalles of the St. Croix in 1895 and 1900. New York created the Catskill Forest Reserve in 1885 and the 700,000-acre Adirondack Park in 1892, and in 1902 California founded Big Basin State Park in the redwood forests near Santa Cruz. The Save-the-Redwoods League in California and the Okefenokee Society in Georgia were both founded in 1918 on the idea of holding land in the public trust. These parks, like the TPR reservations, were pioneering achievements in land stewardship, but in each case they embraced land of national significance or, as with the Catskill Reserve and Adirondack Park, land critical for watershed protection.[82]

It was the TPR that introduced the more subtle understanding that ordinary landscapes were worthy of protection, largely for the enjoyment of those who lived nearby. Rather than focus on sublime natural features and primeval expanses, the TPR and the Metropolitan Park Commission collected an assortment of neglected riverbanks, tangled swamps, rockbound glens, windy mountaintops, bits of woodland and meadow, and other landscapes left behind in the rush to develop cities and suburbs. These were places that, unlike the national parks and the few state parks then in existence, bore the deep press of human history and held cultural as well as natural meaning. Andrew Green, president of the American Scenic and Historic Preservation Society, pointed out that the labor of subduing nature invested this land with a "history upon which to look back and in which to take pride." They were, as Kent Ryden writes, small places that represented "the way people experience natural landscapes in their daily living." Nature was neither abstract nor monumental; rather, it was familiar and representative. The reserves were, as Thoreau would have it, places for intimate immersion in nature.[83] TPR campaigns popularized the idea that ordinary places were meaningful, a realization that began with the campaigns for estate landscaping and village improvement in the middle years of the century.

By the 1920s county and state parks were common—a consequence of the increased mobility of the automobile age—but as historian Ethan Carr writes, it was the TPR that provided the conceptual basis for this preservation achievement "by adapting . . . municipal landscape park work to the scale and context of a regional park." In this sense, the TPR was clearly ahead of its time. Years later, Herbert Evison wrote in the *New York Times* that back in 1891, "nobody . . . foresaw twenty-odd million automobiles rushing up and down the highways of the United States, . . . [in a] restless search . . . for new travel objectives."[84] The impulse to preserve rural landscapes emerged out of the nineteenth-century embellishment of country estates, the improvement of village landscapes, and the innumerable descriptions of New England village life in novels, poetry, art, and essays. It was championed by landscape theorists like Andrew Jackson Downing, Charles Sprague Sargent, Frederick Law Olmsted, Sylvester Baxter, and Charles Eliot, and it was popularized by the trustees' early campaigns in the Boston environs and along the Massachusetts coast. This aesthetic impulse was rekindled in the 1960s by a host of local preservationists seeking to protect their neighbors from suburban sprawl. The idea of conserving an ordinary landscape, whether an estate, a village green, a suburban neighborhood, a city park, a rural reservation, or a natural habitat, was New England's most significant—and most democratic—contribution to American environmental activism.

CHAPTER 3

Stewardship Strategies
The Trustees in the Twentieth Century

By the close of the nineteenth century Boston and its suburbs had acquired some seventeen thousand acres of parks, reserves, parkways, protected river banks, and public seashore, almost all within the span of a decade. The Greater Boston park system, according to regional planner John Nolen, surpassed "not only anything which this country has produced, but in many respects anything similar in Europe as well." With these preserved sites in the hands of the Metropolitan Commission, the TPR turned to the outlying areas of Massachusetts, hoping to create, as the *Boston Herald* put it, a continuous "chain of pleasure grounds" accessible from any point in the state. The need was growing urgent. "The old Bay State may well be proud of the parks in Boston and vicinity," one expert pointed out in 1900, "but she ought to hang her head in shame when she sees the provisions made for working people in other cities." For almost two decades the TPR made little headway in these outlying areas, but after a detailed survey of potential recreational lands in 1929, it adopted a strategy of aggressive acquisition. As the number of reservations grew, the trustees struggled to define the principles that would guide private land preservation into the future. In its half century of experimentation, the TPR reached three overarching decisions: it would continue to acquire and preserve representative landscapes, it would open these landscapes for public use, and it would cede responsibility for protecting them to local volunteers. Beyond these generalities, however, lay a vast gray area in which the TPR confronted complex issues involving the rise of auto-based recreation, the democratization of its management structure, the maintenance of its historic buildings, the uncertainties of ecological preservation, and the balance between open public access and protecting delicate natural or cultural features. The TPR emerged from this era of experimentation with a clear set of preservation policies suited not only to its own commitments but also to the preservation movement that was, by the 1960s, growing up around it.[1]

The TPR faced two challenges in reaching out beyond the Boston Basin, the first being the sheer novelty of preserving ordinary rural landscapes. By the 1890s cities across the country boasted landscaped parks fashioned after New York's masterpiece, but these carefully engineered green spaces bore little relation to the TPR's goal of protecting regionally representative landscapes. In 1869 Horace Cleveland reminded designers that urban parks should harmonize with the city's surroundings, and some early parks did indeed incorporate regional themes, but as landscape architecture gained professional stature, the balance between regional character and abstract landscaping principles tipped in favor of the latter. City parks became complicated artistic creations. Their "unity and beauty," as landscape theorist Mariana Van Rensselaer wrote, would be impaired if any single feature failed to conform to the overall design. And as John C. Olmsted pointed out, there was generally little in the landscapes adjacent to the city to inspire emulation. "Fires, pasturing, cultivation, wood-chopping, the destruction or driving away of the wild animals, wild birds and insects, and the introduction of others, ... long since eradicated nature ..., leaving at best only a general resemblance to natural scenery."[2] As an idealized reconstruction of nature based on abstract design principles, the urban park provided little guidance for saving representative rural landscapes.

A second challenge was the lack of popular enthusiasm for preserving rural open spaces. City dwellers would support an outlying park, but only if it was accessible by train or trolley. Country folk were even less supportive, since the surrounding woods, lakes, streams, and hills supplied ample recreational space without need of preservation. Farm families spent their summers hard at work preparing for the long winter months ahead and had little time for the type of leisure activity that made parks seem so essential in the cities. "Here in New England, where any kind of pleasure, even domestic, was considered sinful, a playground was the very last thing thought of." The country was still new, Iowan Thomas MacBride explained at an 1897 outdoor recreation conference. "Time has not allowed for much aesthetic development out of doors. You can not expect a man to ... plant flowers until the [buffalo] chips are picked up and the mortar on the walls is dry." Even in rural Massachusetts, where the mortar had been dry for some three centuries, farm communities considered the countryside a workplace rather than an object of recreation or contemplation. Park advocates confronted "centuries of inertia" in the countryside.[3] For these and other reasons, the landscape preservation idea languished outside the city. A 1641 Massachusetts law declared all water bodies of ten or more acres in the state "forever open to the public for fishing and fowling," but for the next two hundred years the idea of protecting recreational access to rural areas lay practically dormant. There were, of course, examples provided by the national parks established in the 1890s, but these offered little precedent for a private statewide organization like the TPR. The virtue of preserving ordinary regional landscapes as pleasure grounds was far from obvious at the end of the century.[4]

The TPR's challenge was to transform the literary and artistic celebration of rural New England into a campaign to preserve rural open spaces. In each of its annual reports it included a quote from Henry David Thoreau: "What are the natural features which make a township handsome?" he had asked in his journal. "A river, with its waterfalls and meadows, a lake, a hill, a cliff or individual rocks, a forest, and ancient trees standing singly." It would be worthwhile, he continued, "if in each town a committee were appointed to see that the beauty of the town received no detriment. If we have the biggest bowlder in the country, then it should not belong to an individual, nor be made into a doorstep." Later writers, artists, and poets heaped praise on the rivers, waterfalls, lakes, hills, cliffs, rocks, forests, and ancient trees Thoreau had in mind, preparing the ground for the TPR's crusade to preserve landscapes extraordinary only in a local context. Landscape architect Frank A. Waugh described the satisfactions of nearby open spaces after a saunter through the trustees' Petticoat Hill Reservation. The sixty-acre reservation was clothed in nondescript second-growth hardwoods, but in local context it was, as Thoreau said, a place that made the township handsome. What could be finer, Waugh wrote, than "walking through the cool forest, resting on the convenient seats, drinking from the big spring, looking out at the inspiring distances." It was representative—a reminder of "what God meant this country to look like." Townspeople everywhere should enjoy this privilege, Waugh thought, but this would require citizen initiative. "If you and your neighbors know what you want, there are forty ways to get it, and all of them better than getting it through Congress."[5] Acquiring these democratic spaces would proceed on a town-by-town basis in a manner consistent with New England history and culture.

In the middle decades of the century, the TPR grappled largely alone with the myriad questions that saving these reminders brought to the fore. There were no precedents for acquiring private lands on the scale the TPR founders envisioned, and once these lands were acquired, it had only the echoing advice of Charles Eliot to guide their maintenance. What, for instance, did "natural" mean in this preservationist context, and how were these lands to be presented to the public as representing the New England landscape at large? Could these democratic spaces be protected from overuse if they proved as popular as the TPR hoped? Historic preservation raised equally perplexing questions. How should these special places be made to represent New England's culture and landscapes? Above all, how would the TPR fund its custodianship over this growing estate? The 1960s and 1970s brought an explosion of land-trust organizing across New England, and the strategies these new preservationists adopted were by no means intuitive; they were predicated on years of TPR experimentation as it pioneered the art of public preservation. The middle decades were indeed a crucial incubation for land preservation in New England.

New Mobility

While prospects for creating a system of reservations might have seemed dim in the TPR's first decade, New England was on the cusp of change. In the decades after the TPR's founding, urban parks faded as a focus of the preservation spirit. The rise of immigrant-oriented machine politics dampened upper-class enthusiasm for park building, and as leading families relocated to the suburbs the focus of preservation shifted outward. But it was the automobile that laid the groundwork for rethinking the park movement. Speaking before a gathering of real-estate brokers in 1895, Charles Francis Adams commented on the growing accessibility of the countryside. Just a decade earlier touring was a privilege confined to wealthy urbanites, but as he explained, trains, trolleys, streetcars, and bicycles had democratized this leisure pursuit. "There are now thousands of people in this city, tied to desk or counter, who from one week's end to the other are counting upon the coming of Saturday and the enjoyment of Sunday in the beautiful country which was formerly to them a sealed book." Transportation advances changed the way urban people thought about their rural surroundings. "Under the stimulus of the wheel," one bicycle enthusiast reported, "the country inn is reviving, the outdoor restaurant appears, opening a new industry to the farmer, and affording a field for picturesque improvement."[6] Preservationists took note.

Country roads had been neglected in the railroad era, but in 1880 the League of American Wheelmen launched a good roads movement, and in 1893 Massachusetts created a commission to oversee construction of a state highway system. At the same time, the National Good Roads Association, an alliance of bicycle clubs, farm associations, and university agricultural departments, began experimenting with plows and steam rollers that could build and maintain durable, dry, and smooth roads to meet the growing demand for access to the countryside. The manufacture of practical and affordable motor vehicles intensified the need for improvements. "Few roads laid out today will be adequate in width, in grade or alignment for future traffic," Charles Downing Lay warned in 1917, "if it increases in the next fifteen years as it has in the last."[7]

By the second decade of the century Massachusetts counted two hundred thousand motor-car owners, with another fifty thousand motorists entering the state on vacation each year. The proliferation of touring and camping facilities, motor hotels, equestrian centers, gas stations, fruit stands, and restaurants accelerated the modernization of rural life as touring became an important part of the New England economy. In response, the state Highway Commission spent millions of dollars improving trunk lines and byways. The 1915 Hill Towns Act allocated special funds to widen, straighten, and grade roads in the four counties west of the Connecticut River on the assumption that better roads would help stem hill-country out-migration. The isolation that once characterized rural New England was growing less intense.[8]

Despite the new mobility, rural New Englanders faced difficult challenges. Between 1880 and 1930 land under cultivation fell from 3.3 million acres to little more than 2 million acres, and the declining number of farms, sawmills, and woodworking shops left commentators in a reflective mood. "The methods of pioneering, as everybody now well understands, have been wasteful," Albert Shaw wrote in 1927. "Forests could have been fully utilized, without impairing the natural process of reforestation. Lands could have been farmed to advantage, without the ruinous consequences of soil exhaustion and erosion."[9] Shaw noticed a more positive trend in New England demographics, however: a reverse migration from the cities into the hinterland. Twentieth-century innovations like automobiles, hard-surfaced roads, telephones, radios, long-distance power transmission, grade schools, and combined-denomination churches improved country life, and small towns, with their fresh air and open spaces, beckoned to the urbanite. Books and magazine articles recommended rural atmosphere as balm for the ravages of city life, and companies like Ford Motor, General Electric, Westinghouse Electric, and General Chemical moved factories and workers out to these more intimate population centers. Massachusetts statistician David Rozman found that one-third of the land in a sample of seventy-one small Massachusetts towns was owned by nonresidents, and the trend was on the rise. This in turn created opportunities for full-time residents in home construction, landscaping, part-time farming, truck farming, and dairying.[10]

Planning for the Automobile Age

Cheaper and more dependable automobiles changed the nature of outdoor recreation. Travel by rail and steamship concentrated tourists at specific destinations, such as spas, seaside resorts, or mountain hotels. Auto travel scattered them across the landscape, spreading the vacation industry to once remote places like Cape Cod, the Berkshire Hills, the White Mountains, and the north Maine woods. Families took to the roads in what Warren Belasco calls the "squatter-anarchist" stage of motor touring, picnicking or camping wherever they pleased along the road.[11] As landowners posted their land and the distinction between private and public became clear, the demand for public and private campgrounds, restaurants, and motor hotels, or motor courts as they were first called, rose. By 1929 every state in the Union with the exception of Colorado and Montana featured one or more state parks.

Despite their patrician disdain for advertising and gaudy roadside architecture, the trustees, to their credit, embraced the idea of auto tourism. Their reservations, annual reports explained, would provide motorists "a quiet restful place to stop and prepare lunches at open air." Local committee members posted larger signs to attract even more visitors but at the same time wondered if their limited facilities could accommodate such an increase. In response, the trustees campaigned for land donations along popular auto touring routes—narrow strips between the highway and a brook, lake, or cliff—and envisioned a day when the map of Massachusetts would be "streaked all over with narrow public reservations of this type."[12] Roadside reservations would complement the democratization of touring that came with the automobile.

The new mobility brought troubling signs as well. When the TPR was chartered in 1891, threats to the integrity of the rural landscape were limited to the reach of the carriage and streetcar. The road improvements of the 1910s and 1920s allowed millions of motorists to "stream into the country on holidays and week ends," and advertisers responded accordingly, erecting billboards and painting cliffs, barns, and boulders with promotional messages. A "dark smudge of tawdry taste"—hot dog and barbecue stands, gas stations, ice cream palaces—spread outward from the city.[13] Roadside beauty was a sensitive issue in New England. As early as the 1860s state legislatures were encouraging cities and towns to appoint tree wardens to regulate the removal of roadside foliage. Trees, preservationists explained, kept roads moist, reduced dust, discouraged weeds, and blocked drifting snow, but mostly they framed and enhanced the scenery beyond the roads. State forestry commissions, formed in the 1880s, provided seedlings for roadside planting, and village improvement societies, tree protective associations, and local women's clubs joined the effort, offering prizes for roadside tree planting and rewards for those who supplied evidence to convict tree vandals. The rise of auto touring merely quickened this concern. The thousands of people who traveled the state's country roads, Charles Sargent reminded readers, "felt a personal interest and proprietorship" in the trees that lined them.[14] Property was a private privilege, but scenery was a public right.

The TPR was quick to champion this public right. At its founding meeting in 1891, Leverett Saltonstall complained that "picturesque country roads" were being desecrated by highway engineers who straightened and widened them and removed the embowering trees. The *Boston Globe* suggested that the legislature designate highways as linear parks, and in 1895 the Massachusetts Highway Commission recommended turning strips of land along the roads over to the TPR. While this never became law, it suggests the organization's stature in the roadside beautification movement. Over the next decades the TPR helped clarify laws regarding shade trees. It urged billboard legislation, published newspaper editorials, and worked with local garden clubs, women's clubs, and improvement associations to ignite the "slumbering sense of the right of the people to the enjoyment of natural beauty."[15]

Urged by the trustees and other organizations, in 1899 the Massachusetts legislature prohibited outdoor advertising in the vicinity of parks. Frederick Law Olmsted Jr. explained: having spent thousands of dollars in creating a park, a city could expect to capture the full value of its investment only if the surrounding neighborhood remained free from "features irritating to the nerves." Finally, in 1918 voters amended the state constitution to legalize billboard regulation, and the legislature passed a law to this effect in 1925. "The great majority of the billboards in Massachusetts now stand in defiance of the law," the TPR declared. Other New England states acted similarly, confirming the public right to roadside scenery.[16]

The Bay Circuit

In a 1922 essay Charles Eliot II, nephew to the TPR's founder and its first paid director, described what he saw as the impact of auto touring on landscape perception and park use. The roads that wove sinuously through the molded terrain and sculpted vegetation of late-nineteenth-century parks drew attention to scenic views and made the parks seem larger and more varied, but from a fast-moving automobile, as Eliot explained, these "aimless wiggles and sharp curves" were "worse than futile." Carefully arranged scenery was equally meaningless when viewed through the window of a rapidly moving vehicle. Automobiles were initially excluded from the national parks, and visitors were conveyed over the crooked and narrow roads by horse-drawn coaches or on horseback. Only after World War I did the Park Service began building roads to accommodate automobiles. In smaller landscaped parks, automobiles made less sense. Arthur Comey, who studied landscape architecture under Frederick Law Olmsted Jr. at Harvard, pointed out that the "former afternoon drive about the pond is now a spin of a few minutes." Either curved roads or automobiles would have to go, and most park promoters recommended the latter. Eliot reasoned that auto travel had opened the entire countryside as a "motorist's park," and under these circumstances it seemed reasonable that auto tourists should yield the landscaped parks to carriage riders, pedestrians, and equestrians—"to whom this open country is not accessible."[17]

Eliot's characterization of the countryside as a motorist's park signaled the TPR's plan for landscape preservation in the automobile age. Building on the success of the metropolitan park system, the TPR proposed a broad network of state and private reservations in a belt encircling Boston at a radius of about fifty miles. The so-called Bay Circuit drew inspiration from the Regional Planning Association of America, formed in 1923 by a group of prominent land-use planners and essayists. Association members were interested, among other things, in finding ways to restrain metropolitan influences that threatened the integrity of the countryside. Like earlier reformers, they admired the beauty of ordinary landscapes created by generations of landscape-savvy farmers. Practical-minded and frugal, farmers understood the importance of soil types, geology, hydrology, terrain, climate, and microclimate and arranged their farms to maximize the benefits of this collection of elements. Their adaptations marked the "characteristic beauty of the New England farm," and implicit in the regional planner's admiration was a concern for the vulnerability of the vernacular landscape. Country and city were antipodes, as association founder Benton MacKaye wrote: "One is inherent, the other is intrusive; one is natural, the other is mechanized; one is art, the other is artifice; one is symphonic, the other is cacophonous." Convinced that regional planning could help maintain city and country each in its appropriate sphere, MacKaye presented his best-known contribution to regional planning—the Appalachian Trail—as a twenty-two-hundred-mile buffer that would contain metropolitan expansion back from the seaboard.[18]

The Appalachian Trail epitomized the idea of using natural and recreational corridors to stabilize the relation between city and country. The trail would provide "breathing space" for those in the most densely populated area of North America and at the same time protect the rural character of the land beyond the trail corridor. In order to deepen local attachments to the land, MacKaye insisted that each section of the trail be financed, planned, and built by local volunteer groups. Through their work, volunteers would learn about stream flow, soil composition, forest growth, and plant and animal life. They would develop a love of nature and encourage others to protect it. With its democratic, grassroots base, the trail would be a movement rather than a landscape feature.[19]

Inspired by the regional planning movement's strategies, Charles Eliot and the trustees laid out a coordinated acquisitions program that would meet the recreational needs of the automobile age and at the same time shield the countryside from the expanding metropolis. As the Planning Association pointed out, automobiles and hard-surfaced roads expanded Boston's recreational hinterland out to a fifty-mile radius. Within this radius Eliot mapped out a ring of proposed parks and reserves that would, like the Appalachian Trail, shelter the land beyond it from metropolitan influences. The Bay Circuit would begin at Duxbury Beach south of Boston and run in a broad arc northward to Plum Island via the Charles River Narrows and Walden Pond. It would be accessible via automobile or interurban railroad to as many as four million people living in or near Boston, and it would include state beaches at Salisbury, Duxbury, and Westport. The idea originated in MacKaye's 1928 book, *The New Exploration*, which among other things recommended a green corridor encircling Boston from South Shore to North Shore. Borrowing from MacKaye's book, the TPR proposed a "townless highway" through the protected corridor with northbound and southbound arteries separated by a band of tightly zoned land and a footpath similar to the Appalachian Trail. The corridor already contained four TPR reservations, six state forests, three state reservations, two Audubon preserves, and a water-supply zone.[20]

The Bay Circuit was a striking innovation. It was one of the first proposed greenbelts in the country and among the first attempts to appeal to multiple recreational constituencies, offering motor parkways, wildlife sanctuaries, geologic and botanic exhibits, historic sites, picnic spots, trails, scenic overlooks, and water access points, with opportunities for swimming, boating, fishing, canoeing, skating, skiing, bicycling, hiking, exploring, horseback riding, and hunting. As a multiple-use recreation area it addressed the imbalance between national parks in the West and population concentrations in the East. It was also the first attempt to protect the broader landscapes through which tourists traveled to their final destinations. In the auto age, the TPR understood, travel to and from a resort was an attraction in itself. Rolling farmlands, winding country roads, and fields lined by stone walls were difficult to protect, but they were central to the state's identity, history, economy, and environment. Each farm, field, meadow, and woodlot was "a little sample or specimen or picture of a particular type of country ... life."[21]

Finally, the Bay Circuit was the first park concept in the country to recognize the automobile as a central ingredient in modern recreation. Touring families could, in a few days, circumnavigate eastern Massachusetts along a route that revealed the entire panorama of Massachusetts natural and cultural history. From the sparse postglacial landscape with its drumlins and kettle holes to the primeval forests of the precontact era, each stop along the way would provide a lesson in the making of New England. The touring family could enjoy the beauty of an upland bog, the relaxing ripple of a woodland stream, and the deep historic ambience of a hill-country village—all in one trip. Paths and trailheads would entice them to leave their vehicles and wander the landscape they discovered through the windshield.[22]

Because land values were still relatively low, the TPR reasoned that public lands could be expanded easily. Trustees appealed to private landowners plagued by vandalism and litter, pointing out that public recreation areas would reduce the threat of trespass. Likewise, public beaches would relieve pressures on shorefront property owners. The Bay Circuit was timely, given the rise in tourist traffic and the proliferation of no-trespassing posters. "The time has passed," Walter Prichard Eaton declared, "when people can be sure of natural recreational facilities without public ownership."[23]

The trustees contacted landowners and local assessors to help refine the plan and published two of MacKaye's pamphlets, *Highway Approaches to Boston: A Wayside Situation and What to Do about It* and his later *Bay Circuit: A Practical Plan for the Extension of the Metropolitan Park System*. In the former he described the commercialized highways leading into Boston as "auto slums," lined with hot-dog stands, restaurants, filling stations, curio shops, and other eyesores, and urged town planners to protect their roads by clustering all such establishments at a few locations where they could function as "servants and not parasites." Between these clusters, the roads would be "freeways" with access heavily regulated.[24]

The trustees presented the Bay Circuit bill to the legislature, but in the worsening economic climate of the early 1930s, the measure was tabled. During the Depression the old Federal-period turnpikes were upgraded into multilane express highways, and as it turned out, the new Route 128 throughway ran roughly along the Bay Circuit route, encouraging the "very conditions which MacKaye's proposal was intended to abate." Although the Bay Circuit died in the legislature, it helped focus the trustees' acquisition efforts, and by 1944 it held eighteen reservations in the proposed corridor. Other conservation organizations contributed as well. At Plum Island they acquired land and lobbied against road-building projects that would open the island to residential development. Town officials in the Bay Circuit area met with conservation commissioner Samuel York and public works commissioner Frank Lyman and stepped up their own local efforts to acquire public lands. The idea was perhaps too ambitious for Depression-era thinking, but it suggested answers to the question regional planners saw as defining the modern era of city-country relations: "Can we make ... something better than a chaos of industrial cross-purposes?"[25]

In January 1940, as the national economy rebounded from the Depression, Governor Leverett Saltonstall appointed another special commission to look into the Bay Circuit idea and determine what the towns and cities in the ring were doing to preserve open space and scenic views. Which of these functions, the committee was to determine, could be handed over to an enlarged Metropolitan District Commission? Again nothing came of the study, but in 1955–56 the plan reappeared in the legislature as a way of meeting the state's growing recreational needs. The study committee proposed a system of shared responsibility between several state agencies and the cities and towns along the Bay Circuit, but again the proposal would have to wait for a more propitious economic and environmentally sensitive milieu.[26] When that time came, the Bay Circuit would be built, like MacKaye's Appalachian Trail, from the ground up, with the towns and local organizations contributing to an open-space preservation effort unlike any in the nation.

Acquisitions, 1929–1945

The 1920s brought growing public interest in nature and outdoor recreation, and to meet the demand, federal agencies opened national forests, Corps of Engineers project sites, and Bureau of Land Management lands to recreationists. States set aside land for parks, and municipalities established auto camps on their outskirts to attract tourists.[27] In 1924 President Calvin Coolidge convened a National Conference on Outdoor Recreation to consider the physical, social, and moral implications of parks and other public open spaces and the federal role in protecting them. The following year trustee Walter Eaton complained to Charles Eliot that Massachusetts had "no sense of state-wide plan" for its recreational resources and suggested that Eliot convene a similar statewide conference. Unlike the western states, where recreational resources were managed by a few state or federal agencies, preserved land in Massachusetts was held by local park authorities, state forestry, highway, fish and game and public works commissions, and private organizations ranging from historical societies to rod and gun clubs. The Appalachian Mountain Club was concerned with hiking trails, Massachusetts Audubon with bird sanctuaries, the TPR with open spaces generally, and the Massachusetts Forest Association with forests. The state's demonstration forests fell under the jurisdiction of the Massachusetts Agricultural College or the Forestry Division, and reservations were controlled by county commissions, special commissions, the Department of Conservation, the TPR, the AMC, Harvard University, the Federation of Bird Clubs of New England, and the Audubon Society. Sanctuaries were managed by municipalities, the Division of Fisheries and Game, or local birding or wildflower clubs. "None of them knows what the others are doing," Eaton added. Outdoor recreation was a $300 million industry in New England, and "the health, well-being and recreation of the inhabitants" coincided with the state's commercial interests. No surveys of statewide public open spaces had been compiled since the 1891 shore-towns study, despite the growth in population, the increase in mobility, and the proliferation of no-trespass signs along the highways. The new national parks in the West were drawing tourists away from New England, and Massachusetts was again falling behind other states in acres of public open space per capita.[28]

On behalf of the TPR, Eliot convened a statewide conference that brought together organizations and agencies involved in conservation, planning, park development, and landscape preservation, and in 1927 Governor Alvan Fuller designated the TPR study group a Governor's Committee on Needs and Uses of Open Space and charged it with developing a coordinated system of recreational and conservation resources. To accomplish this, the committee divided the state by watershed and sent out questionnaires to women's clubs, garden clubs, and other organizations, asking members to describe places they would show to visitors or to which they would go for picnicking, swimming, bathing, canoeing, hiking, fishing, camping, motoring, or horseback riding. The committee grouped the results of this grassroots survey into ecological categories such as ocean beaches, marshes and associated uplands, freshwater wetlands, forests, swamps, and land containing "curious and unusual" formations, such as gorges, glens, and caves. Under the last category the report listed Cat-Hole Cave in New Marlboro, Sunderland's Ice Cave, Winsor Jambs and the Wizard's Glen in Lanesboro, Devil's Den in Williamsburg, and the dinosaur footprints near Holyoke. Geological formations like Rattlesnake Gutter in Leverett and a natural bridge in North Adams were listed, as was Disappearing Brook in Laneboro. The committee also included "primeval environments." Since little in Massachusetts could be considered true wilderness, the committee looked for places where plants and wildlife were reclaiming "their ancient ways." In 1929 the committee issued its report, and the TPR distributed copies to government agencies, conservation organizations, women's and civic clubs, libraries, planning boards, and newspapers. The survey brought to light a rich field of endeavor for preservationist organizations, and in time nearly every site identified was protected by some publicly oriented organization.[29]

The Needs and Uses Study brought results. In 1931, under advisement from the TPR, Governor Joseph B. Ely established a Parks Division in the Department of Conservation to bring the state's lands under a single agency. Guided by the Needs and Uses Study, the state acquired two state parks, eleven reservations, and sixty-nine state forests. Some of these lands had been donated by the TPR, and to this recreational system the trustees contributed their own eight reservations. The Park Division of the Metropolitan District Commission (MDC) added another fifteen. Cities, towns, municipal water boards, volunteer organizations, and various state institutions held an additional two hundred thousand acres of parks, reservations, and public forests.[30]

The study was instructive for the TPR as it highlighted the limitations of the passive acquisitions policy set in place at its founding. After the addition of

Petticoat Hill in 1908, the TPR's strategy of waiting for philanthropic donations languished for the next twenty years. In 1927 Charles Bird, a member of the Committee on Needs and Uses, wrote to Charles Eliot II observing that "with a little effort," the trustees could secure "a lot more reservations." Hill-country outmigration was accelerating, meaning cheap land and willing donors, and good roads put these remote but scenic areas within reach of the touring public. With this prod, TPR secretary Laurence B. Fletcher began traveling around the state offering lantern-slide lectures to recreation commissions, garden clubs, women's clubs, university groups, and civic organizations. Fletcher delivered around fifty lectures each year, and at each gathering he invited the sponsoring club or organization to join the TPR in its preservation efforts.[31]

With Fletcher touring the state, the TPR resolved to acquire at least three new reservations each year by donation or sale, and though a combination of luck and determination it accomplished this goal in the following year. Among other things, it purchased the east bank of the Westfield River Gorge in West Chesterfield. Earlier a group of canoeists and kayakers noticed lumbermen in the woods at the head of the gorge and contacted the TPR, and after a brief funding campaign the trustees negotiated the acquisition. Two years later, it acquired land on Old Town Hill, a drumlin in Newbury with a sweeping view of Plum Island Sound. The owner had refused commercial offers of $15,000 for the property in hopes that it would someday become a park, and after raising funds the TPR purchased the 25 acres in 1929 for $5,000. "A few days after the deed had been signed and delivered," the TPR reported poignantly, the seller "shot and killed himself."[32]

In addition to Fletcher's tours, the organization distributed three thousand copies of its annual report and supplemental bulletins, including pamphlets describing each reservation and explaining the Bay Circuit idea. Fletcher spoke with individual landowners at sites identified as potential donations or purchases and led members on field trips to reservations around the state. In 1934 the TPR added a Committee on Publicity to coordinate the lecture series, which was by this time reaching about six thousand people each year. The annual meetings became more elaborate affairs, featuring speakers and elegant luncheons for as many as three hundred members. By 1935 Fletcher had doubled the number of contributors to the TPR.[33]

Interest in park development continued to increase during the Depression due to publicity surrounding the New Deal conservation initiatives and the work of the Civilian Conservation Corps, which built facilities in some eight hundred state parks and helped promote these public lands as more accessible alternatives to the national parks.[34] With interest in preservation on the rise, in 1933 the trustees acquired the 640-acre Whitney Woods in Cohasset and Hingham with an endowment of $10,000 for upkeep and in 1934 took possession of Halibut Point on Cape Ann—the only publicly accessible shoreline on the cape. The following year it gained a stand of rare native rosebay rhododendrons in the remote and densely wooded lowlands near the upper Charles River. The site, inaccessible until local attendants built a corduroy path across the soggy ground, was not notable for its scenery, but the rhododendrons, rare that far north, needed care and protection. Swamp maples were beginning to shade them out, and they were vulnerable to poaching. The local committee marked boundaries, posted signs, enlarged the parking space, cleared trails, removed fallen timber, and trimmed trees to provide the plants a proper balance of sunlight and shade. The rhododendrons grew taller under this care, but they blossomed less. In 1953 the committee solicited advice from professional tree surgeons and undertook a multiyear program of trimming and cutting to let in more light.[35] Keeping nature "natural," the committee discovered, was not a job to be taken lightly.

In 1935 when shorefront property owners on Salem Bay learned that nearby Misery Island was slated for an oil-tanker port, they purchased 68 acres on the island and gave it to the trustees with a $10,000 endowment for upkeep. Misery Island, as the name suggested, came with a long history of abuse. It had once been the site of a fertilizer plant, and around 1900 its forests were removed to make way for a summer resort and golf course. A fire swept away these buildings in 1926, and the oil-tanker farm proposal appeared a decade later. The TPR accepted the island on the assumption that over time and with some help, it would revert to its natural state.[36]

As the trustees gained a better sense of the maintenance needs on the growing list of reservations, they began turning down donations, but in each case they found an organization or public agency willing to accept the land. In 1907 they helped Harvard University acquire 2,100 acres in Petersham as a demonstration site—later the Harvard Forest. In 1923 they donated the TPR's first possession, Virginia Wood, to the Metropolitan Commission, establishing a precedent for divesting other properties. In 1932 when the Charles Bird family offered 70 acres in Walpole suited for ball fields, tennis courts, and a swimming pool, the TPR met with town officials, who accepted the land and landscaped it as the Bird family directed. That year the TPR similarly declined an offer of Pine Knoll in Sheffield, again better suited as a town park, and

1936 it gave Magnolia Shore to the city of Gloucester. During the decade the trustees helped state and private stewardship organizations acquire or enlarge seventeen major conservation areas, including four state forests, two state parks, the state's Watatic Mountain wildlife Area, and, for the Metropolitan Park District, the Breakheart Hill tract between Saugus and Wakefield.[37]

Democratizing Reservation Management

The TPR's more aggressive posture paid dividends. By the end of the 1930s it had pieced together a network of thirty-six reservations ranging from the remote thirty-acre Bartholomew's Cobble in Sheffield, nationally known for its ferns and wild flowers, to Rocky Woods near Medfield, which offered facilities for skating, skiing, and hiking. Each, the trustees discovered, had its own management challenges, and with the number of reservations growing, the cost of supporting them rose as well. By 1947 Fletcher was traveling some fifty thousand miles across the state each year to raise money for maintenance. He conducted these lengthy trips, he told Bird, because the "big fish" had to be cultivated carefully. "It takes so long to raise $4,000 or $5,000 with small amounts, and I've got to try to start with one-half the money raised with big ones. It is uphill work and exhausting, and I am getting older, but it has to be done. Nothing is more devastating or killing than to do a big business on a shoestring.... So there you are ... We are in the position of the ... boy [on] the bicycle. We've got to keep going or we'll fall off."[38] To keep expenses down, the trustees considered each potential land donation carefully, but even the wildest reservations required some attention, and the TPR, with its Boston-area membership and limited operating budget, was poorly prepared for this work. Acknowledging the diversity of maintenance needs across this far-flung domain, the trustees resolved to give more responsibility to the local committees, which in the mid-1930s were active only in six or so reservations.[39]

Faced with these rising maintenance challenges, the TPR struggled with an issue that would continue to vex community-based preservation organizations: balancing the need for expert leadership—the Standing Committee in this case—with grassroots participation. Before the TPR's founding, Lynn Woods officials had learned to deal with an "unending series" of fires, vandalism, and insect infestations by enlisting community volunteers. The TPR incorporated this expedient in its mission statement, which stipulated that the Standing Committee would "arrange with cities and towns for the necessary policing of the reservations so acquired." To this end, the TPR solicited local historical, natural history, and village improvement societies, and when the Standing Committee accepted a new property, it appointed a committee of individuals living in the area. The local committee would meet at least once a year with the field secretary, and it would describe maintenance activities in a formal report at the end of the year. The local committees were expected to avoid improvements that would look "anything like an ordinary public park," but otherwise they exercised a great deal of discretion.[40] In numerous local interpretations, a theme emerged: local committees would keep the reservations in as natural a state as possible but make them attractive to those living nearby. Given a good deal of latitude, the local committees closed the gap between the upper-class contemplative landscape appreciation on which the TPR was founded and the more active outdoor recreational pursuits typical of all classes in the mid-twentieth century.

In 1934 the trustees established a "Cooperating Society" program, inviting village improvement associations, garden clubs, women's clubs, bird-watching clubs, and other local organizations to affiliate by appointing a local "preservation committee." By the end of the decade around fifty local societies had pledged to share responsibilities on the reservations. Likewise, the TPR formed cooperative management arrangements with statewide organizations such as the Massachusetts Civic Federation, the Society of Colonial Dames, the Massachusetts Civic League, and the Society for the Preservation of New England Antiquities. When the reservations were first established, the trustees were distressed by the lack of local support, but by delegating functions to those familiar with the nearby community, they were able to cultivate a more cooperative mood. Along with their formal duties—clearing and planting trees, maintaining trails and signs, preventing fires—local committees were able to increase the level of support from town officials and local clubs and societies.[41]

Democratizing land-trust management created a small army of enthusiastic preservationists dispersed across this sprawling collection of properties and gave nearby communities a sense of ownership. More important, it put decision making in the hands of those who best knew the property. "Each reservation it seems to me should be considered separately in arrangements for the enjoyment of the public," trustee Robert Walcott explained. Maintenance needs were indeed particularistic. In 1942 Fletcher Steele reported that the Elliott Laurel Reservation in Phillipston, donated a year earlier, needed immediate attention. The donor reported that "rowdy shrubs" and sprouts were crowding out the mountain laurel, filling the glades, and obscuring the vistas. The local committee chair, Olive Simes, who helped endow the thirty-three-acre reservation, admitted that it was "more beautiful ten years ago, shortly after the cattle had been turned out," but she was under the impression that TPR policy was to allow reservations to "grow up wild." Steele advised her to "put it back as it was," confident that the local committee best understood the inherent beauty of the property. The committee borrowed some cattle and restored the vegetation to its original condition. At Petticoat Hill, community representatives asked the local committee for permission to clear trees for a children's sledding run, and the committee granted the request since it "added a source of public enjoyment of the Hill without any lessening of its natural beauty." As Standing Committee members loosened their grip on the reservations, they remained confident that the TPR would continue to operate "with a single mind." Annual reports suggest that relations indeed remained cordial.[42]

Vesting power in the community volunteers was a leap of faith. "The local committees and the Standing Committee are for the most part virtual strangers," a trustee admitted in 1948. The Standing Committee retained authority over accounting, publicity, and facilities, but its members understood that local interest would diminish if the volunteers felt themselves "only to be office boys, as it were."[43] Finding a proper balance between local control and consistency across the reservations was an ongoing matter of discussion.

Saving History

Historic preservation, usually the province of wealthy patrons, professional architects, and restoration experts, tested the TPR's strategy of democratizing maintenance on the reservations. In 1927 Minna G. Goddard donated the boyhood home of her grandfather, poet and journalist William Cullen Bryant, along with 240 acres of farmland with a substantial endowment to care for it. The TPR included historic structures in its mission statement, but as the trustees learned when they accepted the Rufus Putnam home, centuries-old historic buildings were by definition in need of care and rehabilitation. The Bryant estate was located in Cummington, far from the center of public giving in Boston, and the account of the donation circulating in the press incorrectly labeled the TPR a "state" Board of Trustees, implying government funds for upkeep. Given the difficulties of fund-raising, the trustees accepted the gift but left responsibility for the building to Minna Goddard and managed only the surrounding lands. Thus, they avoided questions the Standing Committee was as yet unprepared to answer: How were historic buildings to be preserved, which features were to be retained, how was upkeep to be financed, and how much of this procedure depended on the local committee?[44]

The trustees were not alone in facing these questions. With historical and antiquarian societies on the rise across the East, Boston's upper classes proved particularly active in saving historic homes and buildings. With its Revolutionary War legacy and its nationally significant architectural achievements, Boston quickly moved to the forefront of the historic preservation movement. Preservationists lost the battle to save John Hancock's town house in 1863 and the Brattle Square Church in the early 1870s, but when Boston's Old South Church was slated for destruction in 1872, a group of wealthy Boston women headed by Mary Hemenway raised cash to purchase it. By the 1930s the Society for the Preservation of New England Antiquities, the Daughters of the American Revolution, and local historical and antiquarian societies had preserved and restored around two hundred historic homes in New England, and the TPR felt obliged to do its part.[45]

In the Waltham-Watertown area the TPR cooperated with the Society of the Colonial Dames, the Society for the Preservation of New England Antiquities, and individual donors to purchase the Gore Estate, eighty acres of "English park-like scenery" with a brick mansion built in 1806. A few years later in 1939 it acquired the Old Manse located next to Concord's historic battlefield. The building, with connections to the Emerson and Hawthorne families, had been opened to the public in 1934 but was falling into disrepair. The trustees were wary of the purchase but seeing no other recourse raised $17,500 and campaigned for a maintenance endowment. It was immediately clear that the house needed extensive restoration, and once fully opened to the public it would require a great deal of maintenance. "Can you ... imagine what would happen to your rugs and floors if ten thousand people tramped up into your attic during the course of the summer?" The Old Manse, as a trustee reported, was "an unwanted, but beautiful baby left on our door step."[46]

Leaving ongoing maintenance decisions to the local committee, the TPR collected funds for structural repairs and restoration, but this raised complicated questions. The structure had changed considerably since the days of Emerson and Hawthorne. Was it to be restored as it was when it was first constructed? When the battle at Concord was fought? Or when the Emersons and Hawthornes lived in it? Or was it to be modernized "without much regard for the past"? Architects believed buildings should be restored to the time when they were completed in order to give "maximum expression" to the designer. Others felt buildings should show some signs of weathering for historic authenticity, and still others envisioned an "ancient weathered look" that accented the lives of their most important inhabitants. Critics of this approach thought Old Manse appeared "shabby and neglected" and worried that this would reflect badly on the trustees' custodianship. Preserving historic buildings involved a great deal of interpretation, but failure to set a policy would result in a "hodge-podge—a banal little-of-everything."[47] Rather than resolve this dilemma, the Standing Committee left repairs to local volunteers who better understood Concord's vernacular traditions. The Standing Committee had only a vague secondhand knowledge of the work being done, but it trusted the local committee to keep to a general set of principles. The house would be kept in a "reasonable standard of repair," just as any responsible householder in Emerson's day would have done.[48]

The trustees' most lavish historic acquisition came in 1945 when Florence Higinbotham Crane offered the TPR a thousand acres of dunes and marshland along a mile of shore at Cedar Point in Ipswich in memory of her late husband, Chicago industrialist Richard T. Crane Jr. The beach frontage was particularly welcome because so much of the Massachusetts coastline was in private hands. When Florence Crane died in 1949, she left the remainder of her estate to the trustees, including a fifty-nine-room Tudor-style mansion built in 1928 with a marble swimming pool, lawn, and several gardens. Other family members added even more acreage.

The Crane Reservation presented a monumental challenge. After only three years the beach and grounds were attracting more than two hundred thousand visitors annually, and maintenance costs were soaring. The local committee charged fees for parking and rented the manor house for meetings, benefits, dances, and recitals, but the endowment and income fell short, and the house was in desperate need of repairs. The Standing Committee first considered transforming it into a museum, but found this impractical since there were no furnishings. Another possibility was tearing it down and returning the grounds to "blueberry bushes and juniper trees," but few endorsed this option. Amid complaints from the Ipswich Garden Club about litter on the access road, the trustees labored to define policies for parking, boat launching, toilet facilities, policing, lifeguarding, and use of the marsh area. How, they asked, could they meet the demand for ever-expanding recreational use and at the same time preserve the area's scenic and architectural qualities? How were they to find profitable uses for the estate while protecting it from commercial exploitation? In 1951 they set up a foundation to renovate the gardens, restore the buildings, and offer evening performances by well-known artists like the Kingston Trio, Arthur Fiedler, Dave Brubeck, Duke Ellington, Pete Seeger, Josh White, and Carlos Montoya, all of which added between $70,000 and $76,000 each season to the restoration fund.[49] Over time, the TPR worked through these difficulties and kept the Crane Reservation on a paying basis, but the experience was a cautionary tale as they took on more historic preservation responsibilities.

In 1948 the TPR accepted the historic Mission House in Stockbridge, once home to an Indian parish. Mabel Choate, a wealthy local estate owner, purchased the home in 1929, moved it to Main Street, and had it restored and transformed into a museum. Since maintenance on the house and museum was adequately endowed, the TPR accepted the donation, although with some concerns. By this time the organization was running an operating budget deficit, and with twenty-four reservations to maintain, it decided to acquire no new historic properties without similar endowments.[50] The policy was not without merit. The growing number of state public lands in Massachusetts suggested that all "public reservations" were government funded, and this undermined the TPR's ability to attract donations for its own properties. Occasionally, the TPR considered dropping the term "public" from its name, and it did so in 1953.

Despite misgivings about maintenance costs, in 1955 the organization acquired the Stockbridge studio of Daniel Chester French, who had sculpted the statue for the Lincoln Memorial in Washington and the Minuteman statue in Concord. The sculptor's daughter passed the home and estate to the trustees along with a $3,000 annual appropriation for upkeep. Despite the bequest, the home became a significant financial drain. The TPR organized the Friends of Chesterwood to raise funds and arranged with local garden clubs to care for the grounds, but eventually it deeded the property to a descendant of the sculptor, who in turn donated it to the National Trust with an endowment of $400,000.[51]

In 1959 Mabel Choate offered the TPR her Naumkeag estate, also in Stockbridge. The cottage had been designed in 1885 by renowned architect Stanford White and included the original furniture, china, paintings, engravings, and books. Choate was, according to the *Berkshire Eagle*, "perhaps the last remaining South Berkshire summer resident whose means, inclination, and passion for horticulture allowed her to live in the sumptuous manner of the 'cottagers' of a generation or more ago." She expected the cottage and grounds to be maintained as she left it, "so that our public in the future could realize how people lived in her time."[52]

Like the Old Manse, Naumkeag challenged the trustees' commitment to historic preservation. The forty-eight-acre estate was nationally known for its formal gardens, a collaboration between Choate and Fletcher Steele, a prominent Boston landscape architect and member of the trustees' Standing Committee. One of the first graduates from the Harvard School of Landscape Architecture, Steele was a flamboyant and somewhat arrogant character known for his ability to work with demanding clients like Choate. Given this volatile combination of characters, the trustees were circumspect about acquiring the property. Guardedly, they promised to use the $500,000 Choate left in her will to keep the house and surroundings "at the highest standard which funds available for their maintenance will permit." Not everyone agreed with the decision. Trustee Walter Eaton, a well-known Berkshire Hills conservationist, noted that he was

> struck speechless by the idea.... What on earth do the Trustees want of the Choate place? What would they do with it? It isn't an old house; it isn't a beautiful house, being in Stanford White's late Victorian period, and with all due respect to my friend Fletcher Steele it has one of the most horrendous gardens in the Commonwealth of Massachusetts.... [Choate's father, Joseph Hodges Choate] had no connection with the Berkshires except as a summer resident.... I really can't see why the Trustees should take over this white elephant of a house.

Laurence Fletcher dismissed Eaton's comments as misguided and pushed ahead with a maintenance plan.[53]

At the Mission House, the maintenance endowment was adequate, but miscommunication between the Standing Committee and the local committee proved frustrating. Local committee chair Henry Dwight was instructed to pay Fletcher Steele a consultant fee for mixing an "old-time" paint preparation, but when the results were disappointing, Dwight had the paint scraped off. He received another bill from Steele for advice on the new paint and another from a consultant for "professional services on mixing the paint." Dwight wrote that the local committee agreed to the work, "but if it is going to be run by one individual from Boston [Steele], count us out." Evidently, Laurence Fletcher straightened out the matter, but he was left with a lesson in managing historical buildings: "Local representatives ... are in a better position to know how to run the reservation than we are here in Boston."[54]

With troubles in Stockbridge still brewing, in 1962 the trustees acquired the historic Stevens-Coolidge Farm in North Andover and almost immediately found themselves immersed in a battle with the town's School Building Committee over plans to use the property for a new high school. A prolonged campaign by townspeople defeated the Building Committee, but the controversy added another layer of complication to the TPR's mission.[55]

Upkeep in the Crane Estate, Mission House, Naumkeag, and Stevens-Coolidge Farm raised questions about allowing volunteer local committees to maintain professionally designed gardens, which, like nature itself, are dynamic and require constant attention. The trustees contracted with a faculty member from the Harvard School of Landscape Architecture to survey gardens on these holdings and received word that local committees had allowed them "to run rampant." The consultant recommended an aggressive regimen of pruning, clipping, and thinning. While this work was not overly technical, it nevertheless required a great deal of energy. Naumkeag's caretaker, Robert Crighton, was seventy-eight years old, his assistant was seventy-four, and the part-time workers—teenage boys—required careful supervision. The caretaker could "still put in a day on his knees weeding," but both Crighton and his assistant deserved retirement, Fletcher thought.[56]

By the 1970s it had become clear that while natural reservations could, to some degree, look after themselves, landscaped grounds needed "careful planning and continuing supervision." At Naumkeag, Robert Crighton died in 1970, taking with him forty years of accumulated knowledge of the gardens. This, as TPR director Gordon Abbott wrote, was "the end of an era," or perhaps more aptly the beginning of another.[57] Caring for homes and gardens set the stage for the trustees' entrance into the world of large maintenance endowments, capital campaigns, and preservation grant writing. Although historic preservation issues and grant-funded professional gardening reinforced the TPR's top-down structure, the organization maintained faith in its local underpinnings—in the committees that made the day-to-day decisions that kept the gardens and grounds beautiful and the vegetation on the scattered reservations looking natural.

Environmental Strategies

In the 1930s and 1940s, according to historian Alfred Runte, Americans increasingly viewed their national parks as "the last vestiges of primitive America." The Park Service responded by shifting its emphasis from visitor services to ecological and wilderness management. A similar transition was taking place within the TPR. This first became clear in 1946 when the organization pieced together funds with a grant from the Garden Club of America to purchase Bartholomew's Cobble, a 20-acre pasture on the Housatonic River. Although the area had been a local picnic grounds for generations, the TPR, which managed it jointly with the New England Wildflower Preservation Society, was interested less in visitation than in preserving the vegetation, particularly the several varieties of rare ferns that grew in the Cobble's lime-rich soil. The flora was so unique that the Department of Interior placed the Cobble on the National Register of Natural Landmarks alongside features like the Grand Canyon, the Everglades, and California's coastal redwoods. With a few guidelines from the chair of the Standing Committee, the local warden herded cattle onto the property to protect the meadows from reforestation, leaving just enough cedar to feed the waxwings that visited in the autumn. Under this regime the Cobble assumed "the aspect it had years ago, with the handsome rock faces more conspicuous."[58] Experiments like these heralded the TPR's growing emphasis on ecological management.

The Essex River marshes on the Crane Reservation turned the organization further in the direction of ecological preservation. With 1,315 acres of marsh already on the reservation, in 1955 Charles Eliot II began considering new acquisitions along the Ipswich and Essex Rivers. The marshes, according to the trustees, were valuable for exploring, duck hunting, boating, sailing, and swimming in waters warmed over the mud flats, but most important, they provided habitat for wildfowl, deer, shellfish, insects, plants, birds, animals, and fish. The trustees pointed to the fate of the marshes along the Mystic, Charles, and Neponset Rivers and urged Ipswich landowners to protect their own habitat. With this beginning, the trustees turned to ecological preservation as a primary focus in its preservation policies. In 1967 the organization acquired the Mashpee River Reservation on the lower Cape specifically to protect a rare sea-run brook trout once plentiful in New England streams, and the 1969 master plan for the Crane Reservation prioritized restoring the barrier sand dunes. Visitors were given a folder titled "This Fragile Shore," and the TPR conveyed a similar message to schoolchildren on field trips to the reservation.[59]

The TPR came into its own as an environmental organization as it added close monitoring and careful documentation of resident species to its maintenance master plans. It was encouraged in this direction by its involvement with other preservationist organizations. In the 1960s, for instance, it took on projects in association with the Nature Conservancy (TNC), the Nantucket Conservation Foundation, the Charles River Watershed Association, Massachusetts Audubon, the state Forest and Park Association, and the Fund for Preservation of Wild Life and Natural Areas, among others.[60]

The trustees' commitment to ecological integrity once again complicated their relations with the local committees. The preservation movement generally was riddled with controversy about the extent of intervention into natural dynamics. Having preserved tracts of land, it was often difficult, as Anne Whiston Spirn notes, to "persuade the public that landscape management includes the creative use of the ax as well as the generative act of planting seeds." Was the park or preserve to be managed as a scenic resource, a pleasure garden, a wildlife habitat, or a sacred symbol? As a pioneering preservationist organization, the TPR wrestled with these questions. When the Monument Mountain local committee members decided their woods needed thinning in 1950, they contracted with a forester who, in accordance with professional standards, marked the older trees for cutting. From the home office, Laurence Fletcher suggested cutting only the marked trees that were under six inches in diameter, but Walter Eaton "protested violently . . . against cutting *any* trees." Those the forester considered "over ripe," Eaton felt, should be "permitted to fall and make forest mold, as in nature." While the Standing Committee agreed in principle, the matter was not so clear. The reservation's most striking natural feature was a high cliff on the eastern flank that gleamed almost mystically in the morning sunlight. Over time it had been obscured by scrub growth, and the Standing Committee directed that the "worthless poplars and their ilk" around the base be removed. Again Eaton protested, but in the end the TPR sanctioned a "judicious use of the ax." Aesthetic preference prevailed over natural process.[61]

The TPR hoped to acquire reservations that represented the natural history of Massachusetts, but the Standing Committee recognized, as had Charles Eliot, that nature as they understood it required some degree of maintenance. If nothing was done, Fletcher Steele explained, the "undergrowth would soon clog the place up, fine trees would be smothered, and hurricane timber would lie where it fell. Fire ... could not be stopped when once it got a start." Preservation, he continued,

> does not mean that we are mossback reactionaries who rest content with nature's balance. Not so. We know well enough that Nature is continually fouling her own nest. She nurses a tree to grand old age, then bedraggles it with worms, breaks its bones with ice storms, and takes a fling at it with a hurricane. We depreciate such misconduct and do all we can to stop it. ... We trim and mend the breaks and remove the outrageous debris which Nature keeps piling up in our way. We try to keep our reservations more decent and orderly than Nature would let them be.

This complicated mandate left the local committees with more questions than answers. Dead and dying trees harbored insect "enemies" and encouraged fires, and "upstart vegetation" concealed "the very beauty which the reservations were expected to preserve"; clearly, local committees had license to remove them. In addition, the committees cleared away fallen trees, kept hilltop vistas open, replaced blighted chestnut trees with white pine or hemlock, and destroyed gypsy-moth nests—all with an eye to keeping the reservations natural. The committee at Hutchinson's Field harrowed the meadow each year to eliminate tree seedlings and weeds, and at Goodwill Park they worked with the city to remove white oaks and Norway spruce damaged by insects and replace them with hemlock, dogwoods, shadbush, kalmia, azaleas, and clethra. When fires damaged reservations, the committees replanted with species they deemed appropriate to the region's natural history.[62]

Beyond this, maintenance entered a gray area. On the removal of live trees, there were two schools of thought, as one trustee described them: "one, that you should never cut a tree, ... the other, that it would be handled as any good farmer would handle his crops." Some committees removed trees "long since past their prime," and others cleared out the younger trees to showcase the forest monarchs. The forester at the Bryant Homestead insisted that "his principle was to cut out the oldest and biggest trees in order to give the young ones a chance," but as Fletcher Steele complained, this meant destroying the "most valuable and finest specimens" to leave behind "a comparatively uninteresting residue which would be useful as lumber in another forty years but good for little else meantime." The trustees and local committees generally agreed on leaving the reservation "as Nature would have it," but the devil, as always, was in the details.[63]

Generally ceding these decisions to local committees, the trustees moved cautiously into the era of ecological preservation. Their forests would be thinned, views cleared, trees of special interest preserved, wildflowers encouraged, and cover and food for birds and animals maintained. The reservations would be protected against fire, and perhaps, if these ecological and aesthetic values were ensured, certain trees would be marketed. The TPR sought a balance between ecology, scenery, and recreation, but this was made problematic by the dynamic nature of the vegetation, the immense variation between reservations, the irregular communication between the Standing Committee and local committees, the shortage of technical know-how, and the preferences of the donors. Needless to say, leaving a reservation in its "natural state" was not a clear mandate to the local committees.[64]

Managing Democratic Access

While the TPR was working out the principles of ecological preservation, it faced new challenges with its policy of open public access to the reservations. As auto touring grew more popular in the postwar years, park commissioners and rangers across the country struggled to balance visitor needs with ecological imperatives. Early on, the trustees gave little thought to rules of conduct for recreationists. Given the strict standards of etiquette among Victorian upper classes, rules seemed unnecessary; visitors used parks and reservations as places of contemplative enjoyment, just as Charles Eliot or Frederick Law Olmsted would have intended. "On the whole, our visitors were so well trained by normal circumstances that all of them acted as wardens, each one as interested to preserve our lands as the trustees themselves." Moreover, their numbers were small. As late as 1948 TPR president Roger B. Greeley was pondering ways to get more people on the reservations. Regulations could come later, he advised, when attendance became "physically destructive or by mere force of numbers self-defeating."[65]

Nevertheless, the warning signs were there. When automobiles and better roads made reservations more accessible, trustees began asking local committees to give more thought to guarding "our helpless birds, animals, and plants." As early as 1912 the almost inaccessible Rocky Narrows Reservation was being "very much used," the local committee reported, "we regret to say, not always in the spirit in which it was intended." By 1921 the staff at nearby Medfield Hospital was complaining of odors from campsite refuse. At Misery Island, the local committee was overwhelmed by the task of policing campfires, providing sanitary facilities, and removing trash. The committee began charging fees to reduce casual visitation, but numbers nevertheless rose from twenty-five hundred in 1936 to twelve thousand in the mid-1960s. On reservations close to Boston, local committees were forced to enlarge picnic areas and parking lots. Monument Mountain volunteers added a small picnic ground on the highway, hoping to confine the litter problem to a single place.[66]

In 1935 the trustees purchased the 7-acre Dinosaur Footprints Reservation on the banks of the Connecticut River near Holyoke. They had been interested in the property since Ada Heine of Smith College wrote to Eliot in 1924, calling attention to the tracks and warning that vandals were "trying to hammer them out of the rocks." In 1950 local committee members reported enthusiastically that "with proper publicity the Footprints could be made a definite tourist attraction," but in the very next sentence they complained about the growing litter problem. At the 130-acre Lowell estate in Mashpee on Cape Cod visitors seemed less interested in the reservation's magnificent stand of ancient holly trees than in the site's potential as a picnic grounds, and by the 1960s the local committee was overwhelmed by the "perennial problem of trash, vandalism, and just plain dirty habits." At a time when the warden was struggling to contain gypsy-moth and leaf miner infestations, repair toilets, and guard against holly-berry harvesters, the endless round of digging beer cans out of the cat briar and retrieving picnic tables dumped into the ponds was more than a minor annoyance. The committee decided against posting directional signs on the highway, hoping this would limit use to "people who are really interested." Reports like these underscored the dilemma of democratic access to features trustees regarded as priceless. The TPR continued to rely on public responsibility, but the burden of this policy fell heavily on the local committees.[67]

The tension between public use and preservation became clear in the debate over the more popular recreational facilities. To defray maintenance costs, committees sometimes sold sundries and snacks and offered other amenities, even though this seemed contrary to the image of a natural retreat. The 400-acre Rocky Woods Reservation in Medfield, only eighteen miles from Boston, was the most notable example of this trend. The trustees purchased the reservation as a nature-study area, but since it contained no features "so fragile and rare that they must be guarded from destruction," the local committee decided to augment its appeal. They enlarged the parking area, graveled the road, cleared trails, installed a forty-foot hilltop observation tower, enlarged the pond for boating and skating, and built an amphitheater for natural history lectures and a music-in-the-woods program. For skiers they cleared runs and installed a rope tow, and for skaters a warming hut and lights by the pond. By the mid-1950s the reservation was accommodating between fifteen hundred and two thousand skaters on Sundays, and the local committee reported that "its income and expenses have both reached such proportions that the whole operation must be considered as a straight-forward business proposition and managed accordingly." At Monument Mountain the committee decided on a more modest alternative: each visitor received a descriptive folder, a souvenir card, and an envelope to enclose a contribution.[68]

Policies like these created divisions in the TPR. Fletcher Steele, chair of the Standing Committee, advised local committees against encouraging visitors who were "solely pleasure bound." The reservations were there to appeal to "mature, sensitive individuals . . . who . . . learned to stroll instead of tramp, and can observe what lies along the way; [and] those who are content to sit in shade and watch the waves rather than lie half-naked in the blistering sun." There was no practical way to limit casual visitation, he admitted, but the committees need not "inveigle people into our empty acres on any pretext in order to justify our existence." He cautioned against playgrounds, bathhouses, food concessions, and other "amusements" and recommended limiting the number of picnic tables and parking spaces. At the Crane Reservation, a fifteen-hundred-car parking lot sprawled across what would have been an "untouched landscape," and elsewhere overuse left woodland springs muddied, meadows trampled, and birds and animals less "contented on our land." The reservations were meant for nature lovers, bird-watchers, artists, botanists, and geologists primarily. "We became somewhat confused . . . about our major purpose, which is to encourage study and appreciation of our collection of valuable natural and historical objects." Steele was outspoken, but his defense of the Olmsted ideal suggests an uncertainty about democratic spaces within the organization. Overall, relations remained cordial between the Standing Committee, with its more philosophical approach to visitation, and the local committee members who dealt directly with the visitors, but the balance between preservation and public access remained a matter of debate throughout the reservation system.[69] This was a dilemma Charles Eliot simply did not envision when he proposed the TPR in 1890.

Reassessments: Defining a Preservation Policy

By the 1950s the TPR's preservation strategies were in need of review. Each reservation jealously guarded its own treasures, but for different social, financial, or ecological reasons, and recreational needs had grown more complicated than they were when the TPR was first contemplated. City parks accommodated new forms of recreation like baseball, tennis, ice skating, boating, wading, swimming, hiking, bicycling, and zoo-going, and the old-style landscaping suffered under these new demands. The Boston Fens, an Olmsted masterpiece, lapsed into disorder, and the meadows in Franklin Park gave way to a municipal golf course, stadium, and parking lot. Rather than visit city parks, those who wished to commune with nature traveled by car to a nearby state park or forest, which the Civilian Conservation Corps had likely equipped with hiking trails, picnic and camp sites, and other facilities. The trustees realized the growing system of state parks could accommodate public demand for relaxation, amusement, and outdoor play, but they saw a need for reevaluating their own mission in light of these changing recreational uses. "We feel that we must shift with the public's interest," the annual report declared in 1947. Meeting popular needs meant adding picnic tables, parking lots, and here and there a ball diamond, sandbox, or skating pond, but how far should the trustees go in this direction?[70]

There was another important trend for the TPR to consider. In the first half of the twentieth century it alone carried the nongovernmental preservationist banner, but by the 1950s there were other models to choose from. Among the larger of these was the Nature Conservancy, an offshoot of the Ecological Society of America, created in 1916. Aware of the discipline's need for pristine study areas, the Ecological Society formed a Committee for the Preservation of Natural Conditions for Ecological Study under the chairmanship of University of Illinois zoology professor Victor E. Shelford, and in 1926 the committee published *The Naturalists' Guide to the Americas*, an ambitious survey of preserves and preservable areas still in their "natural condition" in North America. In the process of locating these areas, participants realized their obligation to keep them as natural as possible as places where researchers could study plant and animal interactions "under normal conditions in ... primeval habitats and original associations." The authors noted that the national forests contained a great deal of land of little value for timber or forage, but important for recreational and scientific purposes, and recommended setting these aside to serve as classrooms, genetic storehouses, research sites, and benchmarks for measuring ecological change. Among other things, the guide laid out a detailed scientific rationale for wilderness preservation.[71]

Some members of the Ecological Society considered Shelford's activist tone unprofessional, and in 1946 the committee broke away to become the Ecologists' Union, dedicated to preserving land of critical ecological importance. In 1950 the union's director, Richard Hooper Pough, attended a conference in England on the National Trust, and in 1951 the Ecologists' Union reemerged as the Nature Conservancy with essentially the same mission. The organization received its first land donation in 1952 near East Haddam, Connecticut, and two years later purchased sixty acres of forest in New York. By 1965 the conservancy had twenty-five chapters and went on to become the largest land-preservation organization in the world. In addition to preserving land, it sponsored educational projects, published literature, founded nature education centers, and maintained a revolving loan fund to help smaller trusts or public agencies acquire land.[72]

Another notable land-preservation organization was the Friends of Our Native Landscape, founded in 1925 in Chicago by Jens Jensen, a key member of the Prairie School of landscape architecture. Like the Ecological Society, the Friends hoped to preserve native landscapes, but it justified this mission in ethical rather than scientific terms: "Man is a child of nature and the farther he is removed from his original source, the more he lacks spiritually and materially. Man forever needs to return to the primitive, the world not of his making, for inspiration." Jensen proposed a network of reservations representing the midcontinental landscape—prairies carpeted with flowers, marshes stretching to the horizon, slow-moving rivers, rugged cliffs, and other pieces of "true and unadulterated" America. In addition to the Nature Conservancy and the Friends, the Society of American Foresters created a Committee on Natural Areas in 1947 to preserve examples of each significant forest type in the country. Ducks Unlimited, Defenders of Wildlife, state Audubon chapters, and several mountaineering, hiking, and conservation organizations also held land under various forms of stewardship.[73]

These organizations were interested in land that was either primeval or ecologically critical. The Trustees of Reservations held to a more diffuse mandate, and this flexibility was better fitted to the local land-trust movement that emerged in the 1960s. The TPR's distinguishing characteristic was, simply put, its "sheer dedication to the task of saving diminishing reserves of open space," be they natural, cultural, or a mix of the two. As local land trusts moved into this niche in the preservationist movement, the TPR formed a Future Policy Committee to consider its relation to the smaller land trusts appearing across New England. The committee laid out three options. In view of the many preservationist organizations appearing on the scene, it considered a moratorium on new acquisitions in order to concentrate on managing those in hand. The more popular among the trustees' fifty-three reservations faced staggering visitor numbers, and many were due for ecological or architectural restoration. In 2000, for example, the TPR made a painful decision to tear down a 1905 mansion called Grayling Hall in Leominster because it would have cost millions to renovate. State natural resources commissioner Charles Foster suggested selling some properties to other conservation organizations in order to concentrate on those of "museum quality."[74]

The second option was to seek grant money for a staff lawyer and development specialist and serve as a clearinghouse of information for new trusts. The TPR was already acknowledged as "a grandfather of sorts, helping local and regional land trusts," and some thought this role should be incorporated into its mission statement. Smaller organizations were "badly outgunned" by developers, and the TPR, having worked for more than seventy years on acquisition, management, interpretation, and financing strategies, could help balance the odds. This, however, proved a heavy burden. In 1973 alone trustees visited thirty properties to advise local preservationists, and given the growing management pressures on their own lands, they decided not to advertise their services to the movement at large. They continued to offer workshops and advise individual landowners and trust officers, but the clearinghouse role eventually fell to other more specialized organizations such as the state's Forest and Parks Association, the Council of Conservation Commissions, the Bay State Historical League, and the national Land Trust Alliance. After due consideration, the TPR chose a third option. With demand for open space growing, it would continue its acquisitions policy and at the same time ensure "the best possible care" of its existing reservations. It would take a "hard-boiled" look at the suitability of any new properties and consider them primarily from an ecological point of view.[75]

In 1967 the Trustees of Reservations (TOR), as it was now called, moved its offices to the Pierce House in Milton, a recent donation adjacent to the Hutchinson's Field Reservation, and hired Gordon Abbott as director. Abbott had been editor of the *Gloucester Times* and *Beverly Times* and had headed the state branch of the Nature Conservancy, the Conservation Law Foundation, and the Charles River Watershed Association. Intent on professionalizing the TOR, Abbott asked each local committee to prepare a master plan and establish procedures for protecting the reservation's "special qualities."[76]

The plans varied from reservation to reservation, but they generally showed a deepening commitment to ecological preservation. In a world of fast-paced recreation, Steele's contemplative vision of outdoor activity seemed somewhat outmoded, but in fact the local committees sensed a rediscovery of nature among visitors. To encourage this, they published books and pamphlets to help visitors identify objects of interest—glacial erratics, foxes' dens, squirrels' nests, cellar holes, trees, shrubs, ferns, and wildflowers. Committee members at the Notchview Reservation, in consultation with several agencies and organizations, including the US Forest Service, established a demonstration forest with field seminars, an interpretive trail, and a visitor center. The local committee at the Charles W. Ward Reservation worked with Phillips Academy students to build a nature trail through what once would have been considered a boggy wasteland, and at Bartholomew's Cobble the guided tour, as one wildflower enthusiast reported, was "well worth every mosquito bite."[77] Encouraged by rising public interest in the environment, the TOR moved forward with its ecological orientation.

Approaching the Environmental Era

In 1933 the TPR began inviting distinguished conservationists to address its annual meetings, and in each case the speaker interpreted the TPR's mission as part of an emerging environmental ethos. In his 1948 talk, Edward Weeks, editor of the *Atlantic Monthly*, drew attention to the growing threat to the nation's natural treasures. In New Jersey, his home state, Weeks had watched the "wave of suburbia" roll over community after community. He found inspiration in the western national parks, but it was a love of the landscapes around him that instilled an appreciation for the TPR's work. Walter Prichard Eaton, known for his tributes to the Berkshire Hills, warned in a 1952 address that the iconic New England landscape was "in danger of vanishing under the wheels of our motor cars," and three years later Lieutenant Governor Sumner G. Whittier restated the importance of setting aside examples of Massachusetts scenery in a rapidly modernizing state. Too often, he warned, "the thing made by the hand of God becomes desecrated by the hand of man." At the 1946 annual meeting, Fairfield Osborn, soon to publish the widely read *Our Plundered Planet*, warned that wasting vital resources threatened the future of the entire planet and called for a new commitment to conservation, although, as he said, "there might be a better word for it than 'Conservation.'"[78]

Osborn's new conservation made perfect sense to the trustees, who for more than a half century had urged others to protect nature, not in far-off national parks but in their own backyards. When the organization was created in 1891, its founders despaired at how little thought Massachusetts citizens gave to their surroundings. They enjoyed hunting, fishing, and picnicking in the nearby woods and waters but felt no personal obligation to protect these familiar places.[79] Over the course of the twentieth century, the trustees transformed this love of nature into a sense of stewardship, and at the dawn of the environmental era, their volunteers and visitors were well prepared to take on responsibility for saving the places that made up their daily experience.

Responding to the popular enthusiasm for nature preservation evident in their annual addresses, the TOR continued its acquisitions with a special eye to protecting sensitive ecological areas. Its acquisitions included an island off Marblehead, a hill in Dover, and, together with local preservation organizations, the Cape Poge Wildlife Reservation and the Wasque Reservation on Chappaquiddick Island.[80] The highlight of the decade, however, was the 250-acre World's End Reservation on Hingham Bay, only fourteen miles from Boston. The peninsula was not without its ecological treasures, but its recreational value was enormous. It offered a spectacular view of the Boston skyline, and with its five miles of shoreline and its drumlin hills, it was ideally suited for those in search of nature within a few minutes' drive from the city. In the 1880s Frederick Law Olmsted had designed a subdivision on the property, and although the estate was never developed, the peninsula featured five miles of winding roads and trees laid out in the Olmsted fashion. In fact, a *New York Times* story related, "Considering the many years the shrubs and trees, all planted as seedlings before the days of tree movers, have required to mature, it is possible that the area is just now growing up to Olmsted's far-sighted vision." During the 1960s the city of Hingham proposed a municipal golf course, and in 1965 a consortium of public utilities considered building a nuclear power plant on the site. Two years later the Metropolitan Area Planning Council and Hingham Conservation Commission recommended acquisition by a land trust. The Hingham commissioners contacted the trustees and the Walker family, owners of the property, and the campaign for preservation began.[81]

In 1967 the trustees concentrated all their energies on World's End. The fund-raising campaign, spearheaded by Samuel Wakeman and fueled by an immense amount of enthusiasm in Hingham and surrounding towns, gained momentum. Volunteers contacted businesses and residents and mailed out thousands of brochures. Newspapers and radio and TV stations sent out a plea for funds. Children chipped in with coins, and on December 28, 1967, attorney Thomas G. Taylor phoned with the news that the trustees were the "new owners of World's End."[82]

Immediately, the trustees turned to the perennial question: How was the reservation to be maintained? Given the peninsula's proximity to Boston, managing people would be a priority, and this raised a host of questions. Should the property be fenced? What kind of vehicles would be admitted? Would dogs be allowed to run free? Would swimming be permitted, with or without lifeguards and bathhouses? "We have time to do the job well, thank heavens, for World's End should be our masterpiece. And let it not be said too often, the residents of Hingham and ... the South Shore are watching intently to see what we do and how we do it." After seventy years of confronting thorny questions like these, the TOR was well prepared for the challenges World's End presented, and by the mid-1980s the reservation was hosting some sixty thousand visitors each year. The TPR added one more chapter to the emergent philosophy of private land stewardship.[83]

This particular chapter was significant because it presaged a dramatic change in the TOR's acquisitions strategies over the coming decades. The 1929 Needs and Uses Survey touched off a heady era of acquisitions for the trustees, much of this coming through donation or below-market purchase, but as executive director Frederic Winthrop pointed out, "the days of organizations like ours receiving lands is limited. Land has become so valuable, it's hard for anyone to think of donating it." The TOR could no longer wait for next piece of scenic or historic property to fall from the galaxy of landed aristocrats Charles Eliot appealed to in the 1890s. Purchasing a valuable seafront property on Boston's doorstep had required a massive public campaign and coordination with several other private organizations and public agencies—tactics the TOR had tested in various ways since 1929. As the *Boston Globe* reported in 1986, this was the new reality for the land-preservation movement: "soaring land prices ... are forcing the Trustees ... to devise new techniques for protecting open space." The organization's membership had doubled over the previous four years, and its annual giving had quadrupled, both the result of a growing media presence and a membership that had grown well beyond the old Brahmin founders in size, vigor, and diversity. In 1986 the organization counted eighty-five hundred members with about five hundred volunteers and sixty paid staff and an operating budget of $4.5 million. Its two most popular properties, the Crane Beach Reservation and World's End, attracted five hundred thousand and sixty thousand visitors each year, respectively. The TOR continued to pursue carefully chosen tracts of land, but it also experimented with new ways of protecting and maintaining them. In 1986, for instance, it purchased a 188-acre farm in Dover next to an existing reserve. It divided the property into six house lots instead of the twenty-five to fifty developers had proposed, then set aside land adjacent to the reserve and preserved the farm that had been in continuous operation for more than three hundred years. As it had since its founding, the TOR adjusted to modern realities.[84]

By 2004 the TOR maintained 94 reservations with a combined 23,389 acres and held easements on another 210 properties. These were mostly natural areas, but the TOR showed equal concern for its domesticated landscapes— its farms, pastures, cutover woodlots, historic homes, and, more recently, urban community gardens and other downtown open spaces. Its twin goals, preservation and public use, were shaped to new environmental and cultural developments, but as always the TOR campaigned to protect "the diffused beauty," as Benton MacKaye put it, of the blended rural landscape.

This commitment to second-nature landscape would become the hallmark of community-based preservation activities in the decades to come. In his 1952 address, Walter Eaton had challenged the trustees to "contrive some method to conserve certain Massachusetts villages, or at the least, certain landscapes which have the pleasant human flavor of old New England, and yet seem so much a part of the natural scene." He was thinking not so much of a Colonial Williamsburg but of a working village that represented a distinctive New England way of life. There were examples all across the state "where active and independent life still goes on, but which speak to you of a more tranquil and characteristically Yankee past." This would seem overly nostalgic to some among Eaton's listeners, but the hope of preserving rural landscapes like these was at the core of the grassroots land-trust movement that appeared just a decade later.[85]

In the late 1960s, local land trusts, town-size versions of the TOR, launched a campaign to preserve the pleasant human flavor of old New England in campaigns that followed the lead of the Trustees of Reservations. In 1891

Charles Eliot brought to life a plan that anticipated suburban expansion out into the Boston Basin, and when these suburbs spilled out across eastern Massachusetts and into the Berkshire Hills, preservationists equally as bold in local context took up the banner of saving open spaces. Beginning with a few pioneering organizations in the 1950s, land trusts became the face of the New England environmental movement in the 1980s. Like the TOR, they were driven by a mission to preserve representative landscapes—not only the ancient woods that clothed the New England back country but also the broad, rolling farmlands, winding country roads, and out-of-the-way villages that made the region so distinctive.[86]

The trustees pioneered the idea of saving ordinary open spaces. It remained in some senses a top-down organization, but its mission—providing public access to the state's natural and cultural treasures—was essentially democratic, and it realized this mission by enlisting help from ordinary citizens all across the state. Through its local committees and local alliances with village improvement societies, women's clubs, and other civic organizations, it became the first conservation organization in the nation to cultivate a mass constituency for landscape preservation. The TOR did indeed inspire a Thoreauvian commitment on the part of the Massachusetts citizenry, and it did much to transform outdoor recreation into environmental consciousness. Well before the environmental movement set its sights on clean water and clean air, the TOR was protecting the land through which this water flowed and over which the air glided.[87]

CHAPTER 4

The Land-Trust Explosion
Grassroots Preservation in the 1960s and 1970s

In October 1969 the *Fitchburg Sentinel* ran a feature on the town's Laurelwood Garden Club, whose members had launched a campaign to refurbish a local park. It was refreshing, the *Sentinel* correspondent noted, to see local people taking initiative at a time when society depended so heavily on the government for services like these. Three decades later, New Hampshire resident Jay Smith took on a similar task in landscaping a vacant lot in Portsmouth that became known as "Jay's Pocket Park." When Smith died, his neighbors joined together with the city to raise $50,000 to purchase the land, which was slated for condominium development. Accomplishments like these were minor eddies in the current of change sweeping through New England towns in the late twentieth century, but they were, as the Fitchburg correspondent insisted, worthy of note. It was a pleasure to watch ordinary women and men working with "extraordinary zeal" to protect and improve open spaces. "Anyone who can bring beauty and loveliness to this soiled planet of ours deserves the finest of tributes."[1]

The Laurelwood women and Jay Smith's neighbors exemplified a grassroots movement that began with campaigns like these and evolved into a nationwide network that conserved millions of acres of land for scenic, recreational, and ecological reasons. When the Trustees of Public Reservations was founded in 1891 there were few precedents for acquiring land to place in public trust. Around fifty such organizations appeared in the 1950s, sponsored mostly by local birding clubs, and between 1965 and 1975 nearly two hundred new organizations appeared, mostly in New England. By the end of the century this number had grown to more than a thousand. While national organizations like the Sierra Club and Wilderness Society were campaigning to save the great outdoors, these local trusts were hard at work protecting a smaller outdoors in and near towns and cities across the country.[2] New England's first land trusts emerged out of the chaotic suburban growth of the 1960s and 1970s. Anticipating the open air and free movement associated with rural life, city folk moved to the suburbs, but found these amenities growing scarce as more people crowded into their communities. Land trusts appeared when state and local institutions proved incapable of guaranteeing the cultural expectations that drew people out onto the urban periphery.

The preservation movement brings to mind the epic campaigns for national parks in the 1890s and wilderness areas in the 1960s, but these dramatic events obscure a history of local land stewardship that goes back at least to Henry David Thoreau's spirited defense of his own town's open spaces. In 1879 Felix Oswald summarized Thoreau's preservationist plea in a *North American Review* article: "In every township let space of, say, fifty acres ... be appropriated [as] ... an oasis to be forever consecrated to shade-trees, birds' nests, picnics, and playing children." Three decades later, New York landscape designer Harold Caparn proposed a nationwide system of locally designated open spaces that would highlight the distinctive flora and fauna of each region. "It is surely possible to leave enough of the streams and templed hills of New England, the mountain forests of the Alleghanies [sic], the middle country below them, the vegetable seas of the prairies, the scenery of the coasts, of the Great Divide, and the Pacific Slope."[3] Land trusts were grounded in this locally oriented preservationist impulse.

Like the TOR reservations, local trust lands were volunteer operations. Donella Meadows, Dartmouth professor and well-known critic of unbridled growth, discovered land trusts in 1983 when she learned that a New York developer was planning to subdivide three hundred acres of woods and fields near her home. "I thought of getting some neighbors to buy it jointly, but I didn't know how to begin. But in that thought ... I had stumbled upon the idea of a land trust." Meadows and her neighbors contacted the Society for the Protection of New Hampshire Forests, and the organization negotiated a below-market purchase that allowed the landowner a large charitable tax deduction. The SPNHF borrowed money, bought the land, and repaid the loan by reselling it in three parcels: one to an abutting farmer, a second to the town for a park, and a third to another developer with an easement that allowed only two homes on the site. Meadows's neighbors were so impressed they formed their own land trust. "No tools available to communities now are strong enough to stop growth," she summarized, but ordinary people operating through local associations could guide it "to lands that can best support it and away from lands that have other important purposes." Meadows described the rapid growth in land-trust numbers as an "explosion" of grassroots activism—a bottom-up movement far different from the national preservation campaigns aimed at saving the great outdoors.[4]

Open space is a perceptual vacuum—a place of possibilities born of the need for unstructured settings in a world of manicured lawns and concrete buildings. As urban planner Kevin Lynch explained, open space means different things in different times and to different people. It can be a void, a view, a vacant lot, a meeting place free of social barriers, a natural area, an opportunity for release or for sport or recreation, a chance for spontaneous interaction with nature, an inspiration, or an occasion for adventure. Space is "open if it allows people to act freely," and when acted on collectively, it can convey power, mobilize citizens, and revitalize neighborhoods, or it can add to the profits of developers and speculators.[5]

In the 1960s those active in the land-trust explosion saw open spaces as affirmation of their rural identity and assurance that their community had not yet become "suburbanized." In the next decade open spaces took on new meaning as land trusts absorbed the rhetoric and rationale of the emerging environmental movement. Open space in the 1970s meant ecological integrity, habitat preservation, and watershed protection.[6] In the decades to follow, these meanings would change again, but this chapter focuses on the evolution of open-space values as trusts responded first to the challenge of suburban growth, then to the call for saving the environment.

A Land-Use Crisis on the Urban Fringe

In his widely read book, *Bulldozer in the Countryside*, Adam Rome traces the origins of environmental thinking to the suburb. Rapid postwar development, he shows, triggered a series of environmental crises, and coming to grips with these problems laid the foundations for a critique of unbridled growth. Rome offers a compelling interpretation of the origins of environmental consciousness, and land-trust activity fits easily into his paradigm. As he suggests, the burgeoning postwar suburb was wrapped in powerful cultural symbols relating to the vision of an older and more rural America. These images set the stage for Donella Meadows's land-trust explosion.[7]

Postwar suburban expansion was fueled by rising working-class and middle-class incomes, improved commuter transportation, low-interest mortgage loans, and falling construction costs as home building entered an era of mass production. "Hours were shortened and paychecks fattened," Charles Little summarized in 1968. "Everybody wanted a house in the country." During the racially troubled 1960s, suburbs grew as middle-class white urbanites fled to outlying towns protected from racial mixing by exclusionary zoning ordinances and discriminatory mortgage rules. Housing tracts, accompanied by an auto-dependent infrastructure of gas stations, fast-food chains, and regional malls, spread across a vast and amorphous "interurbia" twenty or thirty miles deep around large cities. This development consumed only 5 percent of the total landmass in the forty-eight contiguous states, but it occurred in the living space of more than 75 percent of the population, and it changed the texture of community life.[8]

Despite their eagerness to move to the suburbs, Americans generally disparaged the changes this migration brought. As a TOR newsletter summarized, suburbs "devastated the forest, metropolitanized the village, and motor-slummed the wayside." Land-use planner Ian McHarg explained the paradox at the heart of this suburban conundrum.

> Today a million acres of land each year are transformed from farmland to hotdog stand and diner, gas station, rancher and split level, concrete, asphalt, billboards and sagging wire, shopping centers, parking lots and car cemeteries. Development occurs without reference to natural phenomena, on flood plains, marshes, and steep slopes. Woods and forests are destroyed without remorse, streams culverted, ground and surface water polluted, floods and droughts exacerbated. Yet the instinct which has resulted in this enormous despoliation of nature is based upon a pervasive and profoundly felt need for more natural environments.

Others described suburbs as a "grand experiment gone awry" or a "catastrophic mistake" that "ripped our natural living space to shreds and replaced it with a tawdry, disorganized maze that is neither pleasant to look at nor economical to use."[9]

The suburban building boom came at considerable environmental cost, and the reckoning began almost immediately. Developers drained wetlands and floodplains, leveled hillsides, filled creeks, and cleared forests, leaving new developments prone to floods and erosion. Septic systems set in soils too dense, too thin, or too porous brought groundwater pollution and chronic failures, and keeping lawns green taxed municipal wells and reservoirs. Once scenic byways became high-speed connectors, all but obliterating an important icon of rural life. Americans, Elizabeth Mooney insisted in her *Country Adventures*, should cherish the simple beauty of a country road; they were "not making any more of them." Streams and rivers were polluted by garden pesticides, fertilizers, construction site runoff, and septic system leakage. According to a southern New Hampshire planning commissioner, less than 12 percent of the region's water supply recharge area was in public hands. "We have about 20 years to get a lot of these important lands protected—or they're gone." Traffic congestion, noise, and overcrowded schools frustrated residents who moved to the suburbs seeking isolation and tranquility. How, residents asked themselves, had their community "achieved the traffic of a metropolis and the culture of a cow town?"[10]

The image of the suburb as a country retreat was deeply rooted in romantic literature, and suburbanites grew anxious about the commercial and residential intrusions that challenged this mythology. "Residential crowding is a deeply disturbing sensation," the American Institute of Park Executives explained, "so intense that at times it approaches a feeling of suffocation." The lack of open spaces in the suburbs was a crisis in the making. People were living longer, working less, retiring earlier, and, with modern appliances and processed foods, doing less work around the home. Where indeed would they spend all this leisure time? According to the institute, this was "one of the knottiest social problems of our age."[11]

In the immediate postwar years suburban expansion was slower in New England than elsewhere due to a slump in textile and shoe manufacturing, but the rate of growth accelerated with the expansion of the semiconductor industry in the 1970s. In Massachusetts a spectacular economic turnaround pushed the Boston suburban frontier outward. Interstate 495, built in 1957, doubled the size of the Boston metropolitan area during the semiconductor boom, and other arterials spun the "sprawl frontier" westward into Worcester County, southeast to Cape Cod, and north over the New Hampshire line. Southeastern Connecticut experienced similar pressures when corporate offices and industries migrated out of New York City, and Rhode Island was squeezed between suburban and exurban expansion from New York and Boston. In towns within this expanding suburban umbra, historic centers were altered by commercial development, and highway approaches were transformed into a succession of strip malls.[12]

As late as the 1960s New Hampshire seemed well beyond the expanding suburban frontier, but with completion of Interstate 93 it became the fastest-growing state in New England. Pastures and forests disappeared at a rate of twenty thousand acres a year. Towns scrambled to pass zoning ordinances, and to encourage this in 1977 Governor Hugh Gregg commissioned a film titled *Your Town, Your Choice*. Narrated by Orson Welles and circulated to towns around the state, the film featured a fictive farm couple facing the prospect of selling out to a New York developer. "My father and my grandfather made something of that place," the farmer worried. "They worked damned hard to do it." The couple contacted the select board and various state and volunteer organizations and settled on a formula that kept the land in cultivation and preserved the village character of the town. Communities could not avoid change, the film advised, but careful planning could make it more acceptable.[13] The governor's efforts inspired several towns to compile growth-management plans, and the procedure became mandatory for all communities shortly after.

Maine's southern coast, once a quiet world of small fishing villages and saltwater farms, was by the late 1960s "squarely in the headlights of development hurtling up the I-95 corridor." Coastal towns with limited infrastructure braced for "that hypothetical day in July when all the tourists/residents flush at the same time." Elizabeth Lane, president of the Great Works Regional Land Trust in York, had moved to Maine from Maryland where without relocating she had gone from "having a house in the middle of a field to living in a suburb of more than 100,000 people." She realized, as she said, that "if we didn't work hard in Maine, the same thing would happen here."[14] Vermont encountered the "Massachusetts Overspill" when Interstate 91 extended up the Connecticut Valley in 1958. Five years later, Governor Philip Hoff established a Central Planning Office, and that year a group of educators, naturalists, farm and forestry advocates, and government officials founded the Vermont Natural Resources Council, dedicated to protecting the state's small-town atmosphere and its "bounteous but vulnerable ecology."[15]

Towns farther north remained safely beyond the suburban frontier, but northward extensions of the Interstate Highway System and upgrades on state roads made this remote territory accessible. With travel times reduced, northern New England experienced a boom in resort and vacation-home development.

New Hampshire lakeshores, once a retreat for vacationing blue-collar workers, became havens for the wealthy as modest rental cottages and camps fell to the bulldozer. Lawn fertilizer, overtaxed septic systems, and straight pipes added to the lake-pollution problem. Rural New England became a "land-use battleground" in which developers and speculators faced off against local residents, environmentalists, and newcomers hoping to close the door behind them.[16]

The rapid transition from town to suburb unnerved New Englanders. In contrast to the centuries-old villages that defined rural New England through most of its history, the new suburbs were sterile and uninspiring, and at times they brought disaster. A developer in Redding, Connecticut, built forty-two homes on a wetland, and the first rain left adjacent property owners knee-deep in mud and silt. A York, Maine, resident complained that contractors piled twelve feet of fill on an adjacent lot, and the runoff layered her lawn in slimy mud. In Williamstown, Massachusetts, a mobile home park had to be evacuated repeatedly when a huge development nearly a mile away caused floods. Local planning boards, overwhelmed by a 200–300 percent rise in subdivision applications, frequently missed flaws in site plans that led to consequences like these. According to Rome, suburban land-use problems "inspired the kind of grass-roots activism that became the heart of the environmental movement." Home owners across the country were "banding together to fight, block by block, sometimes tree by tree, to save a small hill, a tiny brook, a stand of maples."[17]

Tools for Towns

Federal agencies and state legislatures gave little thought to planning issues in the postwar years, and thus it was on the towns, as a Massachusetts planning commission put it in 1969, "that the great burden of land use transformations falls." In Europe land-use planning was a national or regional affair, but America held to the "inalienable right to create ugliness and disorder for private greed," as Ian McHarg put it. Handicapped by weak zoning regulations, by volunteer planning boards, and by tax structures dependent on commercial growth, towns were caught "flat-footed" by the great demographic shifts of the 1960s and 1970s.[18]

In the 1930s and 1940s planning experts had urged the federal government to impose some order on metropolitan growth, but when Congress failed to act, they turned to the municipalities. The leading theorist in local land-use control was William Whyte, a *Fortune* magazine editor who in 1958 left his position to conduct a yearlong study of public open spaces. Whyte published *Securing Open Spaces for Urban America* in 1959 and followed this with his seminal *The Last Landscape* in 1968. Early on he considered it unrealistic to expect small towns to deal with the massive demographic restructuring brought on by postwar suburbanization. Towns legislating in isolation, he thought, would produce a kind of "conservation sprawl" that would encourage developers to leap across municipal boundaries seeking land with the fewest constraints. Later Whyte was convinced that anything done with local needs in mind would benefit the whole region. While he recognized the importance of regional planners like Lewis Mumford and Ian MacKaye, he also understood that most people would consider planning on that scale too radical. "My emphasis," he wrote, "is on the micro-environment." He suggested a number of practical options shaped to specific local circumstances: zoning ordinances, comprehensive planning, performance standards, preferential taxation for farmland and forests, flexible zoning codes, conservation easements, cluster housing development, visual buffers, building-design guidelines, setbacks, timed utilities development, incentives for cluster development, and targeted public purchases to protect aquifers, wetlands, wildlife habitat, and floodplains. Whyte's conservative and practical approach, easily adaptable to local circumstances, won him an audience. Communities could solve the open-space problem, he pointed out, without directly challenging long-sacred property rights. Inspired by Whyte's formulations, state planners wrote up practical guidelines for town planning boards in the 1970s, and states passed growth-management laws requiring each town to prepare a comprehensive plan to protect its "village character."[19]

As their populations surged, small towns on the metropolitan rim experimented with Whyte's planning tools, requiring, for instance, open-space provisions in site plans and building out municipal sewer and water lines incrementally to consolidate growth.[20] Cluster zoning, Whyte pointed out, would allow compact development with outlying land left open. This in turn would keep streets quieter, reduce construction costs, encourage affordable housing, and lower expenses for water and sewerage connections, snow removal, garbage pickup, and road maintenance. In Billerica, Massachusetts, a developer submitted plans for sixty-five new homes on one of the largest remaining open spaces in town. Town officials adjusted zoning regulations to allow denser development, keeping half the parcel open. As one study put it, cluster zoning was "simply the old New England Village brought up to date."[21]

Still, growth control was controversial. Massachusetts, for instance, required a two-thirds vote of either a city council or a town meeting to pass zone changes. These limitations often meant that local land trusts, as Jean Hocker of the Land Trust Alliance phrased it, would become the "first line of defense against unbridled development and loss of open space."[22]

The Land-Trust Movement in New England

In 1959–60 several states passed laws designed to expand the powers of the municipality in matters of open-space preservation. California's 1959 Open Space and Scenic Land Acquisition Act provided matching funds for local land acquisitions, and by 1962 ten states had adopted similar legislation. Voters in New York, New Jersey, Pennsylvania, and Wisconsin approved multimillion-dollar bond issues to fund state acquisition programs, and the federal government offered matching grants under various Housing Act amendments.[23] States reacted to the land-use crisis in different ways. Some preferred statewide or multitown growth-management programs, others protections for ecologically sensitive areas, and in some cases municipalities joined together to coordinate sewer, water, and street extensions to control growth. Mid-Atlantic states encouraged counties to develop boundaries around densely developed areas to discourage farmland conversion. Portland, Oregon, adopted comprehensive metropolitan growth management; California, Rhode Island, and Massachusetts passed coastal-zone management programs; Maine implemented a Land Use Regulation Commission for its unincorporated townships; and Hawaii and Vermont established strict statewide zoning regulations.[24]

In its early phases, the land-trust movement was largely a New England phenomenon. The region's resources were thinner and more compact than those to the west, meaning that problems like erosion, deforestation, overfishing, and scenic blight were serious concerns long before westerners faced similar limitations. New Englanders began experimenting with various conservation measures in the mid-1900s, and by the late 1950s they were well positioned to introduce innovative forms of community-based land preservation. This, coupled with an equally venerable tradition of local control, conditioned New Englanders to see the community as a primary locus of land preservation. The Trustees of Reservations was an important reason for this preference, but long before the organization's founding New England towns were in the habit of protecting open space for a variety of reasons. In the colonial era towns had reserved certain lands in common in order to allocate resources like pasturage, salt and meadow hay, timber, and fuel wood, and in the mid-nineteenth century village improvement societies and volunteer forest and park associations provided additional stewardship models. Municipal water companies purchased and managed forestland around their reservoirs to ensure water purity, reduce soil erosion and siltation, and moderate runoff. Even small towns could hold thousands of acres around their reservoirs, and it was here that some of the region's earliest experiments with reforestation and sustained-yield harvesting took place.[25]

A more significant example of community land holding was the town forest, an idea that harked back to the colonial commons but grew more prominent as communities acquired land through tax forfeitures, farm abandonment, gifts, purchases, and transfers from other municipal agencies such as poor farms and watershed protection zones. Towns in other parts of the country owned forests, but the concept was deeply rooted in New England, where state laws encouraged communities to acquire and reforest abandoned farmlands. By the mid-twentieth century 41 Massachusetts towns had taken advantage of this legislation along with 120 towns in Vermont, 188 in New Hampshire, and 170 in Maine. On average, these forests occupied only about a hundred acres in each town, but as Alice Brandeis pointed out, these public lands carried a powerful message. "The very smallness of the wood lots and their nearness are the essential factors in bringing them close to the life of the town and the life of each citizen."[26]

In addition to these precedents, New England's localized political culture encouraged community-based land preservation. The land-trust movement, as Emily Bateson and Nancy Smith point out, "derived its vigor from the same tradition as the town hall meeting: the sovereignty of an empowered people who care about their community and their land." Small towns made up much of the New England demographic, and energetic community participation in town meetings provided a supportive context for grassroots preservation efforts. Strong pride in place further encouraged the preservation impulse. New England towns evolved gradually and organically through centuries of social interaction. Each home was unique in framing, exterior design, roof pitch, and window sequence, yet each contributed to an overall harmony resulting from generations of individual builders working within with the region's vernacular architectural traditions. These long-established villages contrasted sharply with the monotonous uniformity of the contemporary subdivision. Clusters of ranch, colonial, or split-level homes and concrete commercial buildings, virtually indistinguishable in town after town, could "utterly eliminate the rural ambience for miles around." Equally important, particularly in more rural areas, was a subtle sense of tribalism. Mainers, for instance, grew increasingly concerned in the 1970s as their land was bought up by "out-of-staters." Demographers estimated that 80 percent of the state's land base was owned by outsiders, and only 3 miles of the state's 4,058-mile coastline were in public ownership. In 1973 the legislature considered levying a three-dollar-per-acre tax on large tracts of land closed to the general public to soothe the smoldering resentment toward nonlocals. Land trusts provided a less radical means of assuring Mainers their state was safe from these interlopers.[27]

The New England land-trust movement gained momentum in March 1957 when Ipswich citizens, as part of a campaign to protect their marshlands, asked the legislature for a law enabling towns to form conservation commissions in order to inventory natural and recreational resources, assess community needs, and offer local officials perspective on conservation issues "unhampered by . . . day-to-day demands." Massachusetts passed a law to that effect later that year. Rhode Island passed a similar act in 1960, and Connecticut followed in 1961, New Hampshire in 1963, Maine in 1965, New York in 1967, New Jersey in 1968, and Vermont in 1977. The laws once again positioned the towns as the first line of defense against unplanned growth. Land stewardship, as one report concluded, would be dependent henceforth "on bottom-up, or grass-roots activism."[28]

In Massachusetts Lincoln and Ipswich formed commissions almost immediately, and members went to work drafting wetlands regulations and comprehensive plans and writing grant proposals for land acquisition. Other towns were slower to respond due to uncertainties regarding the commissioners' role. State natural resources commissioner Charles H. W. Foster distributed the *Manual for Town Conservation Commissions* and helped form the Massachusetts Association of Conservation Commissions, and in 1960 the state established a Self-Help Conservation Program to provide technical assistance and matching funds for local land purchases. That year saw 25 new commissions formed, and the number grew steadily to 275 by 1969, representing 80 percent of the state's towns.[29]

The commissions first appeared in the Boston suburbs, where one critic described them as a tool for "further insuring the rural facade of wealthy communities and preventing change." The charge of elitism became less frequent as more remote towns formed commissions. In these outlying areas commissioners represented a "new type of conservationist" that included not just local elites but also ordinary folk—hunting and fishing enthusiasts, birdwatchers, housewives, businessmen, teachers, and retirees. Over time town officials found that a single office responsible for all conservation concerns made sense, and as the commissions matured, they took on more responsibilities. They researched conservation issues to advise other municipal boards; passed technical information on forestry, wildlife, and water and soil conservation to town officials; monitored wetlands; sponsored long-range planning discussions; published brochures; and coordinated field trips and other events with schools, garden clubs, historical societies, and outdoor clubs. Lunenberg's commission conducted an aerial survey and suggested ways to protect 15 percent of the town from development.[30] Work like this paved the way for local land trusts. In Ipswich, for example, the commissioners urged citizens to consider donating land to the town or the Trustees of Reservations: "Your conservation commission is asking specifically that before you decide to sell or build on your land you at least contact the Commission. It is entirely possible that we can help you keep your land open. It is, in fact, our responsibility to do so." The commissions in some cases helped form land trusts, thinking that donors would be more willing to give land to an organization separate from governmental agencies.[31]

Land trusts, like conservation commissions, first appeared in areas where development pressures were most intense. Lincoln, some fifteen miles from Boston, experienced a 91 percent population increase between 1960 and 1970 and was one of the earliest towns in Massachusetts to form a trust. Lincoln had been using a one- and two-acre minimum lot size to slow the town's "rampant development," but townspeople realized that this approach drove up housing costs, spread development over a larger area, and marked Lincoln as a "rich man's town." To remedy this, the conservation commission devised a multipronged approach to growth management that restricted development along the historic Revolutionary War road, protected local watersheds, and set performance standards for the business district. Lincoln citizens created a land trust in 1957 and a Rural Land Foundation in 1965. The latter purchased property using loans from its members and then resold the land with development standards that included low- and moderate-income homes and ample open space. By bringing together the conservation commission, the trust, the foundation, and the good faith of local developers, Lincoln carved out a middle way between freezing out newcomers and abandoning the town to uncontrolled development.[32] Concord, also situated on the Route 128 corridor, entered the suburban growth era with an active Planning Board, a conservation commission, and a detailed zoning ordinance. The commission made several purchases along the Sudbury River and in 1958 asked citizens to form a land trust to manage them. The trust acquired an additional six hundred acres near a new manufacturing plant hoping to concentrate industrial facilities in the area, where they would be less likely to "conflict with the open, rural character of Concord." By 1967 nearly a quarter of the town was under some form of local, state, or federal conservation ownership or restriction.[33]

Maine's first land trust was founded on Monhegan Island in 1954, and the idea spread to the mainland when Interstate 95 connected the southern coast to Boston two years later. Trusts worked steadily to secure "a meadow here, a deer yard there, boggy wetlands, prime birding areas, sometimes just a patch of green in a sea of concrete"—enough to remind locals "what the fast-growing town looked like before developers turned it into a bedroom suburb."[34] Rhode Island's first trust came somewhat later with the Block Island Conservancy formed in 1971 and the Sakonnet Preservation Association in Little Compton in 1972, and Connecticut's first trust was the Madison Land Conservation Trust established in 1964. By 1977 Connecticut's sixty-six trusts protected altogether some five thousand acres. The Aspetuck Land Trust alone managed seventeen hundred acres of land and easements in four southern Connecticut towns.[35]

New England became the epicenter of the land-trust explosion due to its TOR legacy, its community stewardship traditions, its localized democratic participation, its conservation commissions, and its strong sense of place. From this region the movement spread outward, first through rural New England and then to the West, where vast areas of federal land had long overshadowed local measures at land stewardship. By the end of the 1970s land trusts were a national phenomenon, taking their place among environmental organizations as the most effective means of protecting nature in the more heavily populated regions of the country.

Sustaining the Land Trust Movement

Once established, trusts had to move quickly to gain credibility in the community, and their ability to do so was essential to the growth of the movement generally. Most, in these early years, were formed to save a particular property threatened by developers, and they remained viable only if they were able to shift quickly to a wider agenda that kept them in the public eye. "The trust is so new, people don't know about it," a Tolland, New Hampshire, officer explained shortly after its founding. With a Ford Foundation grant, the trust inventoried open spaces across the town and aggressively sought donors. Each new acquisition added to its credibility.[36] This approach was easier if the organization was led by someone with prior conservation experience, and overlapping leadership was in fact common in local conservation circles. Retired New Hampshire dairy farmer Jeffrey Smith was a founder of the Nissitissit River Land Trust, a member of the Hollis Conservation Commission, a steering committee participant in the Nashua River Watershed Association, director of the educational nonprofit Beaver Brook Association, and a member of the Cooperative Extension Service, among other duties. In Connecticut the Redding Land Trust's Philip Barske was also a member of the Redding Garden Club, the Audubon Society, and the Fairfield Conservation Commission. The Aspetuck Land Trust was cofounded by Richard Quinton, a well-known nature photographer and lecturer who was also director of forestry for the Bridgeport Hydraulic Company, a Parks and Recreation commissioner, an adviser to the Fairfield County Soil and Water Conservation District, and chairman of the Mayor's Conservation Advisory Council. Pittsfield native Donald Miller, founder of the Berkshire County Land Trust and Conservation Foundation, published the *Berkshire Eagle* and was a member of the Pittsfield Industrial Development Corporation, the Pittsfield Park Commission, the Berkshire Hills Conference, the State Board of Natural Resources, and the Massachusetts Forests and Parks Association.[37] Résumés like this reveal a deep current of experience flowing through the nascent land-trust movement.

Encouraging visitor use was another means of ensuring community-wide visibility. In its workshops, the TOR advised against a mere "silent commitment" to land preservation, and local trusts acted on this advice by hosting trail maintenance and cleanup days, giving classroom talks, creating ecology curricula, holding workshops for landowners and developers, and sponsoring nature walks, canoe trips, bird-watching tours, and summer teachers' institutes. The Tiverton Land Trust in Rhode Island sponsored a "Photo Day" for high school and elementary school students, and the trust in Manchester, Connecticut, offered butterfly-banding and mushroom-identification demonstrations and conducted seasonal walks with titles like "Rituals of Spring in a Pond Environment."[38] The Dunstable Rural Land Trust in Massachusetts hosted a winterfest with ice fishing, snowshoeing, cross-country skiing, and sleigh rides, and the

Acton Conservation Trust advertised a fall color tour led by botanists from the Arnold Arboretum.[39] Activities like these not only energized trusts and raised their visibility but also served as an important source of local environmental education. An active trust could do much to raise nature-awareness in its host community.

Measuring the Value of Open Spaces

In 1966 developers approached seventy-nine-year-old Billerica farmer Gilbert Griggs, proposing to build a shopping center on his land. Griggs measured out the meaning of his farm in personal and community terms and contacted the local land trust, town officials, several state agencies, and the national Trust for Public Land to counter the developers' offer. Together these organizations raised funds to preserve the land, and later he and his neighbors conducted a similarly ambitious campaign to save an adjacent property from a proposed Walmart development.[40] Projects like these required enormous resolve on the part of landowners, trust volunteers, and public officials, and the motives behind this effort are important to understanding the popularity of the land-trust movement. Meanings are difficult to unravel, however. The Becket Quarry and Forest Preserve in Berkshire County, for example, campaigned to protect historic artifacts as well as a stretch of second-growth woods west of Springfield. The Chester & Hudson Granite Quarry, abandoned in 1946, left behind hundreds of industrial artifacts, including a blacksmith shop and a fifty-five-foot derrick. Volunteers found history a compelling reason to preserve the property, and their purchase became an open-air museum, a demonstration forest, and a recreation area all in one. More commonly, citizens were moved to rescue land deemed important to the community's "quintessential rural New England" character. Ashby, Massachusetts, selectman Michael McCallum explained during a campaign to save nearby Mount Watatic that his neighbors "just want to make sure [the mountain] . . . stays an open space. It's why most people live out here. We don't have the restaurants and movie theaters. Our people like to live in a rural town."[41]

The incentive behind this first pulse of land-trust activism, as McCallum suggests, was a preference for open land over commercial growth. That suburbs became the epicenter of the early land-trust explosion is not surprising. Even close to the cities, they retained a surprising amount of open space—forest groves, left-behind meadows, undeveloped lakeshores, and occasionally a working farm—and these were important reminders of the towns' rural beginnings. For more than a century writers had presented the New England village as a kind of human-ordered climax community—a cluster of simple, clapboard-sided homes arranged around a green, where tree-shaded streets radiated outward into a countryside of tilled fields, meadows, and forests. This iconic image lingered even as disappointed suburbanites were gleaning insights into their lives from books like Sloan Wilson's *The Man in the Gray Flannel Suit* (1955), John Keats's *Crack in the Picture Window* (1956), and Paul Goodman's *Growing Up Absurd* (1960). Residents, even new arrivals, were easily united to protect these tokens of their towns' rural past.[42] Greenwich, Connecticut, as one trust officer explained, was "situated within the largest metropolitan area of the United States" yet remained distinctive due to its open spaces. A Bethlehem, Connecticut, bookstore owner expressed a similar preference; she and her neighbors lived in what they considered a small town, and they wanted it "to stay a small town." As one land-trust official explained, "The livability of a town is almost a function of how much open space there is in it." Residents understood intuitively which of these spaces were important and which could be given over to development. The former were symbolic sites—places that "prompt us to say daily, 'that's why I live here.' . . . We would feel its loss if it were not there."[43]

Preservationists had their own ideas about the meaning of open space, but typically they presented their projects to the community in financial terms. Voters in Woodbridge, an affluent New Haven suburb, were persuaded to endorse a $1.5 million preservation bond issue in good part because it was less expensive than the municipal services would have cost if the property had been developed. Leominster likewise spent $63,000 for open-space preservation on the understanding that five houses built on the same land would cost the town $60,000 annually in educational expenses alone. Open space also could bring financial benefits for donors. The New Canaan Land Conservation Trust in Connecticut succeeded because its director, a tax lawyer, made a "high art of finding tax advantages to ease the financial burden of a large land donation." Arguments like these lacked the sharp rhetorical edge of many environmental challenges to property rights, but the low-profile approach won community support.[44]

Not all donors were interested in tax benefits. Why, a *Nashua Telegraph* correspondent wondered, with real-estate prices spiraling all through southern New Hampshire, would some landowners insist on preventing "their shady lanes from becoming shopping centers and their rolling hillsides from turning into housing developments"? Richard Alt, a tree farmer who donated twenty-one acres of classic New England scenery—stone walls, a stream, and a breathtaking view of the White Mountains—supplied the answer: "It all has to do with the reasons you buy the land in the first place." In Alt's view, the land's pleasing prospect was worth more than its resale value.[45] Variations on Alt's understanding of land value were as numerous as the donations themselves. Typically, donors were third- or fourth-generation landowners who no longer used the land for its original purpose but carried a deep attachment to the property. Faith Hutchins Webster, a descendant of Maine pioneer Richard Talpey, offered an easement on her Cape Neddick farm to keep it "forever . . . open and free of development." Dracut farmer Mary Lou Smith Healey found satisfaction in knowing her land would remain as it had since the early 1800s. Two brothers in Rye, New Hampshire, donated a wooded area where they spent their childhood "with our friends having the time of our lives." A donor in Cape Porpoise, Maine, told trust officers that her husband had spent years after a devastating fire in 1947 planting trees, clearing trails, and building benches. "I can't bear the thought of people cutting down those trees," he remarked just before he died. A Kennebunk couple donated land to honor the husband's father, who purchased parcels on various occasions simply to preserve them. "If it was pretty, and wild, and appealed to him . . . he just liked it to be there, undeveloped and empty, where nobody could put up No Trespassing signs or fill it with 'progress.'" Nanci Worthington, a self-proclaimed "land-rich, cash-poor, tree-hugging, dirt-worshipper," was moved by a love of nature: "I . . . wanted to be sure that the myriad rare and endangered species on it would be left alone—as well as the vernal pools, the above-ground springs and the nearly century-old forest. Mostly, I did not want anyone to mess with the place that has so often been my sanctuary and salvation." Donors evaluated their property in deeply personal ways, and land trusts were usually able to align these values with those of the community.[46]

Along with village atmosphere, trusts valued land for its recreational potential. When the congressional Outdoor Recreation Resources Commission convened in 1958, it expected a clamor for more national parks, but instead respondents expressed a desire for "available open space on the fringe of fast-growing urban areas." Local trusts met this need by preserving the small recreational areas familiar to nearby townspeople. As one volunteer explained, "Government by itself won't save the pocket of woods we played in as children or the little woods where we picked blueberries." Communities needed room for simple, unstructured recreational activities—day hiking, picnicking, boating, bird-watching—and this was something suburban planning seldom took into account.[47]

Not all trusts were willing to share these recreational opportunities. Suburbia was built on the idea of private space, whether an exclusionary zoning ordinance, an enclosed backyard, a country club, or a gated community, and trusts sometimes absorbed this instinct. The Greenwich Land Trust publicized the outstanding sand beaches on its Shell Island reservation but posted the island perimeter and patrolled it to warn off "unauthorized visitors." The land trust in Darien, Connecticut, was founded in 1960 by a group of landowners abutting a fifteen-acre parcel slated for development. With encouragement from Charles Lindbergh, who owned a cottage in the area, the fifty or so residents raised $52,000 and purchased the property to ensure the homogeneity of their neighborhood. Outsiders seeking access were instructed to contact a custodian committee, a measure that effectively reserved the land for those living around it. Maine's Kittery Land Trust asked the town to close the parking lot at its Seapoint Beach property to nonresidents in order, as they said, to prevent littering. In Westport, Connecticut, the Glendinning Company faced public resistance to its request for a zoning change for its new corporate offices and in a "promotional extravaganza" offered to donate twenty-five acres around the site to the Aspetuck Land Trust, formed two years earlier. Neighbors dropped their resistance to the development, but the company stipulated that public visits to the Twin Bridges Nature Preserve would be restricted to two days a year and charged the trust with providing "surveillance of the area." Some Connecticut trusts were denied federal matching grants because they were unwilling to admit nonresidents. Charles Little explained: "Images of hoodlum gang members with boom boxes, of lurking silverware thieves, and even of marauding *liberals* came easily to the minds of some."[48]

Land trusts in towns farther out on the urban periphery were less concerned with carving out private reserves. Townspeople in Harrisville, New Hampshire, for instance, rejected a landowner's offer of an easement on his six hundred acres because he demanded that the town close the road leading into it, and the Berkshire County Land Trust and Conservation Fund refused land donations when owners demanded restricted access. Some trusts discouraged visitation for environmental reasons. Sandy Point in Little Narragansett Bay was set aside as a nesting ground for shorebirds, and in 1988 the trust began collecting a modest entrance fee hoping to deter all but the true nature lover. "If you love it, you'll pay a few extra dollars, and you'll take better care of it."[49]

Motives for land preservation were mixed, but critics frequently interpreted the term "rural atmosphere" to mean exclusion of those who did not fit the New England village stereotype of race and class homogeneity. A history of exclusionary zoning laws, minimum lot sizes, square-footage requirements for housing, and prohibitions on multifamily homes, all based in part on attempts at race and class exclusion, suggests that towns near expanding metropolitan areas used growth control and open-land acquisition as a way of ensuring that surrounding neighborhoods would retain their property values and their uniform residential character. The bedroom communities along Route 128, populated largely by professionals and technicians working in the electronics industry, often zoned out apartments, two-family homes, and other forms of affordable housing. Fairfield County, Connecticut, was notorious for large-lot minimums, with some zones reserved for two- and even four-acre lots.

Land preservation could be folded into this exclusionary legacy, particularly as other tactics were challenged in the courts. In many cases preserving "village atmosphere" carried the subtle expectation that, as one critic put it, only "the very nicest people ... would build the very nicest custom built houses." Edward Higbee characterized early open-space campaigns along the metropolitan fringe as "gold-plated rusticity on a Madison Avenue income," and a *New York Times* commentator complained that it was "only the rich who can preserve the views outside their house, while reaping tax breaks, even though it can be argued strongly that the greater good is well served despite a whiff of inequity." According to demographer Peter Francese, preservation was "often a cover" for excluding low- and moderate-income families. Preserved open space did raise land values on adjoining properties, but some argued that these higher property values benefited taxpayers elsewhere in the community or that growth management actually reduced taxes by easing pressures on municipal services. And even Francese agreed that saving wetlands and unique landscapes was a valuable contribution to the community.[50] In any event, this rather undemocratic facet became less evident as the movement spread outward from the metropolitan fringe to areas where rural atmosphere was simply a given.

Environmental Campaigns and New Perspectives

During the 1960s land trusts labored to preserve the Arcadian ambiance that supposedly distinguished their towns from the bland suburban world growing up around them. While this intent lingered, it was superseded in the 1970s by new goals linked to the emerging environmental movement. Environmental thinking added another layer of community value to private property. Tax maps alone, environmentalists pointed out, were too one-dimensional to account for all the meanings attached to a property. "If we were to look at other kinds of maps, for example where rivers rise and where they flow or the range of a red fox or the sky paths of orioles or the mysterious journeys of eels, there would be very different patterns indeed, and our manmade lines would not only be irrelevant but would collide with the natural patterns on these other maps." Assigning meaning to fox habitat or oriole paths challenged deeply held principles of private ownership and entitlement, and protecting these values in a region with some of the most expensive real estate in the country required careful negotiation. When the local land trust in Dracut, Massachusetts, opposed plans for a golf course and 230 high-end homes abutting the town's wildlife sanctuary, select board members insulted trust members as "angry abutters, dumb farmers and tree huggers." Still, in the end the developer agreed to reduce the number of house lots, donate land to the trust, and offer the trust an option on purchasing eighty additional acres. Using a federal loan, the trust completed the purchase, leaving the developer free to subdivide land fronting the golf course.[51]

Environmentalism, as a national movement, was part of postwar America's search for a better quality of life. A series of well-publicized environmental disasters in the 1970s added urgency to the movement, but in New England it began more incrementally as a decades-long campaign to control water pollution. Since the early twentieth century New England rivers had carried a heavy burden of sewage, industrial fibers, metalworking chemicals, dyes, tanning liqueurs, canning residue, and other pollutants, but since more remote rivers and streams remained pristine, this brought little protest, and hard times in the textile industry left legislators reluctant to impose regulations. For these and other reasons, New Englanders largely ignored the caustic fumes and oxygen-starved waters downriver from their industrial cities.

In 1920 Rhode Island formed a water-quality commission to devise standards for pollution control. Connecticut followed in 1925, as did the other New England states in the 1940s and early 1950s. The commissions classified waters from pristine to virtual sewer, and by prohibiting additional discharges in each classification they hoped to stabilize water quality. Although these standards were raised occasionally, in the 1940s residents began pressuring state legislators for accelerated cleanup.[52] Caustic hydrogen sulfide fumes from the oxidizing waste were blackening paint on riverside buildings and tarnishing silverware the homes. In 1941 business owners along the lower Androscoggin River, host to dozens of paper and textile mills, formed "action clubs" and took their complaints to the governor. They received little immediate satisfaction, but their organizations marked the beginnings of grassroots environmental protest in New England. When public health officers began drawing connections between pollution and infant diarrhea, enteritis, infantile paralysis, and poliomyelitis, women's groups joined the protest.

Democratic governors like Edmund Muskie in Maine and Philip Hoff in Vermont pushed for higher classification standards, and a broad base of support emerged, including tourist interests, small businesses, parent-teacher associations, civic and garden clubs, fish and game leagues, conservation societies, union locals, Jaycee Wives, League of Women Voters and women's club chapters, and the Daughters of the American Revolution. Congressional testimony by similar coalitions across the country resulted in the federal Water Quality Acts of 1965 and 1966, which provided matching funds for municipal treatment plants. Pushed by the legislature and courts, corporations followed with their own treatment systems.[53]

In the late 1960s, environmental goals broadened to include protecting endangered species, removing toxic contaminants, saving wilderness areas, battling dam projects, and banning clear-cutting in national forests. In various ways, each of these issues was grounded in a concern for landscape integrity. As Theodore Roosevelt said in a 1903 speech at Stanford University, "There is nothing more practical in the end than the preservation of beauty." Presidential commissions over the next several decades reiterated the point, and by the 1960s citizens were conditioned to consider healthy and visually pleasing environments a foundation for environmental politics.[54]

In May 1965 President Lyndon B. Johnson spoke at a White House Conference on Natural Beauty, urging Americans to "protect the countryside and save it from destruction." This, he thought, would require a new form of conservation that embraced not only specific natural resources but "the total relation between man and the world around him." New conservationists would extend the stewardship principles behind the national parks movement to their own neighborhoods. Beauty, Johnson explained, "must not be just a holiday treat, but a part of our daily life." Johnson's Council on Recreation and Natural Beauty went on to survey the nation's environmental assets, from city neighborhood to remote wilderness, with suggestions for new stewardship initiatives. Preserving the beauty and integrity of nearby landscapes was a prominent theme in the resulting report. The Highway Beautification Act of 1965, championed by Lady Bird Johnson, encouraged states to regulate billboards, junkyards, and other roadside blights; provided federal funding for scenic easements, trails, and overlooks; and encouraged planners to control growth in the urban hinterlands. States responded with advisory commissions on land preservation and highway beautification. The emphasis on preserving nearby landscapes set the stage for a profound transition in land-trust goals.[55]

Johnson's conference, coming on the heels of Rachel Carson's provocative 1962 *Silent Spring* and a host of environmental crises relating to smog, solid waste accumulation, species extinction, clear-cutting in the national forests, and fallout from nuclear testing, laid the foundations for a decade of landmark environmental legislation. The Clean Water Act Amendments of 1970 and 1972 set nationwide water-quality standards and provided matching grants for municipal water-treatment facilities, and over the next decade municipal, state, and federal agencies and private industries spent more on clean water than the federal government spent on building the entire forty-five-thousand mile interstate highway system. The return on this investment was significant. By the late 1970s even the most industrialized rivers were once again home to fish and other aquatic life. In New England environmentalists moved seamlessly from clean-water campaigns to land preservation. In 1971 Rhode Island created a Coastal Resources Management Council, and Massachusetts, New Hampshire, Maine, and Connecticut followed with similar laws protecting coastlines, rivers, forests, and air and water quality.[56]

Land Trusts in the Environmental Era

The new state and federal environmental laws mandated citizen input, and activists responded by testifying, attending meetings, submitting comments, demonstrating, and challenging corporations in the courts. In the wake of this unprecedented citizen participation, an estimated five hundred thousand grassroots organizations appeared across America, addressing issues ranging from environmental protection to rent and crime control, urban gardening, public service, women's health, art and cultural affairs, and housing rehabilitation. This grassroots awakening included hundreds of land trusts battling against the "ever-advancing sea of shopping malls, housing developments, fast-food restaurants, [and] highways."[57]

The term "environment" appeared in trust mission statements as early as the mid-1960s, but it was the environmental awareness of the next decade that reshaped the land-trust mission. These goals would differ from those of national preservationist organizations like the Sierra Club and Wilderness Society, and given their special niche, they offered four advantages as they blended their efforts into the coalescing environmental alliance. The first was their local orientation. The Wilderness Society and Sierra Club also recruited local support in their earlier years, but their focus on protecting vast, pristine open spaces was not of immediate interest to their membership. As landscape historian Anne Whiston Spirn put it, "There is, after all, something that stands between landscapes of city and landscapes of wilderness," and on this continuum land trusts stood for protecting already humanized landscapes in and around the towns that hosted them. For this reason, grassroots participation in local land trusts was far more intense than it was in national environmental organizations.[58] Second, trusts were distinctively flexible in their preservation strategies. Wilderness preservation campaigns, although they did allow some latitude in acreage and degree of human impact, chose their campaigns according to fairly strict guidelines.[59] Land trusts were far more accommodating. In face-to-face negotiations with landowners, town officials, and the local conservation community, trust officers were free to accept land on almost any terms, an advantage often beyond the scope of state or national agencies and larger environmental organizations. Depending on donor preferences and community needs, trusts could manage their lands as scenic vistas, recreational assets, wildlife or wildflower preserves, or sites for affordable housing. Trust officers, who were usually local residents, could "look ahead to see what community members will want to do outdoors [and] plan what needs to be done." This was important, given the vast differences in donor preferences and tactics for land acquisition. A Massachusetts landowner, for instance, offered property first to the state's Division of Fisheries and Game and then to the Department of the Interior, and when neither followed through turned to a local land trust, which accepted the land "without hesitation."[60]

Along with local orientation and flexibility, land trusts enjoyed a community-wide reputation for dependability. Trusts could, as a Connecticut journalist put it, assure donors that the land they offered "was not going to profit anyone." Given the amount of personal sacrifice involved in land donations, trust was an important asset. In 1961 a woman willing to donate land to the city of Chelmsford reminded the select board that back in 1927 the town had received a gift of land and sold it less than a year later to a private developer. To allay her concerns, the select board helped establish the Chelmsford Land Trust. True to its mission, the trust defended the donated land successfully a few years later when town officials proposed building a library on it.[61] Finally, land trusts offered every citizen an opportunity to contribute meaningfully to protecting the environment. Active rank-and-file participation was, in fact, essential to success in almost any project a trust undertook. At a time when national environmental organizations were becoming more centralized and more remote from their constituents, land trusts brought the preservation movement back down to the grassroots level. California environmental historian Raymond Dasmann once remarked that Americans were too mobile to rally around the landscapes in their own surroundings. "Many who act strongly for conservation," he thought, were "concerned with measures designed to take effect far from their own back yards"—in remote wilderness areas, for example. Dasmann perhaps based this impression of environmental consciousness on life in the Los Angeles Basin or Bay Area, where residents lived in one community, worked in another, and shopped in still another. It was easy, in these circumstances, to think of nature as a place apart. Trust volunteers, by contrast, were dedicated to preserving nature in their own communities.[62]

Saving Rivers and Wetlands

Land-use planner Ian McHarg once complained that trusts acquired land unsystematically. "Open space there may be, but . . . systems of open space are not perceptible." In the 1970s preservation strategies became more focused as trusts added an ecological overlay to their campaign to protect rural atmosphere and recreational opportunities.[63] Early on, these environmentally oriented acquisition strategies were built around protecting wetlands and riverbanks. As the Clean Water Acts of the 1970s bore results, citizen-activists realized that river corridors previously shunned due to offensive odors and health concerns were becoming valuable real estate. By the mid-1970s, rivers were noticeably cleaner, and brave souls were venturing into the waters to fish, canoe, kayak, and even swim. Fearing the riverbanks would attract developers, organizations originally created to fight pollution recast themselves as watershed associations. The Connecticut River Watershed Council was founded in 1952 as an antipollution organization, but after the 1972 Clean Water Act Amendments, the council, renamed the Connecticut River Conservancy, expanded its mandate to include shoreside stewardship projects. The council's Terry Blunt pointed to the river's "dramatic comeback" and urged fellow citizens to reconnect with the waters and help protect them. The Nashua River

Clean-Up Committee, created in 1962 to fight pollution, reemerged late in the 1960s as the Nashua River Watershed Association with an agenda that included bankside greenways and protection for the river's extensive wetlands. Preservationists in twenty riverside towns in southern Maine lobbied for a Saco River Corridor Commission in 1973 to set watershed-wide standards for setbacks, frontage, and public access, and in 1983 the Maine Rivers Act applied these specifications to rivers throughout the state. By 1976 New Hampshire's Merrimack River Watershed Council had nearly 80 percent of the shoreline under similar protections. Lowell's land trust completed a greenbelt along the newly naturalized Concord River, and when General Electric announced a multimillion-dollar commitment to removing polychlorinated biphenyls in the Housatonic River in 1969, Berkshire County residents purchased conservation land along the banks.[64]

As the clean-water campaigns of the 1960s became shore-land preservation efforts in the 1970s, land trusts turned their attention to the wetlands that fed these rivers and streams. Wetlands contributed little to securing the community's rural atmosphere or recreational opportunities, but as trusts discovered, they were valuable as wildlife habitat and important in the local hydrological regime. Larger environmental organizations typically overlooked these localized benefits, but land trusts found wetlands easy to acquire and quickly came to appreciate their ecological importance.

By the 1960s wetlands were among the nation's most endangered ecosystems. Before World War II developers were generally unwilling to invest in the engineering necessary to convert swamps, bogs, and marshes into building sites, but as land values rose they found they could use dragline dredges, bulldozers, and other heavy equipment to prepare almost any land for development: "cut down the trees, ... channel the water to the rear, ... top the muck with gravel, and you have a dandy commercial site." Farmers, who had been draining wetlands for a century or more, found these new earthmoving machines useful as well. Of the original 127 million acres of wetlands in the United States, the Soil Conservation Service estimated in 1965 that 45 million acres had been lost, with dire consequences in flooding, erosion, water quality, and habitat loss.[65]

Since at least the Romantic era writers and artists had marveled at the solitary beauty of New England bogs and marshes, but after due appreciation of these aesthetic qualities, most found themselves contemplating, as landscape architect Charles Downing Lay put it in 1912, "some means of making them more useful." Ecological understanding was slow in coming, but in the 1960s popular studies like William Whyte's *Last Landscape*, Ian McHarg's *Design with Nature*, John Teal and Mildred Teal's *Life and Death of the Salt Marsh*, and Gilbert White's *Human Adjustment to Floods* encouraged the perception that wetlands provided a host of important ecological benefits. Tidal marshes, as one study showed, produced as much as ten tons of organic nutrients per acre annually. The spawning fish they sheltered were primary links in the ocean food chain.[66]

In 1955 Charles Eliot II and the Trustees launched a campaign to protect the salt marshes along the lower Ipswich and Essex Rivers adjacent to the TOR's Crane Reservation. Eliot informed marshland owners that the seemingly unproductive tangles of grass and mud in their domain were home to wildfowl, shellfish, insects, plants, birds, water-loving mammals, and fish. Eight years later in 1963 the Massachusetts Department of Natural Resources held hearings to discuss salt marshes in towns along the coast, and that year the state legislature passed the Jones Act, the first statute in the nation requiring developers to seek permits before filling coastal wetlands. The Hatch Law, passed two years later, extended this provision to inland wetlands, and in 1972 these laws were combined into the Wetlands Protection Act. Maine passed a similar law in 1967, and that year Congress directed the Army Corps of Engineers to take environmental considerations into account in their dredge and fill projects. These laws were milestones in environmental regulation, but they contained only vague powers of enforcement, and well into the 1970s the Department of Agriculture still recommended converting wetlands into fields and pastures. Massachusetts left matters of enforcement to local conservation commissions and hoped that landowners themselves would obey the laws "because they don't want their own and other marshes despoiled by careless exploitation and development."[67]

Given these ambiguities, land trusts became a first line of defense against wetland development. They combated popular prejudice by explaining that wetlands stabilized water tables, recharged reservoirs, prevented floods, filtered sediment, protected homes from wildfires, cleansed river systems, provided wildlife habitat, and offered a variety of recreational and nature-study opportunities. According to the Leominster Land Trust's Peter Angelini, protecting these much-maligned places could "save the city millions" in flood-control measures.[68]

The educational campaign bore results. In 1974 a Saco Citizens Coalition in southern Maine saved a 1,160-acre heath on the northern edge of town, aware that "a couple of bulldozers and some drainage pipes" could easily render it a housing tract. Citizens had for generations considered the heath a wasteland, but, as Mayor Berton Braley pointed out, it was a wasteland the city "could not afford to lose." Saco's "everglades" fed a constant supply of water into the town's public wells, filtered and purified the seven streams that ran through the city, and provided valuable wildlife habitat. Locals used it for snowmobiling, hiking, cross-country skiing, and berry gathering. In 1987 the Citizens Coalition convinced the Nature Conservancy to purchase the heath to protect a stand of Atlantic white cedar and provide habitat for a rare butterfly.[69] The heath was saved, and Saco citizens gained a greater understanding of the importance of wetlands everywhere.

In the 1980s the federal government took additional protective measures by prioritizing wetlands in the Land and Water Conservation Fund, and using other agencies to coordinate federal, state, local, and private efforts. The 1990 Farm Bill added a Wetland Reserve Program that provided financial incentives for farmers willing to set aside or restore wetlands. Over time, states removed tax incentives that promoted wetlands conversion and required developers to include wetland conservation and mitigation measures. The idea that these were essential resources, first promoted by the TOR in the 1950s, reached higher levels of government at the end of the environmental era.[70]

Saving Nature

Ascribing ecological meaning to open spaces added a new layer of complications to the land-trust mission. Trusts could maintain a town's rural atmosphere simply by acquiring scattered tracts of open spaces as they came on the market or were offered as a gift. The result was a communitywide patchwork of forests, wetlands, stream banks, and lake shores valued generally for their human benefits. Environmental considerations meant supplementing these spot purchases and random gifts with targeted acquisitions that protected entire ecological zones. The shift from parcel-to-parcel purchase to ecologically strategic acquisitions required a new layer of cooperation between trusts in different communities and between trusts and state and federal agencies—a collaboration that became a signature feature of the maturing land-trust movement.[71]

These changes in strategy began with publication of Ian McHarg's *Design with Nature* in 1969, the year Congress passed the National Environmental

Policy Act. To value land simply as a commodity, McHarg taught, is to overlook its broader functions in stabilizing urban and suburban ecologies. At his University of Pennsylvania laboratory McHarg pioneered a system of land classification based on a set of transparent maps showing ownership, soil type, bedrock foundation, slope, drainage, riparian zones, aquifer-recharge districts, potential recreational areas, historic sites, scenic views, and wildlife habitat. Like a modern Geographic Information Systems projection, the superimposed maps brought all these landscape values together, revealing the complex public and private stake in any single parcel. McHarg explained the importance of each overlay to the overall integrity of the community: vegetation anchored soils to the hillsides; swamps and marshes stored water, prevented floods, filtered streams and rivers, and provided spawning grounds for fish and amphibians; woodlands recharged aquifers and sheltered animals and birds; and meadows nourished flora, birds, and insects. McHarg advised city and town planners to study floodplains, aquifers, watersheds, slopes, and agricultural lands before deciding where to allow development. "If natural processes are maintained in relative equilibrium, all kinds of benefits accrue." His book proved transformative, and as his insights diffused through the planning profession, local preservationists took them up as well.[72]

Among trusts, the TOR and TNC pioneered the idea of ecological assessment by keeping records of plants, trees, birds, and animals on their reservations and by prioritizing sensitive ecological areas in their acquisitions. By the 1970s smaller trusts, sensitive to the multiple meanings of each parcel, were adopting similar strategies. When the Seacoast Land Trust in southern New Hampshire was created in 1998, its first order of business was mapping out fifteen "natural resource elements" in the seven towns it represented so that it might approach acquisitions with a precise understanding of their ecological value. The Lancaster Land Trust in Massachusetts acquired only land that fulfilled "a critical ecological need," and a Biddeford, Maine, trust purchased land to protect the endangered Blanding's turtle. "We are preserving land, not grooming it," Kennebunk Land Trust's Bob Michalkiewicz explained. "The habitat is more important here than public recreation."[73]

The importance of these new acquisition strategies, wildlife specialist Durward Allen wrote in 1966, "can hardly be overestimated," since few national environmental organizations were in the business of saving "remnant bio-types and habitats." Trust officers mapped out their acquisitions carefully, considering factors like hydrological cycles, topographical features, vegetation types, and possible rare or endangered species. The Leominster Land Trust's Peter Angelini worked for a decade, as he said, to put together a three-thousand-acre "jigsaw puzzle" to protect the city's water supply. Realizing the need for "a larger vision," trusts shifted from acquiring isolated individual parcels to piecing together holdings that made ecological sense.[74]

A crisis of sorts at the TOR's Crane Beach Reservation suggests the complicated decisions that went into ecological preservation. In the 1980s when the reserve's deer herd outgrew its food supply, managers planned a small public hunt to cull the herd. Protesters threatened to stand between the hunters and the deer, and the idea was abandoned. Russell Burgess, who raised an orphaned fawn and released it on the reservation, pleaded that "one of the big tragedies of this is that the deer are so trusting. The place will never be the same again." For the next two years, the TOR's regional supervisor followed a "do-nothing" approach," but the resulting deer starvation seemed more cruel than the hunt. Moreover, the herd carried ticks prone to Lyme disease, which threatened attendees at the summertime open-air concerts. Sterilization or relocation proved unrealistic, and the Society for the Prevention of Cruelty to Animals and Division of Fisheries and Wildlife suggested a sharpshooter to eliminate distressed animals. After an exhausting round of legal wrangling, the TOR followed their advice, and by 1990 the herd was back in "excellent health." On other reservations, cutting trees to improve habitat generated similar criticism. Sounding somewhat like a frustrated developer, TOR executive director Frederic Winthrop dismissed the protesters as "classic tree-huggers" who derived their understanding of nature "from some Walt Disney film."[75]

Even without public controversy, ecological preservation could be complicated. It often required restoration, and this in turn meant careful scientific assessment. The Seacoast Land Trust in Portsmouth, for instance, undertook an ambitious community-wide campaign to restore an acquisition known as the Great Bog. The property had been used as a dumping ground for generations, but careful assessment revealed abundant wildlife on site, and in 2001 the trust spearheaded a coordinated, multipronged effort to transform it into "a beautiful natural area for the enjoyment of all Portsmouth and for the wildlife that calls it home." On the upland portion the trust partnered with two utility companies to mulch thirty acres of brush, resulting in a "traditional New England farm-field habitat" for cottontail rabbits, bluebirds, bobolinks, grasshopper sparrows, meadowlarks, and upland sandpipers. The wetland sections sheltered beaver, rabbits, birds, deer, and fishers. With funds from the Department of Agriculture, advice from the state Fish and Game Department, and volunteers from local businesses and the community, trust members hauled out trash, cleared hiking and cross-country skiing trails, and planted native trees and shrubs. Middle school students laid out their own "bluebird trail" with nesting boxes, while volunteers from a local naturalist program posted signs. Others kept the uplands clear of brush using hand tools, mowing machines, herbicides, and controlled fires. When the project was completed in 2005, the land trust sponsored a fund-raising "Bioblitz" with contestants identifying as many plants, birds, and animals as they could in four hours. On other trust lands volunteers diversified second-growth stands, cleared streambeds, and installed nesting boxes, gaining in the process a better appreciation of their community's natural history.[76]

Preservation Easements

In the late 1960s community-based preservationists were content with protecting rural atmosphere and providing recreational opportunities, but in the 1970s they saw their towns' remaining open spaces in a different light. After eighteen years in the conservancy business, southern Maine's Great Works Regional Land Trust had acquired 2,935 acres in fifty-two parcels across six towns. It remained, as a representative said, "a project-driven organization" responding individually to each imperiled landscape and each donor with property to preserve, but it was beginning to view these acquisitions as a preservation matrix rather than a collection of properties. Cultural and natural landscape surveys demonstrated time and again that New England's scenic and ecological legacy derived not from a single natural feature or building but from a broader and more integrated complex that included centuries-old farms, adjacent wetlands and woodlots, forest-shrouded stone walls, winding country lanes, village greens, fields, meadows, and rolling hills.[77] Landscapes like these were the result of intricate patterns of social, cultural, and ecological interaction over decades if not centuries, and saving them required a new level of cooperation between preservation organizations, public agencies, and landowners.

To meet this challenge, local trusts revived an older conservation practice whereby landowners retained ownership of their property but sold the right to develop it. The idea of purchasing development rights had been widely used in Great Britain and was first applied in America by railroad companies to secure rights-of-way across private property. In the 1930s the NPS acquired development rights to Civil War battlefields to ensure working farms would remain as they had appeared during the war. The Park Service also used easements to buffer the Blue Ridge and Natchez Trace Parkways and the Appalachian Trail. The Fish and Wildlife Service sold duck stamps to purchase easements on prairie potholes in the upper Midwest, and the federal Highway Beautification Act of 1965 authorized states to use up to 3 percent of their funds for scenic easements and overlooks.[78]

Easements remained obscure as a land-stewardship tool until 1959 when William Whyte published a technical bulletin for the Urban Land Institute describing them. Private property, as he pointed out, had many public benefits, but scenery, watershed protection, erosion control, and other common goods could not legally justify infringing on the owner's right to profit. "If we want to keep a stream valley open because we like it, the law is very clear. We've got to pay for it." The beauty of easements over outright purchase, he continued, was that land could be "kept alive"—used in a manner that rendered it beautiful or useful to the community in the first place.[79]

In the same year Whyte published his bulletin, the TOR introduced the idea of easements to protect privately owned marshes adjacent to the Crane Reservation in Ipswich. The trustees' Salt Marsh Preservation Committee circulated a model easement agreement with a letter from the Conservation Law Foundation explaining how they worked. Two years later the Nature Conservancy purchased an easement on a property owned by Edward and Mary Hall on the Bantam River in Connecticut. Hall sold the easement, as he told it, so that his grandchildren would "have wilderness to walk in, solitude to feel a little bit frightened in, wild things to see and hear and feel." Whyte's 1968 *The Last Landscape* popularized this form of preservation, and Ian McHarg used it in his planning projects. Land-trust leaders adopted the strategy when they realized that purchasing ecosystems, farmlands, scenic viewsheds, or historic districts would be impossibly expensive.[80]

The use of conservation easements mushroomed in the 1980s due to rising real-estate prices and a shift in preservation strategies away from individual parcels to broader aggregates. Courts cleared away legal misgivings by declaring them binding on subsequent owners. Once an "arcane concept, viewed with suspicion and doubt," easements became a mainstay of the preservation movement. Landowners discovered they could preserve their property and at the same time use it for farming, grazing, gardening, logging, or whatever activity kept the land open. Moreover, easements reduced the value of their land and hence their property taxes. Trusts preferred them because they protected property at a cost lower than outright purchase and because they left the burden of management with the owner. Local officials accepted them because they kept the land on the local tax rolls, albeit at a lower valuation. The popularity of easements also reflected a broader shift in environmental strategies in the Reagan-Bush years as conservationists turned to private market-based solutions. Easements, conveniently enough, assigned a commodity value to ecological benefits. By 2013 some ninety-five thousand easements were in effect covering more than eighteen million acres across the United States.[81]

In a 2005 article, law professor Nancy McLaughlin commented on the thousands of landowners across the country "willing to voluntarily restrict the development and use of their land" and predicted this would become a new paradigm for preservation. McLaughlin's optimism was warranted. Use of easements by this time had become a dominant method of private land conservation. But while easements generated a great deal of enthusiasm, there were drawbacks. They required considerable legal expertise, and this was not often available to smaller trusts, and some preservationists feared that providing monetary compensation for doing the right thing environmentally might weaken the philosophical foundation for traditional state or federal land-use regulations. For government agencies, purchasing easements could be more expensive than simply imposing land-use regulations that might accomplish the same ends. Massachusetts, for instance, spent on average $2,500 per acre for development rights where tighter zoning might have protected an entire class of land. In addition, easement negotiations were typically made in private, and this took conservation out of the realm of public scrutiny. Trust officials could in secret collude with landowners to inflate land appraisals and provide more lucrative tax write-offs. Trusts also incurred an obligation to ensure compliance in perpetuity, and early on there were few standards for monitoring, amending, or enforcing easements. "Future generations," Maine attorney Jeff Pidot wrote, "may not thank us for an unmanageable legacy of untold thousands of easements whose terms, holders, and locations may be difficult to determine, and whose public benefits ultimately could be lost." And finally, as conservation biologists pointed out, easements could pose difficulties if the ecological or cultural conditions that informed them changed. Climate change brought new levels of uncertainty, particularly where easements protected a specific wildlife species. "The notion of conserving communities and ecosystems as they presently exist may soon be obsolete," a 2002 study warned.[82]

Some of this uncertainty was mitigated by new state regulations. In 1969 both Maine and Massachusetts enacted regulations to streamline deed registry changes, and in 1981 Congress passed the Uniform Conservation Easement Act establishing a nationally recognized legal framework for drafting easement contracts. By 2001 forty-eight states recognized the legality of conservation easements and in many cases provided tax subsidies and public financing to encourage them. In 2007 Maine reformed its easement act to require state registration of all agreements. The act prescribed periodic monitoring by easement holders, designated the state attorney general as a backup enforcer, and laid out procedures for terminating or amending agreements. This put Maine, which held more land under easement than any state in the nation, in the forefront of the legislative trend.[83]

Saving Farmlands

Easements gave preservationists a tool for preserving another class of valuable open spaces. Building on the 1929–33 Governor's Committee on Needs and Uses of Open Space, in 1982 the Massachusetts Department of Environmental Management completed a cultural landscape survey of the state. Where the 1933 report centered on preservation-worthy beaches, forests, and mountaintops, the new commission concentrated on the state's rolling fields, saltwater farms, winding country roads, salt marshes, and historic village centers—landscapes at the core of New England regional identity. The 1982 report pointed out in the lower Merrimack valley "farming still survives on the bluffs along the river," and two-hundred- to three-hundred-year-old houses were common. The product of "centuries of human interaction with the underlying natural resources," these priceless heritage landscapes were too large to purchase outright, but could be protected through "indirect means" such as conservation restrictions, design guidelines, public education programs, and easements.[84]

Farmlands everywhere were under siege. Between 1967 and 1975 approximately 23 million acres of agricultural land in the United States were converted to nonagricultural uses. This was a relatively small portion of the nation's 900 million farmland acres, but over a third of this lost acreage was located near expanding metropolitan areas where farms provided important ecological, aesthetic, cultural, and educational benefits. In these areas farmland loss was likely a result of nearby suburban development, which brought rising tax valuations, restrictions on fertilizer and pesticide applications, and zoning ordinances that dictated the types of buildings farm owners could construct. New England farms were particularly vulnerable to these pressures. Being smaller than the national average, they were disadvantaged by competition from western producers, where massive federal irrigation projects subsidized agricultural expansion on a grand scale. Small farmers found it difficult to amortize expensive equipment, and renting additional land in development-prone areas was risky, since farmers needed long-term security to build soil fertility, improve pastures, purchase equipment, and add infrastructure. In short, New England farmers faced mounting pressure to sell out to developers. The amount of agricultural land in the region fell by 62.8 percent between 1950 and 1980, compared with a 13.7 percent decline nationwide.[85]

Given the substantial agricultural surpluses in the 1980s, some analysts downplayed the concern over farmland loss, and New England's 5.1 million acres in farms amounted to only 5 percent of the US total. However, the region's farms were important beyond their relative size, since New England was distant from major food-producing regions. Severe droughts in California in the 1970s along with skyrocketing transport costs during the energy crisis highlighted the region's dependence on outside suppliers for 70 percent of its sustenance. In addition, farms were important in diversifying the region's rural economic base, and they were keystone features in the classic New England landscape—a representation, according to journalist Jerry Harkavy, of what a "fast-growing town looked like before developers turned it into a bedroom suburb." Conscious of this fading heritage, the York Land Trust purchased a Maine farm that was home to ten generations of descendants from the town's first minister, and three years later negotiated a parcel called the Bovine Field, the "last tangible reminder" of the dairy farms that once formed the town's economic base. Farms epitomized the rural character that inspired the early New England land trusts, but by the 1980s they were valued for ecological reasons as well. The mosaic of cropland, meadow, and woodlot ensured soil stability, prevented flooding, recharged groundwater, filtered surface water, and provided plant and animal habitat.[86]

Farms to the north of the suburban frontier were also at risk. Resort and second-home building diffused along the new I-91, I-93, and I-95 corridors, "spoiling views [and] restricting access to many beautiful spots," as a northern Maine resident complained. Farms near ski resorts and around lakes were under enormous pressure, and in many cases easements provided an alternative to development. Vermonter Marjorie Unaitis was offered $120,000 for her 86-acre property but was "loathe to see the farm where she has always lived subdivided and developed." Working with a regional trust, she sold the farm to the town, which in turn rented it to a young couple who eventually purchased the land under easement. Charitable tax deductions helped Unaitis realize some of the original value of the land.[87]

Preserving these ecological values once again complicated the stewardship process. Left unattended, farmlands quickly grew back to monotonous second-growth forests that diminished rather than enhanced their scenic value and ecological benefit. Trusts that purchased farmland faced the challenge of finding new owners or tenants willing to maintain the land in production. In order to "keep the rural character of the town," voters in Portsmouth, Rhode Island, allocated $5 million not only to purchase but to maintain the 92-acre Glen Farm. In matters like these land trusts found allies among historic preservationists, who were also beginning to shift their focus from high-style architecture to vernacular landscapes and from saving isolated buildings to including cultural and natural context—the outbuildings, fences, stone walls, gardens, fields, and woodland edges that represented the history of an entire farm district. Using covenants and deed restrictions, historic preservationists worked with private owners, public agencies, land trusts, historical societies, and state historical commissions to find ways to accommodate rural development while preserving the visual character of the countryside.[88]

Preserving farms was important, but the sheer acreage involved discouraged outright purchase, and preservationists adopted a strategy the TOR had been advocating since the 1950s. Aware that farmers and woodland owners paid taxes on a large land base while asking relatively little in return from the municipality, the Trustees lobbied for special zones with mill rates based on current use rather than highest market value, which generally meant conversion to suburban housing. In the late 1960s Connecticut passed a current-use tax law for farmland and forestland, and other states followed. Vermont's Use Value Assessment Program added special rates for wetlands, vernal pools, and other sensitive areas, and the state's Land Gains Tax imposed a penalty on lands purchased and resold in less than six years. New Hampshire voters endorsed a current-use tax law in 1968, and Maine did so in 1970.[89] Massachusetts launched an Agriculture Preservation Restriction Program in 1977 that provided matching funds for towns or trusts seeking easements to slow the transition from "cows [to] ... condos." In conjunction with local and regional trusts, Rhode Island's Agricultural Lands Preservation Commission, formed in 1978, protected about 20 percent of the state's land area. In addition, states passed "right to farm" laws that insulated farmers from nuisance lawsuits originating from nearby suburbs. University extension services supported farmers' markets and encouraged small farmers to experiment with specialty vegetable production rather than plant low-value staples like onions and potatoes. States conducted "buy local" campaigns and encouraged farmers to diversify their crops, form cooperative marketing arrangements, and adopt sustainable agriculture practices and integrated pest management.[90]

Current-use taxation was not an ideal solution. Connecticut's Public Act 490, passed in 1963, helped save some of the state's four thousand farms, but it cost towns hundreds of thousands of dollars in revenue and drew complaints that banks and other corporations were holding farmlands in current-use valuation for speculative purposes. In 1972 the state levied a substantial recapture tax on current-use property sold for development and in 1978 turned to purchasing easements on farmland threatened by development. The program proved successful; farmers sold their development rights for a variety of reasons, but among them was a commitment to keeping agriculture a "part of life in Connecticut."[91]

Easements could be complicated as well. In 1982 Connecticut purchased development rights to a large farm in Lebanon, and residents, anticipating fields of corn and grain, watched as heavy construction equipment rolled in to lay foundations for barns to accommodate 1.5 million chickens. The General Assembly hastened to amend the law. A similar dispute took place when wealthy New Yorkers with weekend estates in Bridgeport donated more than a million dollars to a local land trust to purchase a ninety-six-acre farm. The trust found tenants to manage the land, but when the estate owner next door discovered the family planned to raise beef cattle, he demanded tighter restrictions. The wealthy donors, as a journalist suggested, were "attracted by agriculture's patchwork landscape but put off by its smells, noises and odd hours." A petition signed by area residents supported the tenants, but this put the trust in a bind, given the estate donors' financial contribution to maintaining "the rural character of this town." State representative Clark Chapin lectured that "you can't just freeze the picture of the farm in time and expect it to stay."[92]

Despite misunderstandings like these, current-use taxation and easements generally worked to the advantage of all parties. The Maine Farmland Trust, in partnership with the state and local trusts, helped designate "forever farms" that protected more than thirty-four thousand acres with easements. These arrangements benefited farmers by providing funds to purchase new equipment or pay down debts. Older couples could lower their land values and taxes and gain assurance that their life work would pass to a younger generation. An exemplary case occurred in 2003 when a recently widowed owner of the Battles Farm in Bradford, New Hampshire, was forced to put her land on the market. In cooperation with the state's Land and Community Heritage Investment Program and other government agencies, the local trust negotiated an easement, and with the infusion of capital the widow and her new husband upgraded their equipment, barns, and processing kitchens and raised grass-fed cow-bison crossbreeds along with chickens, sheep, and pigs in a mostly organic operation. Easements like these could be flexible; in one case the covenant simply stipulated that the farmer develop the land "in ecologically sound ways for the benefit of ... towns and their citizens."[93] Easements did not bring a halt to farmland conversion, but they did slow the process.

The 1980s: New Problems and Bolder Solutions

In April 2001 citizens of North Hampton, a small New Hampshire coastal community of only forty-three hundred inhabitants, gathered in a town meeting and approved a $4 million bond issue to fund their North Hampton Forever initiative. The following year neighboring Stratham appropriated $5 million for similar purposes, while Hollis, a similarly small community on the Massachusetts border, set aside $2 million for land preservation. The following year participants in town meetings across southern New Hampshire set aside more than $13.9 million for similar purposes. At a time when the environment was no longer a top political priority nationally, this small-town commitment to preservation seems extraordinary, but in fact in 2002 voters in seventeen states across the country approved a total of $1.2 billion in state and local funds to protect recreational lands, watersheds, wildlife habitat, farmlands, and other forms of rural and urban open space. As the Land Trust Alliance's Rand Wentworth observed in 2003, "People assume that sprawl is inevitable and that nothing can be done about it. But the million people who are active in America's 1,263 nonprofit local land trusts are doing plenty."[94]

The land-trust movement remained vibrant through the volatile last decades of the twentieth century because it responded so readily to community needs and concerns. At the beginning of the 1980s the Reagan administration reversed a decadelong trend in bipartisan environmental legislation as part of a broader assault on the federal bureaucracy. In this new political climate, trust officers found it more difficult to justify land preservation, particularly in small towns where budgets were tight and property rights sacrosanct. They explained the need to safeguard flood plains, historical sites, and recreational lands and pointed out that trust acquisitions were but a small percentage of the land available for development. The Redding Land Trust, one of the oldest in Connecticut, held a total of 390 acres in 1982, but as its representatives explained, this was only 2 percent of the town's land base.[95] The arguments were sound, but they reflected a defensive mood among trust officers.

The environmental movement was indeed on the defensive in the 1980s. The Reagan election, building on post-Vietnam and post-Watergate cynicism and the conservative reaction to antiwar, civil rights, and feminist rhetoric, realigned the political forces behind the movement. With Republicans moving into the antienvironmentalist camp, Democrats were by default assured of the environmental vote, and accordingly the party was able to shift its focus to political issues that appealed to other constituencies. The Arab oil embargo and the inflationary spiral of the late 1970s undermined environmentalists' attempts to restrain industrial abuse, and with women moving into the workforce in greater numbers, the movement's most active constituency was weakened. Finally, the waning of the counterculture deprived grassroots environmentalism of a rich source of visionary thinking.[96]

The issues grassroots environmentalists faced in the 1980s lacked the intense anticorporate focus that animated earlier campaigns. Remaining environmental problems—non-point-source pollution, soil erosion, groundwater contamination, hazardous waste disposal, pesticide spraying, habitat loss, acid rain, energy conservation—had much higher populist flash points, and here arcane technical expertise counted more than grassroots mobilization. Many activists accepted the idea that these problems could be solved administratively through the new political and legal apparatus they helped create in the 1970s. "Third-wave environmentalism," as Mark Dowie called it, was less confrontational and more dependent on market-based incentives, technological fixes, and regulatory flexibility.[97]

These developments coincided with a growing preference for professionalism and legal negotiation over grassroots mobilizing in the movement at large. Daniel Chiras, a sympathetic critic, noted the symptoms of this "Washingtonization":

a political base composed of "soft members" willing to give money in lieu of personal effort and a narrow focus on "imageable" issues likely to appeal to ephemeral public interest. James Morton Turner traced a similar trajectory in the Wilderness Society. In the 1970s the organization waged its campaigns by mobilizing grassroots support in communities near proposed wilderness areas, but late in the decade officers shifted away from citizen organizing to legal advocacy and Washington-based lobbying. Turner noted, however, that environmental successes in the decade were not limited to "those with the most money or the best political connections." Small groups on the periphery of the nation's wilderness domain played a "pivotal role" in the preservation movement.[98]

This was certainly the case with the land-trust movement. Community-based preservation grew spectacularly between 1980 and 2010. Reagan's antienvironmental rhetoric, as it turned out, was aimed at federal programs rather than local and private initiatives, and in fact in 1986 his administration convened a Commission on Americans Outdoors similar to Lyndon Johnson's earlier Council on Recreation and Natural Beauty. The commissioners heard testimony from more than two thousand witnesses, talked with more than three hundred technical experts, and reviewed nearly a thousand technical reports, and like the commissioners in 1968, they found that most Americans valued local recreational resources as much as they did distant national parks and monuments. As part of the larger Reagan-Bush assault on the Washington bureaucracy, the commissioners hoped to shift responsibility for the land-use crisis from federal agencies to local officials and private organizations. Nevertheless, their conclusions were in line with those in the Johnson commission report. A New Hampshire preservationist summarized these findings: "For most, dramatic unspoiled vistas are the stuff of calendars, vacations, and memories. By definition, most people do not live where big chunks of land have been preserved." The "Great American Outdoors," as the commissioners put it, "is just down the block.... It's the community park, the town commons, the local streamside. The Great American Outdoors is in your backyard, too."[99]

As historians point out, the Reagan years were "tailormade for the growing land trust movement." Given its local orientation and private approach to preservation, the movement thrived in the decade. Between 1980 and 1990 land-trust numbers rose nationwide from 431 to 743, with a combined membership in 1990 of more than 640,000. By 2010 the nation's 1,700 trusts had preserved through gift, purchase, and easement over 47 million acres, a landmass larger than the state of Washington. Trusts could be found from Maine's Bold Coast to California's Big Sur, but New England still accounted for around a third of their number. Massachusetts, the third most densely populated state in the nation, led the nation in the number of trusts. Inspired by growing popular interest in preserving nearby nature, activists wove the land-trust idea into the fabric of the larger environmental movement.[100]

Looking back over the previous two decades in 1996, Leslie Corey of the Connecticut Nature Conservancy marveled at the growing number of land trusts and the changing scale of their projects. By combining forces and employing new techniques, trusts were able to plan their acquisitions across an entire region. A survey conducted in 1994 found that more than half of all land trusts in the nation partnered with other organizations and one or more government agencies to achieve these broader aims, and by this time an impressive array of regional and national organizations stood ready to help local groups coordinate their area-wide projects. Cooperation gave focus to a local trust's acquisition policies; raised the level of enthusiasm among volunteers, residents, and donors; and ushered the trusts into an era of landscape-scale preservation.[101] These alliances prepared the movement for an even larger challenge in the decade to come: protecting urban open spaces in the face of sky-high real-estate prices and conserving entire ecosystems and the numerous plant and animal communities they hosted. These two challenges are the focus of the chapters that follow.

CHAPTER 5

Reimagining Urban Spaces
Preservation in the City, 1980–2000

Open space meant different things in different eras, and the land-trust movement remained viable into the twenty-first century because it adapted to these changes. Preservationists avoided the temptation to mold their acquisitions to preconceived notions of public use or ecological advantage; in essence, they let nearby residents define open-space values for themselves. In the decades after 1980 this flexibility was apparent in two significant ways. First, trust officers and other preservationists responded to changing preferences in outdoor recreation. In the 1980s Americans traveled less on long-distance vacations due to a declining income, rising prices for gasoline and travel services, and longer average workweeks. Responding to these trends and to a growing emphasis on personal health, families turned to near-home open spaces for more casual recreational pursuits like strolling, hiking, jogging, bicycling, canoeing, bird-watching, roller-skating, and cross-country skiing. Linear recreational activities like these required a different type of open space, and accordingly preservationists began piecing together urban-to-rural trail corridors and greenways—popular open-space innovations that brought nature to the doorstep of millions of residents and moved the land-preservation movement closer to the democratic ideals on which the nation's first land trust was founded, namely, unrestricted public access to recreational open spaces.[1]

A second significant change in the meaning of open spaces grew out of a demand for healthier and more enjoyable city environments. Nineteenth-century reformers interpreted urban open spaces as an opportunity for creating landscaped parks that would bring the benefits of nature to the urban masses. In the 1950s these parks fell from favor, and over the next three decades urban open spaces acquired new and far more complicated meanings as they took on the protean texture of the cities' multiracial and multicultural neighborhoods. Working with residents in different neighborhoods, preservationists broadened the meaning of open spaces to meet an amazingly diverse set of needs, and in meeting these needs equitably they took another step toward democratizing the preservation movement. Charles Eliot II wrote in 1958 that saving open space was necessary in "both the city and the region . . . which it serves." In the 1980s preservationists became proficient in saving both, but in entirely different ways.[2] Urban land preservation demonstrated the malleable nature of open-space visions and the need to work with local residents to actualize these visions.

Green Cities, Green Spaces

In the decades before World War II, urban reform meant building parks, beautifying streets and buildings, eliminating graft, and uplifting the immigrant masses. After the war, reformers turned their attention to the physical structure of the neighborhoods. Bewildered by the multiple problems facing inner-city neighborhoods yet buoyed by the successes in federal wartime residential construction, urban planners concluded that the only solution to the city's social problems was, as one put it, "large-scale clearance and redevelopment with new buildings of modern types, arranged in modern patterns." Reformers envisioned wholly new neighborhoods bathed in sunlight and enshrouded in greenery, each with its own library, elementary school, playground, and park, but after passage of the federal Housing Act of 1954, much of this planning enthusiasm went into renewal projects that simply gutted lower-income neighborhoods and replaced them with high-rise apartments, office towers, people-dwarfing superblocks, and vast, empty concrete plazas. In this clean-sweep approach, poor and working-class people were displaced, small businesses ruined, and neighborhood institutions and gathering places destroyed. Multilane connectors extended into the downtown districts to accommodate commuters, further fragmenting older urban communities. Boston became infamous for effacing its working-class neighborhoods in the south and west ends in the 1950s in the hopes of attracting middle-class residents back into the city. There and elsewhere the pattern of small shops and restaurants that gave downtowns their heterogeneous quality gave way before the onslaught of urban renewal.³

In the 1950s the parks movement, once a mainstay of urban reform, was overshadowed by new concerns for redevelopment, and the great turn-of-the-century landscaped parks fell into disrepair. When they were built, these parks were considered an antidote to the dehumanizing artificiality of the urban environment, but by midcentury belief in the social and psychological value of natural landscaping was eclipsed by enthusiasm for physical exercise and structured play. The most urgent need in the larger cities, according to a 1948 study, was "more play lots, more playgrounds and more play fields." In the following decades landscaped parks deteriorated and parkways were stripped of vegetation, defaced by curb cuts and commercial development, and clogged with traffic. Massachusetts Institute of Technology urban planner Anne Whiston Spirn theorized that parks fell out of favor because citizens perceived them not as works of art but as bits of nature left behind in building out the city, but there were other reasons for this changing perception. Rural memories faded among third- or fourth-generation urbanites, and with them went the idea that nature was necessary to enrich the lives of city residents. Spectator sports, organized team sports, and Sunday drives in the country took the place of leisurely strolls through the city park, and in an era when "modern" meant plastic and artificial, landscaping made even less sense. Suburbanites who lavished attention on their own backyards saw little need for parks in the city. By the 1970s large urban parks were more likely to be associated with crime than with peace and tranquility. The original vegetation, aging, trampled, and vandalized, was eclipsed by play and sports areas with low shrubbery designed to discourage unsocial behavior. Deep cuts in park budgets all across the country highlighted the declining importance of the public realm in urban life.⁴

The deterioration of Boston's parks was particularly tragic, given the brilliance of their original conceptualization. The 1950s brought hard times for New England's textile-based manufacturing economy, and for parks this meant a constant round of cuts that left grounds littered, buildings marred with graffiti, trees unpruned, and equipment poorly maintained. The Fenway, Riverway, Jamaicaway, and Arborway were stripped of their landscaping and widened to accommodate commuter traffic. "Today," Spirn wrote in 1964, "the Emerald Necklace is fragmented and tarnished, its parkways sliced by expressway ramps, its bridle paths and promenades converted to car lanes, its parks in decay." Elsewhere, cities squandered the magnificent urban forests that embowered their streets and open spaces. Dutch elm disease eradicated one of the most distinctive townscape features of prewar America, and when these and other trees died they were not replaced.[5]

In the 1960s a group of far-seeing urban planners including Jane Jacobs, Christopher Alexander, and Kevin Lynch reimagined the city from the perspective of the people who lived there. Studies of vibrant inner-city working-class life in so-called slum districts drove home the need to reconsider the remove-and-rebuild approach to revitalization. Cities, the new urbanists urged, should be pedestrian friendly, built to human scale, and fitted out with multiple informal gathering spots and places of discovery. This meant mixing residential and commercial functions, adapting old buildings to new uses, encouraging people-friendly architecture, changing neighborhoods incrementally and creatively rather than precipitously and uniformly, and preserving the cities' "green infrastructure." William Whyte advised planners to "cast a more imaginative look" at unfrequented waterfronts, old utility corridors, neglected rivers and canals, and abandoned lots. Derelict spaces like these could be made into community gardens, green alcoves, play lots, pocket parks, pedestrian or bicycle pathways, or waterfront refuges. Returning streets to pedestrian travel, Ian McHarg added, would help reintegrate all facets of city life—work, home life, recreation, culture, and community.[6]

Creatively adapted, redundant streets and unused spaces could make cities more livable, and this in turn would retain urban populations and relieve the problem of suburban sprawl. Rather than building more expressways to move people out of the cities, planners could design more inviting environments to keep them there. In 1980 Whyte and his students conducted a Street Life Project to document uses of public open spaces in New York City. In a radical departure from the philosophy of large, naturalized urban parks, the students reported that people preferred "not to escape the city, but to partake of it." In short, people were attracted to other people. The most frequented plazas, the students found, were those with a mix of sun and shade and ample places for sitting, not on benches but on steps, walls, and fountain rims. Whyte concluded that city open spaces should be designed to reflect the natural instincts of those who lived or worked in the neighborhoods. On the advice of Whyte and other new urbanists, planners designed people-oriented streets and plazas, small green pocket parks, waterfront promenades, and solar-oriented squares. New zoning laws encouraged small shops, restaurants, theaters, arcades, and other more idiosyncratic gathering places. All this set the tone for a new relationship between urban people and their neighborhood open spaces.⁷

Guided by the same insights, city officials and private preservation organizations reevaluated parks and other public spaces. With environmental consciousness on the rise, planners considered parks from the vantage of improved health, lowered stress, and contact with nature. Parks could also empower citizens if they were involved in the planning process. In 1978 residents in Buffalo, home to the nation's first urban park system, formed the Friends of Olmsted Parks and began a major restoration effort, and by 2004 the organization, now the Buffalo Olmsted Parks Conservancy, was managing the entire system. Residents formed a similar Central Park Conservancy in New York City in 1985, and in Boston the Friends of the Muddy River worked with the city to transform the Fens from an uninviting tangle of brush and weeds into a gardened walkway. Similar groups formed the Emerald Necklace Conservancy in 1998.⁸

Responding to grassroots park advocacy, the Massachusetts state legislature inaugurated an Olmsted Historic Landscape Preservation Program in 1983, and over the next year community, environmental, and business groups came together to form the Boston Greenspace Alliance. Growing interest in parks resulted in a two-year seminar on the future of Boston's open spaces and a widely distributed booklet titled *The Greening of Boston: An Action Agenda*. With this as a guide, Mayor Ray Flynn announced a five-year multimillion-dollar "Rebuilding Boston" plan and appointed William B. Coughlin commissioner of parks and recreation. Aware that community participation was necessary to break the cycle of public apathy and park decline, Coughlin had his staff conduct neighborhood meetings. This resulted in an ambitious schedule of park activities that included arts-and-crafts classes, field sports, sailing lessons, nature walks, kite festivals, bike tours, bird-watching excursions, lunchtime concerts, fitness classes, and a youth park-ranger program. With new funding, Coughlin renovated parks, improved maintenance, and recruited a more diverse and representative staff. Nearly 50 percent of his budget went into improving open spaces in low-income neighborhoods. Mayor Flynn called on private organizations and institutions—businesses, church establishments, schools, colleges—to open up access to their own grounds.⁹

One of the most dramatic additions to the city's open-space inventory was the four-mile linear park linking Back Bay, South End, Roxbury, and Jamaica Plain and serving some of the most diverse neighborhoods in metropolitan

Boston. The South End–Roxbury neighborhood suffered one of the lowest open-space-to-population ratios in the Boston area, but a series of unplanned circumstances changed that. Shortly after World War II the city laid plans for an express highway out of the southwestern district to connect with Route 128. Because the project would displace or disrupt the lives of thousands of low-income residents, activists from across the city protested, and Governor Francis Sargent canceled the project in 1969, but by this time the corridor had been cleared of homes and businesses. The planners and designers assigned to the area "moved beyond the familiar world of architectural drawing boards and lecture halls and took their plans to the street," using slide shows, flyers, meetings, and neighbor-to-neighbor contacts to support residents in articulating their own park visions. With a great deal of grassroots participation, portions of the corridor were transformed into a 120-acre Southwest Corridor Park, the largest open-space development in Boston since Olmsted's time. The park traversed three neighborhoods, transitioning from the stone and brick row houses of Back Bay and South End to the mixed "streetcar suburbs" of Jamaica Plain and the housing projects and apartment buildings of Roxbury and Dorchester. In community meetings, planners discovered different needs "in each mile, and sometimes each block," along the corridor. In response, they laid out an assortment of community gardens, bicycle paths, basketball and tennis courts, sandlots, tot lots, amphitheaters, playgrounds, benches, spray pools, picnic tables, and walking trails. "The Corridor," as historian Karilyn Crockett summarized, became "a connecting point within a socially and economically splintered metropolitan region." Where the highway would have sundered these neighborhoods, the park united them. Neighborhood groups contracted to care for sections of the park, and volunteers met regularly to take on improvement projects. Building the Southwest Corridor Park was an important object lesson in shaping urban open space from the bottom up.[10]

By the time Mayor Thomas Menino launched a "Greening of Boston" program in the early 2000s, a new coalition of urban preservationists had emerged, including city planners and officials, nongovernmental organizations like local land trusts, the national Trust for Public Land, the Boston Greenspace Alliance; and neighborhood activists. Working with these partners, Menino's staff expanded accessible open space, established an Audubon nature preserve at the Boston State Hospital in Mattapan, implemented a comprehensive recycling program, and replaced concrete surfacing with lawns and trees on school yards. This was urban environmentalism "broadly defined," as he said. At the state level, Governor William Weld's Green Ribbon Commission evaluated the state's thirty-two parks and reservations and brought together the Metropolitan District Commission, the Parks and Recreation Division, and various "friends" groups to coordinate their activities.[11]

Open Spaces in the Neighborhoods

Preservationists found other opportunities for transforming urban open spaces into valued community assets. In the decades after World War II, commercial and industrial disinvestment, urban renewal, and the middle-class flight to the suburbs left thousands of acres of land in each of America's great cities vacant. By 1977 Newark, for example, counted more than four thousand abandoned lots, and New York City contained upwards of twenty-five thousand. Boston's fifteen to twenty thousand vacant parcels totaled between three and four thousand acres, mostly in low-income neighborhoods. The unused land suggested new possibilities for renewing the urban environment through public-private preservation partnerships.[12]

In 1968 William Whyte pointed out that planners hoping to maximize public use of open space would do well to "enlarge the perimeter of the space rather than increase the bulk of it." A network of relatively small, well-distributed public spaces would be used more intensively than the same acreage in the large parkland tracts that "look so well on land-use maps." Most of Boston's unused spaces were well under an acre, but as Whyte suggested they offered people throughout the city a chance to enjoy a parklike setting in their own neighborhoods. These small "third places"—gathering spots that were neither home nor work—had an outsize influence on the neighborhoods around them. According to preservationist Mark Primack, they affected "every aspect of our lives in the city—the things we do or don't do, how we think of ourselves, our behavior, often even our reason for living." Kevin Lynch advised planners to "look for beauty and meaning in unaccustomed places," pointing out that the majesty of nature so apparent in the nation's great parks could be "conveyed symbolically, by small devices which recall the large: a fountain for the sea, a dwarf tree for the forest, a moving ray of light for the sun. Such messages can be spoken in very small places." As others pointed out, Japanese landscapers evoked the universe in a tiny backyard setting or even a dish garden. In short, nature could be appreciated not only in remote wilderness areas but also in the interstices of the urban landscape. Boston preservationists began viewing blighted, unused spaces as "an opportunity for civic design unmatched since the 19th century."[13]

Shaped to neighborhood needs, vacant land was an important complement to the city's parks and playgrounds. Because these third places were relatively small, residents could take a hand in transforming them and in the process gain a sense of neighborhood pride and empowerment. City officials supported these grassroots efforts by clearing vacant lots, demolishing derelict buildings, opening up stream banks, and sun-lighting decked-over rivers. In unused lots they erected modular play equipment that could be easily moved and reassembled if the land was slated for another purpose or the needs of the neighborhood changed. Small open spaces became an important feature of urban revival.[14]

Finding new uses for vacant spots drew attention to the cities' natural environment. Traditional ecologists overlooked the built environment in their quest to understand the inner workings of nature, but in the 1980s they took interest in the way nature behaved in an urban environment. As Spirn pointed out, "If cities are to be healthful, vital and delightful places, they must be considered a part of the natural environment." Ian McHarg, who pioneered the new ecological perspective, described the city as a fusion of natural and engineered form. As in other ecologies, disturbances reverberated through the system. Erosion from construction in one place silted up river channels in another, and wastes deposited in one location polluted wells farther down gradient. Viewing the city in ecological terms brought to light numerous natural processes often overlooked in the cityscape. Hearty, fast-growing plants and trees, both native and exotic, sprang up wherever they found a patch of soil. Vacant lots, abandoned industrial sites, and overlooked wetlands and ravines grew back to willow, sumac, ash, cherry, birch, aspen, and box elder and then to longer-lived species like locust, maple, pine, hemlock, spruce, oak, hickory, and sycamore. "Fortuitous meadows . . . support a marvelous variety of butterflies, animals, and birds; . . . poor drainage systems have created small wetlands that help sustain a stable urban hydrologic balance and beneficial microclimate." Boston, the sixth most densely populated metropolitan area in the country, was "full of natural wonders." Peregrine falcons nested in cliffs and barn owls in unused buildings. Deer, foxes, and coyotes wandered the woods; snowy owls sought rodents in the meadows; terns made their homes on abandoned pilings; butterflies, rodents, and birds thrived in the overgrown fields; and upland sandpipers, gulls, oystercatchers, American egrets, snowy egrets, and cormorants made their homes in the coastal marshes. Urban wilds were testimony to nature's resiliency and adaptability.[15]

Cities indeed had a natural history, and preservationists set out to reclaim it. As they pointed out, incidental green spaces benefited not only the nearby neighborhoods but the entire city. They recharged groundwater, prevented flooding, mitigated the heat-island effect caused by sunlight on concrete, stabilized hillsides, prevented erosion, controlled pollution, restored oxygen, and provided habitat for insects, birds, and animals. Urban wetlands settled out silt from upstream excavations, and urban forests slowed runoff during storms and retained water in dry periods. When planners and architects begin to think ecologically, McHarg promised, "a matrix of open spaces of inestimable value for amenity and recreation will result and a structure for metropolitan growth will be revealed."[16]

In 1974 Elliot Rhodeside, chief landscape architect for the Boston Redevelopment Authority (BRA), used a federal grant to survey the city's unstructured green spaces, and two years later Robert Kenney published the survey as *Boston Urban Wilds: A Natural Area Conservation Program*. The results were striking. Woodlands, wetlands, meadows, salt and freshwater marshes, tidal flats, swamps, rock outcroppings, cliffs, and undeveloped hilltops peppered the urban landscape. The project located 4,650 public and private open spaces hidden among the city's streets, buildings, and waterfronts. Of these, 145 sites totaling around two thousand acres were natural, wild, or suitable for rehabilitation. Of those still in private hands, many were too wet, too steep, or too rocky to be developed. The slopes of Bunker Hill, for instance, were undevelopable but suitable for a neighborhood play area, and Roxbury featured an abandoned quarry, a seventy-five-foot cliff, and several wooded hillsides. Outcroppings, abandoned quarries, and steep hillsides in Roxbury, Hyde Park, Roslindale, and Jamaica Plain had been used informally for recreation for generations. The committee discovered several well-vegetated areas among the mills and factories along the Neponset River in Dorchester and Mattapan, and East Boston hosted the city's largest remaining saltwater marshes. Along Chelsea Creek, across the harbor from Boston, an abandoned tank farm and railroad right-of-way supported acres of wild grass.[17]

The BRA defined "wild" loosely as any vegetated open space that would offer residents a predominantly natural experience. The definition varied from neighborhood to neighborhood, depending on the way these residents viewed nature, valued open space, and spent their free time. About forty of the sites that met this pliant designation were publicly owned and were transferred to the city's Conservation Commission or Department of Conservation. Others were protected through floodplain zoning or by federal wetlands regulations. Sites were evaluated according to a complicated mix of social and ecological criteria. Using a "neighborhood-based planning process," project leaders met with residents around the sites and assessed social and recreational needs. In social terms, they ranked sites threatened by development as their first priority and then identified parcels that served Boston's low-income neighborhoods. In ecological terms, undisturbed areas of twenty-five to one hundred acres were high on the list of potential acquisitions, especially saltwater marshes, tidal flats, and tidal creeks. Below this in importance were smaller areas that might need restoration. Others were important because they were "observable clues to Boston's geological history" or because they served ecological functions as habitat or means of conveying water, nutrients, plants, birds, or mammals across the urban landscape. Geographically, the most critical areas were those within or adjacent to low-income neighborhoods or near concentrations of elderly and young people.[18]

In 1977, a year after Kenney issued his report, preservationists established the Boston Natural Areas Network (BNAN), a private charitable organization dedicated to saving as many urban green spaces as possible. The organization worked with city officials and preservation groups to secure parcels according to the 1976 study priorities and acquired around forty-eight acres of private land, with easements and restrictions on other sites. Caring for these sites was a collaborative effort. The Audubon Society conducted educational programs at several, and the Parks Department, with volunteer help, kept the sites clean and the vegetation under control. The Youth Conservation Corps provided park accessories that met the needs of nearby residents, and recruits from the Boston Youth Clean-Up Corps spent summers maintaining the areas.[19]

Boston's urban wilds embraced a broad spectrum of landscapes. At one end was the Puddingstone Garden Urban Wild adjacent to Franklin Park. The small parcel was landscaped in 1960 by the Roxbury Beautification Project, and under the Urban Wilds Initiative it was deemed wild due to a distinctive outcrop of Roxbury puddingstone. At the other end of the spectrum was the Hancock Woods in Roxbury, a forty-six-acre red-maple swamp and woods saved from development by neighborhood protests. One of the last true natural areas in Greater Boston, it was large enough to separate visitors from the noise of the city, and it was a critical link in a matrix of open spaces that included a bird sanctuary, the Arnold Arboretum, and Olmsted Park. Among the city's hidden ecological gems was the Bussey Brook Urban Wild in Jamaica Plain, six acres of marsh, woods, and meadow that provided a sanctuary for both wildlife and nearby residents—a place where "traffic noise . . . fades, to be replaced by birdcalls and the rustling of leaves." Encouraged by acquisitions like this, in 1988 parks commissioner Justine Liff announced that over the coming five years, park space in Boston would expand by 25 percent, with land added by the Central Artery project, the Harbor Islands initiative, the reclamation of landfills, the urban wilds program, and the addition of various vacant lots. The new spaces, she offered, would "be as much a part of today's public dialogue as the massive projects that will create them."[20]

To draw attention to these new green spaces, the city and Massachusetts Audubon sponsored neighborhood-based nature interpretation programs aiming to "awake the curiosity, knowledge, and pride of inner city children about their own parks, urban wilds, and neighborhood vacant lots." Boston's roughly one hundred urban wild units required complicated maintenance decisions given the diversity of flora, fauna, and geological features they harbored and the equally diverse neighborhoods they served, but despite these complexities the program succeeded, and in 1990 the BNAN updated their open-space appraisal and brought more acquisitions into the system.[21]

Encouraged by Boston's example and a growing body of literature on urban nature, trusts throughout New England began acquiring open spaces in and near urban centers. Cities found public uses for relic forests, neglected rivers, ravines, and vacant lots. Industrial-era millponds offered opportunities for reconstructing marshlands, and land left behind in public works projects, derelict industrial sites, blighted vacant lots, inactive dumps, and sand and gravel pits provided new opportunities for greening the civic ecology. The Trust for Public Land's Urban Land Program led the way among national trusts, helping local organizations vegetate their school yards, build urban trails, garden vacant lots, and protect community forests.[22] Urban land preservation required a substantial commitment. The Stamford Land Conservation Trust, for instance, competed with developers for half-acre parcels commanding prices of $1 million or more. Working with city officials and private donors, the trust acquired ninety acres in scattered parcels in the city. Most ranged from one acre to thirteen acres, but the trust offered to take even smaller parcels: "A squirrel could live on it. Bushes can grow on it." In addition to several pocket parks purchased through the federal Urban Redevelopment grants, the trust pieced together the Mill River Greenbelt in the wake of a federally financed dam-removal and river-restoration project. Since the area drained behind the dam was undeveloped, preservation of this recreationally and ecologically valuable open space was relatively inexpensive. Together the Stamford acquisitions put nature "within walking distance" for 80 percent of the city's population.[23]

Smaller trusts joined the urban open-space movement by adding in-town parcels to their acquisitions, often in partnership with grassroots neighborhood organizations or city parks departments. Worcester offered three urban wilds owned by the city, the Ecotarium, the Greater Worcester Land Trust, the Friends of Newton Hill, and Massachusetts Audubon. Each was large enough to maintain its natural character as wetland, oak savannah, or early-succession forest. In Hartford, the Avon Land Trust preserved fourteen acres of wetlands adjacent to a city park. The Kennebunk Land Trust's thirty-eight-acre Mousam River Wildlife Sanctuary offered tranquil, tree-shrouded riverside trails "in the middle of a town that, over the years, has been gradually losing its pastoral identity and charm for the sake of 'progress.'" The nearby York Land Trust joined with other conservation groups and two local lobster fishermen to protect the town's last remaining public dock on land slated for a showpiece home. Their project was well received, and over the next decade the state used conservation funds to acquire dozens of in-town access points to protect the fishing industry.[24]

Greenways: Linking City and Country

Although urban green spaces were typically scattered through the neighborhoods, they could be joined together into greenways, a second major innovation in urban land stewardship. Greenways were corridors of protected land that in most cases linked inner-city neighborhoods to the surrounding countryside, usually following a watercourse, a canal, or an abandoned rail line. The term "greenway" was coined by William Whyte in the 1960s, but the concept originated in Europe as a public promenade connecting points of cultural interest. Frederick Law Olmsted brought this idea to America by designing parkways or sinuous carriage and pedestrian passageways "made interesting by a process of planting and decoration." Olmsted used this device to join Buffalo's three major green spaces—Park, Front, and Parade—as America's first park system and later to knit together Boston's Emerald Necklace. Other early uses of the elongated-park concept included the NPS's 1930 George Washington Memorial Parkway, the 1936 Blue Ridge Parkway, the 1938 Chesapeake and Ohio Canal National Historical Park, and the 1938 Natchez Trace Parkway. Highway engineers sometimes preserved corridors along particularly scenic roadways, such as the Bronx River Parkway or Virginia's Skyline Drive.[25]

The greenway idea also derived from protective corridors along trails dating back to the early days of New England mountaineering. By 1925 the Appalachian Mountain Club and other outdoor groups had completed around four hundred trails extending across 1,221 miles of New Hampshire's mountain terrain, much of it on national forest land or shrouded in protective easements. Connecticut's Forest Park Association created a 700-mile Blue Blaze Trail System in the 1930s with protected corridors along the state's rivers. America's trail system grew considerably in the 1970s when advocates realized abandoned railroad rights-of-way could be converted into level handicap-accessible hiking or biking paths, many with built-in protective corridors. The rails-to-trails movement received federal support as a way of banking right-of-way easements for possible rail use at a later date. With thousands of miles of railroad tracks going out of service every year, the Rails-to-Trails Conservancy, founded in 1986, helped preserve around 3,100 miles of former railroad bed over the next decade.[26]

Maine extended the linear park idea to rivers by creating the Allagash Wilderness Waterway in 1966 as the nation's first state-managed wilderness river preserve. The protective-corridor idea was nationalized in the Wild and Scenic Rivers System and the National Trails System, both established two years later in 1968. In 1990 Charles Little, executive director of the Open Space Institute in New York City, published *Greenways for America*, and in the decade that followed riverside greenways spread across America. Among the first in New England was along the Nissitissit River, flowing through mostly rural lands in Massachusetts and southern New Hampshire. In 1957 the Massachusetts Natural Resources Plan listed the Nissitissit as an important recreational asset, and in 1962 the New England Wildflower Preservation Society drew attention to threats along the river. In 1968, the year Congress passed the Wild and Scenic Rivers Act, Annette Cottrell and others formed the Nissitissit River Land Trust and began acquiring land and easements along critical sections of the river. New Hampshire's Rockingham Land Trust, working with the Trust for Public Land, preserved a 2,300-acre greenway along the Piscassic River, and the Lamprey River Advisory Committee did the same in southeastern New Hampshire. The Souhegan Valley Land Trust worked with local garden, Rotary, and fish and game clubs in thirteen towns to protect land along Purgatory Brook, and other New England examples included the Concord River Greenway Park in Lowell, the Connecticut River Greenway in western Massachusetts, and the Ten Mile River and Blackstone River greenways in Rhode Island.[27]

Preserving urban as opposed to wild rivers required an act of imagination not unlike Charles Eliot's plan for Boston's heavily industrialized Charles, Mystic, and Neponset. By contrast to America's well-loved wild and scenic rivers, urban watercourses were typically fenced off, neglected, polluted, and thoroughly engineered, yet as the hydrologic veins of the city they performed important ecological functions, and to far-sighted planners neglected riverbanks beckoned as natural retreats around which the urban fabric could be rewoven. As these rivers were cleaned of effluent in the 1970s, planners realized they could be converted into linear parks for walkers, runners, bikers, picnickers, or those who simply enjoyed watching water flow. Restoration brought the greenway idea out of the country and into the city, and because river bottomlands were typically given over to working-class neighborhoods, greening the banks promised benefits for a population not generally served by the cities' park and open-space systems.[28]

Urban greenway projects weathered the 1980s antienvironmentalist backlash because they were hugely popular. They stood at the convergence of rising interest in urban open space and the growing popularity of outdoor exercise. They gave the park idea new vigor in an era of unstable urban budgets by transforming underutilized land into popular recreational spaces, and they attracted far more private funding and volunteer effort than traditional parks. National surveys demonstrated time and again that the open spaces Americans most valued were those "closer to home and work." Greenways, as the authors of these studies pointed out, could be accessed from almost anywhere in the city, and they were adaptable enough to accommodate the recreational needs of almost any neighborhood. As Robert Searns put it, greenways made "every doorstep a trailhead." With the cost of urban real estate skyrocketing, greenways required less land than traditional parks, and they could be built on relatively inexpensive property along riverbanks, waterfronts, and abandoned utility and rail lines. Although the numbers are somewhat illusive, scholars calculate that by the early 1990s more than five hundred greenways had been built or were under construction across America.[29]

Greenways were popular and cheap to build, but they required a great deal of foresight and complex interorganizational planning. As the nation's most ambitious project of its kind, the Hudson River Valley Greenway best exemplified the complexity of piecing together such a system. The project began in 1988 when the state legislature commissioned the Hudson River Valley Greenway Council to create a protected corridor along the river from New York City to Albany. The council and its private and public partners investigated every possible opportunity for linking riverside parks, preserves, old estates, and historic sites between the two cities. In numerous public meetings participants identified sites suitable for boat launches, foot and canoe trails, bikeways, and interpretive facilities. The resulting 154-mile greenway brought together 150 state, local, regional, and national organizations encompassing nearly six hundred thousand acres of river frontage and upland, including one hundred historic landmarks, eighty-nine historic districts, and nearly seven hundred thousand acres of agricultural land.[30]

In Massachusetts the Charles River Reservation project, begun in 1971, brought together a similar coalition that included the Boston Metropolitan District Commission, the Charles River Watershed Association, the Trustees of Reservations, the Harvard Department of Landscape Architecture, the Massachusetts Audubon Society, and several local preservation organizations and state and federal agencies. The Charles River begins at Echo Lake in Hopkinton and passes through culverts, past textile mills, and under power lines as it meanders northward to the Rocky Narrows, an early acquisition by the Trustees of Reservations. From there it continues on through Waltham and Boston and out into Boston Harbor, some eighty miles from its source. Despite the semiwild shores of the upper river, the Charles was among the most degraded rivers in America, "strangled with highways, choked with landfill, clogged with debris, polluted with human waste, and poisoned with industrial chemicals." Cemented over, scoured, restructured, and lined with parking lots and chain-link fences, the river had lost its identity as a natural system.[31]

Bostonians could hardly imagine their city without the Charles River as backdrop. Recognizing this, in 1893 Charles Eliot suggested lining the banks with parkland to create an elongated river reservation, and over the next century the MDC accumulated land along the river in increments. In 1931 the commission created an esplanade funded through private donations, but six years later traffic engineers sliced through the new park to create Storrow Drive, consuming half the park's land and most of its serenity. In the early 1960s the League of Women Voters formed a Charles River study group, and in 1965 its members joined with others to form the Charles River Watershed Association (CRWA). The association enlisted the conservation commissions and other groups in towns along the river. Since the watercourse flowed through the heart of Boston and included 20 percent of the state's population in its drainage basin, the CRWA nicknamed it the "People's River." To enhance the recreational opportunities along its banks, the CRWA enlisted cleanup crews to fish cars, bicycles, tires, shopping carts, and tons of "God knows what" out of the river, and by the end of the century the water quality above Waltham had improved remarkably. As odors and obvious effluents dissipated, the lower river attracted boaters and bankside recreationists. In the 1990s the CRWA and MDC completed a public pathway along the lower river from the Esplanade to Needham and extended the Esplanade eastward to the harbor front.[32]

In 1987 the MDC and partner organizations began work acquiring riverside land and piecing together public open spaces to extend the Charles River Walkway to Waltham, Watertown, and finally, fifteen years later, Newton. The MDC developed master plans for the Upper Charles River Reservation in 1994 and 1998, factoring in easements, gifts of land, and $9 million in federal and state money. Using map overlays showing ownership, vegetation, hydrology, land uses, and visual values, the MDC negotiated with more than a hundred owners and abutters and linked together land owned by the trustees, the Audubon Society, the towns of Sherborn and Medfield, and the Medfield State Hospital. The result was a twenty-mile system of footpaths, cultural interpretation sites, and scenic overlooks. To complete the greenway, the MDC reclaimed public land usurped by home owners and businesses for parking lots, patios, storage sheds, and other intrusions. In some cases businesses offered to maintain the greenway sections their intrusions had formerly blocked. By 1998 hikers could walk from the inner city out past riverside wetlands teeming with birdlife and into the suburban wilds under canopies of oak and pine. The reservation was a place where children could learn about nature in their own communities, exploring places previously hidden away behind shopping malls, brush, and fences. That the river flowed through some of Boston's most prosperous suburbs "certainly helped the Association's cause," historian Scott Carlin points out, as did the timing of the river cleanup, which coincided with the state's semiconductor boom. The several affluent towns along the river gave the CRWA "a level of visibility that other watershed associations lack."[33]

While this work proceeded, the CRWA and local groups worked to attract people back to the river. The rock group the Standells had released "Dirty Water" in 1966, and the song became a theme of sorts for the city when the Red

Sox began playing it after winning home games in 1997. Despite the recovery effort, the Standells' depiction of the Charles lingered, so to promote the river's new recreational status, the CRWA held an annual swim and sponsored canoe races and fishing derbies. A participant familiar only with the downtown basin noted he was "pleasantly surprised during the race to see just how rural it can get." Fishing parties, canoeists, and even swimmers hesitantly returned to the river, and to attract more walkers and runners, the MDC added brick sidewalks, boardwalks, footbridges, flower beds, native plants, benches, lighting, and shade trees.[34]

Creating a greenway along Boston's other river, the Neponset, was more complicated. The Charles was the "People's River" because it was Boston's most visible natural landmark; the Neponset, hidden behind factory and mill buildings, brush, chain-link fences, shopping malls, and highway bridges, was the city's "Hidden River." While the Charles flowed through Boston's wealthier suburbs, the Neponset was bordered by neighborhoods of diverse and rapidly shifting ethnic and racial character. Communities along the lower river were desperate for public open space. Almost a quarter of the population lived below the poverty level, few owned cars, and recent immigrants were reluctant to use recreational amenities outside their own neighborhood. Existing parks and playgrounds, with the exception of the Southwest Corridor Park, were in poor physical condition and frequented by drug dealers.[35]

As was often the case, the Neponset River Greenway began with a clean-water campaign. Antipollution legislation in the 1960s and 1970s, buttressed by new municipal water-treatment plants and speeded by deindustrialization, brought a gradual improvement in water quality. Local river activists formed the Neponset Conservation Association in 1967 to encourage the cleanup effort, and in 1985 they renamed their organization the Neponset River Watershed Association to reflect an expanded agenda that included salt-marsh restoration, fish ladders, wildlife refuges, boat launches, walking and biking trails, and park improvements. Convinced that the diverse neighborhood needs along the watershed mandated grassroots involvement, the association's Elizabeth Houghton committed the NRWA to "bottom-up planning," hoping to transform the Hidden River into another People's River. Ian Cooke, the association's executive director, organized fifteen "stream teams" to survey every mile of the Neponset and every stream flowing into it. Teams sampled water, documented nonpoint pollution, and inventoried scenic and ecological features. The "intensely local, one-brook-at-a-time effort" involved thousands of volunteers dedicated to ensuring protection down to the smallest feeder brook. The grassroots effort, according to the Hawes Brook Stream Team's Craig Auston, was "stronger in the Neponset project than the Charles. I like the idea of really exploring your own back yard and getting to know it."[36]

After a decade of community-based discussion, the MDC laid out a path through Dorchester and Milton on an abandoned railroad bed running along the river. In 1985 the MDC acquired marshes and upland on both sides of the upper river and in 2001 built Squantum Point Park on a sandy spit in Dorchester Bay, formerly occupied by a tractor-trailer training school. The BNAN which had coordinated other Boston-area open-space acquisitions, took charge of the Neponset River Greenway and, after hosting more neighborhood discussions, extended it out beyond the railroad right-of-way. While the Upper Charles River Reservation had been largely a top-down effort, the Neponset project drew its energy from volunteers, who insisted that the design reflect the "residential character" of the neighborhoods thorough which it passed.[37] As a linear park cutting across ethnic, race, and class lines, the Neponset Greenway served diverse constituencies with different ways of ascribing meaning to open space. In a 1984 book, biologist E. O. Wilson advanced the principle of biophilia, an understanding that humans, as a species, require regular interaction with the rest of nature in order to remain, as it were, human. Although the concept rings true, it is too rarefied to explain grassroots involvement in projects like the Neponset Greenway. Rivers and their borders are cultural constructions; they take on different meanings as they flow through different neighborhoods.[38] Some residents saw the river as refuge, others as a source of inspiration and contemplation, and still others as an opportunity for exercise or a portal to adventure. For some the foliage-screened banks harbored furtive and dangerous activities, and for others it was a priceless ecological asset. Given this mix of meanings, successful planning depended on neighborhood-by-neighborhood negotiation. Planners shaped these spaces to the needs of nearby residents using some combination of landscaping, hiking and biking trails, greensward, scenic vistas, ecological reserves, playgrounds, picnic grounds, athletic fields, boat launches, and community gardens. The commission met security concerns of residents upriver in Milton, for instance, by adding police patrols. The Neponset and similar urban greenways offered a new model of land stewardship based on cooperation among residents, preservation organizations, and public officials.[39]

Community involvement set in motion a feedback loop in which greenway use encouraged popular demand for even more open space. Preservationists had long argued that encouraging public visitation broadened and deepened the preservationist constituency, and the Neponset organizers acted on this principle. By 2002 the Neponset Greenway Trail ran from Dorchester Bay nearly to the Blue Hills Reservation, linking a collection of public swimming beaches, boat launches, parks, playgrounds, areas of critical environmental concern, and reservations.[40] The project culminated with an annual festival featuring guided canoe trips, fishing lessons, boat cruises, and other activities designed to draw attention to the river's recreational possibilities. A park is "accessible," according to planners, if a user resides within a quarter mile of its edge, and the Neponset River Greenway contained far more edge along its eight-mile course than a traditional park in its circumference. Not only was it accessible to more residents, but it cut across communities both rich and poor, making its access more equitable. It not only democratized open space but helped unify communities along its banks, bringing together people of different cultures, classes, and races—a benefit of green spaces Frederick Law Olmsted recognized as early as the 1870s. "On a town sidewalk strangers may make eye contact, but that's all," recreation specialist Anne Lusk pointed out. "On a [greenway] path ... they smile, say hello, and pet one another's dogs."[41]

As the Neponset project neared completion, it revealed one of the dangers of community-supported greenway projects. The city's newest scenic and recreational asset not only served neighboring communities but also attracted outside investors interested in building luxury apartments, condominiums, and townhouses, including a twelve-story, 280-unit Neponset Landing in Quincy near the recently opened Pope John Paul II Park. According to a state senator, the greenway project brought to light "the majestic beauty of the Neponset River to all of us—including developers," and as one of these developers enthused, "It's so close to the city with all of the state parkland around it. It's like being in the middle of nowhere." Gentrification promised several community benefits, including investment spin-offs, more public services, a stronger political constituency, a larger tax base, and high-visibility community leaders. Diversifying income levels helped break up the "monoculture of poverty" in the lower Neponset neighborhoods. But gentrification also brought potential for escalating real-estate prices and displacement. These impacts were not easily sorted out, but clearly a shadow lingered over the greenway project.[42]

Despite this danger, greenways proved immensely popular in both urban and rural settings across New England. In rural areas the most popular projects included the Eastern Trail in Maine running south of Portland along the

Scarborough Marsh, the Washington Secondary Bike Path in Rhode Island, the Farmington Canal Heritage Trail in Connecticut, and greenways fringing the Connecticut, Housatonic, Nashua, Sudbury, and Saco Rivers. A 2002 inventory brought to light some 19,011 miles of trails and greenways in New England, including the Appalachian Trail, the Connecticut River National Heritage Corridor, and sections of the proposed East Coast Greenway stretching from Maine to Florida. Rural greenways were important in knitting together fragmented ecosystems, conducting wildlife from one protected area to the next, preserving diverse habitats, and providing long stretches of secondary-succession growth for edge-loving plants, animals, birds, and insects.[43]

Urban greenways, like their rural counterparts, were multiple-purpose projects—places for picnicking, walking, jogging, bicycling, roller-skating, horse riding, cross-country skiing, fishing, canoeing, kayaking, or simply escaping the noise and bustle of the city. The healthy recreational activities they invited contributed to the fight against obesity, diabetes, heart attack, stroke, arthritis, and hypertension—diseases common in poor and minority neighborhoods.[44] Urban greenways cut across economic, racial, and ethnic divides, equalizing access to these benefits and allowing people of diverse backgrounds to find their own meaning in nature. They were as close to natural conditions as was possible in an inner-city environment. Cutting across the urban landscape, they illustrated the linkages between riparian buffer, woodland, wetland, and meadow. They encouraged a richer and more nuanced appreciation for nature than traditional parks.[45]

Urban greenways were designed primarily as recreational resources, but they provided important ecological benefits as well. Their varied terrains and diverse plant assemblages offered a broad range of habitats for edge-loving animals. They were home to rapidly reproducing prey species important to urban predators, and they provided corridors allowing wildlife to move between green spaces. Their grasses and trees slowed runoff, prevented erosion, filtered airborne particulates, provided shade, and absorbed solar energy, dissipating the heat reflected off concrete surfaces.[46] They discouraged floodplain development, giving streams room to meander and dissipate energy in flood time. They filtered water running off the streets and helped keep river waters clean. New York City officials built a greenway along Staten Island's marshes and by using the wetlands to filter processed effluent and storm water saved the city around $50 million over a conventional separated storm-water and sewage system. Sorting through ecological services like these inspired a new science of urban ecology devoted to edge effects, hydrological properties, and transmissions between diverse habitats. How much restoration was necessary, ecologists might ask, to ensure functionality in the fragmented city environment? How much redundancy did greenways require to account for changes in these exceptionally dynamic ecosystems?[47]

Urban planners found greenways helpful in breaking up the city's visual monotony; separating conflicting land uses; protecting natural, cultural, and historical features; and increasing visitation to parks and other recreational features. And finally, greenways were important as outdoor classrooms for nature interpretation and community interaction. Unlike park development, greenway design and development typically depended on community volunteers, civic organizers, teachers, and schoolchildren. Projects brought together people of various ethnic, class, and racial backgrounds and taught volunteers, especially children, to see nature as part of their neighborhood environment.[48]

Greenway planning required a keen understanding of both natural and human ecologies. A single greenway could conserve wildlife habitat, encourage health and fitness, mute traffic noise, absorb dust and air pollution, attract tourists, introduce inner-city residents to nature, educate schoolchildren, secure historic sites, improve water quality, and prevent floods. To maximize these multiple benefits, planners carefully weighed the greenway's potential across various natural environments and urban neighborhoods. Landscape architects analyzed the plan's aesthetic effects, hydrologists assessed its potential for flood control, environmental officers appraised its capacity for reducing non-point-source pollution, soil scientists gauged its contribution to slowing sediment flows, and city planners determined its capacity for knitting together fragmented landscapes. To all of this, residents living nearby added their own particular needs and understandings. All parties had to agree on issues like landscaping features, park facilities, and retention or removal of dams, industrial buildings, and other structures that had become part of a river's history. Whether the planners were public or private, grassroots or professional, they had to decide how wild the urban wilderness was to be. Planning a greenway, as one scientist concluded, required "strategic postmodern consensus building among many constituent interests." Without these negotiated understandings, projects courted vandalism, apathy, and forms of public resistance.[49]

Green Grows the City: Democratizing Boston's Vacant Lots

Neighborhood groups were invited to participate in building greenways, but they played a more prominent role in greening the city by planting gardens in vacant lots. Gardening had been part of urban working-class life at least since the English enclosures, and as European cities grew congested, residents joined together to rent and farm small empty plots on the cities' outskirts. In early America working-class and immigrant families tended plots and kept small livestock between or behind the tenements. Based on this tradition, some mayors, beginning in the 1893 depression, encouraged unemployed workers to cultivate their cities' unused land. During the two world wars city dwellers planted Victory Gardens to supplement their diets and demonstrate their patriotism.[50]

The 1970s brought a resurgence in this tradition. The middle-class flight to the suburbs, coupled with downtown disinvestment, left numerous lots vacant, and residents, especially recent immigrants from agrarian countries, seized the opportunity to cultivate these abandoned lands as a supplemental food source. At first, the appropriation of unused land was informal. Residents banded together to plant flowers in the otherwise dreary plots, then to replace the sterile, rubble-strewn soil with loam. "A vibrant kaleidoscope of colors" blossomed, and this was followed by a more serious effort at growing vegetables and fruits. To establish control over land they did not own, gardeners fenced the lots, built paths, and established family plots. Neighborhood groups became associations and sought ways to perpetuate their claims, which were viable only as long as financial considerations discouraged development. The effort, according to Lanae Handy of the South End Lower Roxbury Open Space Land Trust, was "more than just the physical appeal of seeing things growing in the inner city." Gardening opened up a whole new perspective on the neighborhood. "It lets light in."[51]

When the civil rights movement swept through the cities, occupying vacant plots became a form of resistance against absentee owners and aloof city officials. In the mid-1970s a rapid rise in food prices caused by the energy crisis, coupled with a surge in new immigrant arrivals, put the cities' thousands of vacant lots in new perspective. In Boston the BRA realized that gardening kept vacant lots clear of weeds and rubbish, and administrators began working with community organizers to promote the movement. Activist Melvin King, elected to the state legislature in 1972, further legitimized urban gardens in 1974 by sponsoring a Massachusetts Gardening and Farm Act that gave citizens the right to cultivate vacant public land at no cost until a higher use was determined. When Kevin White was elected mayor in 1976, his administration used federal Community Development block grants to clear the lots and provide fencing, water, shrubs, and trees. Working with King, White had National Guard soldiers deliver three thousand yards of topsoil in exchange for a free community-sponsored lunch.[52]

Urban gardens, like greenways, were hybrid developments that brought together preservationist and philanthropic organizations, neighborhood groups, and public agencies. The Southwest Corridor Community Farm, for instance, was set in motion by the Jamaica Plain Ecumenical Social Action Committee, the Roxbury Action Program, and the South End Garden Project; it was built on state-owned land; and it was partially funded through the city's Comprehensive Employment and Training program. Other gardens received similar support from organizations as widespread as the BRA, the School Department, the Housing Authority, the Department of Neighborhood Development, the Suffolk County Extension Service, and the Department of Parks and Recreation. Together, these agencies owned more than a quarter of the properties on which the gardens were located. Activists formed umbrella organizations like the Boston Urban Gardeners, the Highland Park 400, the Southwest Corridor Community Farm, the Lennox Kendall Community Garden, the South End Lower Roxbury Open Space Land Trust, and the Dorchester Gardenlands Preserve. The combined efforts of city officials and grassroots groups, together with established organizations like the BNAN, the Trustees of Reservations, the Trust for Public Lands, Massachusetts Audubon, and the Boston Horticultural Society, secured more than half of Boston's community gardens against development by the mid-1990s. Harvard graduate students drew up designs for gardens, community groups recruited volunteers, garden clubs helped lay them out, and students in college landscape programs helped manage them.[53]

The most important of these umbrella organizations was the Boston Urban Gardeners, founded in 1977 by four Boston groups seeking city support to protect their lots. Using foundation money and Community Action Program and Community Services block grants, BUG volunteers located vacant land; tracked down owners; consulted with individual gardeners; obtained plants, seeds, compost, and manure; promoted farmers markets; and set up a training program at Roxbury Community College. BUG lobbied municipal agencies, which were ambivalent about locking up lots with real-estate prices trending upward, and in 1987 it surveyed vacant land and with BRA help established the South End Open Space Land Trust. By the end of the century Boston led the nation in the number of community gardens, with sixty owned and administered by municipal and state agencies and others under the supervision of nonprofits like BUG, BNAN, the Dorchester Gardenlands Preserve, and the South End Lower Roxbury Open Space Land Trust. The grassroots movement that sprouted in the city's vacant lots bore fruit—and flowers.[54]

In 1990 BUG and the Southwest Corridor Community Farm conveyed their funds and properties to the BNAN. The merger of the three organizations created a unified, city-wide umbrella program staffed with organizers, designers, technical advisers, and landscapers firmly rooted in the neighborhoods they served. In 2014 BNAN affiliated with the Trustees of Reservations, which allowed this venerable preservationist organization to expand its conservation mission into the city. BNAN remained a separate organization with thirty-seven community gardens and several educational and community organizing programs, but the affiliation with the Trustees accelerated nonprofit land acquisition in Boston. Under the Trustees' Seed, Sow & Grow Program, the number of gardens in the city continued to increase.[55]

Back in the early 1970s community gardens were viewed as temporary improvements on weed-filled and littered vacant lots awaiting development. By 1989 Boston's 120 gardens served as essential sources of food and surrogate parks sporting trellises, trees, gazebos, fountains, benches, and barbecue pits. More than half came with trust deeds that guaranteed their status in perpetuity. Across the country a survey of twenty-four cities found 2,318 gardens growing an estimated $1.2 million in produce each season. Creating and maintaining these gardens provided important lessons in neighborhood self-help. When the Clinton Community Garden in New York City was slated for development, neighbors organized a fund-raising campaign, sold square inches of the plot for five dollars apiece, and generated such an outpouring of support from across the country that local officials withdrew the lot from its disposition rolls. The Trust for Public Land helped the gardeners form a land trust, and the funds raised in the square-inch campaign were set aside for capital improvements.[56]

Urban gardeners, as BUG's Charlotte Kahn put it, were "beautifying from within." The gardens enriched the social fabric of the neighborhood as residents interacted over carrots and peas, around barbecues, and in lawn chairs. Immigrants or migrants who grew up in farm country stayed in touch with their past, and neighbors with limited access to supermarkets ate fresh food. Young people learned new skills working in summer programs sponsored by community action organizations or city agencies. Families exercised more, stayed in touch with neighbors, and ate more nutritious food. Neighborhoods were empowered, but mostly, as Jim Alicata of the Massachusetts Department of Food and Agriculture pointed out, "people like to see things grow."[57]

For many, the true value of the garden was cultural affirmation. Immigrants grew crops their parents and grandparents grew and introduced their children to old-country roots. Gardens reflected the mosaic of urban cultures in the city. Italian gardeners laid out compact raised beds, added grape trellises and religious statuettes, and grew tomatoes, zucchini, peppers, greens, onions, beans, cucumber, and basil mixed or in close proximity—a traditional companion planting technique that reduced pests. African American gardeners grew pole beans, string beans, okra, sweet potatoes, tomatoes, cantaloupes, corn, greens, beets, and summer squash sometimes planted in mounded rows as they do in the South. Chinese gardeners were distinctive for their hairy squash and bitter melons and Puerto Rican gardeners for their cilantro. Historian Sam Bass Warner observed that "if you walk about Boston today examining the different community gardens closely, you will find, in one or another plot, almost all the food plants of the world, and most of the gardening techniques of the various peoples and various regions of the earth."[58]

Gardens also reflected the gradual mixing of these cultures. As young professionals moved into the gentrifying neighborhoods and older gardeners passed their plots to the next generation, gardens became less culturally distinct. Gardening was also less social in the 1990s than it had been in the 1970s. "The new gardeners are so busy that they rarely have time to talk with one another." Language barriers discouraged casual interaction, as did subtle cultural tensions. Community gardens were also threatened by rising real-estate values. The movement had taken shape at a time when industrial disinvestment and out-migration left around 30 percent of Boston vacant, but by the 1990s this land was once again developable. Nevertheless, the number of protected gardens was growing. The Trustees of Reservations, the largest nonprofit garden owner in the city, secured 56 of the city's 175 gardens against development, mostly in the South End, Dorchester, Roxbury, Mattapan, Fenway, and East Boston. As some garden plots passed to developers, new opportunities appeared elsewhere, and while some neighborhoods were ethnically homogenized, others welcomed new immigrants with their own gardening cultures. "To infer that cultural practices are being lost all over Boston as a result of demographic change would be inaccurate," one study concluded. With neighborhood cooperation, city support, and outside funding, the gardens continued to serve their economic and cultural functions. A source of community pride, they persisted against the countervailing forces of gentrification and rising real-estate values.[59]

Affordable Housing and Environmental Justice: New Roles for Land Trusts

Transforming vacant lots into permanent gardens posed a dilemma for grassroots preservationists since their neighborhoods also desperately needed these open spaces for affordable housing. In the suburbs the affordable housing crisis was aggravated by large-lot zoning and other ordinances passed ostensibly to preserve rural atmosphere, which all too often implied white, middle-class Yankee demographics. To correct this problem, in 1969 Massachusetts passed an "anti-snob zoning" law that required at least 10 percent of the community's housing stock to be affordable to families earning 80 percent of the local median income. If the goal was not met, affordable-housing developers could circumvent local zoning laws. The controversy cast land-trust acquisitions, often a companion to large-lot zoning, in a less favorable light. Although almost everyone agreed that places with historic, ecological, and scenic value should be preserved, other reasons for open-space preservation seemed less appropriate in an era of skyrocketing real-estate prices, and when civil rights leaders launched a campaign against housing discrimination, this criticism sharpened. A *New York Times* correspondent noted that "more than once, land trusts have been accused of trying to prevent development of unwanted housing—low-income and otherwise—by buying up the land." According to Robert Pirani of the Regional Plan Association in New York, "Land trusts have to understand their responsibilities [and] . . . balance conservation against other kinds of human social needs."[60]

Some preservationists got the message. A southern Berkshire County trust raised money from summer residents to set up a low-interest loan fund for county residents seeking housing. Others worked with developers to build affordable homes in clusters, leaving open space around them. The more direct remedy, however, was a new form of preservation organization called the community land trust (CLT). Like traditional trusts, these were private, nonprofit corporations formed for removing land from the speculative market. They differed, however, in leasing the land to prospective home owners rather than leaving it as open space. Tenants could build homes and other structures and sell them to recoup their investment, but the land itself remained in the hands of the trust.[61]

Much of the credit for the CLT goes to Robert Swann, an activist influenced by the social theories of Henry George, who in the late nineteenth century criticized landlords for profiting off what he called the unearned increment in rising property values. Swann spent five years in prison as a conscientious objector and then went south to help rebuild Black churches firebombed by white supremacists. There he met Slater King, a cousin of Martin Luther King, and together they founded New Communities, a CLT for landless Black sharecroppers in Georgia. Swann authored *The Community Land Trust: A Guide to the New Model for Land Tenure in America*, which became the movement's authoritative text. With back-to-the-land theorist Ralph Borsodi, Swann established the E. F. Schumacher Society, later named the Institute for Community Economics, and through this organization he inspired the founding of CLTs around the world.[62]

The first inner-city CLT was formed by an ecumenical group in Cincinnati in 1980 to combat gentrification in a low-income African American neighborhood. Boston's City-Wide Land Trust and the Lower Roxbury Tenant's Cooperative followed in 1985. The town of Shirley in Massachusetts used state and private funds to preserve forty acres of land for nine low-cost single-family homes for first-time buyers. The Sam Ely Community Land Trust in Maine, the Community Land Trust in western Massachusetts, the Voluntown Peace Trust in Connecticut, and the New Hampshire Rural Land Trust developed similar strategies. City officials, initially suspicious, grew more supportive when they realized that CLTs offered cheap, nonconfrontational solutions to the housing crisis.[63] The city of Bellingham, Washington, for instance, committed $10 million in public funds to help develop a district-wide CLT, and Minneapolis, Minnesota, and Lawrence, Kansas, established interest-free loans forgiven if the CLT met the cities' performance standards. The Hearthstone Land Trust in New Hampshire began in 1978 when a farmer found he could no longer afford to maintain his 220 acres. Rather than sell to a developer, he sold some of the land to a traditional land trust, subdivided other parcels for a CLT, and farmed the remainder. Burlington, Vermont, took the lead in supporting CLTs in 1984 shortly after socialist Bernie Sanders was elected mayor. The city set up a trust to purchase land and build or renovate single-family homes, condominiums, and apartments. Four years after its founding, the trust controlled $3 million in property.[64]

The number of CLTs grew rapidly in the 1980s as a result of sharp rises in housing costs, reductions in federal housing assistance, growing acceptance by public officials and philanthropic funders, and aggressive campaigns from Swann's Institute for Community Economics. The 1990 National Affordable Housing Act provided federal funding for common-land housing, and this boosted confidence among private mortgage lenders and local governments. By the first decade of the new century activists had formed more than 240 CLTs across the country, with the largest number in Washington, California, Florida, New York, and Massachusetts. Burlington's trust, one of the largest in the country, managed fifteen hundred apartments and leased land for five hundred owner-occupied homes.[65]

Affordable housing was part of a broader set of issues affecting poor communities and communities of color, whose neighborhoods not only had fewer parks, gardens, and other environmental amenities but also contained more environmental health hazards, including toxic industrial residues. People of color and low-income residents were three to four times more likely to live in contaminated neighborhoods than their white, middle-class counterparts. The nationally publicized Love Canal protests at Niagara Falls and similar incidents involving chemical plants, waste facilities, and trash incinerators across the country came together as a grassroots movement that included thousands of local organizations. The driving force, as historian Robert Bullard pointed out, was the racial, ethnic, and class segregation of American cities that made poor neighborhoods easy targets for polluters. Ironically, new environmental safeguards increased these inequities by giving wealthier citizens effective legal tools for fighting off industrial hazards, forcing polluters to seek out neighborhoods less likely to mount legal resistance.[66]

Environmental justice, a fusion of environmental and civil rights protest, developed in a complicated social milieu in which problems of toxic contamination and polluted air were intertwined with social problems like joblessness, poor housing prospects, inadequate educational opportunities, substance abuse, official neglect, and deteriorating infrastructure. As in any human ecology, these issues were interrelated, and a crisis in any single area created negative feedback loops that resulted in an overall climate of defeat. Conversely, successes in environmental issues could initiate a spiral of community revival. By the early 1990s inner-city neighborhoods from South Central Los Angeles to South Bronx, New York, were engaging this dynamic of hope.[67]

Mainstream organizations were poorly suited to take on these inner-city environmental issues. Traditionally oriented to wilderness and other public land issues, these organizations were slow to accept the idea that cities also faced environmental problems and that these problems had class and racial implications. Most mainstream organizations assumed a postmaterialist world in which people with relatively high standards of living could focus on quality-of-life concerns rather than matters of food, housing, and income security. While traditional environmentalists were protecting remote stands of old-growth forests and free-flowing rivers, urban activists were fighting to improve the environments in which they lived and worked.[68]

Environmental justice activists needed new organizations adapted to inner-city problems in diverse neighborhoods. Unlike mainstream organizations, which were centralized, professionalized, and national in scope, environmental justice organizations were built from the ground up and remained tied to a single community, each with its own race and ethnic makeup and particular set of issues. Activists reached out to larger environmental groups, as they did to philanthropic foundations, religious organizations, and civic leaders, but they remained independent. The movement—the new voice of inner-city land preservation—was pluralistic, inclusive, and democratic to the core. Activists adopted a more holistic approach to solving environmental issues, which included not only conditions of physical place but also social problems like housing, jobs, health care, policing, municipal services, infrastructure, and education. Open spaces became tools for addressing these problems.[69]

In Boston environmental justice strategies were shaped by the social trauma of urban renewal in the South End. In the early nineteenth century the South End hosted upper-class residents spilling out from Beacon Hill in the years before the Back Bay was developed, but over the next decades the neighborhood's spacious town houses were subdivided and occupied by waves of immigrants and southern migrants. By the 1960s the South End had become the most densely populated, most diverse, and poorest neighborhood in Boston. Still, it was the heart of Boston's Black community, enlivened by nightclubs, pool halls, bars, restaurants, and jazz clubs. In the mid-1960s the BRA declared the South End a slum and in 1965 began demolition, forcing the relocation of about twenty-five thousand people. South End renewal divided the city, with real-estate agents and the BRA on one side and low-income, working-class, and minority residents on the other.[70] Organized protests saved some sections, and in the 1980s new organizations formed to prevent similar destruction in other poor neighborhoods.

Urban activists operated on three principles. First, they realized that the physical, economic, and social problems in the urban neighborhoods were interconnected. As in any ecology, streets, homes, schools, commercial buildings, organizations, and other neighborhood circumstances operated as a complex whole. Addressing inner-city problems required simultaneous, coordinated action on several fronts. Some solutions were as simple as streetside trash receptacles or basketball tourneys to keep drug dealers at bay, and others were more challenging, such as expanding the stock of affordable housing, but each affected the neighborhood in multiple ways. Second, the resolution to these problems would depend on empowering residents rather than appealing to city hall. The South End experience showed the consequences of allowing city planners to dictate solutions, and this message was repeated often in activist rhetoric. Third, organizations tapped into community resources that many outsiders overlooked, including multilingual citizens able to coordinate social and political events, local small-business owners familiar with city hall bureaucracy, underemployed residents willing to help out with community projects, vacant land that could be appropriated for community projects, and "children with dreams and talents to share." The most important of these resources was optimism. Despite the legacy of neglect and discrimination, residents believed their quality of life would improve, and they were willing to take action to see this happen.[71]

The Dudley Street neighborhood, spanning the border between Roxbury and Dorchester, was among the hardest hit by these trends in disinvestment and outmigration. The area contained about thirteen hundred vacant lots, and these attracted more than two-thirds of Boston's trash transfer stations, junkyards, dumpster storage lots, and illegal dumping grounds. Nearby bus and truck depots housed more than a thousand diesel vehicles. Few families had access to a car, and when the city abandoned the elevated transit system that served the two communities in the mid-1980s, residents were left with only limited bus service. Commuter trains ran through the neighborhood, but the Transportation Authority provided no stops near Dudley Street. These and other problems gave rise to the Roxbury-based Alternatives for Community and Environment, launched in 1993, and the Archdale Roslindale Coalition, formed in 1996. The title of the Roxbury Environmental Empowerment Project revealed a strategy common to these organizations: environmental justice campaigns would cultivate young leaders and give them the experience and confidence they needed to take on other civil rights and social justice issues.[72]

The most ambitious and successful of Boston's environmental justice organizations was the Dudley Street Neighborhood Initiative, founded in 1984 initially to block illegal dumping in the area's vacant lots. The DSNI orchestrated a "Don't Dump on Us" campaign aimed at forcing the city to close illegal trash transfer stations, clean up the lots, and remove abandoned cars from the streets. To the surprise of many, the campaign succeeded, and activists went on to force the city to restore the rail stop. With this momentum DSNI broadened its agenda. The organization's concern for neighborhood life was ensured in the bylaws, which mandated an executive board made up of an equal number of Black, White, Latino/Latina, and Cape Verdian members, along with representatives from local businesses, community service agencies, and area churches. The well-attended meetings were translated into three languages. With this backing and a succession of active, outspoken executive directors, the DSNI became "one of the most vocal neighborhood groups in the chorus of organizations vying for City Hall's attention."[73]

Buoyed by funds from the nonprofit Riley Foundation, the DSNI took on the challenge of forcing the city to remediate hazardous wastes in the vacant lots. It promoted lead-poisoning awareness, sponsored annual neighborhood cleanups, hosted multicultural festivals, and set up a summer youth camp. The DSNI's increasingly visible activities attracted young people to help with neighborhood cleanup, peer mentoring, mural painting, summer program staffing, the annual multicultural arts festival, and the community gardens. Some served on the DSNI board of directors and its committees, underscoring the organization's commitment to a shared vision of revitalization. By the 1990s the organization was nationally recognized not only for its accomplishments but also for its effective and inclusive organizational strategies.[74]

In neighborhood surveys conducted by the DSNI and BRA, citizens expressed hopes for a village center in the Dorchester-Roxbury area with an alternative public school, community garden, greenhouse, lifelong learning center, and social services offices. As they envisioned it, the village center would be surrounded by ethnic restaurants, art galleries, boutiques, bookstores, jazz clubs, a theater with films in different languages, and blocks of affordable housing. When the Scott & Duncan furniture factory in Dorchester went out of business, the Federal Deposit Insurance Corporation sold the building to the DSNI for a dollar, and with a $1 million grant the organization cleaned out the industrial chemicals and in 2006 resold the building to the city for office space. The building anchored the village center, creating new jobs and spurring small-business investment. The Dudley center was a grassroots project involving more than 180 residents and organizations, with land-use decisions firmly in the hands of the community itself.[75]

With a $750 million city renovation project slated for the area, the DSNI was racing against the clock to ensure affordable housing before gentrification forced up land values. Boston had the lowest rate of home ownership in the nation and the highest income inequality of any major city, and by the mid-1980s homes in nearby South End, worth $20,000 a few years earlier, were selling as condos for $80,000. Residents in Dorchester and Roxbury worried that a similar wave of development would sweep through their own long-neglected neighborhoods, and indeed speculators were beginning to purchase land in anticipation of a housing rush.[76]

The Dudley Street neighborhood's biggest challenge was "development without displacement"—revitalizing the community without inviting gentrification. DSNI president Che Madyun put it succinctly: "If Roxbury becomes another South End, we'll be pushed out of here before we know what hit us." To this end, the DSNI needed to exercise eminent domain over the neighborhood's vacant lots, taking control of the same legal procedure that had displaced so many in the South End. There were no precedents for granting these powers to a community-based organization, but city councilor Ray Flynn was running for mayor against activist Mel King and needed support in the Black community. Flynn won the election, and after four years of court battles, the BRA granted the DSNI eminent domain rights in privately owned vacant land in the Dudley Triangle. In 1992 the Ford Foundation provided $2 million to buy the land for redevelopment, and with federal, philanthropic, and city funds, the DSNI's adjunct, Dudley Neighbors, Inc., began forcing speculators to sell at current prices rather than wait for gentrification.[77]

Over the next two decades Dudley Neighbors transformed more than half of the thirteen hundred abandoned parcels into more than four hundred affordable houses along with playgrounds, parks, gardens, a greenhouse, an urban farm, a community center, a new school, and a town common, making the organization one of the nation's most acclaimed CLTs. The Dudley Triangle, once a "breeding ground for violent criminals and drug dealers," boasted mixed housing, parks, community gardens, and an ethnically diverse population—hallmarks of a vibrant, equitable, and sustainable community.[78]

Other Boston-area CLTs followed the DSNI's example. The nonprofit Nuestra Comunidad Development Corporation purchased abandoned lots from the city at $500 per parcel, built affordable homes, and converted a former bus yard into a walkable "creative village" with housing units, a grocery store, shops, offices, a public market, and a plaza. The Chinatown Community Land Trust, a coalition of residents, business owners, and activists, shielded the district's historic row houses against gentrification, and the North Dorchester

Beautification Program, Roxbury Action Program, and Dorchester Bay Economic Development Corporation renovated abandoned apartments in neighborhoods on Boston's south side. The City-Wide Land Trust, a network of CLTs formed in the mid-1980s, purchased and rehabilitated buildings as homes and apartments for low- and moderate-income buyers. Staying one step ahead of the speculators, these organizations transformed unused land into a community resource, providing a chance at home ownership for those locked out of the market by rising real-estate prices.[79]

The struggle for affordable housing added one more facet to a long tradition of New England land stewardship. It also highlighted the potential for revitalizing the environmental movement by attracting new constituencies; highlighting racial, ethnic, gender, and class disparities; encouraging diversity in projects and membership; and inventing new organizational models based on grassroots participation. Preservation strategies had changed a great deal since local land trusts first appeared on the scene in the late 1960s. What began as a means of ensuring rural atmosphere in suburban communities expanded in the next decade to include a variety of environmental considerations, and in the 1980s and 1990s the preservation movement shifted to the cities to help revitalize residential neighborhoods with third spaces, urban wilds, greenways, community gardens, and affordable housing. In each of these iterations the preservation movement reflected the changing sentiments of the grassroots organizations that drove it. Urban activists in the early 2000s boldly claimed a new environmental justice motto: "Take a Stand, Own the Land." Preservationists had been proclaiming that sentiment, in different guises, since the Trustees of Public Reservations acquired its first property in 1891.[80]

CHAPTER 6

Middle-Way Preservation in the Era of Ecosystem Management, 1990–2010

During the 1990s New England land trusts faced their ultimate challenge when millions of acres of private timberlands in the Northeast underwent a dramatic change in ownership. Responding to global competition and new corporate tax policies, northeastern pulp and paper producers orchestrated some of the largest private land transactions in American history, and when these lands came on the market, trusts formed complex alliances and achieved preservation successes on a scale never before attempted. Having acquired hundreds of thousands of acres of remote forests in Maine, New Hampshire, Vermont, and New York, trust officers found themselves at the vortex of a changing interdisciplinary science of ecosystem management. Battles over the snail darter in Tennessee and the northern spotted owl in the Pacific Northwest in the 1970s and 1980s drove home the realization that the Endangered Species Act, despite its successes in slowing the rate of extinctions, was not saving the ecosystems that sustained these imperiled species. The next step, preservationists realized, was a strategic system of protecting not an individual species or a specific habitat but an entire ecosystem. As a dominant element in the preservation movement, trusts once again adapted, this time in concert with the new science of ecosystem management.[1]

The history of preservation in New England can be divided roughly into four phases, the first being the early years of the Trustees of Public Reservations, and the second the formation of local trusts in the suburbs. In the third phase, neighborhood activists used trusts as tools for transforming underutilized urban spaces into greenways, gardens, urban wilds, and sites for affordable housing. The fourth phase saw preservationists engaged in the difficult transition from saving land to saving landscapes, a passage that culminated in creating an immense network of reserves and easements in the Northeast from New York's Adirondack Mountains through northern Vermont, New Hampshire, and Maine to the shores of the Gaspé Peninsula. The meaning of open space—its dimensions, values, benefits, and composition—differed across these four phases, but the twin goals of providing unlimited public access and preserving nature remained constant. This chapter considers the fourth phase of New England preservation in the decades between 1990 and 2010 as land trusts redefined open space on a landscape scale and experimented with the highly innovative practice of multijurisdictional management and integrated stewardship across these broader protective networks.

Networking the Land-Trust Movement

Preservationists faced a series of challenges at the end of the century. Real-estate prices were rising and recreational and environmental needs growing more complex. "Parcel-by-parcel protection will never be enough," Jean Hocker of the Land Trust Alliance asserted in 1996. "Whole systems need . . . to be protected—watersheds, viewsheds, habitat, ecosystems, trail systems." Preservationists responded by piecing together incredibly complicated alliances involving local and national trusts, state and federal public agencies, landowners, individual and foundation donors, and a wide range of nonprofit organizations. In 1976 the Trustees of Reservations, which had worked almost alone during the previous eighty years, declared teamwork an "essential ingredient of success," and the sharp rise in real-estate prices over the next two decades made the point self-evident.[2] In 1988 the Connecticut legislature set aside $7 million for conservation purchases, but at a time when shorefront property in Fairfield County sold for $1 million an acre, the gesture was painfully inadequate. In some cases trusts overcame this obstacle as they had in the past—by courting private donations. A development firm in Kennebunk, Maine, for instance, gave a logged-over wetland known as Punky Swamp to the local land trust because it had virtually no commercial value. It did, however, provide habitat for grouse, moose, deer, and cottontail rabbits and filtered water flowing into a nearby river. During a real-estate downturn in 1987, landowners sold a $3 million Kennebunk parcel to a local trust at below-market prices in order to capture corporate tax savings slated to expire at the end of 1988, and during the same downturn a developer in Dover, New Hampshire, abandoned plans for 350 homes around a golf course and recouped part of his investment in tax deductions by donating 402 acres to the state's Land Conservation Investment Program.[3] More commonly, however, trusts acquired multimillion-dollar parcels by joining with other preservation organizations and seeking funding from state or federal sources. Preservationists described this alliance as a "middle-way" approach, neither fully public nor fully private but combining the advantages of both: the financial and legal power of the government and the initiative, volunteer enthusiasm, and administrative direction of the private, nonprofit world. One of the great innovations of the decade, middle-way preservation achieved goals that would have seemed impossible a decade earlier.

These strategies divided the movement into larger trusts taking on ambitious landscape-scale projects and smaller organizations addressing local needs. Small trusts remained viable, but they led a precarious existence. Volunteer staff and high turnover left them poorly prepared to deal with complex financial, legal, and ecological issues or with sophisticated land-development corporations. Part-time officers struggled to meet the multiple demands for educational outreach, fund-raising, lobbying, and land stewardship. According to environmental policy experts Sally Fairfax and Darla Guenzler, one recurring problem in the land-trust movement was that "trusts are so easy to establish that the risk of doing it badly, without proper planning, is high." The Souhegan Valley Land Trust, southern New Hampshire's first local nonprofit preservation group, achieved considerable success in rallying towns to save Upper Purgatory Falls in Hillsborough County, but by 2003 its membership had almost disappeared. Like many small trusts, Souhegan persisted by networking with larger organizations, in this case the Seacoast Land Trust, which subsequently combined with still more trusts to become the Southeast Land Trust of New Hampshire. By joining these regional partnerships, local trusts gained expertise, confidence, and financial clout while adding their own intense conviction and local ecological understanding to a movement that was growing in sophistication and professionalization. Middle-way strategies guided them into the more complex world of landscape-scale preservation.[4]

In 2003 the TOR created a revolving fund to help conservation commissions, land trusts, and other local organizations purchase land. The move was part of a larger trend in the formation of statewide, regional, and national umbrella organizations. In the Berkshire Hills Donald Miller, publisher of the *Berkshire Eagle*, and George Wislocki, a preservationist from New York, formed the Berkshire Natural Resources Council in 1967 and in league with local conservation commissions, trusts, and other preservation organizations established the Berkshire County Land Trust and Conservation Fund, dedicated to operating, as Wislocki said, where it would be "impractical for larger conservation organizations, such as the Trustees of Reservations, and smaller town conservation agencies to involve themselves." The trust published a journal, sponsored conferences and training sessions, and nurtured land trusts in a dozen Berkshire towns. In the 1970s it brought together local trusts, conservation commissions, and other organizations to build a protected corridor along the Housatonic River and along a nine-mile stretch of the Yokun Ridge in the Taconic Mountains.[5]

The Maine Coast Heritage Trust, established in 1970, provided technical assistance to smaller trusts in the coastal areas of Maine and in 1995 created the Maine Land Trust Network to take on this supporting role statewide. The Society for the Protection of New Hampshire Forests served a similar function in that state, as did the Vermont Land Trust, the Massachusetts Land Trust Coalition, the Connecticut Land Trust Council, and the Rhode Island Land Trust Council. The latter was an important source of technical support since only about seven of the state's forty or so trusts had paid staff. In addition, several national trusts stood behind the effort to coordinate trust activity. The Nature Conservancy, the earliest of these, was joined by the Trust for Public Land, the American Land Trust, the Land Trust Alliance, and the American Farmland Trust, while various older conservation and preservation organizations on occasion came to the aid of small trusts by holding workshops, publishing information, offering grants, and providing legal advice. These larger organizations were truly the architects of middle-way preservation.[6]

States as Allies

Middle-way preservation relied on coalitions of private organizations, but its signature characteristic was partnering with public agencies. States became interested in these alliances in the early 1980s as they launched their own preservation initiatives. In 1963 Vermont governor Philip Hoff established a Central Planning Office tasked with, among other things, protecting the "typical Vermont" scene of farms, forests, and villages from billboard advertising, junkyards, and commercial buildings. In 1970 International Paper Company announced plans to build two thousand condominium units in Wilmington, a town of two thousand people. State legislators responded with a Land Use and Development Law—Act 250—that regulated development on tracts greater than ten acres, housing projects that included ten or more units within a five-mile radius, and projects along lakes or rivers, on steep slopes, over water supply and headwater areas, and at elevations above twenty-five hundred feet.[7]

Despite its many restrictions, the act had no provisions for actually preserving Vermont's open spaces, and with speculation escalating, a group of citizens formed the Vermont Land Trust in 1977. Over the next decade a coalition of trust officers, conservationists, and affordable-housing advocates lobbied the state for support, and in 1987 the legislature established a Vermont Housing and Conservation Trust Fund to partner with nonprofits in protecting farms and natural areas and finance affordable housing. The board was funded by a combination of private donations and revenues from a tax on speculative property transfers. Preservation and affordable housing, one observer explained, did not usually overlap since "the very nature of one endeavor frequently excludes the other." Vermont, however, made it work. In a typical maneuver, the Upper Valley Land Trust borrowed funds from the board to purchase a 150-acre farm in Norwich. To pay off the loan, the trust sold one parcel for affordable housing and another for residential development under a conservation easement. The rest was left in open space. Despite some criticism from private apartment owners, the program enjoyed widespread public support. By 2001 the Vermont Land Trust had preserved more than 330,000 acres of farm- and forestland, including 240 farms and 6.5 percent of Vermont's privately owned forest. It rehabilitated historic buildings, revitalized downtown districts, protected recreational resources, preserved ecologically critical areas, and leveraged hundreds of millions of dollars for affordable housing and rehabilitation.[8]

In 1985, at a time when New Hampshire's population was growing faster than any state east of the Mississippi, Paul Bofinger of the Society for the Protection of New Hampshire Forests approached the Business and Industry Association of New Hampshire, the Audubon Society, and the state Fish and Game, Parks and Recreation, and Agriculture Commissions to form a nonprofit Trust for New Hampshire Lands. The legislature, Bofinger pointed out, had made no commitment to land preservation since 1963 when in a "rare moment of largesse" it authorized a $9 million bond issue to expand its park system. No private land trust could compensate for this shortfall, Bofinger realized, but by working together, land trusts, business organizations, trail clubs, conservation commissions, garden clubs, rod and gun clubs, churches, schools, community groups, civic organizations, philanthropic foundations, and the state government could save the "best of what was left of New Hampshire." In 1986 Bofinger's consortium raised nearly $4 million and approached the legislature for additional funding. Preservation was expensive, Representative Judd Gregg admitted, but "the cost . . . of losing . . . the character of this state, its natural beauty, the mountains, the lakes, the streams, the rural environment would far exceed the dollar cost of this bill." In 1987 legislators overwhelmingly endorsed a Land Conservation Investment Program with $20 million in funds. Bofinger deemed this cooperative effort the "New Hampshire way of doing things."[9]

The funding was proportioned between lands of statewide significance—lakeshores, aquifer recharge areas, critical habitat, wetlands, scenic areas—and lands of local significance, with towns submitting proposals for the latter. Below-market sales, donations, and use of easements in lieu of purchases expanded the reach of the program, as did a sharp decline in real-estate prices in the early 1990s. The trust invested $46.4 million to acquire land worth $83.3 million. Funds ran out in 1993, and true to its mission the trust expired, with the equivalent of 1 New Hampshire acre in 57 protected—the highest ratio in New England given the inclusion of the White Mountain National Forest. In 2000 New Hampshire created a Land and Community Heritage Investment Program to support local land-trust activities with funding from the Conservation License Plate Program and fees imposed on deed transfers. The program helped conserve more than 263,000 additional acres of forest- and farmland.[10]

A controversy over public access to beaches spurred similar preservation initiatives in Massachusetts and Maine. After years of traffic congestion along the coast and "elbow-to-elbow people at public beaches," towns and private owners began closing off outside access to the shore. In Massachusetts shore access was governed by laws dating from colonial times. Originally land in the intertidal zone was public property, but in 1641–47 the General Court transferred ownership to abutting landowners to encourage private wharf construction. At the same time, however, the court allowed public access for fishing, fowling, and navigation, and these antiquated terms became the subject of much legal debate as wealthy coastal property owners moved to defend their privacy. Beachgoers took to carrying fishing rods or shell-fishing equipment to gain access. In order to clarify the issue, the Massachusetts legislature proposed an act authorizing the public's right of passage, but in 1974 the Massachusetts Supreme Judicial Court reaffirmed the beach owners' claims.

In 1972, in the midst of the court battle, Massachusetts passed its first open-space bond issue since World War II, and from that point on it continued to make park and reserve acquisitions. In 1984, at the height of the so-called Massachusetts Miracle—the economic boom based on semiconductor production—the state allocated $162 million to increase parks and reserves and three years later passed a $500 million bond measure for public lands. In 1986 the state authorized another $500 million bond to preserve farmland, coastal and floodplain areas, historic sites, and other open spaces. Thinking of the TOR's long-standing commitment to public open spaces, a *Boston Globe* reporter noted that the state's investment was a "valuable supplement to long-standing private efforts toward the preservation of natural assets."[11]

In Maine voters were likewise sensitized to open-space issues by a long court battle over beach access. Moody Beach, a mile-long stretch of sand in Wells in southern Maine, had been used for generations for public recreation, but in 1984 property owners filed a court case against the town, and as in Massachusetts the legislature enacted a Public Trust in Intertidal Land law, ensuring public access. Despite the legislative maneuver, the Maine Superior Court declared in favor of the Moody Beach property owners, and the ruling was upheld in the US Supreme Court in 1989.

In 1987, again in the midst of beach-access proceedings, voters approved a $35 million bond issue to fund the Land for Maine's Future program drafted in part by the Nature Conservancy and Maine Coast Heritage Trust. As in New Hampshire and Massachusetts, the Maine government had ignored the need for public parks for decades, partly because recreationists could hunt, fish, hike, and camp on private timberlands due to the same colonial laws that gave citizens trespass rights in Massachusetts—fish and game were public property. State parks commissioners Laurence Stuart and Ronald Speers in fact refused to acquire parklands even when the legislature allocated funds. As in New Hampshire, the turnabout in state policy had solid support from diverse groups, including wilderness advocates, recreationists, foresters, and the business community.[12]

As in New Hampshire, the agency funded local projects and purchased land directly. Unlike New Hampshire's Land Conservation Investment Program, Maine's commission was not set to expire. It received periodic funding through state bond referenda, and by the end of the century Maine had acquired a stunning assortment of mountain summits, river-access points, lake shores and pond shores, coastal islands and beaches, forests, marshlands, wildlife habitat, working farms and waterfronts, abandoned railroad corridors, and wetlands, altogether some 570,000 acres.[13]

Maine gained another sizable collection of public lands as a result of a series of articles written by Portland journalist Bob Cummings in 1972 pointing to the public reserved lots that had been set aside in each wildland township during the original state land sales to support schools when the towns were incorporated. Since much of the northern and western region remained unincorporated, timberland owners simply absorbed these "school lots" into their own working woods, and the state more or less forgot about them. Reacting to Cummings's report, a group of liberal Republican legislators led by Harrison Richardson, the state senate majority leader, launched a campaign to recover the lots, and after years of litigation state officials and private timberland owners negotiated a settlement under which the undivided public lots in each unincorporated township were consolidated into blocks of wilderness reserves. Ultimately, the settlement returned a half-million acres of wild lands to the people of Maine.[14]

During these same years Connecticut established the Recreation and Natural Heritage Trust Fund, and Rhode Island voters approved an Open Space and Recreation Grants program. Rhode Island later added more funds for open space, farmland, and watershed protection and for restoring Narragansett Bay, placing the state second among those in New England in the percentage of its total land area conserved. Connecticut's Green Plan aimed at protecting 21 percent of the state's land area by the second decade of the century, with around half of this in state-owned parks, forests, and wildlife areas.[15]

Federal Funding

Another boost for middle-way preservation was a surge in federal support for land purchases in the 1990s. The 1937 Pittman-Robertson Aid in Wildlife Restoration Act and the 1950 Dingall-Johnson Fisheries Restoration Act supported state purchases for parks, forests, and game preserves, but the key source of federal funding for preservation was the Land and Water Conservation Fund (LWCF), an outgrowth of the 1958 Outdoor Recreation Resources Review Commission. Congress approved the fund in 1965 using royalties from offshore oil and gas drilling and mineral leases on federal lands. The program, administered through the Bureau of Outdoor Recreation, was used mainly to purchase state parks and wildlife refuges, but a few entrepreneurial trusts tapped into the funds. Under the Ford, Carter, and Reagan administrations, allocations dwindled, and western states, already awash in public lands, offered no support for the program.[16]

Although the LWCF fell short of expectations, other federal agencies, for various reasons, provided matching grants that reinforced the federal commitment to land preservation. In 1986–88 fish and wildlife agencies in the United States, Canada, and Mexico joined in the North American Waterfowl Management Plan in order to stem the loss of wetlands. The NAWMP partnered with state and provincial governments and organizations like Ducks Unlimited, the Federation of State Waterfowl Associations, the Izaak Walton League, the Land Trust Alliance, and scores of local and regional trusts. In addition, the Department of Housing and Urban Development's 1961 Open-Space Program provided matching funds, and the Department of Agriculture's Greenspan program funded purchases of agricultural land under the 1965 Cropland Adjustment Act. Others included the Farmland Protection Program and the Cooperative Endangered Species Conservation Fund both established in the 1980s, the US Forest Service's Forest Legacy Program and the Department of Agriculture's Wetlands Reserve Program created in 1990, and the State Wildlife Grants Program, the Coastal Estuarine Land Conservation Program, and the Community Forest and Open Space Conservation Program created between 2000 and 2008. Of these, the Forest Legacy Program was the most useful. Created to provide funds to state agencies, it indirectly funded private stewardship organizations as well. By 2013 the program helped conserve 682,500 acres of forestland in Maine alone, this being around 30 percent of all land conserved by the program across the country. In addition to these broad funding mandates, the Interstate Commerce Commission helped the National Trails System with purchase of abandoned railroad rights-of-way; the Federal Highway Administration helped maintain boat ramps, scenic overlooks, rest areas, and buffers along scenic highways; and the Department of Agriculture's Watershed Protection and Flood Prevention program helped fund wetland purchases. The 2000 New Markets Tax Credits program supported acquisitions in depressed urban and rural areas. Local trusts employed AmeriCorps volunteers to restore stream banks, remove invasive species, and replant vegetation.[17]

By the early 2000s federal grants had become a mainstay of the land-preservation movement, sustaining local preservation efforts amid skyrocketing real-estate prices. The earliest example of middle-way preservation involved the Sudbury and Concord River marshes in central Massachusetts. In 1928 Concord resident Samuel Hoar purchased 250 acres of wetlands along the Concord River and built dikes to improve waterfowl habitat. In 1944 Hoar donated the land to the federal government, and three years later this became the Great Meadows National Wildlife Refuge. Preservationists in adjacent towns formed the Sudbury Valley Trustees in 1953. The organization worked with local officials to pass protective zoning measures, but with a national wildlife refuge already in the area, they also campaigned for federal funding. The towns, the state, the Trustees of Reservations, the Audubon Society, the Fish and Wildlife Service, and private donors worked together to enlarge the refuge. In 1999 Congress allocated $1.75 million for purchases, and this was matched by the Department of Interior's Migratory Bird Conservation Commission. This "dense mix of public and private efforts," as William Whyte called it, resulted in 3,850 acres of protected wetlands and uplands along the Sudbury, Assabet, and Concord Rivers. Similar middle-way arrangements occurred all through New England.[18] In New Hampshire, for example, several trusts and the SPNHF gained funds from the LWCF and the Forest Legacy Program to preempt a huge luxury subdivision on Lake Tarleton, and the Southeast Land Trust received $2 million from the Coastal and Estuarine Land Protection Program for the Piscassic Greenway. In Maine preservationists convinced the Fish and Wildlife Service to purchase expensive shore lands in Biddeford to enlarge the Rachel Carson National Wildlife Refuge.[19]

Open-space preservation on Block Island in Rhode Island illustrates the way federal funding could magnify the power of grassroots activism. The eleven-square-mile island contained important migratory-bird habitat, three hundred freshwater ponds, and several endangered plant and animal species, but with only six hundred full-time residents, there was little need for land preservation in the early postwar decades. The 1980s brought a boom in summer-home construction, with building permits in the small island community of New Shoreham growing from 264 in 1984 to about 440 in 1987. Townspeople approved a $1 million bond issue for land conservation, and a coalition of environmentalists, real-estate agents, and Chamber of Commerce officials formed the Block Island Land Trust in 1986, funded by a municipal tax on real-estate transfers. These local organizations received additional support from the Nature Conservancy, the state Department of Environmental Management, and the Rhode Island Audubon Society, and with funds from the LWCF and an enlargement of the Block Island National Wildlife Refuge, nearly half the island was permanently protected.[20]

Middle-Way Preservation

Middle-way strategies eased the transition from preserving land to preserving landscapes. Working with coalitions, local trusts gained energy, confidence, and funding. Newfields, New Hampshire, for instance, with a population of just over fifteen hundred, confronted plans for an eighty-nine-unit development covering about 7 percent of the town's total land area. The municipality allocated $2 million to the local land trust to purchase the property, but to muster the remaining $3.5 million, the trust obtained funding from private donors, the national Trust for Public Land, the countywide Rockingham Land Trust, and the Nature Conservancy, and since the area was part of the Atlantic flyway, the trust applied for federal grants under the North American Wetlands Conservation Act, the National Oceanic and Atmospheric Administration's Coastal and Esturarine Land Conservation Program, and Ducks Unlimited. The rest of the funding came from the state's Land and Community Heritage Investment Program and its Water Supply Land Protection Program. With land values soaring, trusts pieced together amazingly complicated funding sources to steadily increase the amount of preserved land in New England.[21]

In southern Maine, middle-way preservation reached a high point when several trusts cooperated to protect a belt of land between Mount Agamenticus in York and the coast. The project began in the 1970s when an Oklahoma oil magnate announced plans to reestablish an abandoned ski area on Mount Agamenticus and build three thousand residential units around it. The developer abandoned the project, but the incident demonstrated the mountain's vulnerability, and a few years later the state purchased seventeen hundred acres in the area. In 1999 the York Land Trust brought together representatives from the Rachel Carson National Wildlife Refuge, the Maine Department of Inland Fish and Wildlife, the Wells National Estuarine Research Reserve, the Trust for Public Land, the Nature Conservancy, the York and Kittery water districts, and several local trusts to form the Mount Agamenticus to the Sea Coalition aiming to establish a protected corridor through several ecosystems to the heights of Mount Agamenticus.[22]

The project was, in the traditional sense, a "scramble" to protect open spaces in a region undergoing rapid development. In 2002, for instance, the coalition purchased the $5.4 million Breckinridge estate on the York River with its twenty-three-room mansion, landscaped grounds, and mile-long river frontage. Despite impromptu purchases like this, the consortium remained mindful of the need to connect the area's various ecologies, which ranged from coastal salt marshes to high-elevation forests. By 2006 some ninety-five hundred acres in the six-town Mount Agamenticus region were under protection—a spectacular accomplishment given the relentless land-development pressures spreading eastward along the coast. Each reservation was valuable for its own reasons, but together they formed a comprehensive ecological mosaic.[23]

These examples mark a turning point in New England preservation. "Instead of simply reacting to emergencies... on an ad hoc basis, public and private partners are now working to identify whole priority areas and to plan in advance who is best positioned to take what role in protecting individual tracts within those larger areas." Chris Elfring, who studied the land trust movement in the late 1980s, concluded that this expansive vision required complicated alliances. "An increasingly popular trend among land trusts is to work in partnership with public agencies." Trusts provided the grassroots enthusiasm, the local knowledge of people and resources, and the flexibility necessary to address local circumstances, while state and federal agencies provided funds to mount more ambitious acquisition agendas. State research units encouraged a scientific approach to acquisition and management, but ecological understanding flowed upward as well. By joining forces with larger organizations and agencies, smaller all-volunteer trusts gained experience in professional administration and ecological management. The number of new trusts formed across the country leveled off in the 1990s, but the acreage preserved by trusts increased dramatically during the same decade, suggesting a time of maturation for the land trusts that came into being in the previous decade.[24]

Greenbelts: The Shift to Landscape-Scale Preservation

The 1990s brought two important innovations that showcased the transition from land preservation to landscape preservation, both made possible by middle-way strategies. In the first of these, planners and preservationists designed greenbelts, or zones of protected woodland or farmland that stabilized land use on the borders of towns and cities. The idea was given modern form by Ebenezer Howard who, as a way of overcoming the bleakness of England's industrial landscapes, proposed moderately sized manufacturing "garden cities" surrounded by zones in which land use was limited to farms, orchards, forests, and public buildings. The idea, incorporated into England's Green Belt Act in 1938, migrated to America as Frederick Law Olmsted's Emerald Necklace and Daniel Burnham's 1909 plan of Chicago's park system. Benton MacKaye designed the Appalachian Trail in part as a greenbelt protecting the mountains from metropolitan expansion. In the late 1940s Ottawa adopted the plan when it purchased land on the city outskirts and combined this with a military reservation to create a National Capital Greenbelt. Toronto followed with its Golden Horseshoe in 2005.[25] Greenbelts gave residents access to nature from almost any neighborhood in the city.

In New England, projects like this were difficult due to fragmented municipal jurisdictions. Still, several towns took steps to bring their public open spaces together into a greenbelt. Cape Elizabeth in Maine initiated a greenbelt plan in 1977 as a way to establish land preservation priorities, provide a communitywide perspective on open space, and encourage funding and donations. In New Hampshire, Concord created a greenbelt by limiting municipal services outside the city limits. Another greenbelt took shape in Boxford, north of Boston, when local residents formed a trust in 1953 to block development on Bald Hill. In 1961 the trust and partner organizations formed the Essex County Green Belt Association and acquired reserves in the marshes and uplands along the Ipswich and Parker Rivers. The association connected these to the Harold Parker State Forest, the Bradley Palmer State Park, and the Boxford State Forest, creating a system with enough wildland "to be the home of half the owls in eastern Massachusetts." The greenbelt drew support from the TOR, and since it included wetlands it was partially funded by the US Fish and Wildlife Service and the state's Fish and Game Division.[26] Over time the trust consolidated all of Essex County's reservations into a greenbelt separating the county from the Boston metropolitan area to the south.

New England's most ambitious greenbelt project was the Massachusetts Bay Circuit. Benton MacKaye introduced the idea in his book *The New Exploration*, proposing a belt of parks and reserves to separate Boston from the rest of eastern Massachusetts, and Charles Eliot II elaborated on MacKaye's idea in a 1929 proposal for a ring of conservancy lands fifty miles out from the city center. The project was put on hold during the Great Depression, but Eliot, who worked as a planner in Washington during the Roosevelt years, was tenacious. In 1954 he and Wayland representative Howard Russell, working with the TOR and several other conservation organizations, convinced Governor Christian Herter to revitalize the project. The state's population had doubled since 1893 when the Metropolitan Park Commission created Boston's rural reservations, and Massachusetts needed a similar matrix of open spaces farther out from the city limits. The campaign was quickened by a series of legal battles over lake and pond access and rising complaints about picnickers and hunters on private property.[27]

The proposal was again tabled in the legislature, this time due to construction of Route 128 along roughly the same corridor. Undeterred, in 1956 the trustees urged legislation calling for a coordinated plan of public and private acquisitions in a zone just outside Route 128. The legislature, lobbied by the TOR, instructed state agencies, private organizations, and town officials to work together to identify potential inclusions in a system of reservations, parks, scenic drives, wildlife sanctuaries, local trust lands, and flood-control and historic districts. Each town formed a local Bay Circuit committee, and TOR president William Greeley predicted the result would be "one of the greatest... large open spaces for public enjoyment ever conceived in this country in a heavily populated area." The legislation brought a greater degree of coordination to the state's recreational resource programs, but the Bay Circuit campaign once again fell short of full financial support.[28]

In 1982 the Department of Environmental Management released a seminal publication titled *Massachusetts Landscape Inventory: A Survey of the Commonwealth's Scenic Areas*, drawing attention to rapid development along Route 128. Shortly after the publication, the legislature allocated $3.25 million to fund a "permanent greenbelt to shape metropolitan Boston's growth." Assuming that local people best understood their own scenic, ecological, and recreational assets, planners relied on town officials, conservation commissions, land trusts, and civic organizations to map out recreational trails and bikeways, river corridors, and scenic roadways. Protecting some of the last unspoiled country roads in eastern Massachusetts was a high priority. Rural routes with lower design speeds, planners explained, could "provide genuinely intimate landscape experiences." By 2005 this public-private partnership embraced land in fifty cities and towns. The ten- to twenty-mile-wide network was the most ambitious attempt at land conservation in Massachusetts history and a testament to the state's extensive network of active and effective land trusts.[29]

In 1990 the TOR, Appalachian Mountain Club, NPS, and state Rivers and Trails Program designed a footpath through the greenbelt and encouraged towns and local trusts to integrate their own trail systems into the plan. Despite areas of dense population, planners managed to thread the trail through a continuous corridor of rural and sometimes wild territory consisting of state parks and forests, Audubon sanctuaries, Trustees of Reservations lands, Boy and Girl Scout reservations, and town and local land trust and conservation commission areas. When completed, the Bay Circuit Trail stretched two hundred miles from Newbury in a broad arc south through Concord to Duxbury, knitting together thousands of acres of protected open space. The project, which depended heavily on easements, drew support from hundreds of volunteers and a wide range of public agencies, private organizations, and landowners.[30]

Greenbelts testified to the growing sophistication of the land-preservation movement. Like greenways, they met a wide range of objectives from floodplain and habitat protection to hands-on ecological education. Designers met these goals, as the Bay Circuit demonstrated, by forming complicated public-private alliances. They brought together neighborhood volunteers, students, scientists, administrators, planners, and public officials and enlisted support across class, ethnic, and racial lines. Greenbelts, like greenways, proved immensely popular, and being in or adjacent to the cities, they touched the lives of thousands.[31]

Heritage Corridors

The second showcase innovation in landscape preservation involved sites of historical importance. Boston enjoyed a venerable tradition of saving historic buildings, with the Old South Church as its first significant preservation success. Built in 1729, Old South was abandoned in 1869 when parishioners migrated from the financial district to the Back Bay. When the property went up for sale in 1872, Boston's leading women launched a fund-raising appeal and purchased the structure from a salvage contractor. Standing on some of the most valuable real estate in America, Old South is the birthplace of the urban preservationist movement.[32]

In the mid-twentieth century Congress extended the NPS's preservation mandate to include heritage landscapes. In 1933 the NPS took charge of Civil War battlefields, and two years later it established a National Register of Historic Places. In 1949 the Park Service helped create the National Trust for Historic Preservation. The National Register and National Trust were limited to protecting individual homes, homesteads, and buildings, but in 1931 citizens of Charleston, South Carolina, established an entire historic district, and Boston followed in 1951 with the Freedom Trail. Using this model, the NPS created the Minuteman National Historic Park in Lexington and Concord in 1959, focused on the running battle between colonials and British regulars that touched off the American Revolution. In designing the corridor—the first national park unit in a suburban environment—planners maneuvered around a busy state highway and removed more than 175 homes and businesses to re-create the historic landscape. Park employees rebuilt old stone walls, cleared ancient farm fields, and reestablished working farms to demonstrate both change and continuity over the previous two hundred years.[33]

Historic districts often included sites that reflected everyday local events, and in the 1970s preserving the history of ordinary people became a central theme in preservation projects. At the University of Pennsylvania and Harvard University, graduate schools in landscape architecture began training students in vernacular landscape identification and preservation. This trend was reinforced in 1976 when Congress created the American Folk Life Center to research, document, and promote folk culture and when folk singers like Pete Seeger, Joan Baez, and the Kingston Trio popularized the musical expression of common people.[34]

Developments like these drew attention to the huge early industrial-era textile mills looming over the rivers of the Northeast. These were particularly interesting given their size, their pioneering role in the Industrial Revolution, and the craft skills evident in their construction. In 1972 the Lowell City Council set aside a "Mill and Canal District," and those interested in this development included school superintendent Patrick Mogan, who suggested reviving the city's flagging local pride by accenting its ethnic heritage and its pioneering role in the Industrial Revolution. Mogan envisioned "a new kind of national park based on labor and industrial history," and his vision was realized in 1975 when Massachusetts commissioned a Heritage State Park commemorating Lowell as the cradle of American industry. Three years later the federal government established the Lowell National Historical Park, which became a model for the Park Service's new approach preserving landscapes. Based on Lowell's success, Massachusetts created an Urban Cultural Park Program to preserve similar historic sites across the state. By 1979 the state boasted fourteen locally administered heritage parks in twenty-one cities and towns.[35]

In 1984 the Park Service launched a National Heritage Areas Program based initially in the Northeast and Midwest—regions historically underserved by national park units. The earliest examples were the Illinois and Michigan Canal National Heritage Corridor, created in 1984 along the Des Plaines River, and the Blackstone River Valley National Heritage Corridor, founded in 1986 in Massachusetts and Rhode Island. Later additions included Pennsylvania's Delaware and Lehigh Canal National Heritage Corridor, the Rivers of Steel National Heritage Area near Pittsburgh, Detroit's Motor-Cities National Heritage Area, and New York's Erie Canal National Heritage Corridor. The heritage areas varied in the way they preserved and conveyed the story of America's past. Features in the MotorCities district, for instance, were scattered across southern Michigan and included such dissimilar sites as the Henry Ford Museum, individual factories, forges, cemeteries, and estates across southeastern Michigan, and a series of local speedways. By 2013 the Park Service managed forty-nine congressionally designated historic areas.[36]

The challenge for the NPS was finding ways to protect nationally significant features scattered across a relatively large area without significantly increasing federal ownership or NPS responsibilities. Having collaborated with local entities on wild and scenic rivers and national trails, Park Service officials realized the key to success was partnering with communities and private organizations around a common goal of boosting economic development and fostering local pride. By enlisting as many partner organizations as possible, they limited federal landownership, and by crossing numerous jurisdictional and organizational boundaries they served multiple purposes, including historic preservation, river restoration, downtown revitalization, and recreational trail development. The Park Service's heritage program pioneered the idea of preserving "lived-in landscapes" that told nationally significant stories about America's past.[37]

The breadth of innovation required to preserve entire historical districts became clear in the Blackstone River Valley National Heritage Corridor, initiated in 1986 and later renamed in honor of Senator John H. Chafee. The mills, factories, and dams that touched off the American Industrial Revolution in the 1790s lay along the forty-six-mile Blackstone River flowing between Worcester and Providence. The corridor passed through twenty-four cities and towns and two states and embraced four hundred thousand acres, with about a million people living near or within its boundaries. Federal and local planners identified the features to be preserved, but rather than follow a traditional strategy of land acquisition, they used a combination of government funding, tax incentives, zoning regulations, land-trust acquisitions, and easements to secure key historic sites and stabilize their immediate surroundings. Planners stressed adaptive reuse of historic buildings, preserving the exterior to provide historic interpretation and modernizing the interior to meet commercial or museum needs. In both conception and management they relied heavily on local participation and community consensus. The prospect of boosting local pride and attracting tourists and investors generated community support.[38]

Connecticut's Quinebaug and Shetucket Rivers Valley National Heritage Corridor, approved by Congress in 2005, demonstrated the broad base of cooperation necessary for preservation on this scale. The two valleys formed a distinctive region of villages, mills, small farms, and forests spread across thirty-five towns with a combined population of nearly three hundred thousand. To preserve this richly textured landscape, the NPS cooperated with the Nature Conservancy, the Universities of Connecticut and Massachusetts, several municipal governments, multiple state agencies, and scores of local businesses, land trusts, and recreational organizations. Town officials, residents, and preservationists worked together to identify the landscape characteristics that defined the region and in 2005 established the Green Valley Institute as a clearinghouse for cooperating organizations and a center for educating landowners, municipal leaders, planning commissioners, contractors, real-estate agents, and others. Communities across New England used this as a model for defining and preserving their own historic districts.[39]

An example of these smaller landscape-scale historic preservation projects was the Mill River Greenway Initiative in Northampton, Massachusetts, a partnership of preservation and businesses groups and civic organizations brought together to commemorate the mills and factories that powered the local industrial revolution. The Boston Society of Landscape Architects and students from Smith College and the University of Massachusetts researched Northampton's industrial past, established interpretative programs that drew attention to the mills' unique architectural features, and suggested ways to restore the partially decked-over river. Lined with parks, paths, and canoe access points, the Mill River became a focus for community revitalization.[40]

The Park Service's heritage projects epitomized a broader shift in the agency from protecting land through top-down initiatives to cooperation with multiple state, local, and nonprofit partners. A 2010 Park Service document titled *Protecting America's Treasured Landscapes* emphasized the important role local citizen groups played in meeting the agency's goals. To its traditional criteria for establishing parks—national significance, feasibility, and suitability for NPS management—it added a new category: potential for partnering with federal, state, and municipal agencies and local preservationist organizations. And to its mission statement it added a goal of achieving preservation on a "landscape or ecosystem level," to be accomplished in cooperation with local agencies and organizations. In its historic corridor projects, the NPS moved closer to the cooperative model that increasingly defined preservation activity in New England and across America.[41]

Preservation in the Northern Forest

With new preservation models at hand and funding from state and federal sources, New England preservationists took on some of the most expansive landscape-scale conservation projects in American history. Most of these occurred in the Northern Forest, a twenty-six-million-acre corridor of temperate broadleaf and spruce-fir woodlands stretching from Tug Hill in New York to the St. Croix River in eastern Maine and including the headwaters of some of the largest rivers in the East: the Mohawk, Hudson, Connecticut, Androscoggin, Kennebec, Penobscot, and Saint John, among others. This was a region of small towns and deep woods, with a population density per square mile among the lowest in the East. "Any large-scale dispersal of industry into the empty areas of the Northeast seems unlikely," a geographer wrote in 1954, due to rugged terrain, poor drainage, high construction costs, lack of existing commercial and industrial infrastructure, poor transportation, and scarce labor and materials. Although ecologists identified several old-growth stands, the forest was by no means pristine, having been cut over several times and farmed in some places before returning to forest. Ownership patterns in the region had been relatively stable for more than a century, but a series of liquidations by pulp and paper companies beginning in the late 1980s threatened a tradition of open recreational access dating back to the early days of the logging industry.[42]

Traditionally, mills acquired forestlands as strategic reserves to insulate their wood flow from market fluctuations, but in the 1980s interest rates rose at a time when stumpage prices were dropping. As the rate of return on the timberlands fell, mill owners chose to divest their holdings. Reduced capital-gains tax penalties, globalization of wood fiber and paper markets, and the declining competitive posture of northeastern paper and lumber mills, many of them dating from the early twentieth century, encouraged these liquidations.

In Maine alone almost half the ten-million-acre north woods changed hands in just eighteen months. At the same time markets for resort- and amenity-based home developments surged due to interstate highway extensions into northern New England, easy access to credit, differentials in home prices between metropolitan areas and the rural Northeast, and the baby-boomer generation reaching retirement age. The Northern Forest, located within an eight-hour drive of seventy million people, saw a pronounced shift from industrial forest to recreational resource. Maine had long ranked first in the nation in the percentage of housing stock in seasonal use, but in the 1990s these investments moved inland from the coast. By 2000 Maine was second in the nation in the percentage of rural land converted to development, and the environmental community braced for further forest fragmentation and a proliferation of no-trespassing signs. Accustomed to unlimited access in these northern timberlands, recreationists feared the worst: "Industrial ownership has been good for Maine people for the past 100 years," one guide explained. "But that is all ending, and people just don't want to see this." Massive land transfers, rising development pressures, mill closures, and interstate highway extensions pointed to an uncertain future in the Northern Forest.[43]

These conditions touched off an acrimonious debate among conservationists, with some arguing for a federally designated wilderness, others for a national park or national recreation area, and still others for conservation agreements with landowners. Maine's resistance to several earlier national park and national forest proposals, beginning with the turn-of-the-century campaign for a Katahdin national park, narrowed options in that state. The Allagash Wilderness Waterway had generated vigorous antifederal sentiment, and in the end the Department of the Interior ceded management to the state. Nor was the Northern Forest suitable for designation under the 1964 Wilderness Act. Although some federal wilderness areas were less than primeval, the idea of remote, pristine conditions was deeply embedded in the wilderness idea, making it difficult to mobilize support for this heavily logged industrial forest. Wilderness qualities, as Michael Lewis points out, were determined "not just by science but also by cultural values." Also, the idea of a single federal designation ran counter to a conservation history marked by hard-fought but incremental adjustments to existing industrial practices. Rather than blanket management policy, preservation in this recovering wilderness would require flexibility to account for its ecological diversity, its centuries-old woodsworking traditions, its local pride of place, its complicated recreational legacy, and a wilderness imagery dating from Henry David Thoreau's visits to the Maine woods in the 1840s and 1850s. Evaluating the region's varied natural dynamics and shifting human uses would require sophisticated tools, constant feedback, and a particularistic knowledge of wetlands, habitat, scenery, nutrient balance, recreational access, and other values. Given these complexities, planning would have to be coordinated regionally, if not locally. It would mean a "new, imaginative and perhaps radically different [way of] thinking and doing" and a great deal of what Aldo Leopold called "intelligent tinkering."[44]

If a national forest, national park, or federal wilderness area seemed out of reach, the Nature Conservancy's success with land donations suggested an alternative. In 1976 the J. M. Huber Corporation deeded to the conservancy the 3,793-acre Crystal Bog on the Seboeis River, one of the largest unspoiled sphagnum-heath bogs in the lower states, and a decade later in 1986 the conservancy gathered $3.1 million from several sources to purchase 12,000 acres of International Paper Company land in the Green and White Mountains in one of the largest cooperative land conservation ventures in history. TNC resold the land to the US Forest Service.[45] Acquisitions on this scale, although improbable for any single land trust, seemed a possible solution in the age of multiorganizational preservationist alliances. Indeed, middle-way preservation was about to yield some of the largest and most innovative conservation land transactions in US history.

The first of these landscape-scale initiatives took place not in the woods but on New Hampshire's Piscataqua River estuary. This vast sunken river valley, the largest estuary on the Atlantic coast, stretches ten miles inland and receives freshwater from seven major rivers. In the postwar decades the river system had been heavily polluted with sawdust, industrial waste, and sewage, but as the waters recovered under the clean-water acts, the area became one of the fastest growing residential regions on the New England coast. In 1973 shipping magnate Aristotle Onassis purchased property to build a refinery port on its shores, and the campaign to block the plan drew national attention. Grassroots opposition defeated the refinery proposal, and trusts began acquiring land around the bay. In 1988, for instance, the Trust for New Hampshire Lands purchased a wildlife sanctuary and went on to acquire more land in partnership with the state's Land Conservation Investment Program. In 1992 the federal government established the Great Bay National Wildlife Refuge under the international North American Waterfowl Management Plan, and two years later a diverse group of state and federal agencies and various trusts and conservation organizations formed the New Hampshire Great Bay Resource Protection Partnership to guard the bay's 150 miles of coastline. With TNC as the lead acquisition agent, the partnership purchased land and easements and by 2004 had protected 6,504 acres around the bay, suggesting possibilities for other large-scale ecological projects.[46]

Even greater challenges were looming in the Northern Forest. In 1982 British corporate raider James Goldsmith acquired Diamond Occidental Corporation and its extensive network of northeastern mills and timberlands. Goldsmith sold the mill properties to the James River Corporation and the timberlands, some 976,000 acres in Maine, New Hampshire, Vermont, and New York, to a French conglomerate, which in 1988 began selling off land to speculators. Claude Rancourt, a Nashua businessman, purchased nearly 100,000 acres of Diamond land in New Hampshire and Vermont and almost immediately offered to sell the 45,000-acre Nash Stream tract in New Hampshire to preservationists at more than double his initial purchase price. New Hampshire senator Warren Rudman threatened Rancourt with federal eminent-domain procedures, and this led to a more reasonable set of negotiations. In view of these circumstances, Congress asked the US Forest Service to establish a Northern Forest Lands Study to assess the future of the region, and governors of the four states formed a similar Northern Forest Lands Council. The two groups, both created in 1989, took on the challenge of finding ways to protect traditional recreational uses and the region's ecosystems and at the same time ensure the best possible climate of investment for the weakening forest industry. While no clear consensus emerged, the path of least resistance led to public-private land conservation purchases and easements.[47]

In the midst of the Northern Forest Lands study, TNC, the SPNHF, and several state and federal agencies came together to purchase 186,000 acres of Diamond land in New York and New Hampshire. The Land for Maine's Future program spent $13.2 million for 800,000 acres from the Diamond liquidation. The largest of these was a 31,500-acre Nahmakanta Lakes region southwest of Baxter State Park. Because the Appalachian Trail passed through the Nahmakanta lands, the NPS contributed $1.5 million toward the purchase.[48] In 1997 Champion International shocked the environmental community by announcing the sale of nearly 300,000 acres of timberland in the Northern Forest. The following year a coalition of government agencies and land trusts, with LWCF funds, absorbed nearly all of this acreage in New York, New Hampshire, and Vermont for a total of $78 million. That same year TNC took the lead in negotiating one of the largest single land-trust acquisitions in US history: 185,000 acres of International Paper Company land along the St. John River in the northwest corner of Maine. Kent Wommack of the conservancy's Maine Field Office explained the decision to raise $35 million for the St. John lands and another $15 million for land elsewhere in Maine: "When we got the news that TNC had the opportunity to buy the property, we looked around the table and thought to ourselves, how could we possibly do this? But as we thought more about it we realized that the real question was, how could we possibly not do it." The St. John River purchase became the standard against which other landscape-scale conservation projects would be measured.[49]

In 1999 Seven Islands Land Company, which managed timberlands in Maine, negotiated with the New England Forestry Foundation for an easement on land belonging to the Pingree family, which had been a presence in the Maine woods since the 1840s when shipping merchant David Pingree began buying up public lands in the state. Over time the growing number of family heirs complicated management decisions. Acting on a desire to keep their lands intact, the Pingrees agreed to a conservation easement on more than 700,000 acres of dispersed holdings along the upper St. John River. Rising to the challenge, the Forestry Foundation gathered funds from federal and state agencies, forty-five foundations, and more than twelve hundred individuals, including a group of Portland fourth graders who collected more than $800 in coins. If TNC's St. John purchase was the largest land-trust acquisition in US history, the Pingree partnership, completed in 2001, was the largest conservation easement. The land included 110 lakes and ponds, more than two thousand miles of river frontage, and some of the wildest lands in the eastern United States. The landowners continued to cut timber under Forest Stewardship Council and Sustainable Forestry Initiative certificates, becoming the largest green-certified forest operators in the Northern Hemisphere. By the early 2000s the New England Forestry Foundation, along with Maine's eighty-four other land trusts, had put more than 1.5 million acres in Maine under easement—nearly a quarter of all easement lands in the United States.[50]

Also in 1999 Georgia-Pacific Corporation sold 440,000 acres on the St. Croix and Machias Rivers in eastern Maine to an investment company. Local residents, anticipating forest fragmentation and lakefront development, formed the Friends of the Downeast Lakes—later the Downeast Lakes Land Trust. Inspired by TNC and the New England Forestry Foundation, the grassroots affiliation of lodge owners, foresters, fishing enthusiasts, and guides raised nearly

$35 million through grants, foundations, and nonprofit alliances to protect 342,000 acres of Georgia-Pacific land. Here again the trust's funding sources were widespread. Philanthropist Elmina Sewall of Kennebunk contributed $6.2 million and bequeathed another $1 million on her death in 2005. Other contributors included the investment firm Wagner Forest Management and Walmart through its "Acres for America" program. The Conservation Fund, National Fish and Wildlife Foundation, National Wildlife Federation, and Nature Conservancy provided funding, as did the federal Fish and Wildlife Service, several local land trusts and state agencies, and the Passamaquoddy Tribe of Indian Township. The trust lands connected with similar conservation land in New Brunswick, making up a contiguous 1.3-million-acre block of trust lands, public lands, and easements.[51]

Similar purchases by the Open Space Institute, TNC, the Trust for Public Land, and state authorities brought conservationists closer to the goal of an "almost unbroken swath of wilderness across the Great Northern Forest." In 2000 businesswoman Roxanne Quimby bought land on the East Branch of Maine's Penobscot River and sixteen years later donated this to the federal government as the 87,563-acre Katahdin Woods and Waters National Monument. Altogether, the flurry of landscape-scale transfers in the 1990s and early 2000s protected some 3.3 million acres across the four-state Northern Forest.[52]

The last great turn-of-the-century land transactions in the Northern Forest took place in the Moosehead Lake region in northwestern Maine. In 2005 Seattle-based Plum Creek Timber Company, which had recently purchased 861,000 acres of Maine forestland, announced a 21,000-acre development proposal calling for nearly a thousand house lots and two resorts on Moosehead Lake. As the largest conversion of woodland to vacationland in Maine history, the proposal drew opposition from conservation organizations, and when it went before the state's Land Use Regulation Commission, which had jurisdiction over unincorporated townships, the required zoning change was denied. To encourage the LURC to accept a revised plan, Plum Creek offered easements on 91,000 acres outside the development area and proposed selling another 34,000 acres to the state or a private conservation organization at bargain prices. After years of public comment, hearings, study, and litigation, in 2009 the LURC approved a modified version of the plan that included a 363,000-acre Moosehead Lake Regional Conservation Easement brokered by the Nature Conservancy and held by the Forest Society of Maine and the state. Plum Creek promised a $1 million fund for construction and management of hiking trails in the region. The Nature Conservancy purchased an additional 15,000 acres for conservation and the Appalachian Mountain Club another 29,500 acres. The 2008–9 recession eroded the market for resort development, however, and in 2016 Plum Creek merged with the Weyerhaeuser Company and dropped plans for the Maine resort complex. Nevertheless, the 363,000-acre easement remained, including in a corridor along the Appalachian Trail from Moosehead Lake to Katahdin—the so-called 100-mile wilderness.[53]

The Science of Ecosystem Management

Managing this fragmented, second-nature wilderness was immensely complicated. Western wilderness management typically involved first-nature lands: vast, roadless areas deemed "untrammeled and free," as the 1964 Wilderness Act put it. This kind of pre-Columbian nature was virtually nonexistent in New England. "We have learned to think that wilderness exists out west," conservationists Emily Bateson and Nancy Smith mused; "can we change our conservation philosophy fast enough to take advantage of the truly breathtaking opportunities we have before us today?" The answer would depend in part on the shifting science of ecosystem management. Rapid revegetation in a humid climate could return even the most abused lands to seemingly wild conditions within a generation or two, and with this in mind, in 1975 Congress passed the Eastern Wilderness Areas Act, which added sixteen new eastern units to the National Wilderness Preservation System. The act, however, provided no guidelines for identifying and managing these smaller and less pristine areas, and eastern preservationists were left with the prospect of rewriting management policy for the newly designated units—and for the lands under state and nonprofit stewardship. Did wilderness require the presence of all the area's original plant and animal species? Could wilderness mean something other than the original climax forest? Could it be smaller than the range of its top predators? Should nonnative species be considered part of the "new" wilderness? Here was an opportunity to rethink wilderness management on a fundamental level.[54]

This was crucial because the eastern wilderness was once again home to a wide range of wildlife species. Beaver, reintroduced in the 1920s, transformed stream systems into wetland homes for fish, birds, amphibians, insects, raccoons, muskrats, mink, otter, and moose. Deer, small mammals, and birds found food and cover in the revegetating farmlands, and fishers, reintroduced to control porcupine populations in the 1950s, rebounded, as did pine martens when trapping was regulated. Lynx, bobcats, and black bear edged outward from their remote forest habitats. Owls and woodpeckers became more common in the maturing forests, and after the ban on DDT bald eagles and ospreys returned to the skies above the renaturalizing wetlands and rivers. Wild turkeys, reintroduced as a game species, proliferated beyond expectations. Coyotes, drawn to the expanding deer herds, reached New York in the 1920s and New England a few decades later, filling a niche formerly occupied by wolves.[55]

In short, much of the Northern Forest was in the process of recovering its ecological integrity, thanks in good part to the vast system of state, federal, and trust lands. Protecting this recovering wilderness differed from classic wilderness management, however. First, New England's wild lands had been used for centuries for a variety of industrial and recreational purposes, and prior claims to the land were strong. Mixing human history into wilderness management complicated policy decisions about logging, hunting, motorized recreation, public access, structure removal, and fire, blowdown, and insect salvage—decisions that could be made virtually by fiat in the more sparsely settled West.[56] Second, New England's wilderness was far more dynamic than those out west. Classic wilderness brought to mind stable, climax ecosystems spread over vast roadless areas and spared almost all human impacts—places where high altitude, severe climate, and limited soil moisture slowed the succession process; here nature seemed eternal. In New England, exotic introductions, rapid revegetation, and loss of top predators made management goals a moving target. In these heavily humanized and dynamic landscapes, active wilderness management was all but mandatory.

A third departure from classic wilderness policy was the relatively small size of the protected areas. New England's patchwork of town, state, federal, and trust lands was matched to the region's smaller physiographic features, its prevailing landownership patterns, and its localized conservation initiatives. Nature writers like Thoreau emphasized the microcosm rather than the macrocosm, and this ideal infused the region's approach to preservation. Natural areas scattered across the region invited a broader spectrum of visitors and encouraged an intimate, as opposed to panoramic appreciation for nature. Land stewardship was tailored to New England's physiographic makeup and culture, but it posed difficult problems for wildlife management.[57]

Fortunately, the science of wildlife management was evolving rapidly, and many of its innovations were useful in this eastern context. The new approaches came in response to the realization that despite all the advances in land preservation over the previous century the nation's ecological matrix remained at risk.

Around a third of the US land area was in public ownership, but most of this was in the West, and much of it was in arid country or at higher elevations where biotic pyramids were flatter and less diverse. Excluding Alaska, only 6 percent of the nation's critical ecosystems were fully protected. In the East the most dramatic conservation initiatives took place in areas where little development would be expected in any circumstances, and despite the good faith of forestland owners, working-forest easements generally did not provide complete biodiversity protection. Preserves were in one estimation "too small, too isolated, and represent too few types of ecosystems to maintain native biodiversity in all its forms." Aware of these limitations and of the growing threat of land conversion, fragmentation, forest fires, insect outbreaks, diseases, and climate change, preservationists searched for more comprehensive solutions.[58]

Classic preservation meant setting aside land in national parks, refuges, wilderness areas, or other enclaves where wildlife could be protected, but in the 1980s ecologists realized just how vulnerable these reservations were—"legally bounded but ecologically porous," as Peter Alagona observed. Species moved constantly in and out of the preserves, and over time whole plant and animal communities might migrate. Predicting the habitat needs of top predators was more difficult that early preservationists imagined. "You cannot just create a park and assume its animals are protected," Florida state biologist Jennifer McMurtray explained. Plants and animals need "room to roam." Given these considerations, biologists rethought the "fortress conservation" strategy; rather than single out particular species or habitats, they would have to save entire ecosystems.[59]

Ecosystem management was not entirely new. In the early 1930s the NPS published a book series titled *Fauna of the National Parks of the United States* in which well-known biologists described the range requirements of various animals within the parks. These estimates were improved a few decades later by radio-collar telemetry. Studies of predators like bears, wolverines, mountain lions, and wolves, and large ungulates like elk, bighorn sheep, and bison helped biologists define ecosystems with much greater precision, and they concluded that "no realistic program of land acquisition would ever come anywhere near to achieving the scope necessary to protect the majority of listed species."[60] A 1988 compendium titled *Ecosystem Management for Parks and Wilderness* fleshed out the new science of ecosystem management just two years before the northern spotted-owl controversy erupted in the Pacific Northwest, pitting environmentalists bent on saving an endangered species against timber companies intent on logging in its old-growth habitat. The flurry of claims and counterclaims crystallized the need for a new scientifically informed strategy for protecting nature.[61]

Ecosystem management rested on two relatively recent scientific formulations. The first was island biogeography, a study of plant and animal dynamics in isolated ecosystems such as islands. These studies demonstrated that multiple breeding populations were necessary to accommodate genetic mixing, promote resiliency, and allow for evolutionary change. Using these new tools, ecologists could estimate minimum viable populations for species in particular ecosystems. The smaller the "island," the greater the risk of species loss. These findings presented an immense challenge for New England wildlife conservationists, since few of the region's reserves were large enough to allow for healthy genetic reproduction.

A second relatively new discovery involved the degree of flux in a natural system. In classic theory, ecologies evolved along a linear path to an optimum "balance of nature" and then remained static unless disturbed, and the goal of conservation policy was to help prevent these disturbances. As ecologist C. S. Holling pointed out in a 1973 article, even without readily observable disturbance, nature was constantly readjusting; indeed, evolution required this instability.[62] Hydrological systems and nutrient flows changed. Wind bursts or lightning strikes opened holes in a forest canopy, and light reaching the soil released a new succession of ferns, grasses, brush, and trees. Insect infestations altered the composition of an entire forest, and subsurface microecologies remained in constant flux. Beaver dams created new habitat for fish, waterfowl, mammals, and birds. Looking at this world through new lenses, biologists saw nature as an ever-shifting tapestry, and this changed the way they thought about preservation. Ecosystem management meant preserving flux rather than preventing it, and this required clear scientific goals and flexible thinking.[63]

Understanding ecosystem dynamics was particularly important in New England, where ecosystems were in a constant state of flux due to high annual precipitation and centuries of logging, farming, and farm abandonment. "The continually dynamic nature of the vegetation pattern," forester David Foster wrote of New England, "is one of the most remarkable aspects of the post-settlement landscape." Climate change added another layer of uncertainty to ecosystem dynamics. Ecologists expected higher temperatures, more precipitation, more frequent droughts, more extreme weather, faster sea-level rise, more dramatic seasonal shifts, and a general northward or upward migration of plants and animals, affecting nearly every plant community and wildlife habitat in the region. Protecting biodiversity in the face of these changes would require large intact wetlands and forests connected to similar ecosystem reserves in other states and provinces, along with multiple examples of each habitat and ecosystem.[64]

On a grand scale, conservation biologists mapped out four "megalinkages" that provided northerly migration routes for plants and animals. The Pacific Spine Megalink joined Baja California to British Columbia, the Continental Spine Megalink ran from the Sierra Madre up the Rocky Mountains to the Brooks Range, the Atlantic Megalink connected the Everglades to the Appalachian Plateau and ran north to the Maritime Provinces, and the Arctic-Boreal Megalink spread from the Upper Great Lakes across the Canadian Shield. Maintaining a "connected landscape" was the best hope for species survival in this volatile situation.[65]

Applying Ecosystem Management

These new insights changed the way preservationists approached the Northern Forest. Umbrella groups like the Vermont Biodiversity Project, New Hampshire Ecological Reserve System Project, Maine Wildlands Reserve Network, and Maine Forest Biodiversity Project joined with older preservationist organizations, state and federal agencies, land managers, landowners, and representatives of the forest products industry to map areas of high species richness and design a comprehensive system of land preservation. As a baseline for protecting its own critical ecologies, in 2001 Massachusetts created a Bio-Map inventorying more than a million acres of wetlands, vernal pools, aquatic and coastal habitats, and forest ecosystems. A 2010 update listed over three thousand natural communities including habitat for several species previously thought to be extinct. Trusts, conservation organizations, and state agencies used inventories like these to define habitat areas large enough to sustain wildlife populations that could disperse into the surrounding countryside.[66]

The inventories included "core" areas that sheltered threatened plants and animals, contained representative ecologies, or harbored keystone species whose impact on an ecosystem was disproportionately large relative to its abundance. Core areas were not necessarily pristine but usually included old-growth components, since some species needed layered canopies, damp forest floors thick with moss and lichen, and snags and downed wood for dens or nests. Core areas provided base measurements for determining ecological change and provided habitat for the carnivores necessary to stabilize prey populations.[67] They were not necessarily coterminous, since most plants and animals can migrate across lands in various states of disturbance. To facilitate this movement, managers also mapped corridors along streams, ridges, or other linear features that linked one core area to another. "Once we change our focus from rescuing isolated critical habitat areas to insuring overall ecological integrity, the connection between patches becomes as important ... as patch size, shape, and type." Corridors allowed offspring predators room to disperse and prevented interbreeding.[68] Finally, ecosystem management required buffers, or blocks of minimally impacted landscape on the skirts of a core area available to wide-ranging species and those less affected by disturbance. Buffers provided ecotones between old-growth and early-succession stands that hosted birds and animals that favored shifting mosaics, sunlight, and warm soils. As a gradient between core and developed areas, buffers insulated against exotic introductions. They could support hunting, fishing, ecotourism, low-density or seasonal housing, and low-impact forestry. A complete conservation system, then, consisted of core areas functionally linked by corridors and buffered by land under some form of stewardship. If the protective system was carefully planned out, nature could thrive in a landscape fragmented by forestry activity, roads, and even suburban development.[69]

Ecosystem management altered preservation strategies in several ways. First, it forced trusts and other preservation organizations to think in terms of systems of reserved land rather than individual parcels—to plan "at very large geographic scales as well as at smaller ones." Each new project had to fit into the larger conservation landscape, and this meant cooperation within a wide community of public and private landowners and different types of land users. This in turn required a variety of management tools ranging from acquisitions and easements to tax incentives, regional planning, forest certification, landowner cooperation, and public education.[70]

Second, ecosystem management encouraged trusts to intervene more directly in their reservations. In its early years the TOR had been actively involved in shaping its natural landscapes, but the practice fell out of favor during the environmental era. In the 1990s land managers realized that let-alone policies did not always yield anticipated results, particularly in New England with its rapid cycles of growth and maturation. In this changing environment, trust managers, once aghast at the idea of messing with nature, relearned the art of restoring degraded habitat, eradicating invasive species, reintroducing native plants and trees, deploying nesting boxes for birds and rock piles for small mammals, clear-cutting to encourage successional growth, planting to control streamside erosion, and mowing or burning to increase habitat diversity, maintain open lands, or reduce fuel loads. This kind of intervention involved complicated choices made with reference to a detailed baseline study and constant monitoring. It also meant rethinking easement stipulations. "The incorporation of active management into conservation easements is a relatively new, but growing, phenomenon," legal scholar Jessica Owley wrote in 2011. To allow for unanticipated ecosystem changes, agreements would have to be flexible.[71]

Third, ecosystem management required a more rigorous scientific assessment. To account for the dynamism that earlier preservationists had overlooked, managers needed precise information about forest type, species composition, population distribution, habitat needs, and potential threats across a broad spectrum of contingencies. Nothing about the core-and-corridor system could be taken for granted. Poorly placed corridors, for instance, could accelerate the spread of diseases, unwanted predators, or invasive nonnative plants.[72] In 1971 the TOR partnered with the New England Natural Resources Center, state Audubon chapters, the Harvard Department of Landscape Architecture, the Nature Conservancy, and the Smithsonian Institution to conduct scientific inventories of critical areas in each New England state, giving trusts a series of benchmarks for protecting these ecosystems. State agencies conducted similar inventories and sent soil scientists, foresters, and fish and wildlife managers to help trusts plan strategies.[73]

Fourth, ecosystem management required the trust and cooperation of private landowners. To achieve this, biologists had to account for social and cultural factors as well as ecological circumstances. In a rapidly shifting political and economic climate, managers were tasked with bringing together numerous public and private stakeholders often traditionally at odds with one another—timberland owners, environmentalists, recreationists, hunters, snowmobile and ATV owners, and municipal officials, among others. To navigate these troubled waters, they needed to understand how each valued the land under consideration. In sum, preservation required an approach that was holistic, interventionist, flexible, scientific, and socially inclusive. The result was a relatively new approach called "adaptive management": using a wide range of tools to respond to dynamic ecological systems, uncertain alliances, and unanticipated changes, whether an invasion by exotic species or a new state or federal administration.[74]

Protecting New England Biodiversity

Ecosystem management was an idea conceived in the West, where natural systems were more stable due to arid conditions and higher altitudes and where huge blocks of public land could be managed under a single set of guidelines. Applying these same principles in New England was challenging, given the rapidly expanding "sprawl frontier," the more changeable ecological conditions, and the complicated mix of private ownerships, trust reserves, and public lands. Fortunately, the core-and-corridor concept was adaptive enough to apply almost anywhere. Corridors could be large enough to allow top predators to migrate to new areas hundreds of miles away or small enough to accommodate wood frogs moving from vernal pools to upland forests. In this context, land trusts, the most flexible of all preservationist tools, played an important role in New England ecosystem management.[75]

During the forestland acquisitions of the 1990s, preservation organizations had protected almost 3.3 million acres between Tug Hill and the Maine Coast, saving, to paraphrase Paul Bofinger, the best of what was left in the Northern Forest. This preservation achievement complemented an existing matrix of older reserves like Maine's 7,600-acre Rachel Carson National Wildlife Refuge and its 200,000-acre Baxter State Park, the Green and White Mountain national forests totaling around 12,000 acres, the 3,000-acre Wachusett Mountain Reservation in Massachusetts, the Adirondack Park, encompassing nearly 6 million acres of public and private land, and the 40,000-acre Silvio O. Conte National Fish and Wildlife Refuge along the Connecticut River. Nearby preserves included the New Jersey Pinelands, Long Island Pine Barrens, Cape Breton Highlands, and Quebec's Gaspé Peninsula. These provided substantial core areas, but ecologists now saw the need to integrate them into larger, more comprehensive networks. This would require linking the Appalachian Plateau in Vermont and New Hampshire to Maine and Quebec in the North, the Adirondack Mountains to the West, and to New Brunswick, Nova Scotia, and the Gaspé Peninsula in the East. In these crucial corridor regions the amount of protected land was actually increasing faster than the amount of developed land, but long-term biodiversity maintenance would require cooperation and planning on a scale never before achieved in the land-trust movement.[76]

Preservationists first determined the bioregional patterns in each New England state. In Maine these included the Western Boundary Plateau, the St.

John River Uplands, the Central Mountains, the Eastern Coastal Region, and the South Coast. The Massachusetts BioMap identified the Taconic Mountains, the Western Marble Valleys, the Berkshire Plateau, the Connecticut River Valley, the Worcester Plateau, the Boston Basin, the Bristol-Narragansett Lowlands, and the Cape and Islands. To identify core areas in these regions, biologists sometimes used indicator species whose range and habitat requirements defined the upper limits for all species in a particular ecosystem. One Massachusetts study, for instance, used river otters for aquatic ecosystems and fishers for forest systems. Biological considerations were adjusted to conform to existing conservation reserves, possible acquisitions and easements, and the potential for partnerships with private owners. The resulting maps were distributed widely so that each town could participate in creating the resulting buffered core-and-corridor system.[77]

In 2009 a collection of public agencies, environmental organizations, and trusts in New York, Vermont, New Hampshire, and Maine initiated the Staying Connected in the Northern Appalachians Initiative. Under the aegis of the Nature Conservancy and the New Hampshire Fish and Game Department, these partners obtained a million-dollar grant from the US Fish and Wildlife Service to identify connectivity corridors running through the Adirondack, Green, and White Mountains; the Taconic and Worcester ranges in Massachusetts; the north woods in Maine; and the Gaspé Peninsula in Quebec. Initiative members gathered data about habitat values, species, road crossings, and other information and provided this to around fifty federal and state agencies, municipal boards, conservation organizations, fish and game clubs, land trusts, and landowners. They held community meetings, gave presentations, sponsored conferences and workshops, and conducted natural history walks and school science programs. This grassroots mobilizing resulted in nearly eighty connectivity projects covering more than 300,000 acres in the four-state area. Regional planning commissions incorporated connectivity provisions into their projects, and towns included them in their land-use ordinances.[78] New England and New York had taken a significant first step in knitting together the hard-won conservation reserves and easements acquired during the timberland transactions of the 1990s.

In Massachusetts the state's best option for core-area protection was the Quabbin Reservoir in the Swift River Valley, which provided water to the Greater Boston area. When the reservoir was completed in 1939, the state put 53,000 acres in and around the reservoir under a watershed protection plan. The upland was made up of second-growth forest interspersed with rebounding clear-cuts and farmlands: a dynamic ecological matrix with suburban development looming on the horizon. The Office of Watershed Management reforested most of the area and in the 1970s began commercial timber harvests based on third-party green certification. Beaver, reintroduced in 1952, created some twelve hundred acres of ponds and marsh, and deer, moose, loons, eagles, wild turkey, and other wildlife migrated in from the north and west. During the 1980s the office accelerated the rewilding process by diversifying habitat types, planting food and cover trees, and mowing or burning to maintain meadows for grassland-dependent species like bobolinks, grasshopper sparrows, Henslow's sparrows, snow bunting, larks, upland sandpipers, deer, foxes, rabbits, butterflies, and wildflowers. Carefully planned logging operations encouraged younger growth essential to some bird and mammal species.[79]

In 2013 a partnership of land trusts and state agencies led by the University of Massachusetts and Massachusetts Audubon Society began work on a corridor designed to link Quabbin and the Wachusett Mountain Reservation. The Quabbin to Wachusett Forest Legacy Initiative (Q2W) connected the state's two largest public landholdings. Around 35 percent of the land area in the projected corridor was already protected, but it also included working farms and villages. The project used $7 million from the federal Forest Legacy Program to leverage other private and public funding, and over the next five years the North Quabbin Regional Landscape Partnership, an informal consortium made up of land trusts, state agencies, the Nashua River Watershed Association, several towns, and multiple landowners, protected some thirty-two hundred acres between the two reservations. Along with habitat needs and predator home ranges, planners considered social and cultural factors. "If people are convinced that the wildlife corridors will help to maintain their image of rural quality, they are more likely to support the concept."[80] The Q2W was a dramatic demonstration that wildlife corridors could be managed in mixed-use landscapes when managers took into consideration not only ecosystem needs but also social scenarios.

Initiatives like these made Massachusetts a leader in middle-way land preservation. Between 1999 and 2005 the state protected substantially more open space than was lost to development: about 110,000 acres versus 47,000 claimed by development. The rate of ecological protection picked up again in 2007 when Governor Deval Patrick invested $280 million to protect around 100,000 acres of land and an astounding 150 new parks. With state matching grants, municipalities stepped up their preservation activities, and between 2008 and 2009 the amount of newly protected municipal land doubled. In the 2010s Massachusetts reached a milestone in permanently protecting a quarter of its land base—around 1.25 million acres that included some 900,000 acres of core habitat and critical natural areas. This was particularly impressive given the Commonwealth's status as the third most densely populated state in the country.[81]

If Massachusetts was the birthplace of the land-trust movement, Maine became one of its greatest practitioners. In 1929 Victor Shelford's *Naturalists' Guide to the Americas* identified Lafayette (Acadia) National Park as the only preserved natural area in Maine. By 2019 Maine land trusts, more than eighty in number, had conserved more than 2.5 million acres, or 12 percent of the state, in fee simple and easement. Together with state and federal lands, these achievements put nearly 20 percent of Maine's land area in conservation ownership and easement—a mix of core and critical habitat, farm and commercial forest easements, wildlife refuges, working waterfronts, snowmobile and ATV trails, and wilderness regions. Maine supported more trust lands per capita than any other state in the Union, despite the state's relatively low population density and low income.[82]

Maine's leadership in land-trust activity derived from the sheer amount of uninterrupted forestland in the state and its scenic and biological richness, together with the fact that state and federal ownership in Maine was relatively low. Maine's 20-million-acre landmass contained the largest block of undeveloped land east of the Mississippi, and given the varied topography, shifting weather patterns, north-to-south length, and maritime and mountain influences, life zones were amazingly diverse. Forest types ranged from temperate hardwood to boreal and alpine. Most of this land had never been fully cleared by farmers or loggers, and thus the species mix had changed little since European arrival excepting the loss of wolves, cougars, and caribou. The vast mosaic of ponds, lakes, rivers, wetlands, alpine habitats, bogs, and dense coastal and mountain spruce-fir forests in the northern two-thirds of the state hosted 139 rare species. With its varied land forms, elevation changes, and microclimates, northern Maine was a critical ecological link in the northeastern US-eastern Canadian biome. This vast forest ecosystem was not only spectacular but also vulnerable, suggesting an urgent need for planning and preservation. "Threats are gathering for the Maine landscape," biologist Robert Baldwin wrote in 2007, "and new conservation action is needed if large swaths of forestland are going to be prevented from slipping to paved roads, housing, and other elements of a developed landscape."[83]

Maine's conservancy lands, impressive though they were, protected only half the habitat types in the state. With this in mind, in 1993 Janet McMahon, a graduate student at the University of Maine working with the Maine State Planning Office, compiled a report titled *An Ecological Reserves System for Maine: Benchmarks in a Changing Landscape.* The following year a group of timberland owners, nonprofit organization leaders, outdoor sports advocates, environmentalists, property-rights defenders, scientists, and state and federal officials came together as the Maine Forest Biodiversity Project hoping to piece together a management system made up of state, trust, and private lands. The proposal was not a formal system but a working understanding among multiple landowners and managers based on a manual titled *Biodiversity in the Forests of Maine: Guidelines for Land Management.* The manual outlined a means of protecting ecosystems in a landscape of shifting timber harvests interspersed with sections of permanently protected lands. Among other recommendations, it suggested large blocks of mature forest with corridors between them and varied harvest plans to provide diverse habitat types. Endorsed by officials in Baxter State Park, Acadia National Park, the White Mountain National Forest, the U.S. Fish and Wildlife Service, the Nature Conservancy, and the Appalachian Mountain Club, the document summarized the techniques necessary to sustain Maine's industrial forest and protect its rich and diverse natural communities.[84]

Local Trusts in an Era of Ecosystem Management

The campaign to preserve whole ecosystems in the Northern Forest was clearly the most spectacular advance in twenty-first-century New England land preservation, but local achievements were significant as well. In a thirty-six-page glossy pamphlet published in 2005 and revised in 2010, a group of ecologists, biologists, conservationists, and historians associated with Harvard Forest laid out a vision for New England in which 80 percent of its working farmlands and forestlands were under some form of protection, including millions of acres of wildlands returning to old-growth status, a larger extent of working forest, and a growing number of smaller reserves arranged according to critical habitat inventories. The Wildlands and Woodlands project suggested tripling the amount of land off-limits to development but stressed that most of this would be working forests or farms. Hundreds of thousands of landowners would forgo "hard conversion"—commercial or residential development—in order to keep the New England landscape sustainable. Although the goal was ambitious, it was not impossible. In fact, preservationists, piecing together a complicated mix of trust and public lands, greenways and greenbelts, farmland and woodland easements, wildlife preserves, and other protective arrangements, had accomplished much of what the report envisioned by the second decade of the new century.[85]

Conservation, as one report summarized, is best served "across a range of spatial scales and reserve sizes," and local land trusts were a vital component in this vast preservation system. Community-based trusts generally operated where the threat of development was most intense, and they protected wetlands, marshes, meadows, woodlands, watercourses, and headwaters high in biodiversity despite their relatively small size. Often overlooked by state and federal land-management agencies, these smaller open spaces, in the aggregate, were immensely important in protecting plant and animal species.[86]

The most important of these locally based biodiversity reserves were greenways, the most heavily used and the most accessible preservation accomplishment in America. Greenways were established principally as recreational resources, but they came into their own as ecosystem management tools after a pulse of scientific studies published in 1993, including *Ecology of Greenways*, edited by Daniel Smith and Paul Hellmund; *Greenways: A Guide to Planning Design and Development*, by Charles A. Flink and Robert Searns; and *Trails for the Twenty-first Century*, edited by Karen Lee Ryan and Charles A. Flink. Together these works provided a sophisticated assessment of buffer dynamics, stream-flow hydrology, habitat use, and other ecosystem services and demonstrated how greenways fit into broader systems of biodiversity protection, particularly where they extended across more than one metropolitan area.[87]

Given the recreational and ecological benefits greenways offered, preservationists imagined combining them into regional or even national networks. The idea of a national system similar to the National Trail and Wild and Scenic Rivers Systems first appeared in the 1985 report of the President's Commission on Americans Outdoors, which spoke of a "living network of greenways" following riverbanks, lakeshores, coastal margins, and abandoned transportation and utility corridors. Towns and cities would be tied together "with threads of green," providing every resident entrée into the natural world. The commissioners envisioned a "giant circulation system" made up of corridors of varying width and purpose and joined together "much the same way as our networks of highways and railroads have been linked." The greenway network would complement the national park and wilderness systems, with the added benefit that a more diverse group of people would participate in its design and management. In a 1995 report, Julius Fabos reminded readers that "nearly all greenway planning ... takes the form of grassroots projects." Despite their increasingly scientific formulation, greenways remained among the most democratic of all preservation efforts in terms of conception and use.[88]

By the early 2000s portions of this network were in place. The Hudson River Valley Greenway linked New York City to Albany and the Mohawk River, and Florida's greenway network ran from Tallahassee down the peninsula through a national forest, a wildlife refuge, and three state parks, stringing together nearly fifteen hundred miles of land and water corridors. Georgia and Oregon were well on their way to realizing similar greenway visions. In 1999 five New England states joined with others along the Eastern Seaboard to plan out an East Coast Greenway stretching from Maine to Florida. Closer to home, planners devised a plan to connect the dense web of protected greenway and trail corridors along the rivers, shores, ridges, and abandoned rail lines of New England. Each state compiled a greenway inventory, and these were combined into a regional composite known as the New England Greenway Vision Plan. The goal was to close the gaps in the region's nineteen thousand miles of existing greenways and trails to allow hikers uninterrupted travel from Long Island Sound to the Maine woods and from Cape Cod to the Berkshire Hills and Green Mountains, taking advantage of the numerous bed-and-breakfast facilities along the way.[89]

To speed completion of the New England system, planners proposed taking advantage of the unique preservationist innovations in each of the six states. Connecticut's Forest Park Association, for example, had created the seven-hundred-mile Blue Blaze Trail System, and in Massachusetts, the 1996 River Protection Act mandated a two-hundred-foot buffer on each side of a river, stream, or brook and a four-hundred-foot protective corridor around the lakes. The intent was to protect water quality, but the legislation suggested a legal basis for greenway extensions along these watercourses. In 1995 Rhode Island began construction of a coordinated greenway system that would serve as a foundation for land-use planning and tourist development. Vermont circumscribed development on land above twenty-five hundred feet—a measure that could guarantee protection for mountaintops and ridge lines across New England. New Hampshire pioneered legislation encouraging public-private partnerships, and Maine developed the nation's most comprehensive legal apparatus for negotiating conservation easements. Like all New England preservation initiatives, the plan relied on "hundreds, if not thousands, of local planning and design efforts." Regional plans elsewhere were impeded by lack of coordination between government agencies and grassroots organizations; New England's middle-way preservation offered a promising path to completion.[90]

Greenway integration on this order would amplify the ecological and recreational benefits of each individual project. As part of a larger system, each would gain wider support, draw more volunteers, attract more funding, and benefit from a broader base of expertise. Combined, they would link together America's ecological systems and contribute immeasurably to public appreciation for, and understanding of the natural world. Greenways, landscape planner Jack Ahern predicted, would become "as prominent on maps as the United States' interstate highway system," outlining the rivers, wetlands, barrier beaches, mountain ridges, and floodplains that made up nature's continental infrastructure. A national greenway system would rekindle the dream Mary Robbins first invoked in 1896: a coast-to-coast "national parkway" leading from one landscaped pleasure ground to another. This would be the ultimate tribute to democratic spaces, not only in wild and remote portions of America but in neighborhoods, towns, and cities across the nation. Greenway projects were living proof that, as Mark Dowie wrote in 1996, "almost daily the environmental imagination is bombarded with new ideas, scientific findings, and paradigms that may one day constitute an authentic ecocentrism." New England pioneered many of these ideas through its creative blend of cultural and natural preservation, its fusion of grassroots and top-down approaches, and its integration of public and private stewardship.[91]

CONCLUSION

National parks, with their towering redwoods, mile-deep canyons, and endless saw-grass prairies, are the most widely admired examples of America's preservation heritage. Nevertheless, we should not overlook the smaller milestones in preservation that in the aggregate left us with millions of acres of trust lands, state and municipal parks, greenways, greenbelts, and sanctuaries for birds, wildflowers, and wildlife. Situated close to our cities and towns, these unassuming accomplishments receive far more visitors than our national parks and wilderness areas. State parks alone welcome more than seven hundred million people each year, more than twice the number visiting our national parks. Moreover, they provide a more intimate experience with the natural world, and, being tailored to local circumstances, they satisfy a more diverse visitor base. Beginning with the foundation of the Trustees of Public Reservations in 1891, preservationists have grown increasingly responsive to the importance of these relatively small parcels in neighborhood life and local biodiversity.[1]

Much of this local and statewide preservation work was accomplished by land trusts, and these, too, are often overlooked as central players in the environmental movement. Land trusts filled a unique niche in preservation politics. Rather than restrict private-sector interaction with nature, as environmental legislation generally does, land trusts encouraged it. As John Wright wrote in 1992, they proved that property owners can be important partners in land stewardship, "if they are encouraged and not coerced." Trusts empowered individuals to act on their best impulses, and for this reason they enjoyed support across a broad section of the public and at all levels of government. As the Land Trust Alliance's Jean Hocker explained, the trusts attracted "people who may not think of themselves as environmentalists, but for whom the land holds a special place in their memories and lives." Through face-to-face deliberation, donors, buyers, sellers, planners, recreationists, property owners, and environmentalists discovered common values and learned to respect each other. This collaborative approach brought spectacular results in the 1980s when preservationists found ways to apply their principles to urban problems, and in the 1990s when they formed interorganizational and interagency alliances to take on landscape-scale projects.[2]

Due in part to this cooperative framework, land trusts remain today among the most stable elements in the environmental coalition. They can operate more or less independently of national political trends by shifting between private, state, and federal funding sources. Their legitimacy rests not with politicians but with the communities that benefit directly from their work. Their constituencies are reliable because trusts adapt to changing community needs. In the 1960s they championed the values of those seeking a rural lifestyle on the suburban fringe, in the 1970s they absorbed the rhetoric of the bourgeoning environmental movement, in the 1980s they responded to the call for open spaces in the inner cities, and when cultural and scientific trends suggested the need for landscape-scale preservation, they joined with state and national agencies and private landowners to protect farmlands, build greenbelts, establish historic districts and heritage corridors, and manage whole forest ecosystems.[3]

The land-trust movement endures because it provides people of all ages, races, ethnicities, classes, and living circumstances an opportunity to participate in meaningful preservation efforts. By the late 1970s most mainstream environmental organizations were headquartered in Washington, DC, where they worked closely with Congress, federal agencies, and the courts. Today these organizations operate on a scale far above their grassroots base. Land trusts, by contrast, remain tied to the communities that host them and continue to depend on dedicated volunteer support for day-to-day operations. Trusts offer ordinary citizens a chance to act on their passion for nature, and they bring to light, time and again, the commitment ordinary people are willing to make to protect cultural, aesthetic, and ecological values in the world around them. In an age when threats to the environment seem overwhelming, they give citizens the satisfaction of protecting nature where it matters most—in their own communities. Trusts are stepping-stones to global environmental consciousness.[4]

Land trusts are important because they preserve both natural and cultural resources. This is especially important in New England, where so much of regional identity depends on blended landscapes: the Maine coast depicted in the short stories of Sarah Orne Jewett, the North Shore harbors represented in Marsden Hartley's paintings, the New Hampshire farms featured in Robert Frost's poetry. Saving second nature is less dramatic than protecting the great earth monuments of the West, but it is a goal worth pursuing at a time when "first" nature is shrinking all across America. In this sense, New England's preservationist achievements remain the region's greatest gift to the American environmental legacy.

The trust movement continues to evolve. In June 2005 a *New York Times* columnist discovered scores of "regular folks" in Salisbury, Connecticut, "writing checks to save a piece of land that is dear to them from development." For years, they had lobbied the state legislature, the national land trusts, and several national environmental groups to no avail. Growing impatient with the existing preservation framework, they began "raising the money themselves." Similarly, in East Lyme the Friends of Oswegatchie Hills saved 700 acres of land that had no other champions, and in East Haddam a "group of worried neighbors" raised funds to purchase 56 acres that the Connecticut Audubon Society had put up for sale. Around a hundred Simsbury residents, supported with a gift from a family trust, raised $1.2 million to purchase the town's 123-acre Dark Hollow. Self-funding seems a limited option given the price of land in the twenty-first century, but who knows where such innovations may end?[5]

The great strength of the environmental movement is its openness to new approaches like these. From solar panels to wilderness preservation, there are countless ways of protecting nature, and each contributes to the overall improvement in our relation to the biosphere. The environmental movement succeeds to the degree it accepts—indeed, celebrates—diversity and innovation, and those who study this movement should likewise embrace its multiple forms. In the eyes of most historians, publication of Rachel Carson's *Silent Spring* in 1962 is a defining moment in the rise of environmental advocacy. William Whyte's *Last Landscape*, published six years later, is rarely considered in a similar light, despite its equally profound effect on the environment. These two books approach nature from radically different perspectives, but each has become an inspiration of historic proportions. We are far from mastering the toxic crisis Carson so brilliantly described in her book, and we are equally far from protecting the open spaces Whyte championed in *The Last Landscape*. There is work to be done, but we need to acknowledge the fact that this work is as varied as the problems we face on a neighborhood, national, and global scale.

NOTES

Introduction

1 Richard W. Judd, *Second Nature: An Environmental History of New England* (Amherst: University of Massachusetts Press, 2014); René Dubos, "The Five E's of Environmental Management," in *The World of René Dubos: A Collection from His Writings*, ed. Gerard Piel and Osborn Segerberg Jr. (New York: Henry Holt, 1990), 406; Charles Eliot II in White House Conference on Natural Beauty, *Beauty for America: Proceedings* (Washington, DC: GPO, 1965), 117.
2 Cody Ferguson, *This Is Our Land: Grassroots Environmentalism in the Late Twentieth Century* (New Brunswick, NJ: Rutgers University Press, 2015), 6, 12.
3 Alfred Todd, "The Esthetics of the New England Town Common" (master's thesis, Massachusetts Institute of Technology, 1950), 9; Garrett Eckbo, "The Link between Man and Nature," *Landscape Architecture Magazine* 56 (July 1966): 267.
4 Richard W. Judd, *Common Lands, Common People: The Origins of Conservation in Northern New England* (Cambridge, MA: Harvard University Press, 1997), 11.

Chapter 1: The Art of Public Improvement

1 Mary Caroline Robbins, "The Art of Public Improvement," *Atlantic Monthly*, December 1896, 742–73. On Robbins's career, see Mary R. S. Creese, *Ladies in the Laboratory II: West European Women in Science, 1800–1900* (Lanham, MD: Scarecrow Press, 2004), 219–20; and Shen Hou, *The City Natural: "Garden and Forest" Magazine and the Rise of American Environmentalism* (Pittsburgh: University of Pittsburgh Press, 2013), 74–76. See also A. McC. Hallock, "The Beauty of Rural England," *Garden and Forest* 7 (May 16, 1894): 198.
2 Robbins, "Public Improvement," 743 (first and third quotes), 745 (second quote).

3 Kirin J. Makker, "Building Main Street: Village Improvement and the American Small Town Ideal" (PhD diss., University of Massachusetts, 2010), 36, 37 (quote).
4 Samuel P. Hays, *Conservation and the Gospel of Efficiency: The Progressive Conservation Movement, 1890–1920* (New York: Atheneum, 1969 [ca. 1959]); Richard W. Judd, *Common Lands, Common People: The Origins of Conservation in Northern New England* (Cambridge, MA: Harvard University Press, 1997); Louis S. Warren, *The Hunter's Game: Poachers and Conservationists in Twentieth-Century America* (New Haven, CT: Yale University Press, 1997); Karl Jacoby, *Crimes against Nature: Squatters, Poachers, Thieves, and the Hidden History of American Conservation* (Berkeley: University of California Press, 2001); Roderick Nash, *Wilderness and the American Mind* (New Haven, CT: Yale University Press, 1967); Alfred Runte, *National Parks: The American Experience* (Lincoln: University of Nebraska Press, 1987).
5 Norman T. Newton, *Design on the Land: The Development of Landscape Architecture* (Cambridge, MA: Harvard University Press, 1971), 660–61.
6 Joseph A. Conforti, *Imagining New England: Explorations of Regional Identity from the Pilgrims to the Mid-Twentieth Century* (Chapel Hill: University of North Carolina Press, 1995); Dona Brown, *Inventing New England: Regional Tourism in the Nineteenth Century* (Washington, DC: Smithsonian Institution Press, 1995).
7 Chris Elfring, "Preserving Land through Local Land Trusts," *Bioscience* 39 (February 1989): 71.
8 Gerald O. Barney, ed., *The Unfinished Agenda: The Citizen's Policy Guide to Environmental Issues; A Task Force Report Sponsored by the Rockefeller Brothers Fund* (New York: Thomas Y. Crowell, 1977), 161.
9 Richard L. Bushman, *The Refinement of America: Persons, Houses, Cities* (New York: Alfred A. Knopf, 1992), xvi; Stephan J. Schmidt, "The Evolving Relationship between Open Space Preservation and Local Planning Practice," *Journal of Planning History* 7, no. 2 (2008): 2.
10 *Burlington (VT) Daily Free Press*, March 16, 1864 (first quote); David Lowenthal, "The Place of the Past in the American Landscape," in *Geographies of the Mind: Essays in Historical Geosophy in Honor of John Kirtland Wright*, ed. David Lowenthal and Martyn J. Bowden (New York: Oxford University Press, 1976), 97 (second quote). See Judd, *Common Lands*, 69, 77.
11 Steven Stoll, *Larding the Lean Earth: Soil and Society in Nineteenth-Century America* (New York: Hill and Wang, 2002), 30, 35, 191–94; Richard W. Judd, *Second Nature: An Environmental History of New England* (Amherst: University of Massachusetts Press, 2014), 77, 205; Judd, *Common Lands*, 76.
12 Kent C. Ryden, *Landscape with Figures: Nature & Culture in New England* (Iowa City: University of Iowa Press, 2001), 49, 152 (quote).
13 Mary E. Woolley, "The Development of the Love of Romantic Scenery in America," *American Historical Review* 3 (October 1897): 61, 63–65; David Jacobson, *Place and Belonging in America* (Baltimore: Johns Hopkins University Press, 2002), 78–79; Raymond Williams, *The Country and the City* (New York: Oxford University Press, 1973), 18–20, 24, 37, 46.
14 Bushman, *Refinement of America*, ix.
15 Sara Josepha Hale in Robert C. Bredeson, "Landscape Description in Nineteenth-Century American Travel Literature," *American Quarterly* 20 (Spring 1968): 92 (first

quote); Conforti, *Imagining New England*, 113 (second quote). See Runte, *National Parks*, 11; and Eric Kaufmann, "'Naturalizing the Nation': The Rise of Naturalistic Nationalism in the United States and Canada," *Comparative Studies in Society and History* 40 (October 1998): 671.

16 Gordon G. Whitney, *From Coastal Wilderness to Fruited Plain: A History Environmental Change in Temperate North America, 1500 to the Present* (New York: Cambridge University Press, 1994), 56–57; William Cronon, "The Trouble with Wilderness; or, Getting Back to the Wrong Nature," in *Uncommon Ground: Rethinking the Human Place in Nature*, ed. William Cronon (New York: W. W. Norton, 1996), 76–78; Nash, *Wilderness and the American Mind*; Paul S. Sutter, *Driven Wild: How the Fight against Automobiles Launched the Modern Wilderness Movement* (Seattle: University of Washington Press, 2002), 14; Mark Stoll, "Religion 'Irradiates' the Wilderness," in *American Wilderness: A New History*, ed. Michael Lewis (New York: Oxford University Press, 2007), 35.

17 Runte, *National Parks*, 20; Angela Miller, "The Fate of Wilderness in American Landscape Art: The Dilemmas of 'Nature's Nation,'" in Lewis, *American Wilderness*, 104 (quote), 105; Angela Miller, *The Empire of the Eye: Landscape Representation and American Cultural Politics, 1825–1875* (Ithaca, NY: Cornell University Press, 1993), 72.

18 Nash, *Wilderness and the American Mind*, 84, 88–89; Richard W. Judd, "Thoreau's Maine Woods and the Problem of Wildness," in *Rediscovering the Maine Woods: Thoreau's Legacy in an Unsettled Land*, ed. John J. Kucich (Amherst: University of Massachusetts Press, 2019), 94, 107.

19 Norman Foerster, *Nature in American Literature: Studies in the Modern View of Nature* (New York: Macmillan, 1923), 145 (first quote), 146; Ralph Waldo Emerson, "American Scholar," in *The Selected Writings of Ralph Waldo Emerson*, ed. Brooks Atkinson (New York: Modern Library, 1950), 228 (second quote). See Judd, *Second Nature*, 161; and Miller, *Empire of the Eye*, 16.

20 Miller, *Empire of the Eye*, 12, 14, 35; Stephen Daniels, *Fields of Vision: Landscape Imagery and National Identity in England and the United States* (Cambridge: Polity Press, 1993), 156–58.

21 Susan Fenimore Cooper, *The Rhyme and Reason of Country Life* (New York: Putnam, 1854), 33 (first quote); Judith K. Major, *To Live in the New World: A. J. Downing and American Landscape Gardening* (Cambridge, MA: MIT Press, 1997), 21 (second quote). See Edward Foster, *The Civilized Wilderness* (New York: Macmillan, 1975), 111; and Makker, "Building Main Street," 42–45.

22 Egbert Hans in *Lowell (MA) Sun*, April 22, 1931. See Horace Bushnell, "The Age of Homespun: A Discourse, Delivered at Litchfield, Conn., on the Occasion of the Centennial Celebration, 1851," in *Centennial Celebration*, by Litchfield County (Hartford, CT: Edwin Hunt, 1851); Henry Ward Beecher, *Norwood; or, Village Life in New England* (New York: Charles Scribner, 1868); James Truslow Adams, *The American: The Making of a New Man* (New York: Scribner's Sons, 1943), 42, 44–45; Joseph Wood, "Build, Therefore, Your Own World: The New England Village as Settlement Ideal," *Annals of the Association of American Geographers* 81 (March 1991): 32; Conforti, *Imagining New England*, 148–49; Miller, *Empire of the Eye*, 16; and Jacobson, *Place and Belonging*, 78–79.

23 Stoll, *Larding the Lean Earth*, 199 (quote). See Fiske Kimball, "The Beginnings of Landscape Gardening in America," *Landscape Architecture* 7 (July 1917): 187; Tamara Plakins Thornton, *Cultivating Gentlemen: The Meaning of Country Life among the Boston Elite, 1785–1860* (New Haven, CT: Yale University Press, 1989), 4–5, 22–23, 191, 198, 200–204; Alexander Von Hoffman, *Local Attachments: The Making of an Urban Neighborhood, 1850 to 1920* (Baltimore: Johns Hopkins University Press, 1994), 67; and Judd, *Second Nature*, 191–92.

24 Richard Cloues, "Where Art Is Combined with Nature: Village Improvement in Nineteenth-Century New England" (PhD diss., Cornell University, 1987), 173 (first quote); Blake Harrison, *The View from Vermont: Tourism and the Making of an American Rural Landscape* (Burlington: University of Vermont Press, 2006), 24 (second quote); Thornton, *Cultivating Gentlemen*, 119, 155, 172 (third quote). See Von Hoffman, *Local Attachments*, 65; and Daniel Denison Slade, *The Evolution of Horticulture in New England* (New York: G. P. Putnam's Sons, 1895), 138–39, 141.

25 "The Significance and Dignity of Country Life," *Horticulturist and Journal of Rural Arts* 19 (August 1864): 316 (quote), 317. See "Rural Taste," *Horticulturist and Journal of Rural Arts* 24 (May 1869): 148; Brown, *Inventing New England*, 16; and Bushman, *Refinement of America*, 5, 9–15.

26 Barr Ferree in Robin S. Karson, *A Genius for Place: American Landscapes of the Country Place Era* (Amherst: University of Massachusetts Press, 2007), xvi, xvi (quote), xviii. See Daniels, *Fields of Vision*, 99.

27 "Visitor," "Landscape Gardening as Applied to Rural Cemeteries," *Horticulturist and Journal of Rural Arts* 17 (December 1862): 556. See Newton, *Design on the Land*, 249–50, 258–59, 427; "Country Residences of Our Merchant Princes," *Horticulturist and Journal of Rural Arts* 25 (September 1870): 278–79; David Schuyler, *The New Urban Landscape: The Redefinition of City Form in Nineteenth-Century America* (Baltimore: Johns Hopkins University Press, 1986), 2; Cloues, "Where Art Is Combined with Nature," 153–56, 159–60; and Bushman, *Refinement of America*, 128–30.

28 Rochelle L. Johnson, *Passions for Nature: Nineteenth-Century America's Aesthetics of Alienation* (Athens: University of Georgia Press, 2009), 131–32; Elizabeth Barlow Rogers, *Landscape Design: A Cultural and Architectural History* (New York: Harry N. Abrams, 2001), 326; Karson, *Genius for Place*, 3; Sarah P. Stetson, "Andre Parmentier: Little-Known Pioneer in American Landscape Architecture," *Landscape Architecture Magazine* 39 (July 1949): 186.

29 Major, *Downing*, 21.

30 Samuel Parson in Karson, *Genius for Place*, xxi. See Major, *Downing*, 81; David Schuyler, *Apostle of Taste: Andrew Jackson Downing, 1815–1852* (Baltimore: Johns Hopkins University Press, 1996), 38, 40, 53; George William Curtis, "Memoir," in *Rural Essays*, by Andrew Jackson Downing, ed. Frederika Bremer (New York: George P. Putnam, 1858), xxv; and Deloris Hayden, *Building Suburbia: Green Fields and Urban Growth, 1820–2000* (New York: Pantheon Books, 2003), 16.

31 Cloues, "Where Art Is Combined with Nature," 156–57, 228 (first quote); Slade, *Evolution of Horticulture*, 126, 150 (second quote), 151, 154 (third quote); Charles S. Sargent, "The Debt of America to A. J. Downing," *Garden and Forest* 8 (May 29, 1895): 211 (fourth quote). See William Webster, "Landscape Gardening as an Art," *Horticulturist and Journal of Rural Arts* 24 (February 1869): 47; Andrew Jackson

Downing, *A Treatise on the Theory and Practice of Landscape Gardening Adapted to North America* (New York: Willey and Putnam, 1841), 11–13, 14; and Mary Caroline Robbins, "Park-Making as a National Art," *Atlantic Monthly*, January 1897, 89.

32 John Archer, "Country and City in the American Romantic Suburb," *Journal of the Society of Architectural Historians* 42 (May 1983): 150 (first quote); Slade, *Evolution of Horticulture*, 164 (second quote); Downing, *Rural Essays*, 209, 211 (third quote), 231 (fourth quote), 237–38.

33 Downing, *Rural Essays*, 212 (first quote); Slade, *Evolution of Horticulture*, 158, 160 (second quote). See Schuyler, *Apostle of Taste*, 95, 105; and Johnson, *Passions for Nature*, 112–15.

34 Conforti, *Imagining New England*, 132–35; William Butler, "Another City upon a Hill: Litchfield, Connecticut, and the Colonial Revival," in *The Colonial Revival in America*, ed. Alan Axelrod (New York: W. W. Norton, 1985), 24–28; Wood, "Build, Therefore, Your Own World," 36; Wood, "New England's Legacy Landscape," in *A Landscape History of New England*, ed. Blake Harrison and Richard W. Judd (Cambridge, MA: MIT Press, 251–67.

35 Cloues, "Where Art Is Combined with Nature," 91 (quotes), 290, 372–73, 302.

36 Clark W. Bryan, *The Book of Berkshire, Describing and Illustrating Its Hills and Homes* (Great Barrington, MA: Clark W. Bryan, 1887), 26 (first quote); Liberty Hyde Bailey, *The Outlook to Nature* (New York: Macmillan, 1911), 66–67 (second quote).

37 Butler, "Another City upon a Hill," 19–21, 36 (second quote), 45 (first quote). See Judd, *Second Nature*, 243–44; W. Barksdale Maynard, "'Best, Lowliest Style!': The Early-Nineteenth-Century Rediscovery of American Colonial Architecture," *Journal of the Society of Architectural Historians* 59 (September 2000): 339; Conforti, *Imagining New England*, 203–9; and Frank A. Waugh, "A Comparison of Town Plans," *Landscape Architecture* 11 (July 1921): 161, 164.

38 Geoffrey Champlin, "The Decline of New England," *North American Review* 146 (May 1888): 587–88. See Nathaniel H. Egleston, *The Home and Its Surroundings; or, Villages and Village Life with Hints for Their Improvement* (New York: Harpers, 1884 [ca. 1878]), 20–23.

39 W. Robinson, "American Horticulture as Seen by an Englishman," *Horticulturist and Journal of Rural Arts* 26 (January 1871): 27 (first quote); Charles H. Moore, "Materials for Landscape in North America," *Atlantic Monthly*, November 1889, 673 (second and third quotes); Robert Morris Copeland, "Landscape Gardening," *Horticulturist and Journal of Rural Arts* 24 (March 1869): 80, 81 (fourth quote). See Liberty Hyde Bailey, *The Country Life Movement in the United States* (New York: Macmillan, 1911), 23; "Rural Improvement Societies," *Garden and Forest* 1 (May 23, 1888): 145; "Village and Country Road-Side," *Horticulturist and Journal of Rural Arts* 20 (November 1865): 341–42; Schuyler, *Apostle of Taste*, 113; Hallock, "Beauty of Rural England," 198; Champlin, "Decline of New England," 589; and Charles S. Sargent, "The Effect of Country Life upon Women," *Garden and Forest* 6 (January 4, 1893): 1–2.

40 Mary Catherwood Robbins, "Village Improvement Societies," *Atlantic Monthly*, February 1897, 213. See Conforti, *Imagining New England*, 241–48.

41 George E. Waring, *Village Improvements and Farm Villages* (Boston: James R. Osgood, 1877), 15. See Makker, "Building Main Street," 20–23; "Societies of Rural

Art and Rural Taste," *Harper's Bazaar*, September 4, 1875, 570; Robbins, "Village Improvement Societies," 217; Kirin J. Makker, "Mary G. Hopkins and the Origins of Village Improvement in Antebellum Stockbridge, Massachusetts," *Landscape Journal* 34, no. 1 (2015): 1–14; Parris Thaxter Farwell, *Village Improvement* (New York: Sturgis & Walton, 1913), 14–16; and "The Birthplace of Village Improvement Associations," *Village: A Journal for Village Life* 1 (December 1906): 6–7.

42 Robbins, "Village Improvement Societies," 216; Charles S. Sargent, "The Improvement of Villages," *Garden and Forest* 2 (March 27, 1889): 145; Egleston, *Home and Its Surroundings*, 60–64, 210–11, 145–49, 232–33.

43 Robbins, "Village Improvement Societies," 213, 214; Makker, "Building Main Street," 81, 88, 114–17; Farwell, *Village Improvement*, 5, 7, 10, 56.

44 Waring, *Village Improvements*, 138 (first and second quotes); Farwell, *Village Improvement*, 20 (third quote); "The Influence of the Central Park upon Public Taste," *Horticulturist and Journal of Rural Art and Rural Taste* 19 (August 1864): 238 (fourth quote). See Susan Fenimore Cooper, "Village Improvement Societies," *Putnam's Magazine*, September 1869, 362; and Robbins, "Public Improvement," 747.

45 Cooper, "Village Improvement Societies," 360 (first quote); Robbins, "Village Improvement Societies, 212 (second quote); Waring, *Village Improvements*, 16 (third quote). See Charles S. Sargent, "Women as Landscape Architects," *Garden and Forest* 5 (October 12, 1892): 482; and Henry T. Williams, "Rural Taste," *Horticulturist and Journal of Rural Arts* 27 (December 1872): 353–55.

46 Cooper, "Village Improvement Societies," 361 (first quote); Makker, "Building Main Street," 24, 141, 148, 351 (second quote), 154, 157; annual report in Cloues, "Where Art Is Combined with Nature," 991 (third quote), 992; Farwell, *Village Improvement*, 17, 48 (fourth quote).

47 Waring, *Village Improvements*, 11, 12 (first and second quotes); Egleston, *Home and Its Surroundings*, 132 (third quote); Frederick Law Olmsted Jr., *Village Improvement*, Massachusetts Civic League Leaflet, no. 5 (Boston: Massachusetts Civic League, 1905), 9 (fourth quote).

48 Cloues, "Where Art Is Combined with Nature," 1021 (first quote), 1023, 1080, 1144 (second quote); Mark Stoll, *Protestantism, Capitalism, and Nature in America* (Albuquerque: University of New Mexico Press, 1997), 41 (third quote); See *Report of the Country Life Commission*, Sen. Doc. 705, 60th Cong., 2nd sess. (Washington, DC: GPO, 1909), 8–9, 13.

49 Ian McKay and Robin Bates, *In the Province of History: The Making of the Public Past in Twentieth-Century Nova Scotia* (Montreal: McGill–Queen's University Press, 2010), 21. See Matthew McKenzie, *Clearing the Coastline: The Nineteenth-Century Ecological & Cultural Transformation of Cape Cod* (Hanover, NH: University Press of New England, 2010), 154–55, 157, 158; Brown, *Inventing New England*, 27–28, 61; Harrison, *View from Vermont*, 20–27, 64–65, 71, 76; Albert S. Carlson, "Recreation Industry of New Hampshire," *Economic Geography* 14 (July 1938): 255–56; George H. Lewis, "The Maine That Never Was: The Construction of Popular Myth in Regional Culture," *Journal of American Culture* 16 (June 2004): 93–95; and John Brinckerhoff Jackson, *American Space: The Centennial Years, 1865–1876* (New York: W. W. Norton, 1972), 105.

50 Nathaniel S. Shaler, "The Landscape as a Means of Culture," *Atlantic Monthly*, December 1898, 778. See Bredeson, "Landscape Description in Nineteenth-Century

American Travel Literature," 89; and Gail S. Davidson, "Landscape Icons, Tourism, and Land Development in the Northeast," in *Frederic Church, Winslow Homer, and Thomas Moran: Tourism and the American Landscape*, ed. Barbara Bloemink et al. (Washington, DC: Smithsonian Institution Press, 2006), 3, 37.
51 Harrison, *View from Vermont*, 20–21, 24, 55, 111, 115; Judd, *Second Nature*, 243; Miller, *Empire of the Eye*, 13; Brown, *Inventing New England*.
52 David Lowenthal, *George Perkins Marsh: Prophet of Conservation* (Seattle: University of Washington Press, 2000); 297, 304 (quote).
53 *Maine Farmer*, August 25 (quote), October 24, 1864. See Calvin Chamberlain, "Man a Destructive Power," in *Thirteenth Annual Report of the Maine Board of Agriculture, 1868* (Augusta, GA: Owen & Nash, 1868), 114–16; Richard W. Judd, "George Perkins Marsh: The Times and Their Man," *Environment and History* 10 (May 2004): 169–90; Steven Stoll, "Farm against Forest," in Lewis, *New American Wilderness*, 65; and Stoll, *Larding the Lean Earth*, 177.
54 Julius H. Ward, "White Mountain Forests in Peril," *Atlantic Monthly*, February 1893, 248 (first quote); Bernhard E. Fernow in Peter B. Lord, "The Rhode Island Conservation Story," in *Twentieth-Century New England Land Conservation: A Heritage of Civic Engagement*, ed. Charles H. W. Foster (Petersham, MA: Harvard Forest, 2009), 222 (second quote); Charles S. Sargent, "The Forestry Report of the Tenth Census," *Garden and Forest* 4 (January 1, 1890): 1 (third quote). See G. E. W., "The Wood Pulp Supply and Our Spruce Forests," *Garden and Forest* 9 (September 9 1896): 363; Will Lindner, "Choices, Chances and Close Calls: How Vermont Grew to Value Its Natural Environment," *Vermont Environmental Report* (Summer 2003): 20; and "The Critical Moment in the White Mountains," *New York Times*, November 21, 1892, 4.
55 Joseph Edgar Chamberlain, "Will the Land Become a Desert?," *Century Illustrated Magazine* 31 (February 1886): 533 (first quote), 536 (second quote); Charles S. Sargent, "The Money Value of Rural Improvement," *Garden and Forest* 2 (January 22, 1890): 37 (third quote); Charles S. Sargent, "The Defacement of Scenery," *Garden and Forest* 5 (December 7, 1892): 577 (fourth quote). See J. B. Harrison, "The Forest—Forestry in New England," *Garden and Forest* 2 (February 20, 1889): 92; B. E. Fernow, "Hygienic Significance of Forest Air and Forest Soil," *Garden and Forest* 6 (January 18, 1893): 34; Harrison, *View from Vermont*, 47–48; and Kimberly A. Jarvis, *From the Mountains to the Sea: Protecting Nature in Postwar New Hampshire* (Amherst: University of Massachusetts Press, 2020), 31–59.
56 Downing, *Rural Essays*, 123 (first quote); Egleston, *Home and Its Surroundings*, 7 (second quote), 31, 40–41; Cooper, "Village Improvement Societies," 360 (third quote); L. E. Holden, comments, in *Second Report of the Park and Outdoor Art Association* (Boston: Rockwell and Churchill Press, 1898), 88 (fourth quote); Schuyler, *New Urban Landscape*, 36 (fifth quote); Michael Rawson, *Eden on the Charles: The Making of Boston* (Cambridge, MA: Harvard University Press, 2010), 177 (sixth quote). See Eliot Lord, "A Village 'Hub,'" *Village: A Journal for Village Life* 1 (December 1906): 10; S. Perry in J. S. Hough, "Relative Influence of City and Country Life," *Penn Monthly*, January 1870; Henry Philip Tappan, *The Growth of Cities: A Discourse Delivered before the New York Geographical Society* (New York: R. Craighead, 1855), 8; and James I. Machor, *Pastoral Cities: Urban Ideals and the Symbolic Landscape of America* (Madison: University of Wisconsin Press, 1987), 150.

57 Slade, *Evolution of Horticulture*, 129 (first quote), 131 (second quote). See James C. O'Connell, *The Hub's Metropolis: Greater Boston's Development from Railroad Suburbs to Smart Growth* (Cambridge, MA: MIT Press, 2013), 17–18, 28, 42, 60, 70–73; Charles J. Kennedy, "Commuter Services in the Boston Area," *Business History Review* 36 (Summer 1962): 155–58; Henry C. Binford, *The First Suburbs: Residential Communities on the Boston Periphery, 1815–1860* (Chicago: University of Chicago, 1985), 91–93, 146–48; Deloris Hayden, *Building Suburbia: Green Fields and Urban Growth, 1820–2000* (New York: Pantheon Books, 2003), 74; Alexander Von Hoffman, *Local Attachments: The Making of an Urban Neighborhood, 1850 to 1920* (Baltimore: Johns Hopkins University Press, 1994), 11–12, 24–25, 29, 40; and Mona Domosh, *Invented Cities: The Creation of Landscape in Nineteenth-Century New York and Boston* (New Haven, CT: Yale University Press, 1996), 30, 33.

58 "Riverside Park, Chicago," *Horticulturist and Journal of Rural Arts* 25 (November 1870): 325 (advertisement, first quote); Charles N. Lowrie, "Suburban Home Grounds," in *Second Report of the Park and Outdoor Art Association* (Boston: Rockwell and Churchill Press, 1898), 84 (second quote), 87–88 (third quote). See Archer, "Country and City in the American Romantic Suburb," 139–40, 152–55.

59 O'Connell, *Hub's Metropolis*, 26–27, 28 (quote), 48–49, 77–79, 85, 87, 103, 107.

60 Brian Donahue, "Remaking Boston, Remaking Massachusetts," in *Remaking Boston: An Environmental History of the City and Its Surroundings*, ed. Anthony N. Penna and Conrad Edick Wright (Pittsburgh: University of Pittsburgh Press, 2009), 123; Stoll, *Larding the Lean Earth*, 202; Richard W. Judd, "Exurbia Meets Nature: Environmental Ideals for a Rootless Society," in *Landscape and the Ideology of Nature in Exurbia: Green Sprawl*, ed. Kirsten Valentine Cadieux and Laura Taylor (New York: Taylor & Francis, 2012), 60–77.

61 *Boston Transcript*, n.d., ca. January 1892, Charles Eliot Scrapbook, Trustees of Reservations Archives & Research Center, Sharon, MA, 67 (quote). See Cynthia Zaitzevsky, *Frederick Law Olmsted and the Boston Park System* (Cambridge, MA: Belknap Press, 1982), 58–60; Hou, *City Natural*, 103; Sam Bass Warner, *Streetcar Suburbs: The Process of Growth in Boston, 1870–1900* (Cambridge, MA: Harvard University Press, 1962); and Eric A. Macdonald, "The Art Which Mends Nature: The Discourse of American Environmental Design in *Garden and Forest*, 1888–1897" (PhD diss., University of Wisconsin–Madison, 2006), 267.

62 Charles S. Sargent, "The True Purpose of a Large Park," *Garden and Forest* 10 (June 2, 1897): 212. See Sargent, "Art and Nature in Landscape-Gardening," *Garden and Forest* 10 (May 19, 1897): 191.

63 Macdonald, "Art Which Mends Nature," 21, 276 (first quote), 337–38; Charles S. Sargent, "The Beautiful in the Surroundings of Life," *Garden and Forest* 5 (November 9, 1892): 529 (second quote). See Sargent, "A Reclaimed Swamp," *Garden and Forest* 5 (October 19, 1892): 494; Sargent, "The Love of Nature—I," *Garden and Forest* 5 (April 27, 1892): 193–94; and Hou, *City Natural*, 112.

64 Franklin Waugh, *The Natural Style of Landscape Gardening* (Boston: Richard G. Badger, 1917), 51 (quote). See Hou, *City Natural*, 123; and Macdonald, "Art Which Mends Nature," 207–8, 214–15, 321, 352.

65 Mariana Griswold [Mrs. Schuyler] Van Rensselaer, *Art Out of Doors: Hints on Good Taste in Gardening* (New York: C. Scribner's Sons, 1897), 252 (second quote), 254, 255 (first quote), 56, 260. See Hou, *City Natural*, 55, 70; and Frederick Law Olmsted

Sr. and J. B. Harrison, *Landscape Architecture* 3 (July 1913): 151 (note: Olmsted died in 1903; the report is a reprint).

66 Charles S. Sargent, "The Artistic Aspect of Trees," *Garden and Forest* 1 (December 12, 1888): 493. See Macdonald, "Art Which Mends Nature," 92–93; Charles S. Sargent, "The Administration of Public Parks," *Garden and Forest* 2 (February 6, 1889): 61; and Charles S. Sargent, "The Field of Landscape-Art," *Garden and Forest* 10 (April 28, 1897): 161.

67 O'Connell, *Hub's Metropolis*, 53.

68 Macdonald, "Art Which Mends Nature," 25–26, 307.

69 Charles Mulford Robinson, *The Improvement of Towns and Cities; or, The Practical Basis of Civic Aesthetics* (New York: G. P. Putnam, 1906), 132 (quote), 33–34.

70 Schuyler, *New Urban Landscape*, 64, 65 (Downing quote); 66–67; Robinson, *Improvement of Towns and Cities*, 154 (second quote). See Machor, *Pastoral Cities*, 148; Zaitzevsky, *Olmsted*, 76; Runte, *National Parks*, 2; and Judd, *Second Nature*, 224.

71 Schuyler, *New Urban Landscape*, 54, 40–41, 50–54, 334–36; Sargent, "Debt of America to Downing," 211; Rogers, *Landscape Design*, 332; "Visitor," "Landscape Gardening as Applied to Rural Cemeteries," *Horticulturist and Journal of Rural Arts* 17 (December 1862): 556–57; D. D. Slave, "Rural Cemeteries," *Horticulturist and Journal of Rural Arts* 23 (April 1868): 97.

72 Downing, *Rural Essays*, 150 (first quote); Frederick Law Olmsted, *Public Parks: Being Two Papers Read before the American Social Science Association in 1870 and 1880* (Brookline, MA, 1902), 91 (second quote). See Rogers, *Landscape Design*, 337.

73 Olmsted, *Public Parks*, 15 (quote). See Peter Walker and Melanie Simo, *Invisible Gardens: The Search for Modernism in the American Landscape* (Cambridge, MA: MIT Press, 1994), 14; Frederick Law Olmsted, *Walks and Talks of an American Farmer in England* (Columbus, OH: J. H. Riley, 1859), 70, 72; Karson, *Genius for Place*, 10; and Zaitzevsky, *Olmsted*, 20–22.

74 Andrew Menard, "The Enlarged Freedom of Frederick Law Olmsted," *New England Quarterly* 83 (September 2010): 518 (first quote); Olmsted, *Public Parks*, 46 (third quote), 60 (second quote). See Frederick Law Olmsted, *Civilizing American Cities: A Selection of Frederick Law Olmsted's Writings on City Landscapes*, ed. S. B. Sutton (Cambridge, MA: MIT Press, 1971), 80; Geoffrey Blodgett, "Frederick Law Olmsted: Landscape Architecture as Conservative Reform," *Journal of American History* 62 (March 1976): 870; Karson, *Genius for Place*, 10–11; and Machor, *Pastoral Cities*, 170–71.

75 "Horticola," "Landscape Gardening as a Profession," *Garden and Forest* 1 (April 18, 1880): 87 (first quote); Charles S. Sargent, "The Administration of Public Parks," *Garden and Forest* 2 (February 6, 1889): 61 (second and fourth quotes); Blodgett, "Olmsted," 870 (third quote); "The Influence of Central Park upon Public Taste," *Horticulturist and Journal of Rural Arts* 19 (August 1864): 237 (fifth quote). See Roy Rosenzweig, *Eight Hours for What We Will: Workers and Leisure in an Industrial City, 1870–1920* (New York: Cambridge University Press, 1983), 127–28.

76 Domosh, *Invented Cities*, 33. See Rawson, *Eden on the Charles*, 22–29, 33, 64–65.

77 Horace W. S. Cleveland, *The Public Grounds of Chicago: How to Give Them Character and Expression* (Chicago: C. D. Lakey, 1869), 8 (first quote), 9 (second quote), 10 (third quote), 11 (fourth quote), 10 (fifth–eighth quotes). See Karl Haglund, *Inventing the Charles River* (Cambridge, MA: MIT Press and Charles River Conservancy, 2003), 80.

78 Cleveland, *Public Grounds of Chicago*, 10; Haglund, *Inventing the Charles River*, 86, 93.
79 Mary V. Frye, "The Historical Development of Municipal Parks in the United States: Concepts and Their Application" (PhD diss., University of Illinois, 1964), 74. See Rogers, *Landscape Design*, 349–50; Harold A. Caparn, James Sturgis Pray, and Downing Vaux, eds., *Transactions of the American Society of Landscape Architects from Its Inception in 1899 to the End of 1908* (Harrisburg, PA: J. H. McFarland and Mt. Pleasant Press, 1912), 44; and Zaitzevsky, *Olmsted*, 35–37, 44–45.
80 *Springfield (MA) Republican*, February 6, 1901 (first quote); John Hanson Mitchell, *Paradise of All These Parts: A Natural History of Boston* (Beacon Press, 2009), 144, 145 (second quote); Anne Whiston Spirn, "Landscape Planning and the City," *Landscape and Urban Planning* 13 (1986): 438 (third quote). See Whiston Spirn, "Reclaiming Common Ground: Water, Neighborhoods, and Public Places," in *The American Planning Tradition: Culture and Policy*, ed. Robert Fishman (Washington, DC: Woodrow Wilson Center Press, 2000), 306–7.
81 Olmsted, *Public Parks*, 52 (quote), 74–75. See Arthur A. Shurtleff, "The Boston Park System," *Journal of Geography* 2, no. 6 (1903): 307–8; Newton, *Design on the Land*, 293; Zaitzevsky, *Olmsted*, 55, 57, 63–68, 70–73, 82–85, 88, 91, 97; and Blodgett, "Olmsted," 886.
82 Robbins, "Park-Making as a National Art," 87 (first quote); Downing, *Rural Essays*, 242 (second quote); Sylvester Baxter, "A Great Civic Awakening in America," *Century Illustrated Magazine* 64 (June 1902): 255 (third quote). See Farwell, *Village Improvement*, 4–5.
83 *Boston Herald*, October 16, 1890 (first quote); Robbins, "Public Improvement," 742 (second quote), 750. See Frederick Law Olmsted, "Parks, Parkways and Pleasure-Grounds I," *Garden and Forest* 8 (May 15, 1895): 192; and Sean McCarrick Fagan, "An Analysis of the Evolution of Theory and Management in the Trustees of Reservations" (master's thesis, University of Pennsylvania, 2008), 22–23.

Chapter 2: Awakening the Preservation Spirit

1 Sheafe Satterthwaite, "Topics: Keeping New England's Heritage in Trust," *New York Times*, August 9, 1968; Gordon Abbott Jr., *Saving Special Places: A Centennial History of the Trustees of Reservations: Pioneer of the Land Trust Movement* (Ipswich, MA: Ipswich Press, 1993), 12.
2 Abbott, *Saving Special Places*, 3, 10 (quote), 11. See Frederick John Pratson, "Yankee Heritage Is Secured without Government Aid," *Smithsonian*, June 1977, 94.
3 Michael Rawson, *Eden on the Charles: The Making of Boston* (Cambridge, MA: Harvard University Press, 2010), 234. See Michael Holleran, *Boston's "Changeful Times": Origins of Preservation & Planning in America* (Baltimore: Johns Hopkins University Press, 1998), 3–4, 39–42, 50–55.
4 Charles S. Sargent, "The Need of More Public Pleasure-Grounds," *Garden and Forest* 10 (January 27, 1897): 31.
5 Charles W. Eliot, *Charles Eliot: Landscape Architect* (Boston: Houghton Mifflin, 1903), 1–4; Keith N. Morgan, "Charles Eliot, Landscape Architect: An Introduction to his Life and Work," *Arnoldia* (Summer 1999): 8.

6 Melanie Louise Simo, *Forest and Garden: Traces of Wildness in a Modernizing Land, 1897–1949* (Charlottesville: University of Virginia Press, 2003), 12. See Eliot, *Eliot*, 10–15, 28.
7 *Boston Transcript*, March 8, 1892, Charles Eliot Scrapbook (online), Trustees of Reservations Archives & Research Center, Sharon, MA (hereafter CES), 71. See Norman T. Newton, *Design on the Land: the Development of Landscape Architecture* (Cambridge, MA: Harvard University Press, 1971) 320; and Eliot, *Eliot*, 32–34, 204.
8 Eliot, *Eliot*, 104 (second quote), 140 (third quote), 157 (fourth quote), 219–23, 231, 321 (first quote).
9 Newton, *Design on the Land*, 236–38, 239 (first quote), 240–41; Charles Eliot in Morgan, "Eliot," 9 (second quote).
10 Charles Eliot in Parris Thaxter Farwell, *Village Improvement* (New York: Sturgis & Walton, 1913), 8 (first quote); Eliot, *Eliot*, 32, 54 (second quote).
11 Charles Eliot in Eric A. Macdonald, "The Art Which Mends Nature: The Discourse of American Environmental Design in Garden and Forest, 1888–1897" (PhD diss., University of Wisconsin–Madison, 2006), 307. See Eliot, *Eliot*, 15–30.
12 Eliot, *Eliot*, 217 (second quote), 313 (first and third quotes), 314.
13 Eliot, *Eliot*, 314 (first quote); Charles Eliot, "Beauties of the Maine Coast," CES, 16 (second quote).
14 Eliot, *Eliot*, 217, 218 (quote), 304.
15 Charles Eliot in Mary V. Frye, "The Historical Development of Municipal Parks in the United States: Concepts and Their Application" (PhD diss., University of Illinois, 1964), 92 (first quote); Eliot, *Eliot*, 228 (second and third quotes), 231 (fourth quote), 267. See Morgan, "Eliot," 13–15; Steven T. Moga, "Marginal Lands and Suburban Nature: Open Space Planning and the Case of the 1893 Boston Metropolitan Parks Plan," *Journal of Planning History* 8 (November 2009): 312; Donald George Jones, "Recreating the Wilderness: The Cultural Landscape of Lynn Woods, a Late Nineteenth-Century Public Park in Lynn, Massachusetts" (PhD diss., Boston University, 1994), 68; and Macdonald, "Art Which Mends Nature," 358.
16 *Boston Herald*, December 17, 1891; Charles S. Sargent, "The Waverly Oaks," *Garden and Forest* 3 (February 19, 1890): 85; Charles Eliot, "The Waverly Oaks," *Garden and Forest* 3 (March 5, 1890): 117.
17 Eliot, "Waverly Oaks," 117 (first quote); Charles S. Sargent, "Wasted Effort in Forest-Reform," *Garden and Forest* 3 (March 5, 1890): 109 (second quote); *Boston Post*, May 1, 1890, CES, 1 (third quote). See Eliot, *Eliot*, 316.
18 *Salem (MA) Gazette*, August 18, 1891, CES, 43 (first quote); *Boston Herald*, ca. February 1893, CES, 97 (second quote). See *Boston Herald*, ca. December 1891, CES, 65; and *Boston Herald*, July 9, 1892, CES, 86.
19 *Boston Post*, ca. May 1892, CES, 10 (first quote); *Springfield (MA) Republican*, September 2, 1891, CES 47 (second quote); *Boston Post*, May 28, 1890, CES, 10 (third quote); "Beautiful and Historical Places," Circular no. 2, CES, 30a (fourth quote); John Ennekin in *Boston Transcript*, March 8, 1892, CES, 71 (fifth quote); *Transcript*, March 8, 1892, CES, 71 (sixth quote). See *Boston Transcript*, May 26, 1890, CES, 9; *Worcester Daily Spy*, February 5, 1891; "The Preservation of Beautiful and Historical Places in Massachusetts," CES, 31; *Boston Post*, March 11, 1891, CES, 34; and Chapter 196 Acts of the Legislature of Massachusetts 1890, CES, 41e.

20 Eliot, *Eliot*, 321–25, 332–35, 343; "Notes and Queries," *New-England Historical and Genealogical Register* 45 (January 1891): 83; *Garden and Forest*, July 2, 1890, CES, 41f; *Boston Herald*, May 25, 1890, CES, 7; *First Annual Report of the Trustees of Public Reservations*, 1891 (hereafter ARTPR), 6–7, 15, 18.

21 *Boston Journal*, March 10, 1891; Stephen T. Riley, "Charles Francis Adams (1835–1915), Conservationist," *Proceedings of the Massachusetts Historical Society* 90 (1978): 28–35; "The Trustees of Reservations," CES, 41b–41c; "An Act to Incorporate the Trustees of Public Reservations," CES, 33.

22 Farwell, *Village Improvement*, 144–47; "Waldemere—Seaside Residence of P. T. Barnum," *Horticulturist and Journal of Rural Arts* 27 (October 1872): 288–90; Charles Mulford Robinson, *The Improvement of Towns and Cities, or The Practical Basis of Civic Aesthetics* (New York: G. P. Putnam, 1906), 159–60; Charles S. Sargent, "The Preservation of Natural Scenery," *Garden and Forest* 3 (July 23, 1890): 354; Abbott, *Saving Special Places*, 9.

23 Robert McCullough, *The Landscape of Community: A History of Communal Forests in New England* (Hanover, NH: University Press of New England, 1995), 35, 88, 149; Jones, "Recreating the Wilderness," 164, 214–18; 221–22, 127, 232, 236, 254; M. C. Robbins, "New England Parks," *Garden and Forest* 4 (August 12, 1891): 374; "The Free Public Forest," ca. September 1895, CES, 131.

24 Metropolitan Park Commissioners, *A History and Description of the Boston Metropolitan Parks* (Boston: Wright & Potter, 1900), 8–9; "Middlesex Fells," *Massachusetts Ploughman and New England Journal of Agriculture* 41 (June 10, 1882): 2; "Parks in and Near Large Cities," *Century* 45 (April 1893): 952–53; "Laws of New York," CES, 22; "New Hampshire Forestry Commission, 1889," CES, 24.

25 "Our Forest Reservations," *Boston Transcript*, March 10, 1894, CES, 109. See Ethan Carr, "The Twentieth-Century Landscape Park," *George Wright Forum* 13, no. 1 (1996): 11; and *Boston Transcript*, October 27, 1894, CES, 113.

26 Eliot, *Eliot*, 317, 447, 448 (quote). See Charles S. Sargent, "The Massachusetts Trustees of Public Reservations," *Garden and Forest* 10 (September 22, 1897): 369; and Morgan, "Eliot," 15.

27 *Springfield (MA) Republican*, May 2, 1891, CES, 36 (first quote); *Springfield (MA) Republican*, March 9, 1891, CES, 34 (second quote). See *Boston Herald*, August 1, 1893.

28 Eliot, *Eliot*, 345; *Fourth ARTPR* (1894), 14–15; Sean McCarrick Fagan, "An Analysis of the Evolution of Theory and Management in the Trustees of Reservations" (master's thesis, University of Pennsylvania, 2008), 12–14.

29 Cynthia Zaitzevsky, *Frederick Law Olmsted and the Boston Park System* (Cambridge, MA: Harvard University Belknap Press, 1982), 18; *Boston Herald*, June 1, 1893; Moga, "Marginal Lands," 317.

30 *Boston Transcript*, August 17, 1895, CES, 128. See *Boston Herald*, March 31, 1893, CES, 99; *Boston Herald*, September 28, 1891, CES, 53; *Boston Herald*, ca. February 1893, CES, 97; *Boston Post*, May 1, 1890, CES, 1; and Eliot, *Eliot*, 342.

31 "To the Rescue," *Boston Transcript*, August 17, 1895, CES, 128 (first and second quotes); Charles S. Sargent, "Natural Beauty in Urban Parks," *Garden and Forest* 10 (June 30, 1897): 251 (third quote). See *Boston Transcript*, June 23, 1892, CES, 81; Karl Haglund, *Inventing the Charles River* (Cambridge, MA: MIT Press and Charles River Conservancy, 2003), 131; Eliot, *Eliot*, 208–9; and Macdonald, "Art Which Mends Nature," 243–46.

32 *Boston Post*, August 8, 1891, CES, 39; Haglund, *Inventing the Charles River*, 120.
33 *Boston Herald*, September 6, 1891, CES, 51 (first quote), 52; Charles Eliot, "A Massachusetts Forest," *Garden and Forest* 4 (August 26, 1891): 405 (second quote). See Sylvester Baxter, "A Trust to Protect Nature's Beauty," *American Monthly Review of Reviews* 23 (January 1901): 42–48; Newton, *Design on the Land*, 326; Shen Hou, *The City Natural: "Garden and Forest" Magazine and the Rise of American Environmentalism* (Pittsburgh: University of Pittsburgh Press, 2013), 81; Haglund, *Inventing the Charles River*, 120; Elizabeth Barlow Rogers, *Landscape Design: A Cultural and Architectural History* (New York: Harry N. Abrams, 2001), 351; and Sylvester Baxter, "The Boston Metropolitan Park Movement," *Garden and Forest* 5 (February 20, 1892): 62.
34 Charles Eliot in Newton, *Design on the Land*, 323; 324 (first quote); *Boston Herald*, April 1, 1893, CES, 101 (second quote). See *Boston Herald*, January 24, 1892, CES, 61; Charles Eliot, "The Boston Metropolitan Reservations," *New England Magazine* 21 (September 1896): 117; Charles Eliot, "Report of the Landscape Architect," in *Report of the Board of Metropolitan Park Commissioners* (January 1893), House doc. no. 150, 92; and Moga, "Marginal Lands," 323.
35 *Boston Herald*, December 17, 1891 (first quote); Charles S. Sargent, "The Boston Metropolitan Park Commission," *Garden and Forest* 5 (September 7, 1892): 421 (second quote).
36 *Boston Herald*, June 3, 1892; Riley, "Charles Francis Adams," 28–30, 35; Governor's Advisory Commission on Open Space and Outdoor Recreation, *Report and Recommendations* (Boston, 1969), 8; Metropolitan Park Commissioners, *History and Description*, 15; Charles S. Sargent, "Boston's Proposed Metropolitan Park System," *Garden and Forest* 6 (February 8, 1893): 61–62.
37 Charles Eliot in Charles S. Sargent, "Boston's Proposed Metropolitan Park System," 61 (quote). See Newton, *Design on the Land*, 325–28; Charles Zueblin, "The Civic Renaissance: Metropolitan Boston," *Chautauquan* 5 (January 1904): 483; Sylvester Baxter, "Parks and Playgrounds of Greater Boston," *Boston Herald*, September 25, 1904; *Boston Herald*, ca. December 1891, CES, 65; and Eliot, "Report of the Landscape Architect," 89-91.
38 *Boston Herald*, September 6, 1891, CES, 52 (first quote); "Secretary's Report" in Metropolitan Park Commissioners, *Report*, 2 (second quote), 105 (third and fourth quotes).
39 Eliot, "Report of the Landscape Architect," 105 (first and second quotes).
40 B. E. Fernow, "Aesthetic Forestry," in *Second Annual Report*, by American Park and Outdoor Art Association (Boston: Rockwell and Churchill Press, 1898), 146 (first quote); Eliot quoted in Carr, "Twentieth-Century Landscape Park," 1996, 18 (second and third quotes). See Michael P. Conzen and George K. Lewis, *Boston: A Geographical Portrait* (Cambridge, MA: Ballinger, 1976), 5; and David Schuyler, *The New Urban Landscape: The Redefinition of City Form in Nineteenth-Century America* (Baltimore: Johns Hopkins University Press, 1986), 144.
41 "Parks in and Near Large Cities," 953; Haglund, *Inventing the Charles River*, 135; Lawrence W. Kennedy, *Planning the City upon a Hill: Boston since 1630* (Amherst: University of Massachusetts Press, 1992), 94; Sylvester Baxter, "Boston's New Metropolitan Parks," *Garden and Forest* 7 (January 17, 1894): 22.
42 William T. Pierce, "The Metropolitan Park System of Boston," in *First Annual Report*, by American Park and Outdoor Art Association (Louisville, KY, 1897), 63;

Charles S. Sargent, "Park Work Near Boston," *Garden and Forest* 9 (April 29, 1896): 171; Zueblin, "Civic Renaissance: Metropolitan Boston," 482–84; *San Diego Union*, November 27, 1902; James C. O'Connell, *The Hub's Metropolis: Greater Boston's Development from Railroad Suburbs to Smart Growth* (Cambridge, MA: MIT Press, 2013), 94.

43 Arthur A. Shurtleff, "The Boston Park System," *Journal of Geography* 2, no. 6 (1903): 314 (first quote); Ellen Wright in Walter Kittredge, "The Middlesex Fells: A Flourishing Urban Forest," *Arnoldia* 70, no. 3 (2013): 3 (second quote). See "In the New Roads," n.p., October 1894, CES, 120; Rawson, *Eden on the Charles*, 235, 243–51; "A Noble Trust," *Independent* 53 (March 7, 1901): 574; and *Boston Transcript*, May 30, 1892, CES, 78.

44 "In the New Roads," n.p., October 1894, CES, 120 (quote). See *Boston Transcript*, June 23, 1892, CES, 81; and *Boston Herald*, March 4, 1994.

45 Charles H. Dalton in *Boston Herald*, May 20, 1900. See Charles S. Sargent, "Park Work near Boston," *Garden and Forest* 9 (April 29, 1896): 171; "Trolleys in the Wild Parks," n.p., CES, 140; and Charles Eliot, *Vegetation and Scenery in the Metropolitan Reservations of Boston: A Forestry Report Written by Charles Eliot and Presented to the Metropolitan Park Commission, February 15, 1897* (Boston: Olmsted, Olmsted, and Eliot, 1897), 7.

46 Fernow, "Aesthetic Forestry," 145–46 (all quotes).

47 Eliot, *Eliot*, 710, 711 (second quote), 716 (first quote). See Richard Brewer, *Conservancy: The Land Trust Movement in America* (Hanover, NH: Dartmouth College and University Press of New England, 2003), 18; and R. Bruce Stephenson, *John Nolen, Landscape Architect and City Planner* (Amherst: University of Massachusetts Press, 2015), 33–34.

48 Eliot, *Vegetation and Scenery*, 9–10, 11 (quote), 14, 18–19, 10. See Charles S. Sargent, "The Metropolitan Parks of Boston," *Garden and Forest* 8 (May 1, 1895): 121, 172.

49 Eliot, *Vegetation and Scenery*, 18, 19 (quote).

50 Robinson, *Improvement of Towns and Cities*, 153 (first quote); *Boston Transcript*, October 27, 1894, CES, 113 (second and third quote). See *Boston Transcript*, ca. January 1892, CES 70; and Metropolitan Park Commissioners, *History and Description*, 9, 14.

51 Rawson, *Eden on the Charles*, 265, 270 (first quote), 276; Eliot, *Vegetation and Scenery*, 10 (second quote); Eliot, *Eliot*, 657.

52 *Ninth ARTPR* (1899), 16–17; Fernow, "Aesthetic Forestry," 144–45.

53 *Cambridge Tribune*, October 27, 1894, CES, 117; Charles S. Sargent, "The Charles River at Boston," *Garden and Forest* 7 (May 16, 1894): 191–92; "Cambridge Aldermen Favor the Charles River Dam," n.p., CES, 117; James C. O'Connell, "How Metropolitan Parks Shaped Greater Boston, 1893–1945," in *Remaking Boston: An Environmental History of the City and Its Surroundings*, ed. Anthony N. Penna and Conrad Edick Wright (Pittsburgh: University of Pittsburgh Press, 2009), 175–76; "Revere Beach as a Park," n.p., November 15, 1895, CES, 130; Shurtleff, "Boston Park System," 313.

54 *Boston Herald*, September 28, 1891, CES, 53 (first quote); *Kansas City Star*, April 4, 1897 (second quote); Mira L. Dock, "Forest Reservations," in *Sixth Annual Report*, by American Park and Outdoor Art Association (Rochester, NY: Democrat and Chronicle Press, 1902), 20. See Abbott, *Saving Special Places*, 24–25.

55 "The Attempt to Save Niagara," *Century Illustrated Magazine*, April 1885, 954 (quote). See "Parks in and Near Large Cities," 953; *Boston Herald*, July 6, 1893; *Third ARTPR* (1893), 14; Howard Potter, "Preserve the Adirondacks," CES, 25a; *Boston Transcript*, May 24, 1890, CES, 6; Mary Caroline Robbins, "The Art of Public Improvement," *Atlantic Monthly*, December 1896, 749; and Charles S. Sargent, "The Value of Good Roads," *Garden and Forest* 4 (March 25, 1891): 134.

56 *Boston Herald*, March 1, 189, CES 99 (first quote); *Springfield (MA) Republican*, September 2, 1891, CES, 47 (second quote); Appendix I [John B. Harrison], "A Report upon the Public Holdings of the Shore Towns of Massachusetts," *First ARTPR* (1891; hereafter "Report of the Shore Towns"), 49, 61, 56 (third quote). See *First ARTPR* (1891), 17; and *Boston Post*, November 12, 1891, CES, 60a.

57 "Report of the Shore Towns," 32 (first and second quotes), 44, 60; *Boston Transcript*, ca. November 26, 1891, CES, 61 (third quote). See *Salem (MA) Gazette*, November 26, 1891, CES, 61; Franklin Waugh, *The Landscape Beautiful: A Study of the Utility of the Natural Landscape, Its Relation to Human Life and Happiness* (New York: Orange Judd, 1910), 229–30; *Boston Transcript*, May 26, 1890, CES, 9; and *Cape Ann Breeze* (Gloucester, MA), August 21, 1891, CES, 45.

58 *Springfield (MA) Republican*, September 2, 1891 (first quote); Mrs. J. H. Robbins, "A Typical New England View," *Garden and Forest* 4 (December 9, 1891): 578 (second quote). See "Report of the Shore Towns," 45; and J. B. Harrison, "The State and the Forest," *Cosmopolitan*, July 1892, 305.

59 "Report of the Shore Towns," 59 (first quote); Charles S. Sargent, "Public Holdings in Massachusetts," *Garden and Forest* 7 (September 5, 1894): 351 (second quote). See Matthew McKenzie, *Clearing the Coastline: The Nineteenth-Century Ecological & Cultural Transformation of Cape Cod* (Hanover, NH: University Press of New England, 2010), 138–39.

60 J. B. Harrison, "In the Shore Towns of Massachusetts," *Garden and Forest* 4 (November 18, 1891): 549 (first quote); "Report of the Shore Towns," 26, 41, 50 (second and third quotes), 54–55. See *Boston Herald*, December 30, 1894.

61 "Report of the Shore Towns," 21, 23 (second quote), 27 (first quote). See *Third ARTPR* (1893), 27; *Gloucester (MA) Times*, August 25, 1891, CES, 45; and *American Architect and Building News*, October 13, 1894.

62 "Report of the Shore Towns," 29–30, 37, 55 (first quote), 57 (second quote). See *Boston Herald*, December 30, 1894; *Beverly (MA) Citizen*, March 26, 1892; and *Mount Desert Herald* (Bar Harbor, ME), June 6, 1890, CES, 12.

63 "Report of the Shore Towns," 30 (first quote), 37 (second and third quotes).

64 *Mount Desert Herald*, June 6, 1890, CES, 12 (first quote); *Cape Ann Breeze* (Gloucester, MA), August 14, 1891, CES, 42 (second quote); "Report of the Shore Towns," 45 (third quote), 60. See *Springfield (MA) Republican*, September 2, 1891, CES, 47; and *Boston Herald*, December 30, 1894.

65 Trustees of Public Reservations, *Report of the Trustees of Public Reservations, on the Subject of the Province Lands*, HR 339, February 1893, in *Second ARTPR* (1892), 6 (first quote), 7; *New York Evening Post*, September 18, 1891, CES, 49 (second quote). See *Boston Herald*, September 19, 1891; and Baxter, "Trust to Protect Nature's Beauty," 44.

66 Trustees of Public Reservations, *Report on the Subject of the Province Lands*, 6, 7, 9–12 (quote). See "The Province Lands at Provincetown," *First ARTPR* (1891), 65–68; *Boston Herald*, June 25, 1892; and *Springfield (MA) Republican*, October 27, 1891.

67 *New York Evening Post*, September 18, 1891, CES, 49 (first quote); *Provincetown (MA) Beacon*, September 19, 1891, CES 50 (second quote). See *Boston Herald*, September 19, 1891; *Provincetown (MA) Beacon*, October 3, 1891, CES, 54; and *Provincetown (MA) Advocate*, September 17, 1891, CES, 55.

68 *Provincetown (MA) Advocate*, October 1, 1891, CES 55 (first quote); *Provincetown (MA) Post*, September 5, 1891, CES, 48 (second quote); *Boston Herald*, March 1, 1893, CES, 98 (third quote). See *Provincetown (MA) Beacon*, April 16, 1892, CES, 69; *Boston Herald*, September 19, 1891, CES, 48; *Boston Herald*, June 20, 1892, CES, 79; 48: *Provincetown (MA) Post*, September 5, 1891, CES 48; and *Boston Herald*, March 1, 1893, CES, 98.

69 Baxter, "Trust to Protect Nature's Beauty," 44 (quote). See Trustees of Public Reservations, *Report on the Subject of the Province Lands*, 14; Commonwealth of Massachusetts, *Report of the Committee on Conservation Relative to the Supervision of the Province Lands*, HR 2191, December 7, 1949 (Boston: Wright & Potter, 1950), 7–8, 14; Abbott, *Saving Special Places*, 18; and *Boston Herald*, August 29, 1894.

70 *Boston Transcript*, June 22, 1893, CES 104 (first quote); *Boston Herald*, November 15, 1891 (second quote). See *First ARTPR* (1891), 12–13; *Third ARTPR* (1893), 12; *Ninth ARTPR* (1899), 19–20; Eliot, *Eliot*, 344, 349; and Fagan, "Theory and Management of the Trustees," 17.

71 *Fourth ARTPR* (1894), 13, 14 (second quote), 15 (third quote), 16–17; *Fifth ARTPR* (1895), 13–14, 18 (first quote); *Tenth ARTPR* (1900), 18–19, 20 (fourth quote), 21. See *Eighth ARTPR* (1898), 14–17; *Ninth ARTPR* (1899), 14–15, 18; Charles S. Sargent, "The Massachusetts Trustees of Public Reservations," *Garden and Forest* 10 (September 22, 1897): 369; Abbott, *Saving Special Places*, 54–55; *Cleveland Plain Dealer*, August 5, 1896; *Boston Herald*, September 19, 1893; and *Worcester Spy*, October 11, 1894.

72 *Seventeenth ARTPR* (1907), 18; Fagan, "Theory and Management of the Trustees," 18–21; Brewer, *Conservancy*, 34; Baxter, "Trust to Protect Nature's Beauty," 46–48.

73 "Trustees of Public Reservations," *Forest and Stream* 40 (June 22, 1893): 25 (first quote); *Ninth ARTPR* (1899), 18 (second quote). See *Ninth ARTPR*, 16–19; *Sixteenth ARTPR* (1906), 14–15; and *Seventeenth ARTPR* (1907), 14.

74 O'Connell, *Hub's Metropolis*, 95; L. E. Holden, "Address," *Fourth Annual Report*, by American Park and Outdoor Art Association (n.p., 1900), 4; William H. Rivers, "Massachusetts State Forestry Programs," in *Stepping Back to Look Forward: A History of the Massachusetts Forest*, ed. Charles H. W. Foster (Petersham, MA: Harvard Forest, 1998), 150; *Ninth ARTPR* (1899), 20–21; Sargent, "Massachusetts Trustees of Public Reservations," 369.

75 *New York Post*, March 27, 1895, CES, 125 (first quote); "Preserving the Palisades," n.p., October 12, 1895, CES, 128 (second quote). See [*New York Post?*], ca. April 1985, CES, 126; and "How to Save the Palisades," n.p., ca. August 1894, CES, 112.

76 *Boston Herald*, November 24, 1892. See "Noble Trust," 574; Mrs. Charles F. Millspaugh, "Tree Protection in the United States," *Chautauquan* 41 (June 1905): 326; and Jim Collins and Richard Ober, "New Hampshire: Common Ground," in *Twentieth-Century New England Land Conservation: A Heritage of Civic Engagement*, ed. Charles H. W. Foster (Petersham, MA: Harvard Forest, 2009), 89–94.

77 *Boston Herald*, July 9, 1909; Brewer, *Conservancy*, 29.

78 John Hakola, *Legacy of a Lifetime: The Story of Baxter State Park* (Woolwich, ME: Baxter State Park Authority, 1981).
79 O'Connell, *Hub's Metropolis*, 95; *Tenth ARTPR* (1900), 24; National Resources Board and National Park Service, *Recreational Use of Land in the United States*, pt. II, *Report on Land Planning* (Washington, DC: GPO, 1934), 30; Carr, "Twentieth-Century Landscape Park," 15–16; Robinson, *Improvement of Towns and Cities*, 156–57; O'Connell, *Hub's Metropolis*, 95.
80 *Boston Herald*, December 30, 1894; Riley, "Charles Francis Adams, 25, 27; Charles S. Sargent, "The Park Movement in the United States," *Garden and Forest* 6 (May 24, 1893): 221–22.
81 Mark Stoll, *Protestantism, Capitalism, and Nature in America* (Albuquerque: University of New Mexico Press, 1997), 148; Alfred Runte, *National Parks: The American Experience* (Lincoln: University of Nebraska Press, 1979), 65, 67, 118.
82 National Resources Planning Board, *Public Land Acquisition in a National Land-Use Program*, pt. 1, *Rural Lands* (Washington, DC: GPO, 1940), 5, 22; National Conference on Outdoor Recreation, *Proceedings, January 20–21, 1926*, 70th Cong., 1st sess., SD158 (Washington, DC: GPO, 1928): 40, 45–47.
83 American Scenic and Historic Preservation Society, *Annual Report of the American Scenic and Historic Preservation Society to the Legislature of New York, 1896–1900* (New York: State Printer, 1900), 29 (first quote); Kent C. Ryden, *Landscape with Figures: Nature & Culture in New England* (Iowa City: University of Iowa Press, 2001), 19 (second quote), 20. See Sylvester Baxter, "A Great Civic Awakening in America: The Organized Instruments for the Creation and Preservation of Beauty in Public Places," *Century Illustrated Magazine* 44 (June 1902): 261; *Boston Transcript*, ca. April 21, 1892, CES, 74; and Franklin Waugh, *The Natural Style of Landscape Gardening* (Boston: Richard G. Badger, 1917), 8–29.
84 Carr, "Twentieth-Century Landscape Park," 19 (first quote); Herbert Evison, "Park Lands of States Increased in Number," *New York Times*, April 21, 1929, 136 (second quote).

Chapter 3: Stewardship Strategies

1 John Nolen, "The Parks and Recreation Facilities in the United States," *Annals of the American Academy of Political and Social Science* 35 (March 1, 1910): 8 (first quote); *Boston Herald*, May 20, 1900 (second quote); Frederick Law Olmsted Jr., "Public Advertising," in *Fourth Report of the American Park and Outdoor Art Association* (Chicago, 1900), 7 (third quote). See Massachusetts State Planning Board, *Progress Report on State Planning for Massachusetts* (Boston, 1936), 327.
2 Horace William Shaler Cleveland, *The Public Grounds of Chicago: How to Give Them Character and Expression* (Chicago: C. D. Lakey, 1869), 7 (first quote); Mariana Griswold [Mrs. Schuyler] Van Rensselaer, *Art Out of Doors: Hints on Good Taste in Gardening* (New York: C. Scribner's Sons, 1897), 195 (second quote); John C. Olmsted, "The True Purpose of a Large Public Park," *First Report of the Park and Outdoor Art Association* (Louisville, KY, 1897), 12 (third quote).

3 "The Listener," n.p., n.d., Charles Eliot Scrapbook (online), Trustees of Reservations Archives & Research Center, Sharon, MA (hereafter CES), 36 (first quote); Thomas H. MacBride, "Rural Parks in a Prairie State," in *First Report of the Park and Outdoor Art Association* (Louisville, KY, 1897), 37 (second quote); L. H. Bailey, *The Nature-Study Idea: Being an Interpretation of the New School-Movement to Put the Child in Sympathy with Nature* (New York: Doubleday, Page, 1903), 34 (third quote). See "Parks for American Villages," *Village: A Journal for Village Life* 1 (January 1907): 69–70; *Fifty-Seventh Annual Report of the Trustees of Public Reservations* 1947 (hereafter *ARTPR*), 6; Nolen, "Parks and Recreation Facilities," 4; and Frederick Law Olmsted [?] to M. Lissner, February 12, 1912, box 1, folder 14, "Letters F. Steele, M. Choate," Charles W. Eliot II Papers, Trustees of Reservations Archives & Research Center, Sharon, MA (hereafter CWEII).

4 National Resources Board and National Park Service, *Recreational Use of Land in the United States*, pt. II, *Report on Land Planning* (Washington, DC: GPO, 1934), 14.

5 Frank A. Waugh, "Petticoat Hill for Example," *Outlook*, August 23, 1922, 679 (first quote), 680 (second quote). See Charles S. Sargent, "The Value of Rural Beauty," *Garden and Forest* 4 (July 8, 1891): 313; and Charles M. Loring, "President's Annual Address," *Fourth Report of the American Park and Outdoor Art Association* (Chicago, 1900), 28–29.

6 "Plan for Parks Is Complete," n.p., November 15, 1895, CES, 130 (first quote); Mary Caroline Robbins, "The Art of Public Improvement," *Atlantic Monthly*, December 1896, 746 (second quote). See "What the Electric and the Bicycle Give Us," n.p., ca. March 1895, CES, 130; and Scott Carlin, "Rediscovering Boston Harbor: The Political Geography of Urban Environmental Agendas" (PhD diss., Clark University, 1995), 119–20.

7 Charles Downing Lay, "Highways and Country-Planning," *Landscape Architecture* 7 (April 1917): 133.

8 *Boston Sunday Globe*, August 6, 1916; David Rozman, *Recreational and Forestry Uses of Land in Massachusetts* (Amherst: Massachusetts State College, 1933), 14; Blake Harrison, *The View from Vermont: Tourism and the Making of an American Rural Landscape* (Burlington: University of Vermont Press, 2006), 89, 92–93; *Lowell (MA) Sun*, December 4, 1922; Charles Zueblin, "The Civic Renascence: The Return to Nature," *Chautauquan*, (May 1904): 261; Massachusetts Historical Commission, *Historic & Archaeological Resources of the Boston Area: A Framework for Preservation Decisions* (Boston: Massachusetts Historical Commission, 1991), 94; *Boston Herald*, June 27, 1892, CES, 84.

9 Albert Shaw, introduction to *New Towns for Old: Achievements in Civil Improvement in Some American Small Towns and Neighborhoods*, by John Nolen and Charles Davock Warren (Cambridge, MA: Marshall Jones, 1927), xvi. See Wilbert L. Anderson, *The Country Town: A Study of Rural Evolution* (New York: Doubleday, Page, 1914), 27–28, 63.

10 Shaw, introduction, xxi (first quote); Anderson, *Country Town*, 184 (second quote). See Nolen and Warren, *New Towns for Old*, 2, 4, 7–9, 115–17; "The Village," *Village: A Journal for Village Life* 1 (December 1906): 3; Rozman, *Recreational and Forestry Uses*, 3, 5–6, 12–15; and Harrison, *View from Vermont*, 53–55.

11 Paul S. Sutter, *Driven Wild: How the Fight against Automobiles Launched the*

Modern Wilderness Movement (Seattle: University of Washington Press, 2002), 19, 31 (Bellasco quote). See Federated Societies on Planning Parks, *What about the Year 2000?* (Harrisburg, PA: J. Horace McFarland, 1929), 6, 9–10; *National Conference on Outdoor Recreation*, 42–43, 45–47, 50; *Boston Sunday Globe*, August 6, 1916; and National Resources Board and National Park Service, *Recreational Use of Land*, 65, 84, 94.

12 *Concord (MA) Enterprise*, March 15, 1939 (first quote); "To the Rescue," *Boston Transcript*, August 17, 1895, CES, 128 (second quote). See *Twenty-Fourth ARTPR* (1914), 16; and *Forty-Seventh ARTPR* (1937), 32.

13 Charles S. Bird, *Fifty-Eighth ARTPR* (1948), 13 (first quote); Winn Everett, "Saving the Beauty of a State for Posterity," *Leisure*, September 1936, box 1, folder 14, CWEII (second quote). See Ecological Society of America, *Preservation of Natural Conditions* (Springfield, IL: Schnepi and Barnes, 1922), 10; and "Riverside Drive Defacement," n.p., ca. February 15, 1896, CES, 135.

14 Charles S. Sargent, "Preservation of Natural Beauty," *Garden and Forest* 9 (August 19, 1896): 331. See Bailey, *Nature-Study Idea*, 98–99; Henry Baldwin, "A Shade Tree Chronology," *Forest Notes* 128 (Spring 1977): 6, 8; Charles Mulford Robinson, *The Improvement of Towns and Cities; or, The Practical Basis of Civic Aesthetics* (New York: G. P. Putnam, 1906), 124–25; and "The Age of Disfigurement," n.p., ca. June 1893, CES, 106.

15 Springfield (?), May 25, 1890, CES, 6 (first quote); Charles S. Sargent, "The Defacement of Scenery," *Garden and Forest* 5 (December 7, 1892): 577 (second quote). See *Fourth ARTPR* (1894), 18; *Fifth ARTPR* (1895), 14; *Eighth ARTPR* (1898), 18–19; *Ninth ARTPR* (1899), 22; "Laws of Massachusetts Relating to Public Open Spaces," *First ARTPR* (1891), 69–83; *Forty-Third ARTPR* (1933), 3–4; and *North Adams (MA) Transcript*, January 2, 1929.

16 Frederick Law Olmsted Jr., "A Summary of the Report of the Committee on Methods of Checking the Abuses of Public Advertising," in *Proceedings*, by American Park and Outdoor Art Association (n.p., 1900), 50–53 (first quote); "The Billboard Interests Assail the Law and Constitution of Massachusetts: What Can We Do about It?," box 2, folder 2 (1924–26), CWEII, (second quote). See George Kriehn, "The Abuses of Advertising and Their Correction," in *Proceedings*, 47; William H. Whyte, *The Last Landscape* (New York: Doubleday, 1968), 51; Harrison, *View from Vermont*, 108; and "The Campaign against Billboards," *Village: A Journal for Village Life* 1 (January 1907): 45.

17 Charles W. Eliot II, "The Influence of the Automobile on the Design of Park Roads," *Landscape Architecture* 13 (October 1922): 28 (third quote), 29, 32 (first quote); Arthur C. Comey, "Adapting a Park to Modern Needs," *Landscape Architecture* 11 (July 1921): 178 (second quote). See Marion Clawson, "The Crisis in Outdoor Recreation," *American Forests* (March 1959): 27; Wesley Ward, "Charles W. Eliot 2nd and His Continuing Legacy," *Special Places: A Newsletter of the Trustees of Reservations* (Spring 1993): 1–3; and Charles Downing Lay, "Notes on the Influence of Automobiles on Town, Country, and Estate Planning," *Landscape Architecture* 10 (October 1919): 90.

18 Arthur A. Shurtleff, "A New Hampshire Farm Group of 1805," *Landscape Architecture* 8 (October 1917): 20–21, 22 (first quote); Benton MacKaye, *The New Exploration: A Philosophy of Regional Planning* (1928; reprint, Urbana: University of Illinois

Press, 1962), 10, 14–15, 150 (second quote). See Mark Luccarelli, *Lewis Mumford and the Ecological Region: The Politics of Planning* (New York: Guilford Press, 1995), 75–77; Kristin Larsen, "Cities to Come: Clarence Stein's Postwar Regionalism," *Journal of Planning History* 4 (February 2005): 35; Federated Societies on Planning Parks, *What about the Year 2000?*, 14–15, 71; Lewis Mumford, "Regionalism and Irregionalism," *Sociological Review* 19 (October 1927): 283–84; Robert L. Dorman, *Revolt of the Provinces: The Regionalist Movement in America, 1920–1945* (Chapel Hill: University of North Carolina Press, 1993), 123; 129; 139; and Edward K. Spann, *Designing Modern America: The Regional Planning Association of America and Its Members* (Columbus: Ohio State University Press, 1996) 19, 20–22.

19 See National Conference on Outdoor Recreation, *Proceedings* (Washington, DC: GPO, 1926), 126 (quote), 127.

20 *Fitchburg (MA) Sentinel*, October 12, 1962 (quote). See Trustees of Public Reservations, *The Bay Circuit: A Practical Plan for the Extension of the Metropolitan Park System* (Boston: Trustees, 1937), 5; Walter Prichard Eaton, "Report on Open Space," ca. 1929, box 2, folder 13, CWEII; *Report of Governor's Committee on Needs and Uses of Open Spaces* (Boston, 1929), box 2, folder 4, CWEII; and MacKaye, *New Exploration*, 181–82.

21 Trustees of Public Reservations, *Bay Circuit*, 4, 10 (quote). See Corey W. Medeiros, "The Massachusetts Bay Circuit" (master's thesis, University of Massachusetts Boston, 2015), v, 2–4; and Massachusetts Department of Environmental Management, *Massachusetts Landscape Inventory: A Survey of the Commonwealth's Scenic Areas* (Boston: Department of Environmental Management, 1982), 3.

22 *Thirty-Ninth ARTPR* (1929), 28–30; Laurence B. Fletcher to "115 Senators and Representatives within the Metropolitan Park District" (letter), March 4, 1941, and Bernard Peterson, "New Park System Program Aims at 25 Mile Extension," *Boston Transcript*, March 8, 1941, both in Records of the Trustees of Public Reservations (hereafter TPR Records), vol. 7 (1940), Trustees of Reservations Archives & Research Center, Sharon, MA.

23 Walter Prichard Eaton, "Report on Open Space," ca 1929, box 2, folder 13, CWEII.

24 Benton MacKaye, *Highway Approaches to Boston: A Wayside Situation and What to Do about It* (Boston: Trustees of Public Reservations, 1931), 4, 5 (first quote), 11, 12 (second quote). See *Thirty-Ninth ARTPR*, 9; "Report of the Massachusetts Landscape Survey," *Fortieth ARTPR* (1933), 23–44; Medeiros, "Bay Circuit," 33–35, 40–41; and James C. O'Connell, *The Hub's Metropolis: Greater Boston's Development from Railroad Suburbs to Smart Growth* (Cambridge, MA: MIT Press, 2013), 160.

25 *Fitchburg (MA) Sentinel*, October 12, 1962 (first quote); MacKaye, *New Exploration*, 24 (second quote). See Massachusetts Historical Commission, *Historic & Archaeological Resources*, 110; *Thirty-Ninth ARTPR*, 6; and "Executive Committee Meeting," January 18, 1928, box 2, folder 4, CWEII.

26 Fletcher to "115 Senators and Representatives." See Medeiros, "Bay Circuit," 48–49, 52.

27 James C. O'Connell, "How Metropolitan Parks Shaped Greater Boston, 1893–1945," in *Remaking Boston: An Environmental History of the City and Its Surroundings*, ed. Anthony N. Penna and Conrad Edick Wright (Pittsburgh: University of Pittsburgh Press, 2009), 181–82; Sutter, *Driven Wild*, 37, 40–41, 53.

28 Walter Prichard Eaton to Charles W. Eliot II, July 27, 1925, box 2, folder 2, CWEII

(first and second quotes); Charles S. Bird and Laurence B. Fletcher, *Report of the Governor's Committee on Needs and Uses of Open Spaces* (Boston, 1929), 2–4 (third quote), 5. See Federated Societies on Planning Parks, *What about the Year 2000?*, 10; Theodore Roosevelt II to Charles Eliot, 2nd, July 11, 1925, box 1, folder 9, CWEII; "Letters from Open Space members, 1925–1926," box 1, folder 15, CWEII; Charles W. Eliot II to Theodore Roosevelt II, July 21, 1926, box 1, folder 15, CWEII; "Report Compiled by Charles Sumner Bird Jr., to Governor Alvan T. Fuller," November 1927, box 2, folder 4, CWEII; "Public Forest Reservations of Massachusetts," November 20, 1924, box 2, folder 2, CWEII; Bernard Peterson, "Building a Greater State, " *Boston Transcript*, n.d., box 2, folder 4, CWEII; and Charles W. Eliot II to George S. Lee Jr., August 7, 1925, box 1, folder 6, CWEII.

29 *Forty-Third ARTPR* (1933), 12 (second quote), 33–34, 39, 40 (first quote). See Gordon Abbott Jr., *Saving Special Places: A Centennial History of the Trustees of Reservations: Pioneer of the Land Trust Movement* (Ipswich, MA: Ipswich Press, 1993), 29–31; *Boston Transcript*, November 4, 1927, box 1, folder 6, CWEII; Charles W. Eliot II, "Draft—Program—Trustees Notes by Charles W. Eliot—November 16, 1959," box 1 folder 6, CWEII; C. E. Melville to Prof. Charles W. Blood, April 8, 1925, box 2, folder 10, CWEII; "The Massachusetts Landscape Survey questionnaire," box 2, folder 7, CWEII; *Boston Evening Transcript*, September 28, 1933, box 2, folder 7, CWEII; "An Act to Establish a Division of Parks in the Department of Conservation," box 2, folder 4, CWEII; Samuel A. York to Laurence B. Fletcher, November 21, 1933, box 2, folder 5, CWEII; "A Meeting of the Governor's Committee on Needs and Uses of Open Spaces," minutes, June 8, 1933, box 2, folder 5, CWEII; *Thirty-Ninth ARTPR* (1929), 30; *Fitchburg (MA) Sentinel*, October 7, 1933; and *Greenfield (MA) Recorder Gazette*, November 10, 1933.

30 Rozman, *Recreational and Forestry Uses*, 18; *Forty-Fifth ARTPR* (1935), 5–7.

31 Charles S. Bird to Charles W. Eliot II, March 8, 1927, box 1, folder 5, CWEII. See *Springfield Union*, April 27, 1915; *Concord (MA) Enterprise*, March 15, 1939; and *North Adams (MA) Transcript*, April 7, 1938.

32 *Thirty-Ninth ARTPR* (1929), 11–12, 13 (quote). See Sean McCarrick Fagan, "An Analysis of the Evolution of Theory and Management in the Trustees of Reservations" (master's thesis, University of Pennsylvania, 2008), 29; Abbott, *Saving Special Places*, 55–57; and *Fortieth ARTPR* (1940), 11, 14.

33 *Forty-Fourth ARTPR*, (1934), 2; *Forty-Fifth ARTPR* (1935), 8; *Forty-Seventh ARTPR* (1937), 5; Abbott, *Saving Special Places*, 286.

34 National Resources Board and National Park Service, *Recreational Use of Land*, 32; Langdon Smith, "Democratizing Nature through State Park Development," *Historical Geography* 41 (2013): 207–9.

35 Clarence M. Gordon to L. B. Fletcher, March 8, 1933, TPR Records, vol. 3 (1933); 105-A-B; "A Suggested Policy for Medfield Rhododendron Reservation," March 7, 1950, box 3, folder 5, CWEII; *Forty-Fifth ARTPR* (1935), 40–42, *Fiftieth ARTPR* (1940), 33–34; *Sixty-Eighth ARTPR* (1958), 34; *Sixty-Third ARTPR* (1953), 32. Note: In 1953 the TPR became the Trustees of Reservations. For reasons of consistency, I will continue with the designation *ARTPR*.

36 Abbott, *Saving Special Places*, 59; *Forty-Fifth ARTPR* (1935), 5–6.

37 Nolen and Warren, *New Towns for Old*, 32–33, 35, 38–39, 41, 44. See *Fortieth*

ARTPR (1933), 12; *Forty-Fourth ARTPR* (1934), 4–5, 22; *Forty-Fifth ARTPR* (1935), 1; and *Forty-Sixth ARTPR* (1936), 4–5, 29–32, 38.

38 L. B. Fletcher to Charles S. Bird, July 22, 1947, box 1, folder 13, CWEII (quotes). See Fagan, "Theory and Management in the Trustees," 24.

39 Fletcher Steele to William Ellery, November 17, 1941, TPR Records, vol. 7 (1940); "Committee on Nominations and Organization," n.d., TPR Records, vol. 13 (1955 and 1956), 2.

40 Robert McCullough, *The Landscape of Community: A History of Communal Forests in New England* (Hanover, NH: University Press of New England, 1995), 251(first quote); "Beautiful and Historical Places," Circular No. 2, CES, 30c (second quote); *Forty-Fourth ARTPR* (1934), 29 (third quote). See *Forty-Sixth ARTPR* (1936), 2; *Fifty-Sixth ARTPR* (1946), 8; and *Sixty-Third ARTPR* (1953), 13.

41 *Forty-Fourth ARTPR* (1934), 2 (first quote), 5 (second quote). See *Twenty-Second ARTPR* (1918), 18; *Twenty-Eighth ARTPR* (1918), 18; *Twenty-Ninth ARTPR* (1919), 15–17; *Thirtieth ARTPR* (1920), 16–17; and *Forty-Sixth ARTPR* (1936), 2.

42 Robert Walcott to Charles S. Bird, March 11, 1948, box 2, folder 10, CWEII (first quote); Laurence B. Fletcher, "Elliott Laurel Reservation, Phillipston," TPR Records, vol. 11 (1950 and 1951), (second quote); Fletcher Steele, "Report on Policies for the Reservations," n.d., box 2, folder 10, CWEII (third quote); *Forty-Fifth ARTPR* (1935), 42 (fourth quote). See *Fifty-Second ARTPR* (1942), 8.

43 R. B. Greeley, "The Public and Our Reservations," March 8, 1948, box 3, folder 5, CWEII (quotes).

44 Fagan, "Theory and Management in the Trustees of Reservations," 27–28; *Lowell (MA) Sun*, August 24, 1929.

45 *Salem (MA) Register*, August 13, 1891, CES, 42; William H. Tishler, "Historical Landscapes: An International Preservation Perspective," *Landscape Planning* 9 (1982): 92, 94–95; James M. Lingren, "'A Spirit That Fires the Imagination': Historic Preservation and Cultural Regeneration in Virginia and New England, 1850–1950," in *Giving Preservation a History: Histories of Historic Preservation in the United States*, ed. Max Page and Randall Mason (London: Routledge, 2004), 108; Michael Holleran, *Boston's "Changeful Times": Origins of Preservation & Planning in America* (Baltimore: Johns Hopkins University Press, 1998), 9–10, 43–44, 47; Marc Callis, "The Beginning of the Past: Boston and the Early Historic Preservation Movement, 1863–1918," *Historical Journal of Massachusetts* 32 (October 2004): 130–31; "History in Old Houses," *New York Times*, July 4, 1937, 14.

46 *Forty-Fifth ARTPR* (1935), 1 (first quote), 2, 5; *Fifty-Sixth ARTPR* (1946), 32 (second quote); *Acton Concord Enterprise*, March 15, 1939 (third quote). See *Forty-Eighth ARTPR* (1938), 13; *Forty-Ninth ARTPR* (1939), 10; and *Fifty-Eighth ARTPR* (1948), 15.

47 Fletcher Steele, "Report on Policies for the Reservations," n.d., box 2, folder 10, CWEII (first, second, and fourth quotes); *Fifty-Ninth ARTPR* (1949), 17 (third quote), 18. See Robert E. Cook, "Is Landscape Preservation an Oxymoron?," *George Wright Forum* 13, no. 1 (1996): 51–52; and *Fifty-Third ARTPR* (1943), 12.

48 *Sixty-Third ARTPR* (1953), 35 (quote). See Fletcher Steele, "Report on Policies for the Reservations," n.d., box 2, folder 10, CWEII; and Robert Walcott to Charles S. Bird, March 11, 1948, box 2, folder 10, CWEII.

49 *Sixty-First ARTPR* (1951), 12 (quote), 13. See *Fifty-Eighth ARTPR* (1948), 15;

Fifty-Ninth ARTPR (1949), 5–6, 8; *Sixty-Second ARTPR* (1952), 33; Ipswich Garden Club (Miriam W. Titcomb) to Trustees, August 1, 1950, TPR Records, vol. 11 (1950 and 1951); "Coordinator's Report," March 14, 1963, TPR Records, vol. 17 (1963 and 1964; note: for consistency's sake, I continue to use "TPR" after the organization changed its name in 1953); David C. Crockett, Charles W. Eliot, and Fletcher Steele, "Report of Committee on Policy Considerations," TPR Records, vol. 15 (1959 and 1960); Crockett, Eliot, Steele, "Report of Committee on Policy Considerations, when Mrs. Crane Bequeathed Castle Hill in 1949," box 3, folder 5, CWEII; *Seventy-Seventh ARTPR* (1967), 42–44; Fagan, "Theory and Management in the Trustees of Reservations," 32; and "Letters from Peter Hornbeck and Loring Conant 1961," CWEII, box 1, folder 2.

50 Abbott, *Saving Special Places*, 66, 69 (quote). See *Fifty-Eighth ARTPR* (1948), 4, 6–7, 14; and *North Adams (MA) Transcript*, October 4, 1948.

51 *Sixty-Fifth ARTPR* (1955), 8; *Sixty-Ninth ARTPR* (1959), 23; Fagan, "Theory and Management of Trustees of Reservations," 33–34; *Seventieth ARTPR* (1960), 23.

52 *Berkshire Eagle* (Pittsfield, MA), December 13, 1958, box 1, folder 13, "Letters from M. Choate re: Mission House . . . , 1958–1989," CWEII (first quote); *Sixty-Eighth ARTPR* (1958), 53 (second quote).

53 Charles W. Eliot II to William Roger Greeley, December 2, 1956, box 1, folder 11, CWEII (first quote); Walter Eaton in L. B. Fletcher to Charles S. Bird, July 22, 1947, box 1, folder 13, CWEII (second quote). See *Times-Union* (Rochester, NY), April 27, 1969 (Fletcher Steele obituary), box 1, folder 13, CWEII; *Berkshire Eagle* (Pittsfield, MA), December 11, 1989, and *Berkshire Eagle* (?)(Pittsfield, MA), December 18, 1858, box 1, folder 13, CWEII; and Charles W. Eliot II to William Roger Greeley, December 2, 1956, and Laurence Fletcher to Mabel Choate, October 24, 1947, box 1, folder 13, CWEII.

54 Henry W. Dwight to Laurence B. Fletcher, June 19, 1953 (first, second, and third quotes), and Laurence Fletcher to Mabel Choate, July 13, 1953 (fourth quote), both in box 1, folder 13, CWEII.

55 Mary Anne Guitar, *Property Power: How to Keep the Bull-Dozer, the Power Line, and the Highwaymen Away from Your Door* (Garden City, NY: Doubleday, 1972), 54–55, 58; *Seventy-Fourth ARTPR* (1964), 47.

56 Gordon Abbott Jr., "Director's Report," October 3, 1969, TPR Records, vol. 21 (1969) (quotes). See Peter L. Hornbeck to Gordon Abbott, December 27, 1977; Hornbeck to Theodore Chase, April 21, 1978(?), box 1, folder 2, CWEII.

57 Peter L. Hornbeck to Theodore Chase, April 21, 1978 (?), box 1, folder 2, CWEII (first quote); "Director's Report," TPR Records, vol. 22 (1970) (second quote).

58 Alfred Runte, *National Parks: The American Experience* (Lincoln: University of Nebraska Press, 1979), 109 (first quote); *Sixty-Fourth ARTPR* (1954), 22 (second quote). See Abbott, *Saving Special Places*, 73–79; Morgan Bulkeley, "An Extraordinary Cow Pasture," n.p., December 2, 1971, box 1, folder 14, CWEII; "Bartholomew's Cobble: A National Landmark," box 23, folder 11, CWEII; *Fifty-Sixth ARTPR* (1946), 3; *Sixty-Third ARTPR* (1953), 26; and *Pittsfield (MA) Berkshire County Eagle*, September 8, 1948.

59 "Report by CWEII on the Ipswich/Essex Salt Marshes, 1956–1975," box 22, folder 4, CWEII; "A Program to Protect the Ipswich/Essex Salt Marshes, 1972–3," box 22,

folder 9, CWEII; *Seventy-Ninth ARTPR* (1969), 16; *This Fragile Shore: A Program of Sand Dune Protection* (Ipswich, MA: Trustees of Public Reservations, ca. 1972), box 3, folder 6, CWEII.

60 *Seventy-Fifth ARTPR* (1965), 7; *Seventy-Sixth ARTPR* (1966), 13; *Seventy-Seventh ARTPR* (1967), 14, 50; *Seventy-Ninth ARTPR* (1969), 16–17; Abbott, *Saving Special Places*, 108; "Ipswich-Essex Marshes: Proposal for Preservation through Trustees of Reservations," February 1959, box 2, folder 10, CWEII; "Castle Hill Preliminary Maintenance Programs, Crane Reservation, Program of Sand Dune Restoration, Stabilization and Protection, Education-Interpretation Program," box 3, folder 3, CWEII; "Conservation Restrictions: Procedures for Inspection," box 3, folder 9, CWEII.

61 Anne Whiston Spirn, "Constructing Nature: The Legacy of Frederick Law Olmsted," in *Uncommon Ground: Toward Reinventing Nature*, ed. William Cronon (New York: W. W. Norton, 1995), 100 (first quote), 101–2; Walter Prichard Eaton to Laurence Fletcher, August 22, 1950, box 1, folder 14, CWEII (second quote); "Suggested Policy for Monument Mountain," September 23, 1950, box 3, folder 5, CWEII (third and fourth quotes). See Fletcher Steele to Laurence Fletcher, August 6, 1950, box 1, folder 14, CWEII; and Laurence Fletcher (?), "Report on Monument Mountain," August 6, 1950, box 1, folder 14, CWEII.

62 Fletcher Steele, "Report on Policies for the Reservations, ca. 1951, box 2, folder 10, CWEII (first quote); William Roger Greeley in *Fifty-Eighth ARTPR* (1948), 19 (second and third quote), 20. See *Twenty-Seventh ARTPR* (1917), 16–17; *Twenty-Eighth ARTPR* (1918), 19; *Thirty-Fourth ARTPR* (1924), 15; *Forty-Forth ARTPR* (1934), 27–28; *Forty-Ninth ARTPR* (1939), 33; *Fifty-First ARTPR* (1941), 14; and *Fifty-Third ARTPR* (1943), 6.

63 Robert K. Wheeler to Laurence B. Fletcher, August 7, 1950, box 1, folder 14, CWEII (first quote); *Thirty-Sixth ARTPR* (1926), 13 (second quote); Fletcher Steele, "Report to the Standing Committee on Lumbering at the William Cullen Bryant Homestead," TPR Records, vol. 8 (1942) (third quote). See *Sixtieth ARTPR* (1950), 33.

64 R. B. Greeley, "Background Philosophy and General Management Policy," box 3, folder 6, CWEII; Charles W. Eliot II, "The Next Seventy-Five Years: Massachusetts Trustees of Reservations," August 8, 1966, box 3, folder 7, CWEII.

65 Fletcher Steele in *Thirty-Ninth ARTPR* (1949), 16 (first quote); R. B. Greeley, "The Public and Our Reservations," March 8, 1948, box 3, folder 5, CWEII (second quote). See Runte, *National Parks*, 155; and Charles W. Eliot, "Popular Utilization of Public Reservations," in *Proceedings*, by American Park and Outdoor Art Association (Rochester, NY: Democrat and Chronicle Press, 1902), 6–14, 14.

66 Fletcher Steele in *Thirty-Ninth ARTPR* (1949), 16 (first quote); *Twenty-Second ARTPR* (1912), 14 (second quote). See *Thirty-First ARTPR* (1921), 17; *Thirty-Second ARTPR* (1922), 16–17; *Forty-Sixth ARTPR* (1936), 43; *Fifty-Eighth ARTPR* (1948), 21; *Seventy-Seventh ARTPR* (1967), 37–38, 54; and Fletcher Steele, "A Suggested Policy for Misery Island," July 1950, box 3, folder 5, CWEII.

67 Ada A. Heine to Charles W. Eliot, May 4, 1925, box 1, folder 6, CWEII (first quote); *Sixtieth ARTPR* (1950), 32 (second quote); *Seventy-Seventh ARTPR* (1967), 37

NOTES TO PAGES 105–108   255

(third quote), 38 (fourth quote). See Charles W. Eliot 2nd to Professor Ada Heine, April 28, 1924, box 1, folder 6, CWEII; *Fortieth ARTPR* (1930), 7; *Sixty-Ninth ARTPR* (1959), 19–20; and *Seventy-Seventh ARTPR* (1967), 38.

68 *Sixtieth ARTPR* (1950), 11, 12 (first quote); *Sixty-Fourth ARTPR* (1954), 34 (second quote). See Fletcher Steele, "Suggested Policy for the Rocky Woods Reservation," May 29, 1950, box 3, folder 5, CWEII; *Fifty-First ARTPR* (1941), 20–21; *Fifty-Ninth ARTPR* (1949), 42–43; Laurence B. Fletcher, "Minutes of Meeting, Standing Committee," September 13, 1947, TPR Records, vol. 8 (1942); and "Annual Meeting—January 23, 1957," 24–25, TPR Records, vol. 14 (1957 and 1958).

69 Fletcher Steele in *Fifty-Seventh ARTPR* (1947), 8, 9 (third and seventh quotes), 10 (first, fifth, and sixth quotes); Steele in *Sixtieth ARTPR* (1950), 20 (second quote), 21 (fourth quote). See *Fifty-Fifth ARTPR* (1945), 14; and *Fifty-Eighth ARTPR* (1948), 21–22.

70 Charles S. Bird in *Fifty-Seventh ARTPR* (1947), 48. See "Suggested Policy for Monument Mountain," September 23, 1950, box 3, folder 5, CWEII; *Fifty-Fifth ARTPR* (1945), 16; *Sixtieth ARTPR* (1950), 21; Peter Walker and Melanie Simo, *Invisible Gardens: The Search for Modernism in the American Landscape* (Cambridge, MA: MIT Press, 1994), 28; Galen Cranz, *The Politics of Park Design: A History of Urban Parks in America* (Cambridge, MA: MIT Press, 1982), 86–88, 91, 157; Peter C. Baldwin, *Domesticating the Street: The Reform of Public Space in Hartford, 1850–1930* (Columbus: Ohio University Press, 1999), 140–41; and Norman T. Newton, *Design on the Land: The Development of Landscape Architecture* (Cambridge, MA: Harvard University Press, 1971), 298, 304.

71 Peter S. Alagona, *After the Grizzly: Endangered Species and the Politics of Place in California* (Berkeley: University of California Press, 2013), 72 (quote), 74; Ecological Society of America, *Preservation of Natural Conditions* (Springfield, IL: Schnepi and Barnes, 1922), 3. See Victor E. Shelford, *Naturalist's Guide to the Americas* (Baltimore: Williams & Wilkins, 1926), 26–28, 85; and C. F. Korstian, "The Preservation of Natural Conditions in the National Forests," 17–18, and V. E. Shelford, "Union of Interests and Management of Natural Areas," both in Shelford, *Naturalist's Guide*, 42–43.

72 Shelford, "Union of Interests," 42; Guitar, *Property Power*, 219–20; Eve Endicott, *Land Conservation through Public Private Partnerships* (Cambridge, MA: Lincoln Institute of Land Policy, 1993), 18–20; Sally K. Fairfax, et al., *Buying Nature: The Limits of Land Acquisition as a Conservation Strategy, 1780–2004* (Cambridge, MA: MIT Press, 2005), 154.

73 Friends of Our Native Landscape, "A Park and Forest Policy for Illinois" (Chicago: Friends of Our Native Landscape, 1926), in Cook County Forest Preserve Documents (University of Illinois at Chicago), 4 (first quote) 13; Jens Jensen, unidentified letter, n.d. (second quote); Charles W. Eliot II to Jens Jensen, April 11, 1925, and "A Park and Forest Policy of Illinois," all in box 1, folder 15, CWEII. See National Conference on Outdoor Recreation, *Proceedings* (Washington, DC: GPO, 1928), 43.

74 Frederick John Pratson, "Yankee Heritage Is Secured without Government Aid," *Smithsonian*, June 1977, 97, 98 (first quote); Charles H. W. Foster in John C.

Marksbury, "Minutes," December 15, 1975, box 3, folder 7, Notes, Reports and Drafts of Future Policy Committee, 1966–1976, CWEII (second quote). See "The Next Seventy-Five Years: Massachusetts Trustees of Reservations," August 8, 1966, 6–7, box 3, folder 7, CWEII.

75 Peter Howell and Abigail Weinberg, *Western Massachusetts: Assessing the Conservation Opportunity* (New York: Open Space Institute, 2005), 37 (first quote); Charles H. W. Foster to Gordon Abbott, August 27, 1975, box 3, folder 7, CWEII (second quote); Pratson, "Yankee Heritage Is Secured," 97 (third quote). See "The Land Conservation Trust: A Report of Activities, 1972–1973," box 3, folder 4, CWEII; Charles H. W. Foster to Gordon Abbott, August 27, 1975, box 3, folder 7, CWEII; and Peter L. Hornbeck, "Proposed Guideline Statement on Ecological Diversity," November 21, 1977, box 3, folder 6, CWEII.

76 *Seventy-Seventh ARTPR*, (1967), 16. See *Sixty-Eighth ARTPR* (1958), 3; and *Seventy-Ninth ARTPR* (1969), 14.

77 *Seventy-Seventh ARTPR* (1967), 31–32, 33 (quote), 75. See *Fifty-Fifth ARTPR* (1945), 15; *Fifty-Seventh ARTPR* (1947), 24; *Sixtieth ARTPR* (1950), 12; and *Seventy-Ninth ARTPR* (1969), 23, 28.

78 Edward A. Weeks Jr. in *Fifty-Eighth ARTPR* (1948), 26 (first quote); Walter Prichard Eaton in *Sixty-Second ARTPR* (1952), 21 (second quote); Sumner G. Whittier in *Fifty-Fifth ARTPR* (1955), 11 (third quote); Fairfield Osborn in *Fifty-Sixth ARTPR* (1946), 14 (fourth quote). See *Forty-Third ARTPR* (1933), 1.

79 Frank A. Waugh, "Petticoat Hill, For Example," in *Thirty-Second ARTPR* (1922), 24.

80 *Sixty-Fifth ARTPR* (1955), 8; *Sixty-Sixth ARTPR* (1956), 6; *Sixty-Seventh ARTPR* (1957), 7; *Sixty-Eighth ARTPR* (1958), 4–7, 19; *Seventy-Second ARTPR* (1962), 5; *Seventy-Seventh ARTPR* (1967), 39; *Seventy-Ninth ARTPR* (1969), 15.

81 *New York Times*, March 23, 1949 (clipping), box 23, folder 23, CWEII. See William H. C. Walker and Willard Brewer Walker, *A History of World's End*, 2nd ed. (ca. 1973; reprint, Milton, MA: Trustees of Reservations, 1984), xi, 1–3, 11, 40, 54.

82 Gordon Abbott Jr., "Director's Report," January 5, 1968, TPR Records, vol. 20 (1968).

83 Abbott, "Director's Report." See *Seventy-Seventh ARTPR* (1967), 12–13, 17, 81; Abbott, *Saving Special Places*, 91–94; and Walker and Walker, *History of World's End*, viii; ix.

84 Elizabeth New Weld, "First Land Trust Marks Century of Preservation," *Boston Globe*, October 21, 1990, 9 (first quote); R. S. Kindleberger, "Conservation: An Old Land-Saving Group Learns New Tricks," *Boston Globe*, February 21, 1986, 24 (second quote).

85 MacKaye, *New Exploration*, 137 (first quote); Walter Prichard Eaton in *Sixty-Second ARTPR* (1952), 22 (second quote). See Pamela Maria Freese, "Third Sector Land Protection: Planning on Conservation Land Trusts" (PhD diss., University of Illinois at Chicago, 2004), 109–10.

86 Freese, "Third Sector Land Protection," 39, 110; Fairfax et al., *Buying Nature*, 158.

87 Fagan, "Theory and Management in the Trustees of Reservations," 5.

Chapter 4: The Land-Trust Explosion

1 *Portsmouth (NH) Herald*, August 20, 2003 (first quote); *Fitchburg (MA) Sentinel*, October 1, 1969 (second and third quotes).
2 President's Commission on Americans Outdoors, *Report and Recommendations to the President of the United States* (Washington, DC: GPO, 1986), 3.
3 Felix L. Oswald, "Preservation of Forests," *North American Review* 128 (January 1879): 35 (first quote); Harold A. Caparn, "Some Reasons for a General System of State Parks," *Landscape Architecture* 7 (January 1917): 65–66, 68 (second quote), 69–70. See *Greenfield (MA) Recorder*, October 28, 1970; and Mrs. Charles F. Millspaugh, "Tree Protection in the United States," *Chautauquan* 41 (June 1905): 326.
4 Donella Meadows, "Land Trusts: A New Tool for Growth Control," *Nashua (NH) Telegraph*, May 22, 1988 (all quotes).
5 Kevin Lynch, "The Openness of Open Space," in *Arts of the Environment*, ed. Gyorgy Kepes (New York: George Braziller, 1972), 108 (quote), 109.
6 Lawrence Levine, "Land Conservation in Metropolitan Areas," *Journal of the American Institute of Planners* 30, no. 3 (1964): 205; Terry Bremer, "Portrait of Land Trusts," in *Land Saving Action: A Written Symposium by 29 Experts on Private Land Conservation in the 1980s*, ed. R. L. Brennerman and Sarah M. Bates (Covelo, CA: Island Press, 1984), 17–19.
7 Adam Rome, *The Bulldozer in the Countryside: Suburban Sprawl and the Rise of American Environmentalism* (New York: Cambridge University Press, 2001); Richard W. Judd, "Exurbia Meets Nature: Environmental Ideals for a Rootless Society," in *Landscape and the Ideology of Nature in Exurbia: Green Sprawl*, ed. Kirsten Valentine Cadieux and Laura Taylor (New York: Taylor & Francis, 2012), 61.
8 Charles E. Little, *Challenge of the Land: Open Space Preservation at the Local Level* (New York: Pergamon Press, 1968), 10 (first quote), 12–13, 43; Robert E. Kickinson, "The Process of Urbanization," in *Future Environments of North America: Transformation of a Continent*, ed. F. Fraser Darling and John B. Milton (Garden City, NY: Natural History Press, 1966), 466 (second quote).
9 *Special Places: A Newsletter of the Trustees of Reservations* (Spring 1993), box 23, folder 19, Charles W. Eliot II Papers, Trustees of Reservations Archives & Research Center, Sharon, MA (hereafter CWEII; first quote); Ian L. McHarg, *Metropolitan Open Space from Natural Processes* (Philadelphia: University of Pennsylvania, 1964), iii (second quote); Andrés D. Duany and Elizabeth Plater-Zyberk, "The Second Coming of the American Small Town," *Wilson Quarterly* 16 (Winter 1992): 19 (third and fourth quotes). See Robert D. Yaro et al., *Dealing with Change in the Connecticut River Valley: A Design Manual for Conservation and Development* (Cambridge, MA: Lincoln Institute of Land Policy and the Environmental Law Foundation, 1988), 7; Massachusetts Historical Commission, *Historic & Archaeological Resources of the Boston Area: A Framework for Preservation Decisions* (Boston: Massachusetts Historical Commission, 1991); 104–5; Robert C. Einsweiler and Deborah A. Miness, *Managing Growth and Change* (Cambridge, MA: Lincoln Institute of Land Policy, 1992), 14, 97; Charles W. Greiner, "Open Spaces and the North Shore," June 1, 1966, box 23, folder 14, CWEII; and Edward Higbee, *The Squeeze: Cities without Space* (New York: William Morrow, 1960), xii.

10 Elizabeth C. Mooney in President's Commission on Americans Outdoors, *Report*, 118 (first quote); Cliff Sinnott in *Portsmouth (NH) Herald*, March 2, 2003 (second quote); Duany and Plater-Zyberk, "Second Coming of the American Small Town," 35 (third quote). See Rome, *Bulldozer in the Countryside*, 3, 9, 43, 91, 105, 109, 122; Harvey Molotch, "The City as a Growth Machine: Toward a Political Economy of Place," *American Journal of Sociology* 82 (September 1976): 318; F. Kaid Benfield, "The Runaway American Dream," in *Smart Growth in a Changing World*, ed. Jonathan Barnett (Chicago: APA Planners Press, 2007), 39; Ann Louise Strong, *Preserving Urban Open Space* (Washington, DC: GPO, 1963), 3–4; Higbee, *Squeeze*, 108; Troy D. Hill and Colin Polsky, "Suburbanization and Drought: A Mixed Methods Vulnerability Assessment in Rainy Massachusetts," *Environmental Hazards* 7, no. 4 (2007): 297; William M. Dobriner in Deloris Hayden, *Building Suburbia: Green Fields and Urban Growth, 1820–2000* (New York: Pantheon Books, 2003), 188; and Robert C. Einsweiler in *Managing Community Growth*, U.S. House of Representatives, 103rd Cong., 2nd sess. (Washington, DC: GPO, 1994), 582.

11 American Institute of Park Executives, *The Crisis in Open Land* (Wheeling, WV: American Institute of Park Executives, 1959), 5 (first quote), 9 (second quote). See James C. O'Connell, *The Hub's Metropolis: Greater Boston's Development from Railroad Suburbs to Smart Growth* (Cambridge, MA: MIT Press, 2013), 164.

12 Brian Donahue, "Remaking Boston, Remaking Massachusetts," in *Remaking Boston: An Environmental History of the City and Its Surroundings*, ed. Anthony N. Penna and Conrad Edick Wright (Pittsburgh: University of Pittsburgh Press, 2009), 122 (quote). See Oliver Gillham, *The Limitless City: A Primer on the Urban Sprawl Debate* (Washington, DC: Island Press, 2002), 28–29; Michael P. Conzen and George K. Lewis, *Boston: A Geographical Portrait* (Cambridge, MA: Ballinger, 1976), 53–54; *Fitchburg (MA) Sentinel*, July 27, 1965; J. Mark Davidson Schuster, "Housing Design and New England Regional Character," in *Planning for the Changing Rural Landscape of New England: Blending Theory and Practice*, ed. New England Center (Durham, NH: Center, n.d., ca. 1986), 285–86; Constance Hays, "Vanguard in the Battle for Dwindling Open Space," *New York Times*, April 23, 1992, B1, B8; and O'Connell, *Hub's Metropolis*, 135.

13 *Nashua (NH) Telegraph*, November 30, 1986 (quotes). See George K. Lewis, "Population Change in Northern New England," *Annals of the Association of American Geographers* 62 (June 1972): 318; and Robert D. Yaro and Armando Carbonell, "Reinventing Megalopolis: The Northeast Megaregion," in Barnett, *Smart Growth in a Changing World*, 80.

14 *York (ME) Weekly*, June 15, 2005 (first quote); Jeannie M. Hamrin and Kristina H. Griffin, "Kennebunkport: A Case Study of the 'Delicate Balance' Dilemma," in New England Center, *Planning for the Changing Rural Landscape*, 407, 408 (second quote), 409, 411; *York County (ME) Coast Star*, September 30, 2004 (third quote). See Richard W. Judd and Christopher S. Beach, *Natural States: The Environmental Imagination in Maine, Oregon, and the Nation* (Washington, DC: Resources for the Future, 2003), 98–99, 100–102; Lincoln Institute of Land Policy, *A Land Conservation Strategy for the New England Region* (Cambridge, MA: Institute, 1986), 4–7; and Lee Burnett, "Conservation Wins Some New Allies," *Biddeford (ME) Journal Tribune*, January 4, 1990.

15 Lewis, "Population Change in Northern New England," 317. See Blake Harrison, *The View from Vermont: Tourism and the Making of an American Rural Landscape* (Burlington: University of Vermont Press, 2006), 124–25, 128–30; Robert McCullough, Clare Ginger, and Michelle Baumflek, "Unspoiled Vermont: The Nature of Conservation in the Green Mountain State," in *Twentieth-Century New England Land Conservation: A Heritage of Civic Engagement*, ed. Charles H. W. Foster (Petersham, MA: Harvard Forest, 2009), 140–42; and Eric Damian Kelly, *Managing Community Growth*, 2nd ed. (Westport, CT: Praeger, 2004), 108–9.

16 Tom Daniels in Hayden, *Building Suburbia*, 182. See Norma Love, "Rustic Retreats Vanish under Bulldozer's Blade," *Boston Globe*, December 14, 1986, 80; Little, *Challenge of the Land*, 14–15; Mary Anne Guitar, *Property Power: How to Keep the Bull-Dozer, the Power Line, and the Highwaymen Away from Your Door* (Garden City, NY: Doubleday, 1972), 101; Lewis, "Population Change in Northern New England," 308, 312–15; and Jan Gotteman, "Wild and Free," *Fitchburg (MA) Sentinel and Enterprise*, September 14, 2000.

17 Rome, *Bulldozer in the Countryside*, 146 (first quote), 147 (second quote from *Saturday Evening Post* quoted in Rome). See Lincoln Institute of Land Policy, *Land Conservation Strategy*, 4, 8; *Assabet Valley Beacon* (Acton MA), November 3, 1966; *Greenwich (CT) News*, April 8, 1993; Little, *Challenge of the Land*, 14–15; *Bridgeport (CT) Post*, February 22, 1974; *York (ME) Weekly*, July 7, 2004; and Beverly Zimmerman in *Branford (CT) Review*, May 19, 1966.

18 Metropolitan Area Planning Council and Metropolitan District Commission, *Open Space and Recreation Plan and Program for Metropolitan Boston* (Boston: Metropolitan Area Planning Council, 1969), 10 (first quote); Ian L. McHarg, *Design with Nature* (Garden City, NY: American Museum of Natural History and Natural History Press, 1969), 23 (second quote); Little, *Challenge of the Land*, 10 (third quote). See Mark Luccarelli, *Lewis Mumford and the Ecological Region: The Politics of Planning* (New York: Guilford Press, 1995), 144; Peter F. Cannavò, *The Working Landscape: Founding, Preservation, and the Politics of Place* (Cambridge, MA: MIT Press, 2007), 99; Rutherford H. Platt, "The Loss of Farmland: Evolution of a Public Response," *Geographical Review* 67 (January 1977): 97–101; and Alan Lupo, "Why Rural Outposts Are Under Siege," *Boston Globe*, August 2, 1987, 79.

19 Pamela Maria Freese, "Third Sector Land Protection: Planning on Conservation Land Trusts" (PhD diss., University of Illinois at Chicago, 2004), 246 (first quote); William H. Whyte, *The Last Landscape* (New York: Doubleday, 1968), 349 (second quote). See Open Space Action Committee, *Stewardship: The Land, the Landowner, the Metropolis* (New York: Open Space Action Committee, 1965), 13; Rome, *Bulldozer in the Countryside*, 130, 136; Robert E. Kickinson, "The Process of Urbanization," in Darling and Milton, *Future Environments of North America*, 463–78; and Sally K. Fairfax et al., *Buying Nature: The Limits of Land Acquisition as a Conservation Strategy, 1780–2004* (Cambridge, MA: MIT Press, 2005), 156.

20 Melissa B. Smart, "Trust for New Hampshire Lands: One Town's Implementation," in New England Center, *Planning for the Changing Rural Landscape*, 274; Ann Louise Strong, *Open Space for Urban America* (Washington, DC: Department of Housing and Urban Development, 1965), 36; Randall Arendt, *Rural by Design: Maintaining Small Town Character* (Washington, DC: American Planning Association and

Lincoln Land Institute of Land Policy, 1994), 17; O'Connell, *Hub's Metropolis*, 165–66; *York (ME) Weekly*, March 3, 2004; *Biddeford (ME) Journal Tribune*, February 22, 1973; *Greenwich (CT) News*, December 9, December 22, 1993.

21 *Assabet Valley Beacon* (Acton, MA), February 6, 1969. See *Berkshire Eagle* (Pittsfield, MA), April 24, 1973; *Bridgeport (CT) Post*, August 25, 1973; Strong, *Open Space for Urban America*, 36–37; Outdoor Recreation Resources Review Commission, *Outdoor Recreation for America: A Report to the President and to the Congress* (Washington, DC: GPO, 1962), 150; and Open Space Action Committee, *Stewardship*, 21, 61.

22 Jean Hocker, "Land Trusts: Key Elements in the Struggle against Sprawl," *Natural Resources & Environment* 15 (Spring 2001): 244. See *Bridgeport (CT) Post*, May 12, 1974.

23 American Institute of Park Executives, *The Crisis in Open Land* (Wheeling, WV: American Institute of Park Executives, 1959), 3; Daniel Press, *Saving Open Space: The Politics of Local Preservation in California* (Berkeley: University of California Press, 2002), 1; William H. Whyte, *Open Space Action: Report to the Outdoor Recreation Resources Review Commission* (Washington, DC: GPO, 1962), 2–3; Jeffrey G. Buckland, "The History and Use of Purchase of Development Rights in the United States," *Landscape and Urban Planning* 14 (1987): 245; Jeanne M. Davis and Peter House, *Open Space: Its Use and Preservation* (Washington, DC: USDA, 1968), 1–2; Strong, *Preserving Urban Open Space*, 20; *Bridgeport (CT) Post*, November 11, 1973; *Portsmouth (NH) Herald*, April 16, 1975.

24 Gerald O. Barney, ed., *The Unfinished Agenda: The Citizen's Policy Guide to Environmental Issues* (New York: Thomas Y. Crowell, 1977), 116–18.

25 Richard W. Judd, *Second Nature: An Environmental History of New England* (Amherst: University of Massachusetts Press, 2014), 180–81; Robert McCullough, *The Landscape of Community: A History of Communal Forests in New England* (Hanover, NH: University Press of New England, 1995), 28, 29, 116, 141; Letty Anderson, "Hard Choices: Supplying Water to New England Towns," *Journal of Interdisciplinary History* 15 (Autumn 1984): 214–23; Carol Y. Mason, "Water Supplies of New England," *Economic Geography* 13 (October 1937): 349–51, 360; Minnie E. Lemaire, "Wachusett Reservoir: A Metropolitan Water Supply," *Economic Geography* 13 (April 1937): 183–84.

26 Alice G. Brandeis, "Town Forests of Massachusetts: A Record of Community Achievement," *Journal of Social Forces* 3 (March 1925): 478. See McCullough, *The Landscape of Community*, 88, 137–38, 119, 149, 154, 217–18, 276; Martha West Lyman, Cecilia Danks, and Maureen McDonough, "New England's Community Forests: Comparing a Regional Model to ICCAs," *Conservation and Society* 11, no. 1 (2013): 48–49; Andrew J. W. Scheffey, *Conservation Commissions in Massachusetts* (Washington, DC: Conservation Foundation, 1969), 23, 26; and Harris A. Reynolds, *Town Forests in Massachusetts: Report in Progress*, bulletin 139 (Boston: Massachusetts Forestry Association, n.d., ca. 1924), box 2, folder 2, CWEII.

27 Emily Bateson and Nancy Smith, "Making It Happen: Protecting Wilderness on the Ground," in *Wilderness Comes Home: Rewilding the Northeast*, ed. Christopher McGrory Klyza (Hanover, NH: Middlebury College Press, 2001), 193 (first quote); Charles E. Little, *Greenways for America* (Baltimore: Johns Hopkins University Press, 1990), 31 (second quote); *Biddeford (ME) Journal Tribune*, February 22, 1973

(third quote). See Robert D. Yaro et al., *Dealing with Change in the Connecticut River Valley: A Design Manual for Conservation and Development* (Cambridge, MA: Lincoln Institute of Land Policy and the Environmental Law Foundation, 1988), 5, 17; David Jacobson, *Place and Belonging in America* (Baltimore: Johns Hopkins University Press, 2001), 87–88; Paul Brooks, *The View from Lincoln Hill: Man and the Land in a New England Town* (Boston: Houghton Mifflin, 1976), 65–66, 166; *Lowell (MA) Sun*, September 29, 1989; Frank A. Waugh, "A Comparison of Town Plans," *Landscape Architecture* 11 (July 1921): 161, 164; Howard Dean, "Growth Management Plans," in *Land Use in America*, ed. Henry L. Diamond and Patrick F. Noonan (Washington, DC: Island Press, 1996), 153; Elizabeth Brabec, "Townscape Planning in Hadley, Massachusetts: A Case Study," in New England Center, *Planning for the Changing Rural Landscape*, 400–401; and Massachusetts Department of Environmental Management, *Massachusetts Landscape Inventory: A Survey of the Commonwealth's Scenic Areas* (Boston: Department of Environmental Management, 1982), 9–10.

28 President's Council on Recreation and Natural Beauty, *From Sea to Shining Sea: A Report on the American Environment—Our Natural Heritage* (Washington, DC: Council 1968), 238 (first quote); Christine Negra and Lois M. Frey, *Identifying Factors Leading to Effective Local Conservation Commissions: An Investigation in New Hampshire and Vermont* (University Park, PA: Northeast Regional Center for Rural Development 1998), 4 (second quote). See Scheffey, *Conservation Commissions*, 12, 30–41; Peter B. Lord, "The Rhode Island Conservation Story," in Foster, *Twentieth-Century New England Land Conservation*, 239; *Greenwich (CT) News*, September 12, 1985; and *Concord (MA) Enterprise*, June 23, 1960.

29 Scheffey, *Conservation Commissions*, 30–31, 37, 103, 105–7; Wayne Sherwood, "Conservation Coordinating Committee," December 15, 1971, box 22, folder 6, CWEII; Guitar, *Property Power*, 188–89; *Berkshire Eagle* (Pittsfield, MA), June 21, 1958, October 7, 1960; *North Adams (MA) Transcript*, December 3, 1960.

30 Scheffey, *Conservation Commissions*, 12, 30, 33 (second quote), 34 (first quote), 57–59, 74, 105–7, 123–26. See Negra and Frey, *Effective Local Conservation Commissions*, 45–47, 50–51, 60; Guitar, *Property Power*, 187; Strong, *Open Space for Urban America*, 50–51; *Fitchburg (MA) Sentinel and Enterprise*, August 31, 2005; *Berkshire Eagle* (Pittsfield, MA), August 23, 1973: *Concord (MA) Enterprise*, June 23, 1960; *Assabet Valley Beacon* (Acton, MA), June 9, 1966; *Bridgeport (CT) Post*, April 30, 1967; and *Darien (CT) News*, July 3, 1974.

31 Mrs. Robert Weatherall to CWEII, December 4, 1972, box 22, folder 6, CWEII (first quote); *Biddeford (ME) Journal Tribune*, September 19, 1973 (second quote). See President's Commission on Americans Outdoors, *Report*, 294; *Fitchburg (MA) Sentinel and Enterprise*, September 14, 2000; and *Manchester (CT) Journal-Inquirer*, December 7, 1976.

32 Paul Brooks in *Assabet Valley Beacon* (Acton, MA), October 24, 1968 (first and second quotes). See Brooks, *The View from Lincoln Hill*, 4, 5; O'Connell, *Hub's Metropolis*, 165–66; Allan Morgan in *Boston Sunday Globe*, January 22, 1961, box 1, folder 2, CWEII; Guitar, *Property Power*, 143–44; Rural Land Trust Foundation, *Lincoln: The First Twelve Years* (Lincoln: Rural Land Foundation, n.d.); Robert A. Lemire, "The Codman Estate Transactions, Lincoln, Massachusetts," in Brennerman and

Bates, *Land Saving Action*, 12–13; and *Assabet Valley Beacon* (Acton, MA), November 21, 1968.

33 *Concord (MA) Enterprise*, October 27, 1960. See *Concord (MA) Enterprise*, November 27, 1958; Strong, *Open Space for Urban America*, 51; *Assabet Valley Beacon* (Acton, MA), May 26, 1966; and Scheffey, *Conservation Commissions*, 115–18.

34 *Nashua (NH) Telegraph*, April 28, 1987 (quotes). See R. J. Mere, "We All Lose If We Gamble with the Area's Wildlife Habitat," *York County (ME) Coast Star*, April 4, 2002; and Lee Burnett, "Conservation Wins Some New Allies," *Biddeford (ME) Journal Tribune*, January 4, 1990.

35 Russell L. Brenneman, "Rescuing Connecticut: A Story of Land-Saving Actions," in Foster, *Twentieth-Century New England Land Conservation*, 278, 281; Michael L. Morano, "Demands on Open Space Threaten State's Charm," *Greenwich (CT) News*, May 28, 1987; *Darien (CT) News*, February 24, March 17, 1977; *New York Times*, March 28, 1982, CN4; *Fairfield (CT) Minuteman*, March 25, 2004; Peter B. Lord, "The Rhode Island Conservation Story," in Foster, *Twentieth-Century New England Land Conservation*, 247.

36 *Manchester (CT) Journal-Inquirer*, May 4, 1973. See Jim Hart, "Open Space: Do We Have Enough?," *Westport (CT) Fairpress*, February 29, 1980; and Scheffey, *Conservation Commissions*, 63; *Manchester (CT) Journal-Inquirer*, May 4, 1973.

37 *Nashua (NH) Telegraph*, January 18, 1971, January 27, 1988; *Bridgeport (CT) Post*, July 22, 1970; *Bridgeport (CT) Post*, March 22, 1967; *Berkshire Eagle* (Pittsfield, MA), November 2, 1972; *Manchester (CT) Journal-Inquirer*, September 30, 1976; Guitar, *Property Power*, 215.

38 *Westport (CT) Fairpress*, June 26, 1981 (first quote); *Newport (RI) Journal*, May 7, 2008 (second quote); *Manchester Conservation Trust Newsletter*, Spring 1976, box 23, folder 15, CWEII (third quote). See Jerome Thomas Posatko, "Land Trusts and Land Conservation in the United States: Characteristics, Systemic Analysis, and Implications for Public Policy" (PhD diss., University of Delaware, 1996), 152–53, 180; *Concord (MA) Enterprise*, October 27, 1960; and Jean W. Hocker, "Patience, Problem Solving, and Private Initiative: Local Groups Chart a New Course for Land Conservation," in Diamond and Noonan, *Land Use in America*, 253.

39 *Nashua (NH) Telegraph*, May 21, 1998; *Lowell (MA) Sun*, April 8, 1962, May 19, 1963, April 25, 1968, January 26, 1998; *Assabet Valley Beacon* (Acton, MA), November 4, 1971; *Fitchburg (MA) Sentinel*, September 23, 1969.

40 *Lowell (MA) Sun*, March 7, 1966, August 30, 1994; *Fitchburg (MA) Sentinel and Enterprise*, September 14, 2000.

41 Bob Kranyik, "Community Works," *Fairfield (CT) Minuteman*, August 1, 2002 (first quote); Michael McCallum in *Fitchburg (MA) Sentinel and Enterprise*, June 21, 2003 (second quote). See Jean Hocker in Chris Elfring, "Preserving Land Through Local Land Trusts," *Bioscience* 39 (February 1989): 71; *Berkshire Eagle* (Pittsfield, MA), July 10, 2003, May 20, 2005, August 26, 2006; *North Adams (MA) Transcript*, July 10, 2003; and Guitar, *Property Power*, 131.

42 Massachusetts Department of Environmental Management, *Massachusetts Landscape Inventory: A Survey of the Commonwealth's Scenic Areas* (Boston: Department of Environmental Management, 1982), 38, 42; Judd, "Exurbia Meets Nature," 63; William H. Whyte Jr., "Research and the Open Space Problem," *American Journal*

of Economics and Sociology 21 (October 1962): 405–6; Rome, *Bulldozer in the Countryside*, 120, 123.

43 *Greenwich (CT) News*, September 12, 1985 (first quote); Constance L. Hays in *New York Times*, April 23, 1992, B1 (second quote); Jerry Harkavy, "3,000 Acres Protected in Maine Land Trusts," *Los Angeles Times*, May 24, 1987, 23 (third quote); Mary Lyn Ray in Land for New Hampshire, *Final Report of the New Hampshire Land Conservation Investment Program and the Trust for New Hampshire Lands* (n.p.: Trust for New Hampshire Lands, 1993), 14 (fourth quote). See David Dubbink, "I'll Have My Town Medium-Rural, Please," *Journal of the American Planning Association* 50 (Autumn 1984): 414–15; Scheffey, *Conservation Commissions*, 65; Karel Yasko in White House Conference on Natural Beauty, *Beauty for America: Proceedings* (Washington, DC: GPO, 1965), 83–84; Duany and Plater-Zyberk, "Second Coming of the American Small Town," 27; and Peter F. Cannavò, *The Working Landscape: Founding, Preservation, and the Politics of Place* (Cambridge, MA: MIT Press, 2007), 44.

44 Bill Baldwin, "Tax Breaks Aid Cause of Conservation," *Westport (CT) Fairpress*, June 21, 1978 (quote). See *New York Times*, January 28, 1996, CN1; *Fitchburg (MA) Sentinel and Enterprise*, December 19, 2002; *Fitchburg (MA) Sentinel and Enterprise*, November 30, 2000; *Lowell (MA) Sun*, January 31, 1995; *Assabet Valley Beacon* (Acton, MA), February 6, 1969; *Bridgeport (CT) Post*, February 23, 1966; Einsweiler and Miness, *Managing Growth and Change*, 51; and Richard Brewer, *Conservancy: The Land Trust Movement in America* (Hanover, NH: Dartmouth College and University Press of New England, 2003), 72–73

45 *Nashua (NH) Telegraph*, June 5, 1978 (quotes). See Open Space Action Committee, *Stewardship*, 41; and William Whyte, *Securing Open Space for Urban America: Conservation Easements* (Washington, DC: Urban Land Institute, 1959), 36–37.

46 Faith Hutchins Webster in *York (ME) Weekly*, July 30, 2003 (first quote); *Portsmouth (NH) Herald*, July 29, 2003 (second quote); *Biddeford (ME) Journal Tribune*, January 25, 1990 (third quote); John and Lorinda Bradford in *York County Coast Star* (Kennebunk, ME), July 31, 2003 (fourth quote); Nanci Worthington, "Protecting the Land," *Berkshire Eagle* (Pittsfield, MA), June 30, 2002 (fifth quote). See *Lowell (MA) Sun*, February 20, March 7, 2001; *Exeter (NH) News-Letter*, March 7, 2006; *Bridgeport (CT) Post*, August 7, 1967; Hocker, "Land Trusts," 246; and Robert W. Eisenmenger, *Land Use Changes in the 1960's* (Boston: Federal Reserve Bank of Boston, 1959), 5.

47 President's Commission on Americans Outdoors, *Report*, 9 (first quote); Peter Anderson, "A Dedication to Preservation," *Boston Globe*, December 15, 1991, 77 (second quote). See Outdoor Recreation Resources Review Commission, *Outdoor Recreation for America*, 4; Marion Clawson, "The Crisis in Outdoor Recreation," *American Forests* (March 1959): 22–31, 40–41; (April 1959): 31–32; and Open Space Action Committee, *Stewardship*, 1, box 2, folder 14, CWEII.

48 *Greenwich (CT) News*, December 20, 1990 (first quote); *Bridgeport (CT) Post*, September 29, October 2, 17, 1968 (second quote); Little, *Greenways for America*, 54, 56 (third quote). See *Greenwich (CT) News*, May 23, 1991; *Darien (CT) News*, December 5, 1974; *Westport (CT) Fairpress*, May 11, 1972, May 8, 1974, January 17, 1975, September 22, 1976; *Portsmouth (NH) Herald*, June 22, 2008; Stephan J. Schmidt, "The Evolving

Relationship between Open Space Preservation and Local Planning Practice," *Journal of Planning History* 7, no. 2 (2008): 11–13; and Little, *Challenge of the Land*, 67, 69.

49 *New York Times*, July 16, 1989, CN2. See *Nashua (NH) Telegraph*, July 17, 1996; and *Berkshire Eagle* (Pittsfield, MA), April 10, 1973.

50 Open Space Action Committee, *Stewardship*, 60 (first quote); Higbee, *Squeeze*, 109 (second quote), 110; Christopher West Davis in *New York Times*, October 12, 2003, WE1 (third quote); *Portsmouth (NH) Herald*, March 20, 2005 (fourth and fifth quotes). See Little, *Greenways for America*, 32- 33; Molotch, "City as a Growth Machine," 326–27; Elfring, "Preserving Land through Local Land Trusts," 74; *York (ME) Weekly*, May 18, 2005; O'Connell, *Hub's Metropolis*, 30; and Whyte, *Conservation Easements*, 21–22.

51 Brenneman, "Rescuing Connecticut," 261 (first quote); *Lowell (MA) Sun*, July 29, October 13, 1999, Anna M. Corey Dracut, letter to editor, *Lowell Sun*, October 24, 1999 (second quote), February 11, October 12, 2000, February 20, 2001. See Scheffey, *Conservation Commissions*, 155, 156; Ronald C. Hess and George M. Pomeroy, "The Geographic Distribution of Land Trust Activities in the United States," in *Spatial Diversity and Dynamics in Resources and Urban Development*, ed. Ashok K. Dutt et al. (New York: Springer, 2015), 152; McHarg, *Design with Nature*, 80; and Joseph William Singer, "Property and Social Relations: From Title to Entitlement," in *Property and Values: Alternatives to Public and Private Ownership*, ed. Charles Geisler and Gail Daneker (Washington, DC: Island Press, 2000), 15.

52 Judd and Beach, *Natural States*, 23–25, 29–30, 32–33, 43; Peter J. Coleman, *The Transformation of Rhode Island, 1790–1860* (Providence, RI: Brown University Press, 1963), 76–77; Lord, "Rhode Island Conservation Story," 223–24, 239; William S. Wise, "Pollution Control in New England," *Sewage and Industrial Wastes* 30 (January 1958): 87–90.

53 Judd and Beach, *Natural States*, 34–36, 46–51; Harrison, *View from Vermont*, 203–4, 209.

54 Theodore Roosevelt, *In the Words of Theodore Roosevelt*, ed. Patricia O'Toole (Ithaca, NY: Cornell University Press, 2012), 196. See Negra and Frey, *Effective Local Conservation Commissions*, 50–51; President's Council on Recreation and Natural Beauty, *From Sea to Shining Sea*, 11; Massachusetts Department of Environmental Management, *Massachusetts Landscape Inventory*, 6; and Scheffey, *Conservation Commissions*, 18.

55 President Lyndon B. Johnson, "The Conference Call: Message from the President," in White House Conference on Natural Beauty, *Beauty for America*, 1 (first quote), 2 (second quote), 8–9. See Richard G. Gibbons in President's Commission on Americans Outdoors, *Report*, 119–20; and Metropolitan Area Planning Council and Metropolitan District Commission, *Open Space and Recreation Plan*, 82–83.

56 Lord, "Rhode Island Conservation Story," 244; Randall Arendt, "Retaining Natural Landscapes along the Water's Edge," in New England Center, *Planning for the Changing Rural Landscape*, 220–24; Judd and Beach, *Natural States*, 55, 98–106; *Lowell (MA) Sun*, March 14, 1969; Philip Shabecoff in *Lowell (MA) Sun*, October 30, 1986.

57 Charles H. W. Foster, preface to *Twentieth-Century New England Land Conservation*, ed. Foster, viii. See Harry C. Boyte, *The Backyard Revolution: Understanding the*

New Citizen Movement (Philadelphia: Temple University Press, 1980), 3–5; Cody Ferguson, *This Is Our Land: Grassroots Environmentalism in the Late Twentieth Century* (New Brunswick, NJ: Rutgers University Press, 2015), 8–10; and Posatko, "Land Trusts and Land Conservation," 4, 85–86.

58 Anne Whiston Spirn, "Constructing Nature: The Legacy of Frederick Law Olmsted," in *Uncommon Ground: Toward Reinventing Nature*, ed. William Cronon (New York: W. W. Norton, 1995), 113. See Mark Harvey, "Loving the Wild in Postwar America," in *American Wilderness: A New History*, ed. Michael Lewis (New York: Oxford University Press, 2007), 192; Scheffey, *Conservation Commissions*, 59; Hocker, "Land Trusts," 247; and Freese, "Third Sector Land Protection," 117;

59 James Morton Turner, *The Promise of Wilderness: American Environmental Politics since 1964* (Seattle: University of Washington Press, 2012), 3, 6, 62, 63 (quote). See Bateson and Smith, "Making It Happen," 198.

60 Willard Brown in President's Commission on Americans Outdoors, *Report*, 47 (first quote); *Berkshire Eagle*, July 12, 1975 (second quote). See Charles Matthei, "Criteria for Community Land Trusts," in Brennerman and Bates, *Land Saving Action*, 44; Sally K. Fairfax and Darla Guenzler, *Conservation Trusts* (Lawrence: University Press of Kansas, 2001), 11, 34; US Department of the Interior and Nature Conservancy, *Preserving Our Natural Heritage* (Washington, DC: GPO, 1982), 29; Eve Endicott, *Land Conservation through Public Private Partnerships* (Cambridge, MA: Lincoln Institute of Land Policy, 1993), 8; and Little, *Challenge of the Land*, 59–60.

61 *Bridgeport (CT) Post*, November 11, 1973. See *Lowell (MA) Sun*, April 25, 1968, October 9, 1990; Posatko, "Land Trusts and Land Conservation," 81; and Endicott, *Land Conservation*, 5.

62 Posatko, "Land Trusts and Land Conservation," 4.

63 McHarg, *Metropolitan Open Space*, 7 (quote), 64.

64 Christine Tree in *Boston Globe*, May 15, 1983, 1 (first quote). See Yaro et al., *Dealing with Change in the Connecticut River Valley*, 7; Judd, *Second Nature*, 254; Arendt, "Retaining Natural Landscapes," 222, 225–26; *Lowell (MA) Sun*, March 30, 1991; Patricia P. Schlesinger, "The Birth of the Pemigewasset River Council," in New England Center, *Planning for the Changing Rural Landscape*, 234, 235–39; Gordon Abbott Jr., "Director's Report," February 12, 1967, Records of the Trustees of Public Reservations (hereafter TPR Records), vol. 20 (1968), Trustees of Reservations, Archives & Research Center, Sharon, MA; *Berkshire Eagle* (Pittsfield, MA), August 15, 1969; Peter Howell and Abigail Weinberg, *Western Massachusetts: Assessing the Conservation Opportunity* (New York: Open Space Institute, 2005), 14; Dianne Dumanoski, "Reclaiming the Charles," *Boston Globe*, August 3, 1986, 42; Lisa Grace Lednicer, "Cleanup Makes a Splash in the Charles," *Boston Globe*, July 19, 1987, 24; and Megan Woolhouse, "Tons of Trash Removed in a Cleanup of Charles River," *Boston Globe*, May 4, 2006, 1.

65 Guitar, *Property Power*, 89 (quote), 141; Strong, *Open Space for Urban America*, 9.

66 Charles Downing Lay, "Tidal Marshes," *Landscape Architecture* 2 (April 1912): 101. See National Resources Board and National Park Service, *Recreational Use of Land in the United States*, pt. 11, *Report on Land Planning* (Washington, DC: GPO, 1934), 10; Kitty Robertson, "Fight against Wasters Comes Here," *Ipswich (MA) Chronicle*, January 4, 1966, and Henry Moore, "Coastal Wetland Protection for 3000 Acres in Ipswich?" (clipping), both in box 22, folder 6, CWEII; Commonwealth of

Massachusetts, *Report of the Department of Natural Resources for the Preservation of the Wetlands in the Sudbury and Concord River Valleys* (Boston: Wright & Potter, 1961), 11–12, 15; and Levine, "Land Conservation in Metropolitan Areas," 207.

67 Henry Moore, "State Moves on Marshland" (clipping), box 22, folder 6, CWEII. See Legislative Research Council, *Report Relative to the Preservation of the Natural Environment*, House Document 5301 (Boston, 1971), 39–40, 52; Metropolitan Area Planning Council and Metropolitan District Commission, *Open Space and Recreation Plan*, 41–42; and *Ipswich (MA) Today*, October 16, 1970, box 22, folder 6, CWEII.

68 *Fitchburg (MA) Sentinel and Enterprise*, January 22, 2004. See *Bridgeport (CT) Post*, July 22, 1970; *Assabet Valley Beacon* (Acton, MA), March 27, 1969; *Fitchburg (MA) Sentinel*, July 27, 1965; President's Commission on Americans Outdoors, *Report*, 111, 115–16; and Whyte, *The Last Landscape*, 40–41.

69 *Biddeford (ME) Journal Tribune*, February 27, 1974 (quotes); December 26, 1987.

70 Diamond and Noonan, *Land Use in America*, 69.

71 President's Commission on Americans Outdoors, *Report*, 20; Massachusetts Department of Environmental Management, *Massachusetts Landscape Inventory*, 3; Robert L. Bendick Jr., "State Partnerships to Preserve Open Space: Lessons from Rhode Island and New York," in Endicott, *Land Conservation*, 151.

72 Ian McHarg in Little, *Challenge of the Land*, 20, 21 (quote), 22. See Thomas L. Daniels, "A Trail across Time: American Environmental Planning from City Beautiful to Sustainability, *Journal of the American Planning Association* 75, no. 2 (2009): 182; McHarg, *Design with Nature*, 24, 35–38, 40, 56; and Whyte, *The Last Landscape*, 182–83.

73 *Portsmouth (NH) Herald*, December 5, 2004 (first quote); *Fitchburg (MA) Sentinel and Enterprise*, October 10, 2001 (second and third quotes); Bob Michalkiewicz in *York County (ME) Coast Star*, March 20, 2003 (fourth quote). See Posatko, "Land Trusts and Land Conservation," 80, 178; *Biddeford (ME) Journal Tribune*, August 13, 2008; *Fairfield (CT) Minuteman*, January 27, 2005; *Nashua (NH) Telegraph*, April 3, 1997; and *York (ME) Weekly*, April 5, 2006.

74 Durward Allen, "The Preservation of Endangered Habitats and Vertebrates of North America," in Darling and Milton, *Future Environments of North America*, 22–23, 24 (first quote); *Fitchburg (MA) Sentinel and Enterprise*, January 22, 2004 (second quote); Little, *Greenways for America*, 56–57 (third quote). See John B. Wright, "Land Trusts in the USA," *Land Use Policy*, 9, no. 2 (1992): 86.

75 Edgar J. Driscoll Jr., "Reservation Accused of 'Covert' Plan to Kill 120 Deer," *Boston Globe*, January 6, 1985, 32 (first quote); Marvin Pave, "Reports Say Many Slain Deer Were Near Starvation," *Boston Globe*, June 19, 1985, 19 (second quote); Elizabeth New Weld, "First Land Trust Marks Century of Preservation," *Boston Globe*, October 21, 1990, 9 (third and fourth quotes). See Marvin Pave, "Reservation's Problem: How to Deal with Hungry Deer," *Boston Globe*, December 9, 1984, 42; R. S. Kindleberger, "Castle Hill Sponsors Tick Disease," *Boston Globe*, July 2, 1985, 19; and David Arnold, "Crane Reservation Deer Kill," *Boston Globe*, April 7, 1985, 38.

76 *Portsmouth (NH) Herald*, March 11, 2003 (second quote); Robin Najar in *Portsmouth (NH) Herald*, December 17, 2003 (first and third quotes), January 21, 2004, June 5, 2005 (fourth quote), January 30, 2006. See *Fitchburg (MA) Sentinel and*

Enterprise, October 10, 2001; and *Biddeford (ME) Journal Tribune*, February 16, 2012, April 23, 2013.

77 *York County (ME) Coast Star*, September 30, 2004. See Robert D. Yaro and Randall Arendt, "Rural Landscape Planning in the Connecticut River Valley of Massachusetts," in New England Center, *Planning for the Changing Rural Landscape*, 175–76; Massachusetts Department of Environmental Management, *Massachusetts Landscape Inventory*, 19; and Fairfax and Guenzler, *Conservation Trusts*, 12–13, 177.

78 Fairfax et al., *Buying Nature*, 42; Buckland, "History and Use of Purchase of Development Rights," 242–43; Ann L. Strong, "Easements as a Development Control in the United States," *Landscape Planning* 10 (June 1983): 48.

79 Whyte, *Securing Open Space*, 7 (first quote), 8 (second quote), 12, 16–17, 27.

80 Open Space Action Committee, *Stewardship*, 33. See Conservation Law Foundation of New England, "How to Live with Conservation Restrictions," and "Conservation and Preservation Restrictions," box 3, folder 9, CWEII; *Assabet Valley Beacon* (Acton, MA), November 20, 1969; President's Council on Recreation and Natural Beauty, *From Sea to Shining Sea*, 111; Whyte, *The Last Landscape*, 84–86, 96; Buckland, "History and Use of Purchase of Development Rights," 239; Fairfax et al., *Buying Nature*, 42, Gordon Abbott Jr., *Saving Special Places: A Centennial History of the Trustees of Reservations: Pioneer of the Land Trust Movement* (Ipswich, MA: Ipswich Press, 1993), 135–37; and *Berkshire Eagle* (Pittsfield, MA), July 25, 1970.

81 Strong, "Easements as a Development Control," 47–49, 60. See Hocker, "Land Trusts," 245; US Department of the Interior and Nature Conservancy, *Preserving Our Natural Heritage*, 14–15; Whyte, *Open Space Action*, 17; Virginia A. Keesler, "Conservation Easement Policies across New England" (honors paper, Colby College, 2013), 2; and Amy Wilson Morris, "Easing Conservation? Conservation Easements, Public Accountability and Neoliberalism," *Geoforum* 39 (2008): 1215, 1218–19.

82 Nancy A. McLaughlin, "Conservation Easements: A Troubled Adolescence," *Land Resource and Environmental Law* 26, no. 1 (2005): 56 (first quote); Jeff Pidot, "Conservation Easement Reform: As Maine Goes Should the Nation Follow?," *Law and Contemporary Problems* 74 (Fall 2011): 2–4, 5 (second quote), 14–15; L. Hannah et al., "Conservation of Biodiversity in a Changing Climate," *Conservation Biology* 16 (February 2002): 264 (third quote). See Thomas L. Daniels, "The Purchase of Development Rights: Preserving Agricultural Land and Open Space," *Journal of the American Planning Association* 57, no. 4 (1991): 424; A. M. Merenlender et al., "Land Trusts and Conservation Easements: Who Is Conserving What for Whom?," *Conservation Biology* 18 (February 2004): 67; *New York Times*, October 12, 2003, WE 1; Freese, "Third Sector Land Protection," 177; and Morris, "Easing Conservation?," 1216–17, 1223.

83 Massachusetts Audubon Society, *Losing Ground: Planning for Resilience*, 5th ed. (Lincoln, MA: Audubon, 2014), 9; Metropolitan Area Planning Council and Metropolitan District Commission, *Open Space and Recreation Plan*, 18.

84 Massachusetts Department of Environmental Management, *Massachusetts Landscape Inventory*, 3, 6, 38 (first quote), 42; Yaro et al., *Dealing with Change in the Connecticut River Valley*, 4 (second quote), 7–8.

85 Rutherford H. Platt, "The Loss of Farmland: Evolution of a Public Response,"

Geographical Review 67 (January 1977): 93–101; Daniels, "The Purchase of Development Rights," 421; Donn A. Derr and Pritam S. Dhillon, "Strategies to Maintain Production Agriculture in New England," in New England Center, *Planning for the Changing Rural Landscape*, 79–81; *New York Times*, October 1, 2013, A25.

86 Harkavy, "Maine Land Trusts" (first quote); *York (ME) Weekly*, June 25, 2003 (second quote). See *Portsmouth (NH) Herald*, December 26, 2006; Ian L. McHarg, *Metropolitan Open Space from Natural Processes* (Philadelphia: University of Pennsylvania, 1964), 59; Edward P. Thompson Jr., "Protecting Agricultural Lands," in Brennerman and Bates, *Land Saving Action*, 65; Eisenmenger, *Land Use Changes in the 1960's*, 7–8; and New England Governors' Conference, *Report of the Blue Ribbon Commission on Land Conservation* (Boston: New England Governors' Conference, 2009), 19–21.

87 *New York Times*, November 1, 1987, 59 (first quote); Louis Berney, "Vermont Town Discovers a Way to Save the Farm," *Boston Globe*, July 3, 1983, 1 (second quote). See *Lowell (MA) Sun*, August 12, 1983; *York (ME) Weekly*, November 19, 2003; *Portsmouth (NH) Herald*, August 15, 2003; *Nashua (NH) Telegraph*, November 26, 2002; and Derr and Dhillon, "Strategies to Maintain Production Agriculture," 76–77.

88 *Newport (RI) News*, February 22, 25, 2003. See Nancy Crowe, "Helping Keep Farmland Farmed," *Vermont Business*, February 1987, 62; Pamela W. Hawkes, "Preserving New England's Rural Landscapes: The Property Plan for Eastman Hill, Lovell, Maine," *APT Bulletin: The Journal of Preservation Technology* 28, no. 1 (1997): 12, 15–18; and Richard W. Hale Jr., "Cooperation in Preservation in Massachusetts," *Historic Preservation* 17 (1965): 155.

89 *Boston Globe*, November 3, 1968, box 2, folder 12, CWEII. See "Petition of Charles W. Eliot—Introduced by Rep. Mary B. Newman" 1957, box 2, folder 7, CWEII; Strong, "Easements as a Development Control," 52; Judd, *Second Nature*, 257–58; Jim Collins and Richard Ober, "New Hampshire: Common Ground," in Foster, *Twentieth-Century New England Land Conservation*, 101–3; Maine Legislature, *Joint Standing Committee on Agriculture on Its Study of the Maine Farm and Open Space Law* (Augusta: Maine State Legislature, 1987), 2–4; Thompson, "Protecting Agricultural Lands," 65–67; and Thomas Kenworthy, "Conserving Farmlands May Push State to Greater Food Sufficiency," *Lowell (MA) Sun*, July 1, 1980.

90 *Lowell (MA) Sun*, February 18, 1987 (first quote); Brennerman and Bates, *Land Saving Action*, 67 (second quote). See *North Adams (MA) Transcript*, August 21, 2003; *Nashua (NH) Telegraph*, August 1, 1987; US Department of the Interior and Nature Conservancy, *Preserving Our Natural Heritage*, 22–23; Strong, "Easements as a Development Control," 56; Peter B. Lord, "The Rhode Island Conservation Story," in Foster, *Twentieth-Century New England Land Conservation*, 246; Esther Lacognata and Richard Wood Jr., "The Agriculture Viability Program: Working on the Other End of the Development Pressure," in New England Center, *Planning for the Changing Rural Landscape*, 69; Buckland, "History and Use of Development Rights," 248–50; and Yaro et al., *Dealing with Change in the Connecticut River Valley*, 9.

91 Alvin Powell, *Norwalk (CT) News-Trader*, December 10, 1987 (quote). See *Westport (CT) Fairpress*, August 24, 1977; *Manchester (CT) Journal-Inquirer*, November 23, 1974, March 16, September 21, December 3, 1976, March 15, 1977; Julie D. Belaga, "Do We Want Farms?," *Westport News*, February 27, 1980; Daniels, "Purchase of Development Rights," 421, 424; and Buckland, "History and Use of Development Rights," 249.

92 *New York Times*, July 10, 1999, B7 (first quote), December 14, 2003, CT6 (second quote). See *New York Times*, October 24, 1982, 841.
93 GrowSmart Maine, *Charting Maine's Future: Making Headway* (Augusta, ME: GrowSmart Maine, 2006), 10 (first quote); *Nashua (NH) Telegraph*, August 11, 1980 (second quote). See *Nashua (NH) Telegraph*, January 28, 2011; *Berkshire Eagle* (Pittsfield, MA), June 18, 1974; and *Lowell (MA) Sun*, June 15, 1986, February 18, 1987.
94 Rand Wentworth in *York County (ME) Coast Star*, January 2, 2003. See *Nashua (NH) Telegraph*, March 22, 1998, March 24, 2002; and *York County (ME) Coast Star*, April 17, 2002.
95 *New York Times*, March 28, 1982, CN4, R1; Freese, "Third Sector Land Protection," 166; *Nashua (NH) Telegraph*, February 14, 1981, March 24, 2002; Posatko, "Land Trusts and Land Conservation," 160–61; Negra and Frey, *Effective Local Conservation Commissions*, 30.
96 Hal K. Rothman, *The Greening of a Nation? Environmentalism in the United States since 1945* (Fort Worth: Harcourt Brace, 1998), 5.
97 Mark Dowie, *Losing Ground: American Environmentalism at the Close of the Twentieth Century* (Cambridge, MA: MIT Press, 1996), 4–5, 106 (quote), 108. See Judd, "Exurbia Meets Nature," 65–66.
98 Daniel D. Chiras, *Beyond the Fray: Reshaping America's Environmental Response* (Boulder, CO: Johnson Books, 1990), 129 (first quote); Turner, *Promise of Wilderness*, 7, 13 (second quote), 49, 378. See James Morton Turner, "The Politics of Modern Wilderness," in Lewis, *American Wilderness*, 247, 251.
99 Land for New Hampshire, *Final Report*, 6 (first quote); President's Commission on Americans Outdoors, *Report*, 49 (second quote), 55, 170, 289. See Brooks, *View from Lincoln Hill*, 231–32; and Clawson, "The Crisis in Outdoor Recreation," 40.
100 Fairfax et al., *Buying Nature*, 171. See Posatko, "Land Trusts and Land Conservation," 83–84, 88–93; and Hess and Pomeroy, "Geographic Distribution of Land Trust Activities," 152, 156; Elfring, "Preserving Land through Local Land Trusts," 72. Note: Exact figures on the number of trusts and their holdings vary from account to account, probably due to irregularities in defining a land trust. Hocker ("Patience, Problem Solving, and Private Initiative," 247) points out that there is "virtually no way to tally the number of voluntary groups—large and small, staffed and unstaffed, temporary and permanent—that are affecting the use of land in communities across America."
101 Leslie N. Corey in *New York Times*, June 9, 1996, CN3. See Posatko, "Land Trusts and Land Conservation," 106–8; Sylvia Bates, *Models of Collaboration among Land Trusts* (Topsham, ME: Maine Coast Heritage Trust, 2005), 4; *Lowell (MA) Sun*, February 20, 2001; and *Berkshire Eagle* (Pittsfield, MA), May 17, 1974, December 3, 2006.

Chapter 5: Reimagining Urban Spaces

1 Kevin Lynch, "The Openness of Open Space," in *Arts of the Environment*, ed. Gyorgy Kepes (New York: George Braziller, 1972), 110–11; *New York Times*, November 1, 1987, 59; President's Commission on Americans Outdoors, *Report and Recommendations to the President of the United States* (Washington, DC: GPO, 1986), 33–34; Ted Randich,

"Understanding Urban Wilds: Nature, Culture, and Management" (master's thesis, Clark University, 2017), 25.

2 Charles W. Eliot, "City and Regional Parks and Playgrounds: Preservation of Open Spaces," *Landscape Architecture* 48 (January 1958): 82.

3 Theodore T. McCrosky, Charles A. Blessing, and J. Ross McKeever, *Surging Cities* (Boston: Greater Boston Development Committee, 1948), 52, 76–77, 78 (quote), 79, 192–94. See Michael P. Conzen and George K. Lewis, *Boston: A Geographical Portrait* (Cambridge, MA: Ballinger Publishing Company, 1976), 70–71; Don Alexander, "The Resurgence of Place," *Alternatives Journal* 28 (Summer 2002): 17; and Barry Bluestone and Mary Huff Stevenson, *The Boston Renaissance: Race, Space, and Economic Change in an American Metropolis* (New York: Russell Foundation Publications, 2002), 82, 88. For a concise history of urban renewal in Boston, see Karilyn Crockett, *People Before Highways: Boston Activists, Urban Planners, and a New Movement for City Making* (Amherst: University of Massachusetts Press, 2018), 1–18.

4 McCrosky, Blessing, and McKeever, *Surging Cities*, 248. See James C. O'Connell, "How Metropolitan Parks Shaped Greater Boston, 1893–1945," in *Remaking Boston: An Environmental History of the City and Its Surroundings*, ed. Anthony N. Penna and Conrad Edick Wright (Pittsburgh: University of Pittsburgh Press, 2009), 193–95; Anne Whiston Spirn, "Reclaiming Common Ground: Water, Neighborhoods, and Public Places," in *The American Planning Tradition*, ed. Robert Fishman (Washington, DC: Woodrow Wilson Center Press, 2000), 297; Karl Haglund, *Inventing the Charles River* (Cambridge, MA: MIT Press and Charles River Conservancy, 2003), 304; Peter C. Baldwin, *Domesticating the Street: The Reform of Public Space in Hartford, 1850–1930* (Columbus: Ohio University Press, 1999), 117; Galen Cranz, *The Politics of Park Design: A History of Urban Parks in America* (Cambridge, MA: MIT Press, 1982), 137, 152, 186; Donald George Jones, "Recreating the Wilderness: The Cultural Landscape of Lynn Woods, a Late Nineteenth-Century Public Park in Lynn, Massachusetts" (PhD diss., Boston University, 1994), 69; and Mark L. Primack, ed., *The Greening of Boston: An Action Agenda* (Medford, MA: Carol R. Goldberg Seminar and Tufts University Center for Public Service, 1989), 36.

5 Ann Whiston Spirn, *The Granite Garden: Urban Nature and Human Design* (New York: Basic Books, 1984), 171–72, 173 (quote). See Ann Whiston Spirn, "Constructing Nature: The Legacy of Frederick Law Olmsted," in *Uncommon Ground: Rethinking the Human Place in Nature*, ed. William Cronon (New York: W. W. Norton, 1996), 91; Primack, *Greening of Boston*, 40; and John Hanson Mitchell, *Paradise of All These Parts: A Natural History of Boston* (Boston: Beacon Press, 2009), 149.

6 Alexander, "Resurgence of Place," 19 (first quote); William H. Whyte, *The Last Landscape* (New York: Doubleday, 1968), 318, 319 (second quote). See Ian McHarg, "The Humane City," *Landscape Architecture* 48 (January 1958): 103–5; and Cranz, *Politics of Park Design*, 138–44.

7 William H. Whyte, *The Social Life of Small Urban Spaces* (Washington, DC: Conservation Foundation, 1980), 7, 10, 17–19, 33–38, 47, 100 (quote). See Anthony Walmsley, "Greenways and the Making of Urban Form," *Landscape and Urban Planning* 33 (October 1995): 125; Whyte, *The Last Landscape*, 318, 319; Ada Louise Huxtable, "Open-Space Designs Breathing New Life into Smothered Blocks," *New York*

Times, July 6, 1972, 39; McHarg, "Humane City," 103–5; and Alexander, "Resurgence of Place," 19.

8   O'Connell, "How Metropolitan Parks Shaped Greater Boston," 197; Stephanie Pincetl and Elizabeth Gearin, "The Reinvention of Public Green Space," *Urban Geography* 26, no. 5 (2005): 365; Robert G. Shibley and Lynda H. Schneekloth, "Olmsted Park and Parkway System for the 21st Century," *Proceedings of the Fábos Conference on Landscape and Greenway Planning* (2010): 180; *Boston Globe*, May 19, 1990, 14.

9   Primack, *Greening of Boston*, 14, 16, 20, 117, 126; O'Connell, "How Metropolitan Parks Shaped Greater Boston," 197; *Boston Parks & Recreation Annual Report 1988* (Boston, 1988), 5–12; *Boston Globe*, November 30, 1987, 19; *Boston's Open Space: Ten-Point Policy Plan* (n.p.: n.d.; Boston Public Library digital archive), 1, 4–5; Randich, "Understanding Urban Wilds," 7.

10 Crockett, *People Before Highways*, 65 (first quote), 196 (second quote); Jane Holtz Kay, "In Boston, a Wasteland Is Now an Oasis," *New York Times*, October 13, 1988, C10 (third quote from Ann Hershfang). See Boston Urban Gardeners, *South End Open Space Needs Assessment* (Boston, February 1988), 6, 12.

11 Justine M. Liff, "Planning for a Greener Boston," *Boston Globe*, February 2, 1988, A15 (first quote); Thomas Menino in *Boston Globe*, April 9, 1995, 33 (second quote). See *Boston Globe*, May 25, 1996, 10.

12 Mark Francis, Lisa Cashdan, and Lynn Paxson, *Community Open Spaces: Greening Neighborhoods through Community Action and Land Conservation* (Washington, DC: Island Press, 1984), 2; *Boston Globe*, November 30, 1987, 19; Robert T. Kenney, *Boston Urban Wilds: A Natural Area Conservation Program* (Boston: Boston Redevelopment Authority, 1976), 13–16.

13 Whyte, *The Last Landscape*, 172 (first quote); Lynch, "Openness of Open Space," 112 (second quote), 121; Randall Arendt, *Rural by Design: Maintaining Small Town Character* (Washington, DC: American Planning Association and Lincoln Land Institute of Land Policy, 1994), 5 (third quote); Primack, *Greening of Boston*, 25 (fourth quote); Lynch, "Openness of Open Space," 119 (fifth quote), 121 (sixth quote); Anne Whiston Spirn, "Landscape Planning and the City," *Landscape and Urban Planning* 13 (1986): 434 (seventh quote). See Francis, Cashdan, and Paxson, *Community Open Spaces*, 3, 5–6, 11, 17; Charles E. Little, *Greenways for America* (Baltimore: Johns Hopkins University Press, 1990), 37; and Garrett Eckbo, "The Link between Man and Nature," *Landscape Architecture Magazine* 56 (July 1966): 268.

14 See President's Council on Recreation and Natural Beauty, *From Sea to Shining Sea: A Report on the American Environment—Our Natural Heritage* (Washington, DC: Council 1968), 33–35; Arendt, *Rural by Design*, 4–5; Viniece Jennings, Matthew H. E. M. Browning, and Alessandro Rigolon, *Urban Green Spaces: Public Health and Sustainability in the United States* (Cham, Switzerland: Springer, 2021), 9, 12, 17–18.

15 Anne Whiston Spirn in Steve Curwood, "Shaping the City to Nature's Laws," *Boston Globe*, May 26, 1985, A13 (first quote); Michael Hough, "Design with City Nature: An Overview of Some Issues," in *The Ecological City: Preserving and Restoring Urban Biodiversity*, ed. Rutherford H. Platt, Rowan A. Rowntree, and Pamela C. Muick (Amherst: University of Massachusetts Press, 1994), 41 (second quote); Scott Allen, "Boston's Surprising Natural Wonders," *Boston Globe*, May 23, 1994, 23 (third quote). See Ian L. McHarg, *Design with Nature* (Garden

City, NY: American Museum of Natural History and Natural History Press, 1969), 80.
16 Ian L. McHarg, *Metropolitan Open Space from Natural Processes* (Philadelphia: University of Pennsylvania, 1964). 3. See Primack, *Greening of Boston*, 31; Whiston Spirn, *Granite Garden*, 27, 29, 37; and Sam Bass Warner, *The Way We Really Live: Social Change in Metropolitan Boston since 1920* (Boston: Trustees of the Public Library of the City of Boston, 1977), 52.
17 Kenney, *Boston Urban Wilds*, 3, 22–23, 26, 29, 46–49; Primack, *Greening of Boston*, 54; Whiston Spirn, *Granite Garden*, 201; Boston Redevelopment Program, *Boston Urban Wilds* (Boston: Boston Redevelopment Authority, 1976), 2, 4–5.
18 Kenney, *Boston Urban Wilds*, 35 (quote), 37–38, 40, 44, 46–49. See *Boston's Open Space*, 6; Boston Redevelopment Program, *Boston Urban Wilds*, 3–4; and Randich, "Understanding Urban Wilds," 3–4, 6.
19 Kenney, *Boston Urban Wilds*, 10; Primack, *Greening of Boston*, 54, 74; *Boston Globe*, August 29, 1980, 1; *Bay State Banner*, September 8, 1977, 2.
20 *Boston Globe*, September 21, 1991 (first quote); Justine M. Liff, "Planning for a Greener Boston," *Boston Globe*, February 2, 1988, A15 (second quote). See Shary Page Berg, *Hancock Woods Site Analysis* (Boston: Boston Conservation Commission, 1976), 2, 11; and *Boston Globe*, April 7, 9, February 28, August 25, 1995.
21 *Boston's Open Space*, 7. See Randich, "Understanding Urban Wilds," 34–35; and *Boston Globe*, March 11, 1995, 10.
22 Richard W. Judd, *Second Nature: An Environmental History of New England* (Amherst: University of Massachusetts Press, 2014), 235–36; Francis, Cashdan, and Paxton, *Community Open Spaces*, 8, 14.
23 *New York Times*, March 15, 1995, CN1. See President's Commission on Americans Outdoors, *Report*, 294–95.
24 Dana Pearson, "A Walk in the Woods," *York County (ME) Coast Star*, December 14, 2006. See Rita A. Niro, "Land Trust Receives 14 Acres of Open Space," *Hartford Courant*, February 6, 1996, B2; *York (ME) Weekly*, December 3, 2003; *Portsmouth (NH) Herald*, December 5, 2003, April 29, 2005; Randich, "Understanding Urban Wilds," 1, 19, 26–28; and James F. Thorne, "Landscape Ecology: A Foundation for Greenway Design," in *Ecology of Greenways: Design and Function of Linear Conservation Areas*, ed. Daniel S. Smith and Paul Cawood Hellmund (Minneapolis: University of Minnesota Press, 1993), 23.
25 Frederick Law Olmsted in Anthony Walmsley, "Greenways and the Making of Urban Form," *Landscape and Urban Planning* 33 (October 1995): 84. See Arendt, *Rural by Design*, 263; Robert M. Searns, "The Evolution of Greenways as an Adaptive Urban Landscape Form," *Landscape and Urban Planning* 33 (October 1995): 67–68; Ervin H. Zube, "Greenways and the US National Park System," *Landscape and Urban Planning* 33 (October 1995): 19, 22–23; and Jack Ahern, "Greenways as a Planning Strategy," *Landscape and Urban Planning* 33 (October 1995): 134, 138.
26 Russell L. Brenneman, "Rescuing Connecticut: A Story of Land-Saving Actions," in *Twentieth-Century New England Land Conservation: A Heritage of Civic Engagement*, ed. Charles H. W. Foster (Petersham, MA: Harvard Forest, 2009), 273; Noel Grove, "Greenways: Paths to the Future," *National Geographic*, June 1990, 89–92.

27 Richard W. Judd and Christopher S. Beach, *Natural States: The Environmental Imagination in Maine, Oregon, and the Nation* (Washington, DC: Resources for the Future, 2003), 81–93; *Nashua (NH) Telegraph*, June 10, 1969, January 13, 1970, January 18, February 16, 1971, May 9, 1972, March 28, 1973, August 16, 1984, July 14, 2000; Jim Klein, "The Art of Managing Long and Skinny Places: A Case for Regional Collaboration," *Proceedings of the Fábos Conference on Landscape and Greenway Planning* (2013): 643.

28 John G. Kelcey, "The Green Environment of Inner Urban Areas," *Environmental Conservation* 5 (Autumn 1978): 198.

29 President's Commission on Americans Outdoors, *Report*, 50 (first quote), 51–53; Robert Searns, "Greenways, The Next Step: Every Doorstep a Trailhead," *Proceedings of the Fábos Conference on Landscape and Greenway Planning* (2016): 397–98 (second quote), 400. See Henry L. Diamond and Patrick F. Noonan, *Land Use in America* (Boston: Lincoln Institute of Land Policy and Island Press, 1996), 48–49; Grove, "Greenways," 83; Elisabeth Lardner and Jim Klein, "More than a Trail: Greenways and Heritage Tourism," *Proceedings of the Fábos Conference on Landscape and Greenway Planning* (2010): 513; and Searns, "Evolution of Greenways," 65–70.

30 David S. Sampson, "The Hudson River Valley Greenway and Beyond: How a Word Can Change the Way We Think about Our Land," *Proceedings of the Fábos Conference on Landscape and Greenway Planning* (2013): 513–19.

31 Jack Thomas, "River Renaissance," *Boston Globe*, August 13, 1992, 35.

32 Scott Carlin, "Rediscovering Boston Harbor: The Political Geography of Urban Environmental Agendas" (PhD diss., Clark University, 1995), 146 (first quote); Christina Pazzanese, "Going with the Flow," *Boston Globe*, September 26, 2004, GW1 (second quote).

33 Carlin, "Rediscovering Boston Harbor," 145–46, 168–69, 176 (first quote), 177 (second quote). See Dan Driscoll in Pazzanese, "Going with the Flow"; and Driscoll and Karl Haglund, "Reclaiming the Middle Charles River Reservation," both in Penna and Wright, *Remaking Boston*, 199–202.

34 Robert L. Zimmerman in Doreen Ludica Vigue, "Putting the Charles into the Spotlight," *Boston Globe*, April 23 1995, 3. See Jennifer Kingston Bloom, "A River Whose Time Has Come," *Boston Globe*, January 6, 1991, n.p.; Dianne Dumanoski, "Reclaiming the Charles," *Boston Globe*, August 3, 1986, 42; Lisa Kocian, "It's Step Two for Riverwalk Path," *Boston Globe*, February 25, 2001, 1; and Pazzanese, "Going with the Flow."

35 Simona Lee Perry, "More than One River: Local, Place-Based Knowledge and the Political Ecology of Restoration and Remediation along the Lower Neponset River, Massachusetts" (PhD diss., University of Massachusetts Amherst, 2009), 1, 4–5, 77–81, 82 (quote), 83. See Michael Kenney, "'Back Door River' Awash in History," *Boston Globe*, July 3, 1994, 1; Andrew Caffrey, "Along the Neponset River," *Boston Globe*, July 5, 1988, 1; Jeff Mclaughlin, "Rediscovering the Neponset River," *Boston Globe*, May 5, 1996, 1; and Boston Urban Gardeners, *South End Open Space Needs Assessment* (Boston, February 1988), 30.

36 McLaughlin, "Rediscovering the Neponset River" (all quotes; third quote from Craig Auston). See Perry, "Neponset River," 88.

37 Emily Shartin, "MDC Starts Work on Neponset River Greenway," *Boston Globe*, July 15, 2001, 9.
38 Perry, "Neponset River," 16; Jennings, Browning, and Rigolon, *Urban Green Spaces*, 9; Edward O. Wilson, *Biophilia* (Cambridge, MA: Harvard University Press, 1984).
39 Perry, "Neponset River," 2, 109–12; Driscoll and Haglund, "Reclaiming the Middle Charles River Reservation," 202; Charles River Project, "Model Preservation Planning Program," box 3, folder 4, Charles W. Eliot II Papers, Trustees of Reservations Archives & Research Center, Sharon, MA; *Lowell (MA) Sun*, November 30, 2004.
40 *Boston Globe*, June 23, 2001, A14; Perry, "Neponset River," 12–14, 34.
41 Anne Lusk in Grove, "Greenways," 91. See Anthony Walmsley, "Greenways and the Making of Urban Form," *Landscape and Urban Planning* 33 (October 1995):81; Whyte, *The Last Landscape*, 173, 176, 179; and Governor's Advisory Commission on Open Space and Outdoor Recreation, *Report and Recommendations* (Boston, 1969), 19.
42 Milton state senator Brian A. Joyce (first quote) and Ken Mackin (second quote) in Robert Preer, "Return to the River," *Boston Globe*, February 11, 2007, H1; Melanie Spencer, "Minimizing Displacement in Gentrifying Neighborhoods: An Examination of the Community Land Trust" (master's thesis, Tufts University, 2007), 1, 21, 26 (third quote). See *Boston Globe*, June 23, 2001, A14; and Jennings, Browning, and Rigolon, *Urban Green Spaces*, 23.
43 Daniel S. Smith, "An Overview of Greenways," in Smith and Hellmund, *Ecology of Greenways*, 2, 9; *Nashua (NH) Telegraph*, June 10, 1969, August 16, 1984, January 13, 1970, January 18, February 16, 1971, May 9, 1972, March 28, 1973, July 14, 2000.
44 Juan J. Sanchez, "An Assessment and Analysis of Issues and Patterns Associated with the Utilization of Open Spaces by Latino Immigrants in an Urban Neighborhood in Boston" (PhD diss., Tufts University, 2010), 16–19, 23; Jennings, Browning, and Rigolon, *Urban Green Spaces*, 11.
45 Smith, "Overview of Greenways," 16–17; Smith, "Introduction," in Smith and Hellmund, *Ecology of Greenways*, xii.
46 Thorne, "Landscape Ecology," 29–32.
47 Searns, "Evolution of Greenways," 72–73; Ahern, "Greenways as a Planning Strategy," 135; Lawrence Levine, "Land Conservation in Metropolitan Areas," *Journal of the American Institute of Planners* 30, no. 3 (1964): 207; Thorne, "Landscape Ecology," 23.
48 Walmsley, "Greenways and the Making of Urban Form," 81; Julius Gy. Fabos, "Introduction and Overview: The Greenway Movement, Uses and Potentials of Greenways," *Landscape and Urban Planning* 33 (October 1995): 7; Searns, "Evolution of Greenways," 65–66, 74–78.
49 Ahern, "Greenways as a Planning Strategy," 132 (quote), 135–36. See Searns, "Evolution of Greenways," 66, 73–76; and Perry, "Neponset River," 8, 106, 111, 113, 116–18.
50 Sam Bass Warner, *To Dwell Is to Garden: A History of Boston's Community Gardens* (Boston: Northeastern University Press, 1987), 9, 12 19.
51 Ric Kahn, "A Garden Oasis Takes Root in South End," *Boston Globe*, October 15, 2000, 1(quotes). See Ken Nicholls, foreword to *Community Open Spaces*, ed. Mark, Cashdan, and Paxson, vii; Getta Anald, "Townies Have Room to Grow, in Deed," *Boston Globe*, August 3, 1995, 29; and Warner, *Community Gardens*, 4–5.

52 Carol Stocker, "Still Cultivating the Garden of Ideals," *Boston Globe*, July 5, 1989, 27; Warner, *Community Gardens*, 20–23; Charles A. French, "The Social Production of Community Garden Space: Case Studies of Boston, Massachusetts and Havana, Cuba" (PhD diss., Dartmouth College, 2008), 73.
53 Stocker, "Still Cultivating the Garden of Ideals"; Warner, *Community Gardens*, xi, 28, 31–32, 36–37; Michael Fields, "Rebuilding the Community," *Bay State Banner*, August 10, 1978, 3; French, "Community Garden Space," 102–5; Whiston Spirn, "Reclaiming Common Ground," 303.
54 Primack, *Greening of Boston*, 56–58, 74; Trustees of Reservations, *The Trustees at 125: A Commemoration* (n.p.: Trustees of Reservations, 2016), 34–35; Anne Wyman, "Plotting Greener Use of Vacant Space after 10 Years," *Boston Globe*, September 13, 1987, 54; Michael Rezendes, "Inner-City Gardeners Stand Their Ground in Boston," *Washington Post*, November 9, 1988, A3; Stocker, "Still Cultivating the Garden of Ideals"; Andrew L. Andrews, "Roxbury He Sees Opportunity in Retirement," *Boston Globe*, September 10, 1987, 32; *Boston Globe*, September 25, 1988, A26; Boston Redevelopment Authority, *South End Community Land Trust Report* (Boston, August 12, 1988), 2–3; *New York Times*, August 29, 1985, C3.
55 *Boston Banner*, May 9, 2019, 20.
56 Primack, *Greening of Boston*, 55–56; Carol Stocker, "Harvest of Time," *Boston Globe*, July 25, 1996, G1; David Arnold, "How Their Gardens Grow," *Boston Globe*, May 31, 1993, 13; Boston Redevelopment Authority, *South End Report*, 5.
57 *New York Times*, August 29, 1985, C3 (first quote); Jim Alicata in *Boston Globe* July 16, 1995, 1. See Jill Eshelman, foreword to *Community Gardens*, by Warner, ix; and French, "Community Garden Space," 87, 97, 113–14.
58 Warner, *Community Gardens*, 100. See French, "Community Garden Space," 18–19, 85–86, 93–94.
59 French, "Community Garden Space," 8, 10, 91–92, 106, 109 (quote), 112, 118. See Warner, *Community Gardens*, 34; and Rezendes, "Inner-City Gardeners Stand Their Ground."
60 Constance L. Hays, "Vanguard in the Battle for Dwindling Open Space," *New York Times*, April 23, 1992, B1 (first and second [Robert Pirani] quotes). See Elizabeth New Weld, "First Land Trust Marks Century of Preservation," *Boston Globe*, October 21, 1990, 9; James C. O'Connell, *The Hub's Metropolis: Greater Boston's Development from Railroad Suburbs to Smart Growth* (Cambridge, MA: MIT Press, 2013), 173, 174; and Bluestone and Stevenson, *Boston Renaissance*, 99–100.
61 Boston Redevelopment Authority, *South End Report*, 3–4.
62 Robert Swann, *The Community Land Trust: A Guide to the New Model for Land Tenure in America* (1972; repr., Cambridge, MA: Center for Community Economic Development, 2007), 14–15; *New York Times*, October 11, 1987, R25; James Meehan, "Reinventing Real Estate: The Community Land Trust as a Social Invention in Affordable Housing," *Journal of Applied Social Science* 8 (September 2014): 118–22; John Emmeus Davis, "Origins and Evolution of the Community Land Trust in the United States," in *The Community Land Trust Reader*, ed. John Emmeus Davis (Cambridge, MA: Lincoln Institute of Land Policy, 2010), 22–27; *Berkshire Eagle* (Pittsfield, MA), January 16, 2003; Wendy Priesnitz, "Land Trusts: Conservation and Stewardship for the Benefit of People and the Earth, *Natural Life* (Toronto), May–June 2013, 23.

63 Davis, "Origins and Evolution of the Community Land Trust," 3, 6–7, 27–29, 34, 36; Julie Farrell Curtin and Lance Bocarsly, "CLTs: A Growing Trend in Affordable Home Ownership," in Davis, *Community Land Trust Reader*, 291–92; Sharon Cho, Koko Li, and Tessa Salzman, *Building a Livable Boston: The Case for Community Land Trusts* (Boston: Tufts Field Project and Greater Boston Community Land Trust Network, 2016), 8–9.

64 *New York Times*, November 15, 1987, R25, April 2, 1989, WC1. See *Fitchburg (MA) Sentinel and Enterprise*, July 22, 2004; Peter Howell and Abigail Weinberg, *Western Massachusetts: Assessing the Conservation Opportunity* (New York: Open Space Institute, 2005), 5; *Nashua (NH) Telegraph*, June 29, 1986; *New York Times*, October 11, 1987, R25; Spencer, "Community Land Trust," 15–16; John Milne, "Communities Look to the Land for Housing," *Boston Globe*, May 15, 1988, 29; and Cho, Li, and Salzman, *Building a Livable Boston*, 10.

65 Davis, "Origins and Evolution of the Community Land Trust," 4–5, 33–35; Meehan, "Reinventing Real Estate," 124; *Newport (RI) News*, August 11, 1976; *North Adams (MA) Transcript*, December 14, 2001; *Greenfield (MA) Recorder*, June 17, August 3, 1976; *Kennebec Journal* (Augusta, ME), May 28, 1976.

66 Joseph Margulies, "Communities Need Neighborhood Trusts," *Stanford Social Innovation Review* 17 (Spring 2019): 50, 53; Mark Dowie, *Losing Ground: American Environmentalism at the Close of the Twentieth Century* (Cambridge, MA: MIT Press, 1996), 129, 131; Robert D. Bullard, ed., *Confronting Environmental Racism: Voices from the Grassroots* (Boston: South End Press, 1993), 7.

67 Kelcey, "Green Environment of Inner Urban Areas," 197. See Robert Halpern, *Rebuilding the Inner City: A History of Neighborhood Initiatives to Address Poverty in the United States* (New York: Columbia University Press, 1995), 197.

68 Dowie, *Losing Ground*, 20; Giovanna Di Chiro, "Nature as Community: The Convergence of Environment and Social Justice," in Cronon, *Uncommon Ground*, 301; Martin Melosi, "The Place of the City in Environmental History," *Environmental History Review* 17 (Spring 1993): 3–4.

69 David Schlosberg, *Environmental Justice and the New Pluralism: The Challenge of Difference for Environmentalism* (Oxford: Oxford University Press, 1999), 9, 31; Carlin, "Rediscovering Boston Harbor," 4–6, 11–12.

70 Boston Urban Gardeners, *South End Open Space Needs Assessment*, 14–15; Spencer, "Community Land Trust," 32–35; Kendra A. King, "African-American Community Development Corporation-Led Redevelopment in Boston" (PhD diss., Ohio State University, 2000), 22, 167.

71 Holly Sklar, "Building an Urban Village: The Dudley Street Neighborhood Initiative," *Environmental Action* 28 (Spring–Summer 1996): 34. See Halpern, *Rebuilding the Inner City*, 198; Michael K. Frisby, "Poll in Roxbury Shows Optimism on Quality of Life," *Boston Globe*, March 3, 1985, 29; Luz Delgado, "Restoring Neighborhood Pride in Four Corners," *Boston Globe*, September 26, 1993, 1; Efrain Hernandez, "Becoming Good Neighbors One Step at a Time," *Boston Globe*, September 17, 1991, 20; and Getta Anald, "A Neighborhood Restored," *Boston Globe*, July 22, 1995, 17.

72 Sklar, "Building an Urban Village," 33–34; Daniel Faber, "A More 'Productive' Environmental Justice Politics: Movement Alliances in Massachusetts for Clean Production and Regional Equity," in *Environmental Justice and Environmentalism*:

The Social Justice Challenge to the Environmental Movement, ed. Ron Sandler and Phaedra Pezzullo (Cambridge, MA: MIT Press, 2007), 138.
73 Che Madyun in Alexander Reid, "Dudley Street Neighbors Fight Blight with Hope," *Boston Globe*, January 30, 1988, 21. See Sklar, "Building an Urban Village," 34; *Boston Globe*, November 16, 1993, 22; and Halpern, *Rebuilding the Inner City*, 202–3.
74 Gloria Negri, "A Sense of Renewal Stirs in Roxbury," *Boston Globe*, November 26, 2000, WKC1.
75 Sklar, "Building an Urban Village," 34 (quote), 35. See Derrick Z. Jackson, "Dudley Street's Vision for a Village," *Boston Globe*, July 16, 1997, A 19; Diego Ribadeneira, "Plan Maps Future of Dudley Street," *Boston Globe*, October 26, 1987, 19; Michael K. Frisby, "BRA Drafts a Plan for Advising on Dudley Square Development," *Boston Globe*, July 12, 1985, 23; and Negri, "Sense of Renewal Stirs in Roxbury."
76 John Powers, "Property Values Soar in Dudley Square," *Boston Globe*, July 14, 1985, 25; Bluestone and Stevenson, *Boston Renaissance*, 6; Erick Trickey and Adrianne Mathiowetz, "Fixing a Highway-Shaped Hole in the Heart of Black Boston," *Forefront* (Philadelphia), August 14, 2017, 1–3; *Boston Globe*, November 16, 1993, 22, May 6, 1988, 14; Sklar, "Building an Urban Village," 34.
77 Che Madyun in Reid, "Dudley Street Neighbors Fight Blight with Hope." See Peter S. Canellos, "Neighborhood Hopes to Wield Eminent Domain," *Boston Globe*, October 28, 1988; King, "Community Development Program," 111–12; Bluestone and Stevenson, *Boston Renaissance*, 383.
78 Thomas Grillo, "Praise Greets Orchard Commons," *Boston Globe*, December 2, 2000, E1. See *Boston Globe*, June 6, 1999, G6; Sklar, "Building an Urban Village," 33, 35; Spencer, "Community Land Trust," 42–43; Meehan, "Reinventing Real Estate," 114, 125, 127; and Margulies, "Neighborhood Trusts," 53.
79 Martin Desmarais, "Demolition Set to Begin on Bartlett Yard Site," *Boston Globe*, August 15, 2013, 1, 20. See Sarah Snyder, "Uphams Corner: A Raising of Houses, A Lifting of Spirits," *Boston Globe*, April 18, 1986, 26; Cho, Li, and Salzman, *Building a Livable Boston*, 6; *Bay State Banner*, July 13, 1972, 19; King, "Community Development Program," 102, 108; and Desiree French, "Land Trusts in an Urban Setting," *Boston Globe*, December 19, 1986, 61.
80 Davis, "Origins and Evolution of the Community Land Trust," 23, 26 (quote). See Faber, "More 'Productive' Environmental Justice Politics," 158; and King, "Community Development Program," 29.

Chapter 6: Middle-Way Preservation in the Era of Ecosystem Management, 1990–2010

1 A. M. Merenlender et al., "Land Trusts and Conservation Easements: Who is Conserving What for Whom?" *Conservation Biology* 18 (February 2004): 66; Judith A. Layzer, Sheldon Kamieniecki, and Michael E. Kraft, *Natural Experiments: Ecosystem-Based Management and the Environment* (Cambridge, MA: MIT Press, 2008), 10, 12.
2 Jean W. Hocker, "Patience, Problem Solving, and Private Initiative: Local Groups Chart a New Course for Land Conservation," in *Land Use in America*, ed. Henry L. Diamond and Patrick F. Noonan (Boston: Lincoln Institute of Land

Policy and Island Press, 1996), 252 (first quote); Future Policy Committee, "Beautiful and Historic Places and Tracts of Land," ca. 1976, box 3, folder 9, Charles W. Eliot II Papers, Trustees of Reservations Archives & Research Center, Sharon, MA (hereafter CWEII; second quote). See *New York Times*, March 28, 1982, CN4.

3 *New York Times*, March 20, 1988, 866, August 5, 1990, R15, August 11, 2002, J1; *Portsmouth (NH) Herald*, July 20, 2003; *York County (ME) Coast Star*, February 5, 2004; Eve Endicott, "Preserving Natural Areas: The Nature Conservancy and Its Partners," in *Land Conservation through Public Private Partnerships*, ed. Eve Endicott (Cambridge, MA: Lincoln Institute of Land Policy, 1993), 31–32; *Biddeford (ME) Journal Tribune*, January 4, 1990; *Nashua (NH) Telegraph*, May 11, 1990.

4 Sally K. Fairfax and Darla Guenzler, *Conservation Trusts* (Lawrence: University Press of Kansas, 2001), 36. See Charles H. W. Foster, "Environmental Conservation in Massachusetts: A Twentieth-Century Overview," in *Twentieth-Century New England Land Conservation: A Heritage of Civic Engagement*, ed. Charles H. W. Foster (Petersham, MA: Harvard Forest, 2009), 207–8; and *Nashua (NH) Telegraph*, April 25, 2004.

5 *North Adams (MA) Transcript*, August 15, 1969 (quote), June 14, 1973, December 30, 1977. See *Berkshire Eagle* (Pittsfield, MA), August 14, 16, September 3, 1969, July 25, 1970, August 23, December 31, 1973, December 10, 1974, January 3, December 11, 1976; Endicott, *Land Conservation through Public Private Partnerships*, 202–3; and *New York Times*, May 18, 1969, box 2, folder 12, CWEII.

6 *Bridgeport (CT) Post*, April 4, 1967; "The Land Conservation Trust: A Report of Activities, 1972–1973," box 3, folder 4, CWEII; Virginia A. Keesler, "Conservation Easement Policies across New England" (honors paper, Colby College, 2013), 23; William Poole, "Preserving Urban and Suburban Gardens and Parks: The Trust for Public Land and Its Partners," in Endicott, *Land Conservation through Public Private Partnerships*, 61–63; Jerome T. Posatko, "Land Trusts and Land Conservation in the United States: Characteristics, Systemic Analysis, and Implications for Public Policy" (PhD diss., University of Delaware, 1996), 5–6; Ann Louise Strong, *Open Space for Urban America* (Washington, DC: Department of Housing and Urban Development, 1965), 104; Foster, "Environmental Conservation in Massachusetts," 196; Sylvia Bates, *Models of Collaboration among Land Trusts* (Topsham, ME: Maine Coast Heritage Trust, 2005), 34; *Fitchburg (MA) Sentinel and Enterprise*, February 12, 2004, February 14, 2008; *Berkshire Eagle* (Pittsfield, MA), February 19, 2008; *Westport (CT) Fairpress*, November 5, 1980.

7 Blake Harrison, *The View from Vermont: Tourism and the Making of an American Rural Landscape* (Burlington: University of Vermont Press, 2006), 203–4, 206 (quote), 207–9, 223. See Randall Arendt, "Retaining Natural Landscapes along the Water's Edge," in *Planning for the Changing Rural Landscape of New England: Blending Theory and Practice*, ed. New England Center (Durham, NH: Center, n.d., ca. 1986), 220–24; Robert McCullough, Clare Ginger, and Michelle Baumflek, "Unspoiled Vermont: The Nature of Conservation in the Green Mountain State," in Foster, *Twentieth-Century New England Land Conservation*, 156–59; and Howard Dean, "Growth Management Plans," in Diamond and Noonan, *Land Use in America*, 152.

8 Pamela M. Dennis, "A State Program to Preserve Land and Provide Housing: Vermont's Housing and Conservation Trust Fund," in Endicott, *Land Conservation*

through *Public Private Partnerships*, 177. See Keesler, "Conservation Easement Policies," 25–27; Nora Mitchell and Rolf Diamant, "Stewardship and Sustainability: Lessons from the 'Middle Landscape' of Vermont," *Wilderness Comes Home: Rewilding the Northeast*, ed. Christopher McGrory Klyza (Hanover, NH: Middlebury College Press, 2001), 226, 230; *Nashua (NH) Telegraph*, June 20, 1997; James M. Libby Jr. and Darby Bradley, "Vermont Housing and Conservation Board: A Conspiracy of Good Will among Land Trusts and Housing Trusts," in *Property and Values: Alternatives to Public and Private Ownership*, ed. Charles Geisler and Gail Daneker (Washington, DC: Island Press, 2000), 274–75; and Joyce Marcel, "For Vermont: In Land We Trust," *Vermont Business Magazine* 24 (April 1, 1996): 32.

9 Jim Collins and Richard Ober, "New Hampshire: Common Ground," in *Twentieth-Century New England Land Conservation*, ed. Foster, 101 (first quote), 111–12; Paul Bofinger in Land for New Hampshire, *Final Report of the New Hampshire Land Conservation Investment Program and the Trust for New Hampshire Lands* (n.p.: Trust for New Hampshire Lands, 1993), 3, 4 (second quote), 6; *Nashua (NH) Telegraph*, January 16, March 3 (third and fourth quotes), March 20, April 8, July 6, 1987.

10 Land for New Hampshire, *Final Report*, 5–8, 24; *Nashua (NH) Telegraph*, October 23, 1988; *Lowell (MA) Sun*, October 5, 1986.

11 *Boston Globe*, December 13, 1987, A26. See *Boston Globe*, April 27, 1975, box 22, folder 8, CWEII; "Proposed Legislation Beach Access 1975," Appendix A, An Act to Protect Public Beach Access," box 22, folder 8, CWEII; and "Public Reservations Bill #1080," and clipping, "Finds Public No Longer Has Free Access to Beaches," n.p., ca. 1975, box 23, folder 8, CWEII.

12 Thomas A. Urquhart, "A Certain Persistence of Character: Land Conservation in Maine, 1900–2000," in Foster, *Twentieth-Century New England Land Conservation*, 59–61, 64–66.

13 Lee Burnett, "Conservation Wins Some New Allies," *Biddeford (ME) Journal Tribune*, January 4, 1990; *Biddeford (ME) Journal Tribune*, November 14, 1989; Posatko, "Land Trusts and Land Conservation," 9; *New York Times*, January 26, 2000, CT1; February 14, 1988, CN1; *Greenwich (CT) News*, May 28, 1987.

14 Urquhart, "Certain Persistence of Character," 61–64; Urquhart, *Up for Grabs: Timber Pirates, Lumber Barons, and the Battles over Maine's Public Lands* (Camden, ME: Down East Books, 2021).

15 Keesler, "Conservation Easement Policies," 39, 40–43, 46, 59.

16 Sally K. Fairfax and Darla Guenzler, *Conservation Trusts* (Lawrence: University Press of Kansas, 2001), 9–10; Charles E. Little, *Greenways for America* (Baltimore: Johns Hopkins University Press, 1990), 55; *New York Times*, June 10, 1987, A20.

17 Charles E. Little, *Challenge of the Land: Open Space Preservation at the Local Level* (New York: Pergamon Press, 1968), 34–37; New England Governors' Conference, *Report of the Blue Ribbon Commission on Land Conservation* (Boston: New England Governors' Conference, 2009), 10; Ann Louise Strong, *Preserving Urban Open Space* (Washington, DC: Urban Renewal Administration, 1963), 24–25; President's Commission on Americans Outdoors, *Report and Recommendations to the President of the United States* (Washington, DC: GPO, 1986), 140–41; *Nashua (NH) Telegraph*, February 14, 1981; *Biddeford (ME) Journal Tribune*, August 23, 2007; *Biddeford (ME) Journal Tribune*, July 17, 2007.

18 Andrew J. W. Scheffey, *Conservation Commissions in Massachusetts* (Washington DC: Conservation Foundation, 1969), 127, 128 (first quote), 129–31; William H. Whyte, *The Last Landscape* (New York: Doubleday, 1968), 101 (second quote). See Noel Grove, "Greenways: Paths to the Future," *National Geographic*, June 1990, 98; Foster, "Environmental Conservation in Massachusetts," 193–96; Strong, *Open Space for Urban America*, 51–52; Sally K. Fairfax et al., *Buying Nature: The Limits of Land Acquisition as a Conservation Strategy, 1780–2004* (Cambridge, MA: MIT Press, 2005), 225; *Lowell (MA) Sun*, March 21, 1962; and Commonwealth of Massachusetts, *Report of the Department of Natural Resources for the Preservation of the Wetlands in the Sudbury and Concord River Valleys* (Boston: Wright & Potter, 1961), 6, 15–16.
19 *Nashua (NH) Telegraph*, June 20, 1997, July 18, 1988.
20 Robert L. Bendick Jr., "State Partnerships to Preserve Open Space: Lessons from Rhode Island and New York," in Endicott, *Land Conservation through Public Private Partnerships*, 158–60; *New York Times*, September 20, 1987, R29, June 13, 1993, R13.
21 *Exeter (NH) News-Letter*, May 3, 2005; *Portsmouth (NH) Herald*, January 11, 2004; *Fitchburg (MA) Sentinel and Enterprise*, June 1, November 5, 2000.
22 *York County (ME) Coast Star*, August 18, 2005; Bates, *Models of Collaboration among Land Trusts*, 13; *Portsmouth (NH) Herald*, March 2, 2003.
23 *York (ME) Weekly*, December 24, 2003 (quote), June 15, 2005. See *Portsmouth (NH) Herald*, August 16, 2004; June 25, 2006; May 8, 2008; *Biddeford (ME) Journal Tribune*, December 15, 1988; and *York County (ME) Coast Star*, April 6, December 7, 2006.
24 Endicott, "Preserving Natural Areas," 32 (first quote); Chris Elfring, "Preserving Land through Local Land Trusts," *Bioscience* 39 (February 1989): 74 (second quote). See Hocker, "Patience, Problem Solving, and Private Initiative," 258; *New York Times*, August 11, 2002, J1; Layzer, Kamieniecki, and Kraft, *Natural Experiments*, 27; and Bendick, "State Partnerships to Preserve Open Space," 152.
25 Daniel R. Mandelker, *Green Belts and Urban Growth: English Town and Country Planning in Action* (Madison: University of Wisconsin Press, 1962), 25–28, 33; James Taylor, Cecelia Paine, and John FitzGibbon, "From Greenbelt to Greenways: Four Canadian Case Studies," *Landscape and Urban Planning* 33 (October 1995): 48–50; Marco Amati and Laura Taylor, "From Green Belts to Green Infrastructure," *Planning, Practice & Research* 25 (April 2010): 144.
26 Barbara B. Paine in *Boston Globe*, May 23, 1962, box 2, folder 13, CWEII. See Anthony Romano, *First Annual Report, Essex Greenbelt Association*, and brochure, n.d., ca. 1960–63, box 2, folder 13, CWEII; Thomas L. Daniels, "The Use of Green Belts to Control Sprawl in the United States," *Planning, Practice & Research* 25 (April 2010): 255–56, 258; Oliver Gillham, *The Limitless City: A Primer on the Urban Sprawl Debate* (Washington, DC: Island Press, 2002), 174; Town of Cape Elizabeth, *Greenbelt Plan* (Cape Elizabeth, ME: n.p., 2013); and Thomas L. Daniels, "The Use of Green Belts to Control Sprawl in the United States," *Planning, Practice & Research* 25 (April 2010):259.
27 "Report Establishing 'the Bay Circuit,' 1956," box 5, folder 9, CWEII; *Fitchburg (MA) Sentinel*, October 25, 1955; *Concord (MA) Enterprise*, October 25, 1956.
28 *Concord (MA) Enterprise*, August 23, 1956 (quote), September 6, 1956, August 8, 1957.

See "Draft Program, Trustees Notes by Charles W. Eliot, November 16, 1959," box 2, folder 10, CWEII; *Lowell (MA) Sun*, June 30, 1957, June 26, 1958; *Fitchburg (MA) Sentinel*, October 25, 1955; and *Sixty-Fourth Annual Report of the Trustees of Public Reservations 1954*, 9; *Concord (MA) Enterprise*, January 26, 1956, October 4, 11, 1962.

29 Robert D. Yaro and Armando Carbonell, "Reinventing Megalopolis: The Northeast Megaregion," in *Smart Growth in a Changing World*, ed. Jonathan Barnett (Chicago: APA Planners Press, 2007), 91 (first quote); Richard L. Kent and Cynthia L. Elliott, "Scenic Routes Linking and Protecting Natural and Cultural Landscape Features: A Greenway Skeleton," *Landscape and Urban Planning* 33 (October 1995): 341–55, 353 (second quote). See Wesley Ward, "Charles W. Eliot 2nd and His Continuing Legacy, *Special Places: A Newsletter of the Trustees of Reservations*, Spring 1993, box 23, folder 19, CWEII; Little, *Greenways for America*, 163–66; Massachusetts Department of Environmental Management, *The Massachusetts Bay Circuit Program* (Boston: Massachusetts Department of Environmental Management, 1991), 3–8; Massachusetts Bay Circuit Program, *The Bay Circuit Program* (pamphlet, 1988), n.p.; Corey W. Medeiros, "The Massachusetts Bay Circuit" (master's thesis, University of Massachusetts Boston, 2015), 57–58; *Lowell (MA) Sun*, July 11, 2005; and Metropolitan Area Planning Council and Metropolitan District Commission, *Open Space and Recreation Plan and Program for Metropolitan Boston* (Boston: Metropolitan Area Planning Council, 1969), 87–89.

30 Medeiros, "Massachusetts Bay Circuit," 59–60; James C. O'Connell, *The Hub's Metropolis: Greater Boston's Development from Railroad Suburbs to Smart Growth* (Cambridge, MA: MIT Press, 2013), 168.

31 Lawrence Levine, "Land Conservation in Metropolitan Areas," *Journal of the American Institute of Planners* 30, no. 3 (1964): 207, 213.

32 Richard W. Judd, *Second Nature: An Environmental History of New England* (Amherst: University of Massachusetts Press, 2014), 224–25.

33 J. Glenn Eugster, "Evolution of the Heritage Areas Movement," *George Wright Forum* 20 (June 2003): 55–58; Robert L. Ryan and Theodore S. Eisenman, "Building Connections to the Minute Man National Historic Park," *Proceedings of the Fábos Conference on Landscape and Greenway Planning* (2019): 3.

34 Eugster, "Evolution of the Heritage Areas Movement," 51–54.

35 Eugster, "Evolution of the Heritage Areas Movement," 52, 54 (quote). See Julius Gy. Fabos, Jack Ahern, and Mark Lindhalt, *Blackstone Heritage Greenway Planning and Community Development*, Research Bulletin 745 (Amherst: Agricultural Experiment Station, University of Massachusetts, 1993), 14.

36 Eleanor Mahoney, "Industrial Heritage at Risk," *Proceedings of the Fábos Conference on Landscape and Greenway Planning* (2013): 495.

37 Mahoney, "Industrial Heritage at Risk," 494; Ervin H. Zube, "Greenways and the US National Park System," *Landscape and Urban Planning* 33 (October 1995): 24; Charles L. Tracy, "Working with Communities: U.S National Park Service Community Assistance in Corridor Planning," *Proceedings of the Fábos Conference on Landscape and Greenway Planning* 3 (2010): 425; Daniel N. Laven, Jennifer L. Jewiss, and Nora J. Mitchell, "Toward Landscape-Scale Stewardship and Development: A Theoretical Framework of United States National Heritage Areas," *Society and Natural Resources* 26 (2013): 764, 772.

38 Fabos, Ahern, and Lindhalt, *Blackstone Heritage Greenway*, 1–4, 7; Robert W. McIntosh, Rolf Diamant, and Nora J. Mitchell, "Federal Land Conservation in New England: Crisis, Response, and Adaptation," in Foster, *Twentieth-Century New England Land Conservation*, 330; Eugster, "Evolution of the Heritage Areas Movement," 51, 56–58; Laven, Jewiss, and Mitchell, "Toward Landscape-Scale Stewardship and Development," 765, 770.

39 Tracy, "Working with Communities," 430–31.

40 Reid Bertone-Johnson et al., "The Mill River Greenway Initiative," *Proceedings of the Fábos Conference on Landscape and Greenway Planning* (2013): 410–14.

41 US Department of Interior National Park Service, *Treasured Landscapes* (Washington, DC: National Park Service, 2010), 37 (first quote), 39 (second quote). See Tracy, "Working with Communities," 425, 431; and Mahoney, "Industrial Heritage at Risk," 494.

42 Lester E. Klimm, "The Empty Areas of the Northeastern United States," *Geographical Review* 44 (July 1954): 326, 339, 343.

43 Elizabeth Dennis Baldwin and Richard W. Judd, "Why History Matters in Conservation Planning," in *Landscape-Scale Conservation Planning*, ed. Stephen C. Trombulak and Robert F. Baldwin (New York: Springer, 2010), 38. See Robert J. Lilieholm, Lloyd C. Irland, and John M. Hagen, "Changing Socio-economic Conditions for Private Woodland Protection," in Trombulak and Baldwin, *Landscape-Scale Conservation Planning*, 68–73; Fairfax et al., *Buying Nature*, 244; and Stephen C. Harper, Laura L. Falk, and Edward W. Rankin, *Northern Forest Lands: USDA Forest Service and Governors' Task Force on Northern Forest Lands* (Rutland, VT: US Forest Service, 1990), 1, 10–12, 14.

44 Michael Lewis, "Wilderness and Conservation Science," in *American Wilderness: A New History*, ed. Lewis (New York: Oxford University Press, 2007), 208 (fourth [Leopold] quote), 219, 220 (first quote); Baldwin and Judd, "Why History Matters," 34, 41, 42 (second quote), 43, 50, 60–61; Harper, Falk, and Rankin, *Northern Forest Lands*, 3 (third quote) 41–42. See Richard W. Judd and Christopher S. Beach, *Natural States: The Environmental Imagination in Maine, Oregon, and the Nation* (Washington, DC: Resources for the Future, 2003), 81–93; and William Cronon, "The Trouble with Wilderness; or, Getting Back to the Wrong Nature," in *Uncommon Ground: Toward Reinventing Nature*, ed. William Cronon (New York: W. W. Norton, 1995), 82.

45 *Biddeford (ME) Journal Tribune*, April 20, 1976.

46 Kimberly A. Jarvis, *From the Mountains to the Sea: Protecting Nature in Postwar New Hampshire* (Amherst: University of Massachusetts Press, 2020), 104–35; *Portsmouth (NH) Herald*, January 7, 2004; Collins and Ober, "New Hampshire: Common Ground," 119–21; *Boston Globe*, June 19, 1988, 17.

47 Collins and Ober, "New Hampshire: Common Ground," 113, 115–16; Fairfax et al., *Buying Nature*, 187; McCullough, Ginger, and Baumflek, "Unspoiled Vermont," 161–63; Harper, Falk, and Rankin, *Northern Forest Lands*, 15, 17.

48 *Nashua (NH) Telegraph*, July 29, 1988; Land for New Hampshire, *Final Report*, 13; *New York Times*, August 5, 1990.

49 William J. Ginn, *Investing in Nature: Case Studies of Land Conservation in Collaboration with Business* (Washington DC: Island Press, 2005), 2 (quote), 3. See *New York Times*, December 16, 1998, A26.

50 *New York Times*, March 21, 2001, A12; Fairfax, *Buying Nature*, 222–24; Lilieholm,

Irland, and Hagen, "Changing Socio-economic Conditions," 77; Keesler, "Conservation Easement Policies," 12–13, 17; Sara Clark and Peter Howell, "From Diamond International to Plum Creek: The Era of Large Landscape Conservation in the Northern Forest," *Maine Policy Review* 16, no. 2 (2007): 61–62.

51 Martha West Lyman, Cecilia Danks, and Maureen McDonough, "New England's Community Forests: Comparing a Regional Model to ICCAs," *Conservation and Society* 11, no. 1 (2013): 51–52; *Biddeford (ME) Journal Tribune*, May 20, 2008; *Nashua (NH) Telegraph*, January 13, 1995; Lillieholm, Irland, and Hagen, "Changing Socio-economic Conditions," 78.

52 *New York Times*, June 10, 2002, B1 (quote), B5, March 21, 2001, A12, December 23, 2001, A3.

53 Lillieholm, Irland, and Hagen, "Changing Socio-economic Conditions," 78–79; Clark and Howell, "From Diamond International to Plum Creek," 64; *Portland Press Herald*, November 9, 2015.

54 Emily Bateson and Nancy Smith, "Making It Happen: Protecting Wilderness on the Ground," in Klyza, *Wilderness Comes Home*, 189. See Harper, Falk, and Rankin, *Northern Forest Lands*, vi.

55 Judd, *Second Nature*, 268; Christopher McGrory Klyza, "An Eastern Turn for Wilderness," in Klyza, *Wilderness Comes Home*, 15–16; Stephen C. Trombulak and Kimberly Royar, "Restoring the Wild: Species Recovery and Reintroduction," in Klyza, *Wilderness Comes Home*, 171–72.

56 Klyza, "An Eastern Turn for Wilderness," 8. See Judd, *Second Nature*, 266.

57 Judd, *Second Nature*, 267.

58 Robert Long et al., *Maine Wildlands Network Vision: A Scientific Approach to Conservation Planning in Maine* (Richmond, VT: Wildlands Project, 2002), 8–9, 12 (quote), 13. See Robert F. Baldwin et al., "The Importance of Maine for Ecoregional Conservation Planning," *Maine Policy Review* 16, no. 2 (2007): 74; and Adena R. Rissman, "Evaluating Conservation Effectiveness and Adaptation in Dynamic Landscapes," *Law and Contemporary Problems* 73, no. 4 (2011): 150, 171.

59 Peter S. Alagona, *After the Grizzly: Endangered Species and the Politics of Place in California* (Berkeley: University of California Press, 2013), 5–6, 7 (first quote); Jennifer McMurtray in Grove, "Paths to the Future," 90 (second quote); Fikret Berkes, "Rethinking Community-Based Conservation," *Conservation Biology* 18 (June 2004): 622 (third quote). See Andrew W. Barton, *The Changing Nature of the Maine Woods* (Durham: University of New Hampshire Press, 2012), 164; Stephen C. Trombulak and Robert F. Baldwin, "Creating a Context for Landscape-Scale Conservation Planning," in Trombulak and Baldwin, *Landscape-Scale Conservation Planning*, 2–3; Jack Ahern, "Greenways as a Planning Strategy," *Landscape and Urban Planning* 33 (October 1995): 131–33; Conrad Reining et al., *From the Adirondacks to Acadia: A Wildlands Network Design for the Greater Northern Appalachians* (Richmond, VT: Wildlands Project Special Paper no. 7, 2006), 4; and Craig R. Groves et al., "Planning for Biodiversity Conservation: Putting Conservation Science into Practice," *Bioscience* 52 (June 2002): 500.

60 Alagona, *After the Grizzly*, 234. See Layzer, Kamieniecki, and Kraft, *Natural Experiments*, 21; and R. Edward Grumbine, *Ghost Bears: Exploring the Biodiversity Crisis* (Washington, DC: Island Press, 1992), 42, 57–59.

61 James K. Agee and Darryll R. Johnson, eds., *Ecosystem Management for Parks and*

Wilderness (Seattle: University of Washington Press, 1988), 4–5; R. Edward Grumbine, "What Is Ecosystem Management?," *Conservation Biology* 8 (March 1994): 28–29.

62 C. S. Holling, "Resilience and Stability of Ecosystems," *Annual Review of Ecology and Systematics* 4 (1973): 2, 7, 11, 18; Massachusetts Department of Fish & Game and Nature Conservancy, *BioMap2: Conserving the Biodiversity of Massachusetts in a Changing World* (Boston: n.p., 2010), 51.

63 Jack Ahern, "Sustainability and Cities: A Landscape Planning Approach," *Proceedings of the Fábos Conference on Landscape and Greenway Planning* 3 (2010), 562; Holling, "Resilience and Stability of Ecosystems," 2, 13–14, 16; Rissman, "Evaluating Conservation Effectiveness," 151–52; Layzer, Kamieniecki, and Kraft, *Natural Experiments*, 103, 137.

64 David R. Foster, "Land-Use History (1730–1990) and Vegetation Dynamics in Central New England," *Journal of Ecology* 80 (December 1992): 469. See Janet McMahon, *Diversity, Continuity and Resilience: The Ecological Values of the Western Maine Mountains* (Phillips, ME: Maine Mountain Collaborative, 2016), 11–12; and Massachusetts Department of Fish & Game, Nature Conservancy, *BioMap2*, 10, 13–14.

65 McMahon, *Diversity, Continuity and Resilience*, 11 (quote), 13. See Reining et al., *From the Adirondacks to Acadia*, 40.

66 Massachusetts Department of Fish & Game, Nature Conservancy, *BioMap2*, 4, 6–9, 15–16, 53; Baldwin et al., "Importance of Maine," 72; Stephen C. Trombulak, "Ecological Reserve Design in the Northeast," in Klyza, *Wilderness Comes Home*, 113–18; Bateson and Smith, "Making It Happen," 195.

67 Groves et al., "Planning for Biodiversity Conservation," 504; Jamie Sayen, "An Opportunity for Big Wilderness in the Northern Appalachians," in Klyza, *Wilderness Comes Home*, 131–32; Long et al., *Maine Wildlands Network Vision*, 28; Catherine A. Elliott, ed., *Biodiversity in the Forests of Maine: Guidelines for Land Management* (Orono: University of Maine Cooperative Extension, 1999), 27–29, 79–80; Reed F. Noss et al., "Core Areas: Where Nature Reigns," in *Continental Conservation: Scientific Foundations of Regional Reserve Networks*, ed. Michael E. Soulé and John Terborgh (Washington, DC: Island Press, 1999), 99, 101, 105.

68 John Linehan, Meir Gross, and John Finn, "Greenway Planning: Developing a Landscape Ecological Network Approach," *Landscape and Urban Planning* 33 (October 1995): 181. See Elliott, *Biodiversity in the Forests of Maine*, 114–16; Long et al., *Maine Wildlands Network Vision*, 3; Ahern, "Greenways as a Planning Strategy," 136; and Andy Dobson et al., "Connectivity: Maintaining Flows in Fragmented Landscapes," in Soulé and Terborgh, *Continental Conservation*, 133–34.

69 Reining et al., *From the Adirondacks to Acadia*, 7; Long et al., *Maine Wildlands Network Vision*, 30; L. Hannah et al., "Conservation of Biodiversity in a Changing Climate," *Conservation Biology* 16 (February 2002): 265; Martha Groom, "Buffer Zones: Benefits and Dangers of Compatible Stewardship," in Soulé and Terborgh, *Continental Conservation*, 171–74.

70 Nature Conservancy, *Staying Connected in the Northern Appalachians: Mitigating Fragmentation and Climate Change Impacts on Wildlife through Functional Habitat Linkages; Final Performance Report-Summary* (Boston: Nature Conservancy, 2013), 2. See Rissman, "Evaluating Conservation Effectiveness," 172–73.

71 Jessica Owley, "Conservation Easements at the Climate Change Crossroads," *Law*

and Contemporary Problems 74 (Fall 2011): 226. See Rissman, "Evaluating Conservation Effectiveness," 147, 153.

72 R. E. Daniels, "The Role of Ecology in Planning: Some Misconceptions," *Landscape and Urban Planning* 15 (July 1988): 291, 298; Linehan, Gross, and Finn, "Greenway Planning," 181–82; Groves et al., "Planning for Biodiversity Conservation," 499–500; Grumbine, *Ghost Bears*, 60; Ahern, "Greenways as a Planning Strategy," 136.

73 "Landscape and Natural Areas Project, Annual Report, 1972," box 3, folder 9, CWEII; Posatko, "Land Trusts and Land Conservation," 182; Scheffey, *Conservation Commissions*, 91; *Norwalk Citizen News*, June 29, 1989.

74 Grumbine, "What Is Ecosystem Management?," 31.

75 Massachusetts Audubon Society, *Losing Ground: Planning for Resilience*, 5th ed. (Lincoln, MA: Audubon, 2014) 4. See Long et al., *Maine Wildlands Network Vision*, 13; and Nature Conservancy, *Staying Connected in the Northern Appalachians*, 2.

76 Julius Gy. Fabos, "Introduction and Overview: The Greenway Movement, Uses and Potentials of Greenways," *Landscape and Urban Planning* 33 (October 1995): 6; Massachusetts Department of Fish & Game, Nature Conservancy, *BioMap2*, 6; Reining et al., *From the Adirondacks to Acadia*, 33–40.

77 Long et al., *Maine Wildlands Network Vision*, 33–34, 61, 71; Massachusetts Department of Fish & Game, Nature Conservancy, *BioMap2*, 20–27; Ahern, "Greenways as a Planning Strategy," 149; Linehan, Gross, and Finn, "Greenway Planning," 186; Barton, *Changing Nature of the Maine Woods*, 165.

78 Nature Conservancy, *Staying Connected*, 1-10-11; Mark G. Anderson and Arlene Olivero Sheldon, *Conservation Status of Fish, Wildlife, and Natural Habitats in the Northeast Landscape: Implementation of the Northeast Monitoring Framework* (Boston: Nature Conservancy Eastern Conservation Science, 2011), chap. 1, p. 1.

79 Linehan, Gross, and Finn, "Greenway Planning," 185; Ahern, "Greenways as a Planning Strategy," 149–51.

80 Ahern, "Greenways as a Planning Strategy," 149 (quote), 150–51.

81 Massachusetts Audubon Society, *Losing Ground*, 8, 10–11; Massachusetts Department of Fish & Game, Nature Conservancy, *BioMap2*, 52, 54; Tom Horton, "Speaking for the Trees," *Boston Globe*, October 10, 2010, BGM27.

82 Victor E. Shelford, *Naturalist's Guide to the Americas* (Baltimore: Williams & Wilkins, 1926), 316; Jeff Pidot, "Conservation Easement Reform: As Maine Goes Should the Nation Follow?," *Law and Contemporary Problems* 74 (Fall 2011): 5.

83 Baldwin et al., "Importance of Maine for Ecoregional Conservation Planning," 67 (quote), 69, 71. See McMahon, *Diversity, Continuity and Resilience* 2, 7, 11–12; Long et al., *Maine Wildlands Network Vision*, 1; and Barton, *Changing Nature of the Maine Woods*, 172.

84 Ecological Reserves Study Steering Committee [Janet McMahon], *An Ecological Reserves System for Maine: Benchmarks in a Changing Landscape* (Augusta, ME: Maine State Planning Office, Natural Resources Division, 1993), 2, 14; McMahon, *Diversity, Continuity and Resilience*, 10–11, 14; Elliott, *Biodiversity in the Forests of Maine*, 5, 7.

85 Horton, "Speaking for the Trees."

86 Amber Pitt et al., "Small Parks as Local Social-Ecological Systems Contributing to Conservation of Small Isolated and Ephemeral Wetlands," *Natural Areas Journal* 38 (July 2018): 237–38, 241–42, 243 (quote). See Robert M. Searns, "The Evolution of

Greenways as an Adaptive Urban Landscape Form," *Landscape and Urban Planning* 33 (October 1995): 72.
87 Linehan, Gross, and Finn, "Greenway Planning," 179; Fabos, "Introduction," 2.
88 Fabos, "Introduction," 1 (first and third [President's Commission] quotes), 2 (fourth quote); Grove, "Paths to the Future," 89 (second quote). See Anthony Walmsley, "Greenways and the Making of Urban Form," *Landscape and Urban Planning* 33 (October 1995): 82.
89 Robert L. Ryan and Mark Lindhult, "Knitting New England Together," *Landscape Architecture Magazine* 90 (February 2000): 50–54; Robert L. Ryan, Julius Gy. Fabos, and Mark S. Lindhult, "Continuing a Planning Tradition: The New England Greenway Vision Plan," *Landscape Journal* 21, no. 1 (2002): 165–67.
90 Ryan, Fabos, and Lindhult, "Continuing a Planning Tradition," 171.
91 Ahern, "Greenways as a Planning Strategy," 136 (first quote); Mary Caroline Robbins, "Park-Making as a National Art," *Atlantic Monthly*, January 1897, 87 (second quote); Mark Dowie, *Losing Ground: American Environmentalism at the Close of the Twentieth Century* (Cambridge, MA: MIT Press, 1996), 224 (third quote). See James Morton Turner, *The Promise of Wilderness: American Environmental Politics since 1964* (Seattle: University of Washington Press, 2012), 299, 400; Grove, "Paths to the Future," 80; and Barbara A. Ryder, "Greenway Planning and Growth Management: Partners in Conservation?," *Landscape and Urban Planning* 33 (1995): 429–30.

Conclusion

1 Lary Dilsaver and Terence Young, "U.S. Parks and Protected Areas: Origins, Meanings and Management," *Historical Geography* 35 (2007): 7–8; Langdon Smith, "Democratizing Nature through State Park Development," *Historical Geography* 41 (2013): 207; Amber Pitt et al., "Small Parks as Local Social-Ecological Systems Contributing to Conservation of Small Isolated and Ephemeral Wetlands," *Natural Areas Journal* 38 (July 2018): 243.
2 John B. Wright, "Land Trusts in the USA," *Land Use Policy* 9, no. 2 (1992): 86 (first quote); Jean Hocker, "Land Trusts: Key Elements in the Struggle against Sprawl," *Natural Resources & Environment* 15 (Spring 2001): 247 (second quote). See Judith A. Layzer, Sheldon Kamieniecki, and Michael E. Kraft, *Natural Experiments: Ecosystem-Based Management and the Environment* (Cambridge, MA: MIT Press, 2008), 26; and William J. Ginn, *Investing in Nature: Case Studies of Land Conservation in Collaboration with Business* (Washington, DC: Island Press, 2005), 4.
3 Larry Selzer, "Private Lands: The Future of Conservation in America," in *A Better Planet: Forty Big Ideas for a Sustainable Future*, ed. Daniel C. Esty (New Haven, CT: Yale University Press, 2019), 39.
4 Ashish Kothari, Philip Camill, and Jessica Brown, "Conservation as If People Also Mattered: Policy and Practice of Community-Based Conservation," *Atree* (Ashoka Trust for Research in Ecology and the Environment, India) 11, no. 1 (2013): 4, 9–10; R. Edward Grumbine, "What Is Ecosystem Management?," *Conservation Biology* 8 (March 1994): 33–34.
5 *New York Times*, June 26, 2005, CT1.

INDEX

Acadia National Park, 73, 221
affordable housing, 179–81
Appalachian Trail, 85, 199
Art of Public Improvement, 7–8, 10–12, 17–24. *See also* colonial revival; rural aesthetic; village improvement societies
automobiles, effect of, 80–87

Baxter, Sylvester, 42, 55–57
Baxter State Park, 73–74
Berkshire Natural Resources Council, 190
Boston: Charles River, 168–72; community gardens, 174–80; environmental justice, 182–86; historic preservation, 95, 200–202; Middlesex Fells, 59–60; Neponset River, 58, 170–72; parks, 38–45, 49–51, 54–60, 77–78, 155–64; railroads, 32; South End, 182–83; suburbs, 31–32; and TPR, founding of, 42–45; urban revival, 155–64; "urban wilds," 161–65. *See also* Emerald Necklace; Massachusetts Bay Circuit; Metropolitan Park Commission
Boston Natural Areas Network (BNAN), 163–64
Boston Redevelopment Authority (BRA), 162–63
Boston Urban Gardeners, 176–77

Central Park, 36–38
Charles River Reservation, 168–72
clean water acts, 133–35
Cleveland, Horace W. S., 39
colonial revival, 23–24
Commission on Country Life, 26–27
community-based organizations: democratizing land holding, 93–94, 114–16, 122–28; and easements, 143–44; and environmentalism, 135–37, 151–53; interactions with TPR, 93–94; significance to land stewardship, 5–6, 11–12; as village improvement societies, 22–27
community land trusts, 179–81
Connecticut: farm preservation, 149; greenways, 166; land trusts in, 126; public lands in, 194
conservation: of forests, 28–30; vs. preservation, 8–10; of wetlands, 137–40
conservation commissions, 124–25
country estates, 3, 17–22, 31
Crane Reservation, 96–97, 142

Downing, Andrew Jackson: on landscape design, 20–22; on parks, 36–37
Dudley Street Neighborhood Initiative, 183–86

easements, 143–50
ecological preservation: and Art of Public Improvement, 10–14; of forests, 28–30; national parks, 8–10; preservation organizations, 106–7; by TPR, 100–103, 106–13; of wetlands, 137–40
ecosystem management, 100–103, 211–25
Eliot, Charles W., Jr.: influences on, 45–48; landscaping philosophy of, 48–49, 60–64; Metropolitan Park Commission, founding of, 54–60; and Olmsted, 46, 48–49; TPR, founding of, 49–54
Eliot, Charles W., II: and Massachusetts Bay Circuit, 84–85, 199–200; TPR acquisitions under, 88–89, 100; and wetland preservation, 100, 139
Emerald Necklace, 40–41, 58
environmentalism: clean water acts, 133–35; environmental justice, 181–83; Highway Beautification Act of 1965, 135; during Johnson administration, 134–35; and land trusts, 135–37, 140–43; as national movement, 132–35, 140; during Reagan administration, 151–53; rivers and wetlands conservation, 137–40

farming: and easements, 149–50; preservation of farmlands, 146–50; and rural aesthetic; 12–14; rural emigration, 23–24; and taxation, 148–50
Felt, Charles W., 69–70
forest management, 28–30, 101–3, 205–6

gardening, 174–75, 178
grassroots organizations. *See* community-based organizations
greenbelts, 198–201
greenways, 165–74, 223–25

Harrison, Jonathan Baxter, 65–68
historic preservation: in Boston, 95; of farmlands, 148–50; historic districts, 201–5; National Historic Preservation Act, 8; by National Park Service (NPS), 202–5; by TPR, 94–99
Hudson River School, 16

interstate highway system, 118–20

Johnson, Lyndon B., 134–35

Land and Water Conservation Fund, 194–95
landscape painting, 27–28
landscaping: of country estates, 19–22; park design, 36–41, 54–59; of reservations, 60–64; in suburbs, 31–35. *See also* Central Park; Downing, Andrew Jackson; Eliot, Charles W., Jr.; Olmsted, Frederick Law; Sargent, Charles Sprague
logging. *See* forest management
Lynn Woods, 52

MacKaye, Benton, 85, 87–88, 199–200
Maine: Allagash Wilderness Waterway, 166; easements in, 146; Kennebunk, 188; Land for Maine's Future, 193–94; land trusts in, 126, 139–40, 188, 221–22; Maine Coast Heritage Trust, 190, 193; Monhegan Island, 126; Mount Agamenticus, 197–98; Northern Forest, 205–11; population increases, 119–20, 124; Saco Citizens Coalition, 139–40. *See also* Acadia National Park; Baxter State Park; Mount Desert Island
Marsh, George Perkins, 28–29
Massachusetts: billboard legislation, 83; Blue Hills Reservation, 59, coastal towns, 65–70, 192–93; conservation commissions, 124–26; ecological preservation, 100–103, 196, 219–21; farmlands, 146; historic districts, 202–4; Lowell, 202; Lynn Woods, 52; Middlesex Fells, 65–70; Mill River Greenway, 204; Park Act, 52; Province Lands, 68–70, rural parks in, 74; state forests, 72, 88–92; and TPR, 88–94

Massachusetts Bay Circuit, 84–88, 199–201
McHarg, Ian, 117, 141, 161–62
Metropolitan Park Commission, 56–60, 70–71, 168–71
middle-way preservation, 189–98
Mount Desert Island, 47–48, 73

Nash, Roderick, 2, 9, 15
national parks: 73–74, 84, 100; easements and, 144; historic preservation and, 8, 201–5. *See also* Acadia National Park; White Mountain National Forest
Nature Conservancy, 106–7, 193, 207–9
Naumkeag, 97–99
Neponset River, 58, 170–72
New Hampshire, 73, 119, 149, 191–92, 197, 207–8
Northern Forest, 205–11

Olmsted, Frederick Law: 31, 46, 165; Central Park, 37–38; and Charles Eliot Jr., 48–49; Emerald Necklace, 40–41

parks, 36–41, 51–52, 156–60. *See also* Metropolitan Park Commission; *and specific parks*
Parmentier, André, 20
preservation. *See* ecological preservation; historic preservation; middle-way preservation; urban land preservation
Province Lands, 68–70

Reagan, Ronald: administration, 151–53
Regional Planning Association of America, 84
Rhode Island, 126, 194, 196–97
Roosevelt, Theodore, 9, 26

Roxbury, 158–59, 163, 183–86
Runte, Alfred, 2, 9
rural aesthetic, 8, 10–17, 23–24, 132

Sargent, Charles Sprague, 29, 32–35; *Garden and Forest: A Journal of Horticulture, Landscape Art, and Forestry,* 33–35; Metropolitan Park Commission, founding of, 56–57
Southwest Corridor Park, 158–59
state parks, 75, 82, 226
suburbs, 30–32, 116–20
summer residents, 23–24, 26

tourism, 27–30, 68
Trustees of Public Reservations (TPR): ecological preservation by, 100–113, 141–42; founding of, 42–45, 49–57; historic preservation by, 95–99; land acquisition by, 53–57, 65, 70–76, 88–94, 144; and Massachusetts Bay Circuit, 82–88, 199–201; in mid-twentieth century, 77–80

urban land preservation, 155–65, 175–78
urban wilds, 161–65

Vermont, 119, 190–91
village improvement societies, 22–27, 52, 92–95

Waverly Oaks, 49–51
wetlands, 138–40
White Mountain National Forest, 73
Whyte, William, 120–21, 144, 160
wilderness: 14–15, 33–34, 205–12; Wilderness Act, 8
World's End Reservation, 110–11

www.ingramcontent.com/pod-product-compliance
Lightning Source LLC
Chambersburg PA
CBHW032050230426
43672CB00009B/1547